Financial Innovation and Technology

Series Editor

Thomas Puschmann, Swiss FinTech Innovation Lab, University of Zurich, Zurich, Switzerland

The book series 'Financial Innovation and Technology' features scholarly research on the latest developments in the world of finance such as AI, FinTech startups, Big Data, Cryptocurrencies, Robo-Advisors, Machine Learning, and Blockchain applications among others. The book series explores the main trends and technologies that will transform the finance industry in the years to come. The series presents essential insights into the financial technology revolution, and the disruption, innovation, and opportunity it entails. The books in this series will be of value to both academics and those working in the finance industry.

Gilbert Fridgen • Tobias Guggenberger •
Johannes Sedlmeir • Nils Urbach
Editors

Decentralization Technologies

Financial Sector in Change

Springer

Editors
Gilbert Fridgen
Interdisciplinary Centre for Security, Reliability and Trust
University of Luxembourg
Luxembourg, Luxembourg

Tobias Guggenberger
FIM Research Center for Information Management
University of Bayreuth
Bayreuth, Germany

Johannes Sedlmeir
Interdisciplinary Centre for Security, Reliability and Trust
University of Luxembourg
Luxembourg, Luxembourg

Nils Urbach
FIM Research Center for Information Management
Frankfurt University of Applied Sciences
Frankfurt am Main, Germany

ISSN 2730-9681 ISSN 2730-969X (electronic)
Financial Innovation and Technology
ISBN 978-3-031-66046-7 ISBN 978-3-031-66047-4 (eBook)
https://doi.org/10.1007/978-3-031-66047-4

This Springer imprint is published by the registered company Springer Nature Switzerland AG
The registered company address is: Gewerbestrasse 11, 6330 Cham, Switzerland

To the pioneers of decentralization, whose vision and determination have paved the way for a potentially more inclusive and resilient financial future.

To the students who seek to understand and challenge conventional wisdom, shaping the next generation of financial innovation.

To the practitioners, whose everyday efforts transform theory into tangible business solutions, driving adoption and impact.

To the decision-makers and regulators, who navigate complexities with courage and foresight, steering us toward a more inclusive, equitable, and sustainable world.

To the researchers, whose relentless pursuit of knowledge and drive to scrutinize the status quo fuels progress, illuminating new pathways and possibilities.

May this book serve as a beacon of insight and inspiration, uniting us in our shared quest for a more decentralized financial landscape.

Foreword

"Decentralization Technologies: Financial Sector in Change" is a valuable resource for academics, practitioners, and students exploring the complex digital transformation in finance driven by decentralized technologies.

While the aspirations of decentralized technologies for financial services are simple to understand—-and even noble in their aims—individual and organizational adoptions are complex, thus requiring thoughtful scholarly work. The authors of this collection provide that thought leadership in the context of financial services. Pertaining to aspirations, decentralized technologies provide an alternative Information system (IS) architecture to orchestrate online economic activities. Many people want a new IS architecture to fix the power inequities, privacy invasions, and cybersecurity threats of online centralized control, known as "Web2."

With Web2, users (individuals and organizations) rely on centralized platform providers to access online financial services. Centralized platform providers—like banks and other financial institutions—have control over customers' financial assets. Banks loan out more money to borrowers than they retain in deposits. While fractional reserve banking is allowed because it helps to expand the economy, there are risks. If a large portion of depositors suddenly demand their money back in cash, the bank could go bankrupt. Additionally, borrowers may default on their loans, which happened in droves during the 2008 Global Financial Crisis. The creator of Bitcoin, Satoshi Nakamoto, wrote: "Banks must be trusted to hold our money and transfer it electronically, but they lend it out in waves of credit bubbles with barely a fraction in reserve" (Nakamoto, 2009). Identity theft is another common occurrence with Web2 financial services. Our online relationships with centralized platform providers are managed with accounts and passwords, which are stored—along with our personal data—in the provider's centralized databases. These databases then become prime targets for cyberthieves. The United States (US) Bureau of Justice and the European Union Agency for Cybersecurity (ENISA) reports millions of instances of identity theft each year, representing nearly 10% of these populations. Lack of user control, privacy invasions, and data breaches have led to high levels of user mistrust in financial institutions and in economic markets (Edelman, 2024). Many people believe that the decentralization of economic activities is the best way to restore trust online. Blockchains are the digital infrastructures that support decentralized activities, heralding the next version of the Internet known as Web3.

Web3 financial services work differently than Web2 financial services; they aim to shift the power to users. Users have control over their online relationships and personal information. Rather than Web2's use of accounts and passwords for access control, users access Web3 applications with a digital wallet—no personal information is required for many Web3 applications. Rather than a centralized platform provider storing transactions on a centralized database, transactions are stored on a distributed ledger, which is copied and stored on tens of thousands of peer computers, meaning no single computer is in control. Decentralized architectures are resilient to cybersecurity attacks because the attack surface is diffused across many locations. The only way to infiltrate the network is to commandeer more than 50% of the processing power of nodes. Cybersecurity gets stronger as more nodes are added to the network because hackers will need to attack more nodes (Lacity & Lupien, 2022).

Bitcoin was the first Web3 application for one type of financial service, namely, peer-to-peer payments. It was launched in 2009 and the network itself has never been breached. Three years after Bitcoin's launch, Ripple launched for currency exchange and global payments. Two years after Ripple's launch, Web3 fundraising models called Initial coin offerings (ICOs) emerged. More recently, Web3 versions for borrowing and lending emerged, called Decentralized finance (DeFi). Moreover, many nations are also exploring central bank digital currencies; China, the Bahamas, and Nigeria have already tried them.

While Web3 innovations in financial services deliver on some of Web3's promises, they also introduce new problems. Technologies are developed and deployed in a dynamic political, organizational, regulatory, social, economic, and physical world. New technologies bring new risks; several high-profile blockchain shutdowns at Everledger, TradeLens, we.trade, Marco Polo, B3i, and the Australian Securities Exchange (ASX) contribute to blockchain fatigue among many executive (Gartner, 2019). We need a better understanding of how to deliver the promised value of such complex technologies.

This book, edited by Gilbert Fridgen, Tobias Guggenberger, Johannes Sedlmeir, and Nils Urbach, provides an understanding of many types of financial services. The authors navigate the complexities of decentralized technologies so that scholars and practitioners can achieve the vision for more trusted online economic activities. The chapters critically engage with the current regulatory environment, technological foundations, and potential applications of decentralization in finance.

Many of the chapters' authors are European; Europe is ahead of the United States of America (USA) (where I live) in terms of fostering regulatory frameworks to support "one market" approaches to decentralized systems. In particular, the chapter on Europe's progressive regulations by Tom Barbereau, Linda Weigl, and Nadia Pocher shows a level of regulatory innovation sorely lacking in the USA. For example, the European Parliament supports the electronic Identification, Authentication and Trust Services (eIDAS) regulation, which provides a regulatory digital identity framework. The regulation allows citizens of the European Union to identify and authenticate themselves online without having to rely on commercial providers. Unlike the European Union's "single market" approach, most innovative regulations in the USA are happening at the State level, most notably in Wyoming. The comprehensive chapters on decentralized identity, which my co-authors and I more broadly call "decentralized credentials" (Lacity et al., 2023), DeFi, decentralized carbon-credits, and central bank digital currencies (CBDCs), show not only the promise of these applications but also their tradeoffs and challenges. There are no easy answers.

As financial services continue to evolve under the influence of emerging technologies, "Decentralization Technologies: Financial Sector in Change" offers a rigorous scholarly examination of this progression. It is a valuable contribution to the literature, providing nuanced insights into the challenges and opportunities presented by the integration of decentralization technologies in finance.

Ambassador, Global Blockchain Business Council
Fellow, British Blockchain Association
David D. Glass Chair and Distinguished Professor of Information Systems
Sam M. Walton College of Business, University of Arkansas
Fayetteville, AR, USA
March 2024

Mary C. Lacity

References

Edelman (2024). Edelman trust barometer https://www.edelman.com/trust/trust-barometer.

Gartner (2019). Gartner predicts 90% of blockchain-based supply chain initiatives will suffer 'blockchain fatigue' by 2023. https://www.gartner.com/en/newsroom/press-releases/2019-05-07-gartner-predicts-90--of-blockchain-based-supply-chain.

Lacity, M., Carmel, E., Young, A. G., & Roth, T. (2023). The quiet corner of Web3 that means business. *MIT Sloan Management Review*, *64*(3). https://sloanreview.mit.edu/article/the-quiet-corner-of-web3-that-means-business/.

Lacity, M., & Lupien, S. C. (2022). *Blockchain fundamentals for Web 3.0.* Epic Books/University of Arkansas Press.

Nakamoto, S. (2009). Bitcoin open source implementation of P2P currency. http://p2pfoundation.ning.com/forum/topics/bitcoin-open-source?id=2003008%3ATopic%3A9402&page=1.

Preface

As editors and contributors to this volume, we extend our heartfelt appreciation for the opportunity to present a comprehensive exploration of the symbiotic relationship between decentralization technologies and the financial sector. In curating this scholarly collection, our primary aim is to offer an insightful, multifaceted examination of the transformative landscape where regulatory imperatives and business needs meet technological advancements, reshaping the contours of financial markets. The genesis of this project stems from our collective recognition of a pivotal paradigm shift occurring in the financial sector. The emergence of decentralization technologies, including distributed ledger technology (DLT), digital identities, and federated learning, has spurred a profound restructuring of traditional financial frameworks. The velocity of technological disruption, coupled with an evolving regulatory landscape, compels us to navigate the intricate interplay between innovation technology and markets as well as the effects of policymaking and compliance. This interdisciplinary approach shall help academics, industry professionals, policymakers, and students from different focused backgrounds to gain a balanced view on foreseeable technology adoption.

Part I, titled "Regulatory, Economic, and Technical Developments," scrutinizes the essential triggers that underpin the intersection of decentralization technologies and the financial sector. In our introductory chapter, we set the stage by elucidating the driving forces behind the adoption of decentralization in finance. From the intrinsic value of data in a competitive market to models of cooperation amid competition, we lay the groundwork for a theoretical perspective and an abstract model that permeate the subsequent chapters. Our intent is to provide readers with a contextualized overview, emphasizing the trajectory of decentralization within financial markets. The chapter that follows delves into the intricacies of the European regulatory landscape, contrasting it with counterparts in the USA and China. These insights set the stage for the subsequent exploration of DLT, digital identities, and federated learning in the context of finance.

Moving on to Part II, aptly titled "Technical Foundations," the focus shifts to the technical underpinnings of decentralization technologies. Chapters on blockchain and DLT, decentralized digital identities, and federated learning dissect the intricate mechanisms driving decentralization. From smart contracts and decentralized finance to digital identity wallets and verifiable credentials, our contributors unravel the complexity of these technologies. Moreover, the exploration of privacy-enhancing techniques such as zero-knowledge proofs, multi-party computation, homomorphic encryption, and differential privacy adds a critical layer toolbox for effectively balancing privacy and compliance aspects in decentralized systems.

Part III, "Applications," unveils the real-world implications of decentralization technologies in the financial sector. Chapters on self-sovereign identity for digital Know-your-customer (KYC), the embracement of decentralized finance by the traditional financial sector, the use of decentralization technologies in the context of Environmental, social, and governance (ESG) accounting and reporting, opportunities and applications of federated learning, as well as a discussion of decentralization aspects of central bank digital currencies provide a nuanced examination of decentralized applications. From digital identity solutions and financial inclusion to environmental, social, and governance considerations, this section bridges the theoretical foundations with practical implementations.

The concluding Part IV, "Discussion and Outlook," frames the future trajectory of decentralization in financial applications. Contributors reflect on the technical, organizational, and regulatory perspectives essential for maintaining decentralization. The final chapter critically assesses the energy and carbon footprint implications of decentralization in finance, paving the way for a discourse on the broader sustainability impact. As editors, we have sought to strike a balance between technical depth, socioeconomic implications, and regulatory considerations throughout the book. We hope that this volume serves as both a scholarly resource and a practical guide for academics, industry professionals, policymakers, and students navigating the evolving landscape where finance converges with decentralization technologies. We hope you will enjoy reading the book, and we invite you to contact us for questions, feedback, and discussions.

Esch-sur-Alzette, Luxembourg — Gilbert Fridgen
Bayreuth, Germany — Tobias Guggenberger
Esch-sur-Alzette, Luxembourg — Johannes Sedlmeir
Frankfurt, Germany — Nils Urbach
October 2024

Acknowledgments

We would like to acknowledge funding through the following grants and institutions:

- The Luxembourg National Research Fund (FNR), grant references
  - PayPal-FNR/Chair in DFS/Gilbert Fridgen, grant agreement P17/IS/13342933
  - Project NCER-FT (National Centre of Excellence in Financial Technologies), grant agreement NCER22/IS/16570468/NCER-FT (Cryptoreg)
  - Project FiReSpARX (FinTech/RegTech in Space for Trustful Autonomous Robotic Interaction), grant agreement 14783405
  - Project PABLO (Privacy-preserving Tokenisation Of Artworks), grant agreement 16326754
- Luxembourg's Ministry for Digitalisation
- Luxembourg's Banque et Caisse d'Épargne de l'État (Spuerkeess)
- The European Union (EU) within its Horizon 2020 program, project MDOT (Medical Device Obligations Taskforce), grant agreement 814654
- The Bavarian Ministry of Economic Affairs, Regional Development and Energy for their support of the project "Fraunhofer Blockchain Center (20-3066-2-6-14)"

We also would like to thank all authors, and deeply thank all involved people on the side of Springer who helped us in the proofreading and typesetting process.

Contents

Contributors

Iván Abellán (ivan.abellan@uni.lu) is a doctoral researcher at the Interdisciplinary Centre for Security, Reliability and Trust (SnT), University of Luxembourg. He received his M.Sc. in Advanced Network Security and Digital Forensic from Edinburgh Napier University (UK) in 2020. His research interests are in computer security with a focus on cryptography, blockchain technology, and privacy-related methods. His main research is in the practical design of privacy-preserving artifacts for decentralized systems while balancing compliance and regulatory demands; building on digital identities and blockchain-based applications. His research has been published at conferences such as Financial Cryptography and Data Security (FC), the International Conference on Blockchain and Cryptocurrency (ICBC), and the International Conference on Design Science Research in Information Systems and Technology (DESRIST).

Alexandre Amard (alexandre.amard@uni.lu) is a doctoral researcher at the Interdisciplinary Centre for Security, Reliability and Trust (SnT) at the University of Luxembourg. He received his M.Sc. in Management in International Business. In his research, he focuses on societally transforming technologies such as digital identity, biometrics, and artificial intelligence and how the public sector can harness them for the benefit of its citizens and society, topics that he previously addressed for governments and supranational organizations such as the European Commission and Parliament, and large publicly traded companies. His research has been featured in international conferences, such as the United Nations University's International Conference on Theory and Practice of Electronic Governance (ICEGOV) and the European Conference on Information Systems (ECIS).

Matthias Babel (matthias.babel@fim-rc.de) is a Ph.D. candidate at the University of Bayreuth and a researcher at the Branch Business and Information Systems Engineering of the Fraunhofer FIT. He holds a B.Sc. and an M.Sc. in Computer Science. In his research, he focuses on bridging the gap between state-of-the-art technology and real-world applications in the energy sector to drive the energy transition and decarbonization. Therefore, he studies the practical design of IT artifacts with a focus on distributed systems, digital identities, and applied cryptography. His research has been published in international journals like *Energy Informatics* (EnIcs) and the International Conference on Information Systems (ICIS).

Tom Barbereau (tom.barbereau@tno.nl) is a scientist specialist for the governance of disruptive technologies at the Dutch Organisation for Applied Scientific Research (TNO). Previously, he was a researcher at the Interdisciplinary Centre for Security, Reliability and Trust (SnT) at the University of Luxembourg and a visiting researcher at the Institute for Information Law (IViR) at the University of Amsterdam. He received his M.Sc. in Science & Technology Studies and his Ph.D. in Information Systems Management. His work has been published in international journals such as Technology in Society (TiS), Government Information Quarterly (GIQ), and Philosophy & Technology, as well as the International Conference on Information Systems (ICIS) and the Hawaii International Conferences on System Sciences (HICSS).

Martin Brennecke (martin.brennecke@uni.lu) is a doctoral researcher at the University of Luxembourg's Interdisciplinary Centre for Security, Reliability, and Trust. He received his master's degree in International Economics & Governance from the University of Bayreuth, Germany. In his research, he focuses on the intersection of management and computer science, studying the decentralization of digital infrastructures. Along those lines, he investigates the impact of distributed ledger technologies on digital financial services. His research has been published in the proceedings of the International Conference on Information Systems (ICIS), the Hawaii International Conference on Systems Sciences (HICSS), and the International Conference on Wirtschaftsinformatik (WI).

Joaquín Delgado Fernández (joaquin.delgadofernandez@uni.lu) is a postdoctoral researcher at the Interdisciplinary Centre for Security, Reliability and Trust (SnT), University of Luxembourg. He received his M.Sc. in Artificial Intelligence and his Ph.D. in Computer Science. His research focuses on how distributed artificial intelligence, and in particular federated learning, can be applied to facilitate cross-silo coordination. His research is mainly oriented toward the energy sector, where his research shines on short-term and nation-scale forecasting, and the financial sector, where he mainly focuses on the prediction of household loan defaults. His research has been published in international journals and conferences such as Applied Energy (AppEn), PowerTech, and the Hawaii International Conference on System Sciences (HICSS). He has also had the opportunity to present his work at the United Nations Asia Pacific and the Stuttgart Stock Exchange, among others.

Marvin Ehaus (marvin.ehaus@fim-rc.de) is a research assistant at the University of Bayreuth and the Branch Business and Information Systems Engineering of the Fraunhofer FIT and the Fraunhofer Blockchain Lab. He received his B.Sc. in Business Management. In his research, Marvin Ehaus focuses on emerging technologies such as blockchain, self-managed identities, and advanced cryptography and their impact on organizations that need to share information while retaining data sovereignty.

Simon Feulner (simon.feulner@fim-rc.de) is a researcher at the Frankfurt University of Applied Sciences and the Branch Business and Information Systems Engineering of the Fraunhofer FIT and a doctoral candidate at the University of Bayreuth. He received his B.Sc. in Business Administration and holds M.Sc. in Business Administration and Business & Information Systems Engineering. His research centers around decentralized technologies like blockchain and digital identities. In his research, Simon Feulner especially emphasizes the practical application of such technologies in various domains. His research has been published in international journals like *Electronic Markets* (EM), *Information & Management* (I&M), and leading conferences like the European Conference on Information Systems (ECIS).

Muriel Frank (muriel.frank@uni.lu) is a postdoctoral researcher at the Interdisciplinary Centre for Security, Reliability and Trust (SnT) at the University of Luxembourg. She holds a Ph.D. in Information Systems from Goethe University Frankfurt, Germany. Her research primarily focuses on understanding decision-making with regard to information security, policy compliance behavior, as well as extra-role security behaviors. She is also interested in issues related to identity and access management as well as privacy-enhancing technologies. Her work has been published in several conference proceedings and academic journals, including *Decision Support Systems* (DSS), *Business & Information Systems Engineering* (BISE), and *Computers & Security*.

Gilbert Fridgen (gilbert.fridgen@uni.lu) is Professor and PayPal-FNR PEARL Chair in Digital Financial Services at the Interdisciplinary Centre for Security, Reliability, and Trust (SnT), University of Luxembourg and Coordinator of Luxembourg's National Centre of Excellence in Research on Financial Technologies (FinTech NCER). In his research, he analyzes the transformative effects of digital technologies on individual organizations as well on the relationship between organizations. He addresses especially decentralized and distributed technologies like Distributed Ledgers, Digital Identities, Federated Learning, and the Internet-of-Things. His research involves information systems engineering, IT strategy and (risk) management, as well as regulatory compliance. He frequently publishes in academic journals and conference proceedings in management, information systems, computer science, and engineering, as well in outlets at the intersection of these disciplines. He is editor of major journals in his field and chaired tracks of the most important German, European, and International Conferences of Information Systems.

Vincent Gramlich (vincent.gramlich@fim-rc.de) is a researcher at the Frankfurt University of Applied Sciences and the Branch Business and Information Systems Engineering of the Fraunhofer FIT and a doctoral candidate at the University of

Bayreuth. He received his B.Sc. and M.Sc. in Economathematics. His research centers around leveraging innovative, decentralized technologies like blockchain, digital identities, and other applied cryptography to enable traceability and verifiability of information and assets without relying on central authorities while maintaining system efficiency, data sovereignty and privacy. In his research, Vincent Gramlich especially emphasizes the transfer of cutting-edge technological advances into practical application and is mainly focused on the financial and energy sectors. His research has been published in international journals like *Electronic Markets* (EM), *Energy Informatics* (EnIcs), and the *Journal of Banking and Banking Law* (JBB).

Tobias Guggenberger (tobias.guggenberger@fim-rc.de) is a postdoctoral researcher at the University of Bayreuth and the Branch Business & Information Systems Engineering of Fraunhofer FIT. He holds an M.Sc. in business administration and a Ph.D. in information systems engineering. His research primarily concentrates on the design and management of information systems, leveraging emerging technologies like artificial intelligence (AI) and blockchain. In particular, his work is notably centered on exploring the impact of decentralization and distributed decision-making on the collaborative and value-creation practices of firms. His scholarly contributions have appeared in renowned conference proceedings, including the European Conference on Information Systems (ECIS) and the International Conference on Information Systems (ICIS). His research has also been published in prestigious international journals such as *IEEE Transactions on Engineering Management* (IEEE TEM), *Electronic Markets* (EM), and *Computers & Industrial Engineering*.

Eduard Hartwich (eduard.hardwich@uni.lu) holds a PhD from the University of Luxembourg. He has a background in International Business Administration and Information Technology (B.Sc. from Hochschule Ludwigshafen, M.A. from Munich Business School, and MBA from Florida International University). His research explores the intersection of economic and technological developments, specifically focusing on machine economies and the role of decentralized finance (DeFi). His research focuses on understanding efficient machine economies and the technologies supporting them such as distributed ledger technology (DLT) and non-fungible tokens (NFTs). Additionally, he analyzes how DeFi adoption can create opportunities for enterprises and drive economic growth. His work has been published in prestigious international journals and conferences, including *Internet Research (INTR), Electronic Markets (EM), the International Conference on Information Systems (ICIS), the European Conference on Information Systems (ECIS), and the Hawaii International Conference on System Sciences (HICSS).*

Pol Hölzmer (pol.hoelzmer@uni.lu) is a doctoral researcher at the Interdisciplinary Centre for Security, Reliability and Trust (SnT), University of Luxembourg, specializing in informational security and privacy. He received his B.Sc. in Information and Communication Technologies and his M.Sc. in IT security. His research focus lies on technical aspects of (decentralized) digital identity management systems and (qualified) electronic attestation of attributes.

Alexandra Hoess (alexandra.hoess@uni.lu) is a researcher at the University of Luxembourg's Interdisciplinary Centre for Security, Reliability and Trust. She also closely collaborates with Luxembourg's Ministry for Digitalisation. Alexandra holds a PhD from the University of Luxembourg and has a background in Finance & Information Management (M. Sc. with honors from the Technical University of Munich, the University of Augsburg, and the University of Bayreuth). In her research, she explores the digitalization of public services with a particular focus on the management and design of digital identity systems and the role of blockchain technology therein. Her research has been published in international journals and conferences, such as *Business & Information Systems Engineering* (BISE), the International Conference on Information Systems (ICIS), the European Conference on Information Systems (ECIS), and the Hawaii International Conferences on System Sciences (HICSS).

Lars Keppler (lars.keppler@fim-rc.de) is a research assistant at the Frankfurt University of Applied Sciences and the FIM Research Center. He currently studies computer science and assists the Fraunhofer Blockchain Laboratory at the Branch Business and Information Systems Engineering of the Fraunhofer FIT. As a certified business economist and stock exchange broker, his research focuses on Distributed Ledger Technology in Finance.

Marc-Fabian Körner (marc.koerner@fim-rc.de) is a postdoctoral researcher at the University of Bayreuth, where he received his Ph.D. in Information Systems in 2021. He also leads a research group on Green IS and Digital Decarbonization at the Branch Business & Information Systems Engineering of the Fraunhofer FIT and the FIM Research Center. His research focuses on Green IS and the application of data ecosystems for cross-organizational collaboration, as well as digital identity management in private and public organizations. Additionally, he serves as a reviewer, associate editor, and track chair for several journals and conferences. His work has been published in various conference proceedings and international journals, such as *Business & Information Systems Engineering* (BISE), *Electronic Markets* (EM), and *Renewable & Sustainable Energy Reviews* (RASER).

Jonathan Lautenschlager (jonathan.lautenschlager@fim-rc.de) is a researcher at the Branch Business and Information Systems Engineering of the Fraunhofer FIT and currently pursuing his Ph.D. in Information Systems at FIM Research Center, University of Bayreuth and Frankfurt University of Applied Sciences. In his research, Mr. Lautenschlager works on blockchain technology, decentralized identity management and related fields. He received his M.A. in Media Economics with specialization in media informatics.

Sarah Lichtmannecker (sarah.lichtmannecker@fim-rc.de) is a research assistant at the University of Bayreuth and the Branch Business and Information Systems Engineering of the Fraunhofer FIT. She received her B.Sc. in Business Administration with a major in Information Systems and Information Management. In her research, Sarah Lichtmannecker explores the impact of technological advancements on social dynamics, as well as the innovative evolution of business models in the digital era. Adopting a multidisciplinary perspective, her work examines the ways digital technologies are reshaping human interactions, societal norms, and business strategies; highlighting the interconnectedness of these domains in the digital era.

Renan Lima Baima (renan.limabaima@uni.lu) is a doctoral researcher at the Interdisciplinary Centre for Security, Reliability, and Trust (SnT) at the University of Luxembourg. With a master's in Computer Science and a bachelor's in Control and Automation Engineering, his research spans Robotics, Artificial Intelligence, Reinforcement Learning, Cognitive Robotics, Object Affordance Recognition, Ontology, Agent-Based Systems, Multi-Robot Interaction, and Federated Machine Learning. Renan's multiple international collaborations include work with the European Space Agency (ESA) and long-lasting International Universities. Among past experiences, he developed an Ontological Knowledge-Base system for autonomous software testing in the aviation and aerospace industries and created an incremental framework for teaching cognitive robotic agents to autonomously interact with diverse objects using multimodal multi-fingered grippers to attain various object affordances. Currently, Renan is focused on the FiReSpARX project, where he is developing an architectural framework for space multi-robotic cooperation. This framework integrates governance (RegTech) and autonomous economic decision-making (FinTech) to construct a collaborative multi-robotic system (MRS).

Felix Paetzold (felix.paetzold@fim-rc.de) is a researcher at the University of Bayreuth and the Business and Information Systems department of Fraunhofer FIT. He holds an M.Sc. in Business Administration with a focus on Information Systems and Information Management. His research focuses on the intersection of business administration and information technology, especially in the context of blockchain technology and self-sovereign identity in the digitalization of the energy industry.

Nadia Pocher (nadia.pocher@uni.lu) is a postdoctoral researcher at the Interdisciplinary Centre for Security, Reliability and Trust (SnT), University of Luxembourg. She received her Master of Laws, summa cum laude, from the University of Trento, and her Ph.D. in Law, Science and Technology, excellent cum laude, from the University of Bologna, jointly with a Ph.D. in Law from the Autonomous University of Barcelona and K.U. Leuven. In her research, she focuses on the regulation and compliance of emerging technologies in the financial space, through the lens of techno-legal design. Her interests include AML/CFT in crypto-assets and decentralized finance. Her research has been published in international journals such as *Electronic Markets* and *IEEE Transactions on Network and Service Management* (TNSM), edited books such as Springer's *Handbook on Blockchain*, and conferences such as IEEE Conference on Blockchain and Cryptocurrency (ICBC) and the Atlantic Council's Forum on US-European GeoEconomics.

Emanuela Podda (emanuela.podda@uni.lu) is a postdoctoral researcher at the Interdisciplinary Centre for Security, Reliability and Trust (SnT) at the University of Luxembourg. In her research, she focuses on the regulatory challenges posed by data-driven innovation, including data processing compliance and data governance models. She received her M.Sc. in law and her Ph.D. in law, science, and technology.

Marc Principato (marc.principato@fim-rc.de) is a research assistant at the University of Bayreuth and the Branch Business and Information Systems Engineering of the Fraunhofer FIT. He received his B.Sc. in business administration with a major in information systems and information management. In his research, Marc Principato focuses on blockchains and applied cryptography for data sovereignty, privacy, and scalability in information systems. His research has been published in international journals and conferences such as *Electronic Markets* (EM) and the International Conference on Information Systems (ICIS).

Alexander Rieger (arieger@walton.uark.edu) is an Assistant Professor of Information Systems in the Sam M. Walton College of Business at the University of Arkansas. His research focuses on innovation with emerging technologies in highly structured contexts. His work has appeared or is forthcoming in *Nature Human Behavior*, *Nature Machine Intelligence*, *Information & Organization*, *International Journal of Information Management*, and *MISQ Executive*. He has several years of experience working in industry and consulting for the European Commission as well as various public and private sector organizations in Germany and Luxembourg. He holds a master's degree and a Ph.D. in Information Systems.

Benjamin Schellinger (benjamin.schellinger@web.de) is an affiliated researcher at the FIM Research Center, University of Bayreuth, where he received his Ph.D. in information systems engineering. His research focuses on leveraging digital assets and currencies for the finance sector. Benjamin Schellinger further explores the transformative potential of decentralized finance and the tokenization of assets. He employs a blend of quantitative (e.g., portfolio optimization), qualitative (e.g., structured interviews), and design-oriented methods. His research has been published in international journals, including the *Journal of Business Economics* (JBE), the *Journal of Risk Finance* (JRF), and *Electronic Markets* (EM).

Vincent Schlatt is an affiliated researcher at the FIM Research Center, University of Bayreuth, where he received his Ph.D. in Information Systems Engineering in 2022. His research focuses on decentralized information systems with an emphasis on blockchain technology and self-sovereign identities. Vincent Schlatt further focuses on design-oriented research approaches as well as IT security aspects. His work has been published in international journals, such as *Electronic Markets (EM), Information & Management (I&M), as well as various conference proceedings.*

Johannes Sedlmeir (johannes.sedlmeir@uni.lu) is a postdoctoral researcher at the Interdisciplinary Centre for Security, Reliability and Trust (SnT), University of Luxembourg. He received his M.Sc. in mathematical physics and his Ph.D. in information systems engineering. In his research, he focuses on the use of emerging digital technologies that enhance the verifiability and privacy of workflows in organizations. He does so by designing innovative IT artifacts based on components such as blockchains, digital identity attestations, and zero-knowledge proofs. He also uses methods like quantitative (e.g., performance evaluations) and qualitative (e.g., expert interviews) methods to conduct criteria-based evaluations of the corresponding solutions. His research has been published in international journals such as *Business & Information Systems Engineering* (BISE), *Electronic Markets* (EM), *Information & Management* (I&M), and the *Journal of Network and Computer Applications* (JNCA).

Jens-Christian Stoetzer (jens.stoetzer@fim-rc.de) is a researcher at the FIM Research Center, University of Bayreuth and a doctoral candidate at the University of Bayreuth. He received his B.Sc. and M.Sc. degrees in Business Administration. In his research, Jens-Christian Stoetzer focuses on digital emerging technologies in various domains, with an emphasis on implications for strategic information management. His research has been published in leading international journals and conferences such as the International Conference on Information Systems (ICIS).

Jan Stramm (jan.stramm@fim-rc.de) is a doctoral candidate at the University of Bayreuth and researcher at the Frankfurt University of Applied Sciences and the Branch Business and Information Systems Engineering of the Fraunhofer FIT. He received his B.Sc. and M.Sc. in Business Administration from the University of Bayreuth. In the scope of his research endeavors, Jan Stramm primarily focuses on the domain of strategic management of emergent digital technologies within various operational and organizational contexts. His expertise extends particularly to the strategic integration of blockchain technology and artificial intelligence in operational settings, such as strategic procurement and supply chain management. His research has been published in the proceedings of the Hawaii International Conference on Systems Sciences (HICSS) and the International Conference on Wirtschaftsinformatik (WI).

Tobias Ströher (tobias.stroeher@fim-rc.de) is a researcher at Branch Business and Information Systems Engineering of the Fraunhofer FIT and a doctoral candidate at the University of Bayreuth. He received his B.Sc. and M.Sc. degrees in Industrial Engineering. His research focuses on the use of digital technologies in the energy sector, with an emphasis on sustainability issues such as decarbonization, and has been published in international conferences such as the Americas Conference on Information Systems (AMCIS).

Jens Strüker (jens.strueker@fim-rc.de) is Professor of Information Systems and Digital Energy Management at the University of Bayreuth in Germany. He received his Ph.D. and habilitation in information systems and economics from University of Freiburg, after working as a visiting researcher at SAP Labs, Palo Alto. Jens is Director at the FIM Research Center for Information Management and the Branch Business & Information Systems Engineering of Fraunhofer FIT, as well as Director of the Fraunhofer Blockchain Lab. In research, teaching and practice Jens investigates the potential of digital technologies for decarbonising the (energy) industry. His work has been published in several academic journals such as the Journal of European Information Systems (EJIS), the Communications of the ACM (CACM), Business & Information Systems Engineering (BISE), and Electronic Markets (EM). Jens works intensively with corporations, small and medium sized companies as well as with associations and think tanks. He is a member of various advisory boards of start-ups and supervisory boards. Furthermore, Jens is a regular keynote speaker at events in Europe, Asia and North America.

Nils Urbach (nils.urbach@fim-rc.de) is Professor of Information Systems and Digital Business as well as Director of the Research Lab for Digital Innovation & Transformation at the Frankfurt University of Applied Sciences, Germany. Furthermore, he is Director at the FIM Research Center for Information Management and the Branch Business & Information Systems Engineering of Fraunhofer FIT, as well as Co-Founder and Director of the Fraunhofer Blockchain Lab. Nils Urbach has been working in the fields of digital innovation and transformation for several years. His work has been published in several academic journals such as the *Journal of Strategic Information Systems* (JSIS), the *Journal of Information Technology* (JIT), *MIS Quarterly Executive* (MISQE), *IEEE Transactions on Engineering Management* (IEEE TEM), *Information and Management* (I&M), *Business & Information Systems Engineering* (BISE), and *Electronic Markets* (EM). He advises several companies on digitalization issues and regularly appears as a speaker on this topic.

Maximilian Volland (maximilian.volland@fim-rc.de) is a research assistant at the University of Bayreuth and the Branch Business and Information Systems Engineering of the Fraunhofer FIT. He studies philosophy, economics, law, and computer science. In his research, Maximilian Volland focuses on the digital transformation of the legal sector (legal tech) and the question of how innovative technologies can increase efficiency for courts, law enforcement or law firms. He is also interested in the regulation of disruptive technologies. His research has been published in journals such as *Legal Revolution Journal* (LRZ).

Fabiane Völter (fabiane.voelter@fim-rc.de) is an affiliated researcher at the FIM Research Center, University of Bayreuth, where she received her Ph.D. in Business Information Systems Engineering in 2023. Her research focuses on digitally sovereign information systems. Fabiane Völter thereby emphasizes the management, utilization, and security of IS for digital sovereignty. Her work has been published in various conference proceedings and international journals such as Computers&Security (C&S), Business & Information Systems Engineering (BISE) and the International Journal of Information Management (IJIM).

Linda Weigl (l.weigl@uva.nl) s a postdoctoral researcher at the University of Amsterdam's Institute for Information Law. Her research interests lie in digital sovereignty, digital regulation, and trustworthiness in the digital society. Linda focuses on platform regulation and digital trust dynamics of decentralized infrastructures. She further analyzes how technology-centric solutions can be reconciled with democratic criteria and public values. Her contributions have been published in esteemed academic journals, including Government Information Quarterly (GIQ) and Nature Human Behavior, as well as well-known conference proceedings, notably at the International Conference on Information Systems (ICIS) and the European Conference on Information Systems (ECIS).

Lukas Willburger (lukas.willburger@fim-rc.de) is a researcher and doctoral candidate at the Branch Business and Information Systems Engineering of the Fraunhofer FIT. He received his B.Sc. in Information Systems and his M.Sc. in Computer Science. His research focuses on leveraging the use of innovative methods to minimize data in digital processes. This includes, in particular, works on secure digital and self-sovereign identities and federated learning. His research has been published in international journals like *Energy Informatics* (EnIcs) and conferences such as the European Conference on Information Systems (ECIS).

Till Zwede (till.zwede@fim-rc.de) is a researcher and doctoral candidate at the University of Bayreuth and a researcher at the Branch Business and Information Systems Engineering of the Fraunhofer FIT and the Fraunhofer Blockchain Lab. He received his B.Sc. and M.Sc. in Business Administration. His research centers around leveraging innovative, decentralized technologies like blockchain, digital identities, and other applied cryptography to enable the traceability and verifiability of information and assets without relying on central authorities while maintaining system efficiency, data sovereignty, and privacy. In his research, Till Zwede especially emphasizes the transfer of cutting-edge technological advances into practical application and is mainly focused on the energy sector, and sustainability and carbon information in product lifecycles. His research has been published in international journals like *Energy Informatics* (EnIcs) and conferences such as the International Conference on Information Systems (ICIS) and the Hawaii International Conference on System Sciences (HICSS).

Acronyms

AI	Artificial intelligence
AICPA	American Institute of Certified Public Accountants
AML	Anti-money laundering
AMLA	Anti-Money Laundering Authority
AMM	Automated market maker
API	Application programming interface
ARP	Address resolution protocol
ASIC	Application-specific integrated circuit
ATM	Automated teller machine
AWS	Amazon Web Services
B2B	Business-to-business
BBS	Boneh-Boyen-Shacham
BCBS	Basel Committee of Banking Supervision
BFT	Byzantine fault tolerance
BIS	Bank for International Settlements
BLE	Bluetooth low energy
CA	Certificate authority
CBDC	Central bank digital currency
CDD	Customer due diligence
CeFi	Centralized finance
CEX	Centralized exchange
CFT	Combating the financing of terrorism
CL	Camenisch-Lysyanskaya
CPMI	Committee on Payments and Markets Infrastructure
CRL	Certificate revocation list
CSP	Cloud service provider
CSR	Corporate social responsibility
DAO	Decentralized autonomous organization
DApp	Decentralized application
DeFi	Decentralized finance
DEX	Decentralized exchange

DGA	Data Governance Act
DID	Decentralized identifier
DL	Deep learning
DLP	Discrete logarithm problem
DLT	Distributed ledger technology
DMA	Digital Markets Act
DNS	Domain name services
DORA	Digital Operational Resilience Act
DP	Differential privacy
DPP	Digital product passport
DSA	Digital Services Act
E2E	End-to-end
EBA	European Banking Authority
EC	European Commission
ECB	European Central Bank
ECC	Elliptic curve cryptography
ECDLP	Elliptic curve discrete logarithm problem
ECDSA	Elliptic curve digital signature algorithm
ECSC	European Coal and Steel Community
EEC	European Economic Community
eID	Electronic identity
eIDAS	Electronic Identification, Authentication and Trust Services
eIDAS2	European Digital Identity Regulation
eKYC	Electronic KYC
EMD2	Electronic Money Directive 2
EOA	Externally-owned account
ERC	Ethereum request for comments
ESG	Environmental, social, and governance
ESSIF	European self-sovereign identity framework
ETF	Exchange traded fund
EU	European Union
EUDIW	European digital identity wallet
Euratom	European Atomic Energy Community
EV	Electric vehicle
FATF	Financial Action Task Force
FCA	Financial Conduct Authority
FDS	Fraud detection system
FHE	Fully homomorphic encryption
FI	Financial institution
FiDAR	Regulation on Financial Data Access
FIU	Financial intelligence unit
FL	Federated learning
FRI	Fast Reed-Solomon interactive oracle proofs of proximity
FSB	Financial Stability Board
FT	Fungible token

FTL	Federated transfer learning
GDPR	General Data Protection Regulation
GHG	Greenhouse gas
GRI	Global Reporting Initiative
GSIA	Global Sustainable Investment Alliance
HE	Homomorphic encryption
HIPAA	Health Insurance Portability and Accountability Act
HTTPS	Hypertext transfer protocol secure
IAM	Identity and access management
IASB	International Accounting Standards Board
ICO	Initial coin offering
ICT	Information and communication technology
IdM	Identity management
IFS	Integer factorization problem
IID	Independent and identically distributed
IMF	International Monetary Fund
IOSCO	International Organization of Securities Commissions
IoT	Internet of Things
IPO	Initial public offering
IRA	Inflation Reduction Act
IS	Information system
ISP	Internet service provider
IT	Information technology
KYB	Know-your-business
KYC	Know-your-customer
LEA	Law enforcement agency
LED	Data Protection Law Enforcement Directive
LP	Liquidity pool
LPT	Liquidity pool token
MAC	Medium access control
MAS	Monetary Authority of Singapore
MEV	Maximal extractable value
MiCAR	Markets in Crypto Assets Regulation
MiFID II	Second Markets in Financial Instruments Directive
MiFIR	Markets in Financial Instruments Regulation
MITM	Machine-in-the-middle
ML	Machine learning
MLA	Money laundering act
MLOps	Machine learning operation
MPC	Multi-party computation
NATO	North Atlantic Treaty Organization
NFC	Near-field communication
NFT	Non-fungible token
NHS	National Health Service
NIST	National Institute of Standards and Technology

NIZKP	Non-interactive zero-knowledge proof
non-IID	Non-independent and identically distributed
OCSP	Online certificate status protocol
OECD	Organisation for Economic Co-operation and Development
OIDC4VP	Open ID Connect for verifiable presentation
P2P	Peer-to-peer
PET	Privacy-enhancing technology
PII	Personally identifiable information
PKC	Public key cryptography
PKI	Public key infrastructure
PoA	Proof of authority
PoS	Proof of stake
PoW	Proof of work
PQC	Post-quantum cryptography
PSD2	Revised Payment Services Directive
PSD3	Payment Services Directive 3
PSP	Payment service provider
PSR	Payment Services Regulation
PUE	Power usage effectiveness
QR	Quick response
QWAC	Qualified website authentication certificate
RBA	Risk-based approach
RSA	Rivest-Shamir-Adleman
RTGS	Real-time gross settlement
RTR	Real-time reporting
SASB	Sustainability Accounting Standards Board
SEC	Securities and Exchange Commission
SecAgg	Secure aggregation
SIOP	Self-issued OpenID provider
SKC	Symmetric key cryptography
SNARK	Succinct non-interactive argument of knowledge
SRI	Socially responsible investing
SSI	Self-sovereign identity
STR	Suspicious transaction report
TEE	Trusted execution environment
TLS	Transport layer security
TradFi	Traditional finance
TTP	Trusted third party
UK	United Kingdom
UML	Unified modeling language
US	United States
USA	United States of America
UTXO	Unspent transaction output
VC	Verifiable credential
VP	Verifiable presentation

WTO	World Trade Organization
zk-SNARK	Zero-knowledge succinct non-interactive argument of knowledge
zk-STARK	Zero-knowledge scalable transparent argument of knowledge
ZKP	Zero-knowledge proof
zkVM	Zero-knowledge virtual machine

Part I
Regulatory, Economic, and Technical Developments

Chapter 1
Introduction: Decentralization Technologies in Finance

Gilbert Fridgen, Tobias Guggenberger, Johannes Sedlmeir, and Nils Urbach

Abstract This chapter first gives a brief overview of the evolution of the financial sector, highlighting key milestones such as the introduction of automated teller machines (ATMs), the rise of online and mobile banking, and the impact of FinTech innovations and open banking regulations. It then explores the paradigm shift initiated by Bitcoin and blockchain technologies toward decentralized financial services. The subsequent discussion of potential benefits and challenges of adopting decentralization technologies underscores the dynamic interplay between technological advancements and financial services. As such, the chapter sets the stage for a deeper exploration of the impact of decentralization technologies on the financial sector.

1.1 Historical Overview of the Impact of the Digital Transformation on the Financial Sector

The path of digital transformation in the financial sector represents a reflection of the dynamic interplay between technological innovation and financial services.

G. Fridgen · J. Sedlmeir (✉)
Interdisciplinary Centre for Security, Reliability and Trust (SnT), University of Luxembourg, Esch-sur-Alzette, Luxembourg
e-mail: gilbert.fridgen@uni.lu; johannes.sedlmeir@uni.lu

T. Guggenberger
FIM Research Center, University of Bayreuth, Bayreuth, Germany

Branch Business & Information Systems Engineering of Fraunhofer FIT, Bayreuth, Germany
e-mail: tobias.guggenberger@fim-rc.de

N. Urbach
FIM Research Center for Information, Frankfurt University of Applied Sciences, Frankfurt am Main, Germany

Branch Business & Information Systems Engineering of Fraunhofer FIT, Bayreuth, Germany
e-mail: nils.urbach@fra-uas.de

G. Fridgen et al. (eds.), *Decentralization Technologies*, Financial Innovation and Technology, https://doi.org/10.1007/978-3-031-66047-4_1

Over the last decades, digital technologies have vastly changed the way we perceive the financial industry and interact with financial services. This evolution already began in the 1960s with the introduction of ATMs. ATMs fundamentally changed the traditional banking landscape by allowing customers to conduct basic banking transactions, such as cash withdrawals, deposits, and balance inquiries, outside of bank branches and outside of normal business hours. This innovation not only ushered in a new era of convenience and accessibility in customer service but also laid the foundation for the digitization of selected financial services and marked the first significant step toward self-service banking platforms (Arner et al., 2015).

Arguably even more disruptive than the introduction of the ATM was the diffusion of the Internet in the 1990s, which catapulted the financial sector into the realm of online banking. This period was characterized by a significant change in the way financial transactions were conducted. Banks started offering their customers a range of services over the Internet, allowing them to manage their financial activities remotely (Arner et al., 2015). This period also saw the successful emergence of innovative online payment systems such as PayPal, which played a crucial role in reshaping online transactions and commerce. These developments not only expanded the scope and reach of financial services but also introduced a new level of convenience and efficiency to financial management, paving the way for a "digital-first" approach to banking and finance (Bhattacherjee, 2001).

The digital transformation of the financial sector has been further accelerated by the ubiquitous use of smartphones and the subsequent development of mobile banking applications. Mobile banking applications have transformed smartphones into portable banking terminals, allowing users to perform a wide range of financial transactions with just a few taps on their edge devices (Claessens et al., 2002; Mallat et al., 2004). Near-field communication (NFC) capabilities for contactless payments further increased the convenience of mobile phone-based payments, and improved authentication features (e.g., passkeys offering sophisticated cryptographic key management with trusted execution environments or embedded secure elements and biometric unlocking) have substantially reduced security threats (Kruzikova et al., 2022). Today, a large share of bank customers use mobile applications to manage their banking services, and the majority of bank customers use mobile applications to manage their banking services. This shift to mobile banking underscores the growing demand for financial services on the go and highlights the critical role of technology in meeting consumers' changing expectations for immediacy and convenience.

The rise of FinTech companies and the emergence of open banking, catalyzed in particular by regulatory initiatives such as the Revised Payment Services Directive (PSD2), have also created a new competitive landscape in the financial services sector (Arner et al., 2021; Zavolokina et al., 2016). Open banking has broken the banks' traditional monopolies over their customers' financial data and created an environment that favors innovation and competition. This regulatory change encouraged the development of a variety of new financial services and applications and enabled third-party providers to access banking data and infrastructure to create value-added services for consumers (Mansfield-Devine, 2016). Concurrently, the

FinTech revolution, driven by technological advances and supportive regulatory frameworks, has contributed significantly to the diversification and democratization of financial services, challenging incumbent institutions to innovate and adapt to the rapidly evolving digital landscape (Puschmann, 2017).

Often considered as important as the emergence of the Internet, the revolutionary launch of Bitcoin in 2009 and the subsequent spread of blockchain and distributed ledger technology (DLT) in the form of cryptocurrencies and decentralized applications (DApps) finally heralded a paradigm shift toward the decentralization of financial services (Gramlich et al., 2023). This "wild west" phase of cryptocurrencies and other crypto-assets facilitated by permissionless blockchains was initially characterized by rapid growth and minimal regulation (Barbereau et al., 2023b). It has marked a significant departure from traditional financial models. While also characterized by several meltdowns, as in the case of the crypto-asset exchange FTX that gave evidence for substantial (systemic) risks in crypto-asset markets (Jalan & Matkovskyy, 2023), recent years witnessed some convergence of the crypto space with the regulated financial environment, as evidenced by the introduction of several new regulatory frameworks (Zetzsche & Woxholth, 2022). These frameworks go far beyond the recent introduction of Bitcoin exchange traded funds (ETFs) (Schmitt et al., 2024): For instance, the Markets in Crypto Assets Regulation (MiCAR) aims to reduce risks for consumers and, at the same time, give businesses the opportunity to provide financial services for crypto-assets within the regulatory domain (Pocher, 2023; Ferreira & Sandner, 2021). The growing, albeit cautious, interest in the adoption of blockchain technology by traditional financial institutions and central banks reflects a maturing ecosystem that seeks to combine the benefits of decentralization with the stability and trust inherent in regulated financial systems (Jalan & Matkovskyy, 2023).

1.2 The Emergence of Decentralization Technologies

The digital transformation in the financial sector, driven by new technologies and the ubiquity of mobile banking, has ushered in a new era of operational efficiency and increased customer engagement (Alt et al., 2024; Puschmann, 2017). These technologies have enabled financial institutions to extract value from analyzing vast data sets, saving costs by automating complex processes, and improving their services for customers by delivering personalized banking experiences. However, this next step of the digital transformation is not without its challenges. Reliance on centralized digital architectures has raised significant concerns about data security, the risk of system outages, and the potential erosion of digital sovereignty in a world where financial services are increasingly globalized and interconnected and, therefore, build important foundations of our society (Codagnone & Weigl, 2023). As such, they are naturally subject to political decision-making. In particular, the dominance of incumbents and legacy systems in the financial sector has led to a perception that competition and innovation are being stifled, necessitating a reassessment of existing paradigms for the delivery of financial services. Finally, there is a growing need for open financial infrastructures that can integrate an increasing number of machines engaging in autonomous economic interactions (Hartwich et al., 2023), as well as millions of people who are still suffering from limited opportunities (particularly in developing countries) because they lack access to the international financial system.

In response to these diverse challenges, a new set of technologies, collectively referred to as decentralization technologies, has emerged as a promising solution. At the heart of these technologies is the principle of decentralization, which aims to distribute control and decision-making, reducing dependence on and trust requirements in central authorities, as well as mitigating several risks associated with centralized systems. In the evolving landscape of the financial sector, the adoption of key decentralization technologies marks a pivotal shift to address some inherent challenges of traditional financial systems and better harness the potential of the digital transformation. This chapter provides an overview of the foundational technologies that are reshaping the fabric of financial services, namely DLT, digital identity wallets, and federated learning (FL). We also include a chapter on privacy-enhancing technologies (PETs) that are often necessary to compensate for increased risks of exposure of sensitive information in decentralized systems, driven, e.g., by higher degrees of transparency, a bigger attack surface, or lower trust in individual stakeholders involved in data processing. Each of these technologies may play a critical role in the transition to a more secure, efficient, and inclusive financial ecosystem.

Blockchain and Distributed Ledger Technology Blockchain and DLT are often used as a synonym for the decentralization movement, providing a distributed, transparent, and immutable record of transactions. This technology underpins all decentralized finance (DeFi) applications, enabling peer-to-peer transactions without the need for central intermediaries (Brennecke et al., 2022). Blockchain's inherent decentralization and fault-tolerant characteristics address critical issues such as single points of failure, censorship, and fraud in traditional financial systems (Feulner et al., 2022). The adoption of blockchain and DLT also extends to financial services beyond cryptocurrency transactions: The programmability features provided by smart contracts open up novel opportunities in many sectors, including supply chains and trade finance and the digital representation of ownership rights for real-world assets ("tokenization"), providing a versatile foundation for innovation in financial services (Sunyaev et al., 2021; Alt et al., 2024).

Digital Identity Wallets At the heart of the decentralized financial landscape is the concept of decentralized digital identity, a key element in connecting transactions in the trustless and pseudonymous environment of cryptocurrencies to real-world trust and accountability (Sedlmeir et al., 2021). In this regard, digital identity wallets are emerging as a pivotal concept, providing a secure and easy-to-use means to manage digital identities and associated credentials. These wallets enable individuals and organizations to store, manage, and selectively disclose verifiable identity information (Sedlmeir et al., 2022a), facilitating seamless access to financial services while safeguarding privacy and data control (Guggenberger et al., 2023). Integrating digital identity wallets into financial applications and smart services can enhance user authentication processes, streamline know-your-customer (KYC) procedures, and underpin the trust mechanisms essential for transactions on decentralized platforms (Schlatt et al., 2022; Richter & Anke, 2021).

Federated Learning As financial institutions navigate the complexities of data privacy and security, FL presents a novel approach to machine learning that aligns with the principles of decentralization. FL enables multiple participants to collaboratively train machine learning models without sharing the underlying data, preserving privacy and data ownership. This technology is particularly relevant in the financial sector, where the need to leverage big data for predictive analytics and risk management must be balanced with strict privacy regulations and the hesitations of financial service providers to share customer data that gives them a competitive edge (Lee et al., 2023). FL facilitates the development of advanced analytical tools and personalized financial services when data-sharing opportunities are limited, enhancing the capabilities of financial institutions while complying with privacy and regulatory requirements and business imperatives (Long et al., 2020).

Privacy-Enhancing Technologies Traditional financial service providers were long reluctant to make full use of their clients' data. Privacy and data protection are paramount, especially in the sensitive area of financial services (Groß et al., 2021). While PETs are not a decentralization technology per se, they are an important building block for protecting individuals' privacy and securing data transactions in decentralized systems, where each individual component is often less trusted regarding the confidential treatment of data they process than a centralized entity. Besides anonymization techniques such as differential privacy, PETs include cryptographic tools for secure computation (e.g., zero-knowledge proofs (ZKPs), multi-party computation (MPC), and fully homomorphic encryption (FHE)), which allow certain data to be processed without revealing it entirely (Garrido et al., 2022). While the technology development was originally pushed through DeFi projects, their adoption provides ample opportunities to the traditional financial industry.

The convergence of these key technologies represents a transformative force in the financial sector, offering innovative solutions to longstanding challenges and unlocking new opportunities for designing and offering financial services. The subsequent chapters of this book will delve deeper into the technical underpinnings, applications, and implications of blockchain/DLT, digital identity wallets, FL, and PETs, providing a comprehensive exploration of their role in shaping the future of finance.

1.3 Introducing Decentralization Technologies into the Financial Sector

The intersection of decentralization technologies and the financial sector heralds a new era of innovation and transformation. While decentralization, e.g., through blockchains, is unlikely to replace banks (Fridgen et al., 2021), centralized finance (CeFi) is undergoing a profound evolution as decentralization technologies, epitomized by DeFi, permeate traditional financial systems (Scharfman & Scharfman, 2022; Gramlich et al., 2022). Even though blockchain might not revolutionize the financial system, blockchain, as well as other cryptographic technologies, might have an evolutionary effect. The fusion of traditional and decentralized finance presents unparalleled opportunities to enhance efficiency, transparency, and accessibility while simultaneously addressing longstanding challenges. From blockchain-enabled efficient cross-border payments in central bank digital currencies (CBDCs) (Pocher & Veneris, 2021) to the integration of compliance elements in smart contracts (Barbereau et al., 2023a), the potential applications are vast and far-reaching. Moreover, openness and composability facilitate the integration of CeFi components into DApps and the exploration of novel synergies between DeFi and traditional finance, underscoring the adaptability and resilience of this evolving ecosystem. As we embark on this journey, it is essential to delve into the transformative implications, navigate regulatory complexities, and uphold ethical standards to realize the full potential of decentralization technologies in reshaping the financial landscape (Schellinger, 2023). In the following, we sketch some of these transformative potentials discussed in the later chapters of the book.

Augmentation of CeFi Services with Decentralization Technologies The augmentation of traditional CeFi services with decentralization technologies is poised to significantly enhance efficiency and interoperability in the financial sector. For instance, blockchain technology can be employed to streamline cross-border payments and settlements, diminishing the time and cost associated with these transactions while enhancing transparency and security. Similarly, smart contracts can automate compliance and regulatory reporting, thereby reducing operational overheads and human errors. This convergence of CeFi and DeFi technologies can not only improve the efficiency of existing financial operations but also open up new avenues for collaboration and innovation across different financial institutions and systems.

Decentralized Applications Augmented by CeFi Components The integration of CeFi components into decentralized applications offers the potential to address some of the limitations of purely decentralized systems, such as liquidity issues and market depth. For example, decentralized exchanges (DEXs) can be augmented with liquidity pools and market-making services from traditional financial institutions, enhancing their functionality and user experience. This symbiotic relationship between CeFi and DeFi components can lead to more robust and resilient financial applications that leverage the best of both worlds.

Exploring New Combinations of DeFi and Traditional Financial Services The fusion of DeFi and traditional financial services is leading to the creation of entirely new combinations and use cases that were previously difficult to imagine. For instance, blockchain technology and digital identity attestations supposedly could enhance environmental, social, and governance (ESG) reporting by providing cryptographically verifiable records of a company's ESG activities, thereby increasing trust and accountability in ESG compliance. Similarly, the integration of digital identity wallets with DeFi platforms has the potential to revolutionize KYC processes, making them more efficient and user-friendly while aligning them with regulatory accountability requirements and ensuring privacy and data protection. Moreover, the application of federated learning in credit risk assessments could, in principle, enable more accurate and personalized credit scoring by leveraging data sources fragmented across users or organizations without compromising individual privacy or data control requirements.

These emerging combinations of DeFi and traditional financial services underscore the transformative potential of decentralization technologies in creating a more inclusive, efficient, and secure financial ecosystem. As we delve deeper into these implications, it is crucial to consider the broader socioeconomic impacts, regulatory challenges, and ethical considerations associated with the widespread adoption of these technologies. The exploration of use cases such as ESG reporting with blockchain, digital identity wallets for KYC, and credit risk assessments with federated learning not only illustrates the practical applications of these technologies but also highlights the need for a collaborative approach in addressing the complexities and opportunities presented by the evolving financial landscape.

1.4 Benefits of Decentralization Technologies

The evolution of the digital transformation in the financial sector, particularly through the lens of decentralization technologies, represents a significant pivot from traditional paradigms underlying financial service offerings to a new, dynamic model that holds profound implications for the global financial ecosystem. This shift, underpinned by technologies such as blockchain/DLT and digital identity wallets, is not merely a technological evolution; it represents a comprehensive restructuring of financial transaction mechanisms, service delivery, and the overall operational fabric of global financial systems. As such, we can derive several distinguished value propositions of decentralization technologies in the financial sector:

Facilitating New Opportunities of Collaboration One of the core value propositions of decentralization technologies, such as blockchain, that previous work has pointed out is that they can facilitate collaboration in the form of cross-organizational digital interactions for which no universally trusted intermediary exists (e.g., for economic, political, technical, personal, or social reasons). The availability of a neutral digital platform (Sedlmeir et al., 2022b) has led to the emergence of innovative solutions in the context of, e.g., medical supply chains (Mattke et al., 2019) or trade finance (Jensen et al., 2019) and attempts of collaboration between competitors that promise efficiency gains and new value propositions (Napirata et al., 2023; Hoess et al., 2024). As control over monetary systems is highly contested from a political perspective, a neutral infrastructure that defines rules for monetary systems and that is largely independent of single corporate or state actors may unlock innovation in the financial sector.

Reimagining Efficiency and Security The promise of enhanced efficiency and security within financial transactions is key to the adoption of decentralization technologies. Blockchain technology stands out by offering streamlined transaction processes that potentially eliminate or significantly reduce the reliance on traditional banking intermediaries, thereby diminishing the time and costs associated with the provisioning of certain financial services. The verifiability provided by blockchain technology instills a higher degree of trust and reliability in financial transactions that can effectively mitigate some of the prevalent risks of fraud and errors that today characterize conventional financial systems. This transformative potential could usher in a new era of financial infrastructures that are not only more efficient but also inherently better protected against cybersecurity threats.

Innovation in Financial Products and Services The move toward decentralization is considered a harbinger of innovation within the financial sector, transcending traditional boundaries to introduce a wide array of financial services and products. Through DeFi platforms, facilitated by permissionless blockchains and smart contracts, the financial sector has witnessed the creation of novel services such as decentralized lending, borrowing platforms, and tokenized assets. These innovations are pivotal in extending the scope and flexibility of financial services, making them more accessible and tailored to a diverse range of consumer needs, thereby fostering a more inclusive financial ecosystem that can reach underserved and unbanked populations. On the other hand, decentralization technologies offer financial service providers an opportunity to collaborate without having to fear increased exposure to a single entity's decision-making driven by market power, revenue considerations, or political pressure. Instead, they promote a collaborative approach that may unlock a higher degree of composability and contribute to reducing the hesitation to collaborate and co-innovate.

Decentralized Platformization With the maturation of decentralization technologies, the adoption of DeFi platforms is poised to become more mainstream, offering robust alternatives to traditional financial services. These platforms advocate for a permissionless approach to finance in which users have the sole custody over their digital assets and can customize any rules to interact with them. This approach challenges the hegemony of traditional financial institutions and necessitates a reevaluation of existing business models and regulatory frameworks to accommodate the emerging DeFi landscape—especially in transaction-oriented parts of the business. At the same time, it necessitates supportive tools such as digital identity wallets to establish a connection with regulated environments and established trust infrastructures.

Personalization and Automation in Financial Services The convergence of blockchain technology with advancements in artificial intelligence (AI) heralds a new frontier in financial services characterized by heightened personalization and automation. Smart contracts can facilitate the precise and reliable execution of financial agreements, while AI and machine learning algorithms may enable the delivery of personalized financial advice and products tailored to individual consumer profiles. In this context, federated learning can help to gain access to the high-quality training data needed for achieving the required accuracy of machine learning models. This integration of decentralization technologies promises to revolutionize customer experiences and operational models in finance, making services more responsive to individual needs and broader market trends. On the other hand, checks and balances to avoid mistakes and contain the impact of approximation errors (e.g., "hallucinations" in large language models (Xu et al., 2024)) will be necessary. The fine-granular delegation of permissions from users and organizations to AI agents using digital wallets may play an important role in this context. Moreover, the verifiable execution of AI algorithms by means of smart contracts may provide new opportunities for decentralized financial applications. However, the amount of storage and computation these models consume is typically too large for direct execution in smart contracts. On the other hand, nondeterminism and the enormous proving overhead incurred by verifiable computation techniques such as succinct ZKPs inhibit the cheap verification of the correct execution of state-of-the-art large language models in smart contracts (Thaler et al., 2022). Nevertheless, improvements in this area have been fast (Srivastava et al., 2024; Modulus, 2024), promising a trajectory toward being practical.

Navigating the transformative path charted by decentralization technologies in the financial sector requires a comprehensive understanding of the intricate challenges, regulatory considerations, and market dynamics that accompany this technological shift. A collaborative, multi-stakeholder approach involving technologists, regulators, financial institutions, and consumers is essential to fully harness decentralization technologies' potential while ensuring a balanced, equitable, and protective financial ecosystem for all participants.

1.5 Challenges of Adopting Decentralization Technologies

The integration of decentralization technologies within the financial sector is accompanied by a broad spectrum of challenges that span technical, economic, and regulatory domains (Sedlmeir, 2023). Addressing these challenges is paramount to ensure the seamless adoption and sustainable growth of services relying on decentralized systems, which promise to redefine the financial landscape. In the following, we discuss selected challenges that appear in the subsequent chapters.

Ensuring Robust Decentralization A primary challenge in the deployment of decentralization technologies is maintaining the delicate balance between decentralized principles and centralization. Centralization can appear at various system levels, including infrastructure, governance, and application layers (Napirata et al., 2023). Inclinations toward centralization are often driven by stakeholders seeking higher degrees of efficiency, control, or value capture. This profound situation necessitates a vigilant approach to system design and governance to avert recentralization in layers where it could undermine the core benefits of decentralization. Historical precedents in blockchain systems have shown many tendencies toward centralization, ranging from the consolidation of mining operations and node hosting to fully managed blockchain services offered by cloud service providers (Sai et al., 2021). These experiences highlight the need for ongoing alertness in this area.

Addressing Energy Efficiency and Sustainability Concerns The operational demands of certain decentralization technologies have raised significant sustainability concerns due to their sometimes high energy consumption (Rieger et al., 2022). The discourse is dominated by the massive energy consumption of blockchain solutions employing the proof of work (PoW) consensus mechanism. While other blockchain networks consume many orders of magnitude less electric energy, the general redundancy of blockchain networks and the relocation of computing from highly specialized centralized entities (e.g., cloud service providers or platform operators) to often less specialized stakeholders or edge devices, and increased communication (e.g., in federated learning) increases energy consumption (see also Chap. 14). Balancing the operational needs of decentralized networks with global sustainability objectives is a critical challenge that requires innovative solutions and a continuous weighing of the benefits (e.g., avoiding the consumption of resources by the digitization enabled through decentralized approaches) against the costs (e.g., higher overall demand for devices, networking infrastructure, and electricity) (Sedlmeir, 2023).

Navigating Security, Data Privacy, and Operational Efficiency Trade-Offs The adoption of decentralization technologies in financial systems necessitates a nuanced approach to balancing operational efficiency with stringent data privacy requirements (Sedlmeir, 2023). This involves developing innovative solutions that safeguard confidentiality in personal data processing without diminishing the quality or security of financial services. Decentralization technologies, while aimed at enhancing system security, also introduce many new vulnerabilities because a larger number of involved devices and stakeholders, as well as less centrally managed coordination and global oversight, may increase the technical attack surface. Misaligned incentives and the "tragedy of the commons" (Cila et al., 2020) can also lead to systemic risks and unintended consequences, underscoring the need for carefully crafted incentive mechanisms that align with the overarching goals of decentralized systems. Continuous security research and fast and robust development and implementation cycles are also necessary to ensure long-term success.

Overcoming Market Adoption Barriers The widespread acceptance and adoption of decentralization technologies among consumers and financial institutions face obstacles related to trust, comprehension, and perceived benefits when considering potentially high upfront costs. Addressing these barriers requires concerted efforts in education, the design of user-friendly systems, and the clear demonstration of tangible benefits that decentralized systems offer over traditional financial models. Similar to centralized platforms, many decentralized systems, such as blockchain-based supply chain management or digital identity wallets, also must cross initial chasms, as value creation may only manifest once a critical mass of adoption is reached.

Addressing Regulatory Uncertainty The dynamic and rapidly evolving nature of decentralization technologies has appeared to outpace existing regulatory frameworks multiple times, leading to a landscape that is still fraught with legal ambiguities and uncertainties. Crafting clear, adaptive, and supportive regulatory environments that accommodate the unique characteristics of decentralized systems while at the same time ensuring consumer protection and system stability remains a significant challenge for policymakers and regulators.

Facilitating Integration with Legacy Systems The coexistence and integration of decentralization technologies with existing infrastructures present considerable technical and operational challenges (Sedlmeir et al., 2022c), particularly in the financial sector. Ensuring compatibility, interoperability, and the seamless integration of new decentralized systems with established financial frameworks is crucial for the continued smooth operation of financial services, necessitating thoughtful consideration in system architecture and design. Corresponding standards necessary to establish reliable interfaces, however, are often at odds with upholding openness and not inhibiting innovation.

Tackling these many challenges demands a collective and strategic effort from all stakeholders within the financial ecosystem. By acknowledging and addressing these issues, the financial sector can navigate the complexities of adopting decentralization technologies, paving the way for a more inclusive, efficient, and resilient financial system that leverages the full potential of the digital transformation.

1.6 Concluding Remarks

In this introductory exploration into the digital transformation in the financial sector, we have traveled the journey from the early days of ATMs to the cutting-edge areas of blockchain and cryptocurrencies. This evolution reflects not only technical advances but also a paradigm shift in the way financial services are designed, delivered, and consumed. The transition from traditional banking to digital platforms offering financial services is characterized by a dynamic interplay between centralized and decentralized tendencies on multiple layers. The early days of the Internet were characterized by a peer-to-peer (P2P) ethos and open protocols. The subsequent transition into the era of centralization in the form of digital platforms was driven by new business models, network effects, and centralized control. Negative aspects of this development raised interest in novel technologies such as blockchains, which may bring us to a tipping point where the forces of centralization and decentralization reach a new balance. The combination of decentralization technologies such as blockchains, digital identity wallets, and federated learning enables decentralized platforms as viable, emerging alternatives to the traditional, centralized platform-based models.

This journey underscores the two-sided nature of the digital transformation in the financial sector. On the one hand, it brings significant benefits, such as increased accessibility, efficiency, and innovation. On the other hand, it also poses complex new challenges related to security, privacy, and regulatory compliance. The emergence of decentralization technologies and accompanying (cryptographic) tools may offer promising solutions to some of the sector's most pressing challenges and advocates for a more transparent, open, and inclusive financial ecosystem.

The following chapters of this book aim to explore the opportunities and challenges of decentralization technologies and provide a comprehensive understanding of their potential to transform the financial sector. As we turn to the main content of this book, we encourage readers to keep an open mind and engage with not only the intricate interplay between apparent synergies but also tensions between technological possibilities, practical realities of implementation, regulation, and adoption. As we delve into the complexities of this transformation, it is important that readers understand the balance between embracing innovation and overcoming the challenges that come with fundamental changes in the financial landscape. The exploration ahead aims not only to give readers an overview of technologies and applications but also to inspire a new vision of the future of the financial sector in which decentralization technologies play a key role in creating a fairer, more innovative, more efficient, and more resilient financial ecosystem.

References

Alt, R., Fridgen, G., & Chang, Y. (2024). The future of FinTech – towards ubiquitous financial services. *Electronic Markets*, *34*(1). https://doi.org/10.1007/s12525-023-00687-8.

Arner, D. W., Barberis, J., & Buckley, R. P. (2015). The evolution of FinTech: A new post-crisis paradigm. *Georgetown Journal of International Law*, *47*. https://ssrn.com/abstract=2676553.

Arner, D. W., Buckley, R. P., & Zetzsche, D. A. (2021). Open banking, open data and open finance: Lessons from the European Union. In *Open banking* (pp. 21–69). Oxford University Press. https://doi.org/10.1093/oso/9780197582879.003.0009.

Barbereau, T., Ermolaev, E., Brennecke, M., Hartwich, E., & Sedlmeir, J. (2023a). Beyond a fistful of tumblers: Toward a multi-layered taxonomy of Ethereum-based crypto-asset mixers. In *Proceedings of the 44th International Conference on Information Systems*. https://aisel.aisnet.org/icis2023/cyber_security/cyber_security/13/.

Barbereau, T., Smethurst, R., Papageorgiou, O., Sedlmeir, J., & Fridgen, G. (2023b). Decentralised finance's timocratic governance: The distribution and exercise of tokenised voting rights. *Technology in Society*, *73*, 102251. https://doi.org/10.1016/j.techsoc.2023.102251.

Bhattacherjee, A. (2001). Understanding information systems continuance: An expectation-confirmation model. *MIS Quarterly*, *25*(3), 351–370. https://doi.org/10.2307/3250921.

Brennecke, M., Guggenberger, T., Sachs, A., & Schellinger, B. (2022). The human factor in blockchain ecosystems: A sociotechnical framework. In *Proceedings of the 17th International Conference on Wirtschaftsinformatik*. https://aisel.aisnet.org/wi2022/finance_and_blockchain/finance_and_blockchain/3/.

Cila, N., Ferri, G., de Waal, M., Gloerich, I., & Karpinski, T. (2020). The blockchain and the commons: Dilemmas in the design of local platforms. In *Proceedings of the CHI Conference on Human Factors in Computing Systems*: ACM. https://doi.org/10.1145/3313831.3376660.

Claessens, J., Dem, V., De Cock, D., Preneel, B., & Vandewalle, J. (2002). On the security of today's online electronic banking systems. *Computers & Security*, *21*(3), 253–265. https://doi.org/10.1016/S0167-4048(02)00312-7.

Codagnone, C. & Weigl, L. (2023). Leading the charge on digital regulation: The more, the better, or policy bubble? *Digital Society*, *2*(1), 4. https://doi.org/10.1007/s44206-023-00033-7.

Ferreira, A. & Sandner, P. (2021). EU search for regulatory answers to crypto assets and their place in the financial markets' infrastructure. *Computer Law & Security Review*, *43*, 105632. https://doi.org/10.1016/j.clsr.2021.105632.

Feulner, S., Guggenberger, T., Stoetzer, J.-C., & Urbach, N. (2022). Shedding light on the blockchain disintermediation mystery: A review and future research agenda. In *Proceedings of the 30th European Conference on Information Systems*: AIS. https://aisel.aisnet.org/ecis2022_rp/13/.

Fridgen, G., Radszuwill, S., Schweizer, A., & Urbach, N. (2021). Blockchain won't kill the banks: Why disintermediation doesn't work in international trade finance. *Communications of the Association for Information Systems*, *49*, 603–623. https://doi.org/10.17705/1cais.04932.

Garrido, G. M., Sedlmeir, J., Uludağ, Ö., Alaoui, I. S., Luckow, A., & Matthes, F. (2022). Revealing the landscape of privacy-enhancing technologies in the context of data markets for the IoT: A systematic literature review. *Journal of Network and Computer Applications*, *207*, 103465. https://doi.org/10.1016/j.jnca.2022.103465.

Gramlich, V., et al. (2022). Decentralized finance (DeFi): Foundations, applications, potentials, and challenges. https://www.fit.fraunhofer.de/content/dam/fit/de/documents/Whitepaper__DeFi__English_Version_2022_07_15.pdf.

Gramlich, V., Guggenberger, T., Principato, M., Schellinger, B., & Urbach, N. (2023). A multivocal literature review of decentralized finance: Current knowledge and future research avenues. *Electronic Markets*, *33*. https://doi.org/10.1007/s12525-023-00637-4.

Groß, J., Sedlmeir, J., Babel, M., Bechtel, A., & Schellinger, B. (2021). Designing a central bank digital currency with support for cash-like privacy. https://papers.ssrn.com/abstract=3891121.

Guggenberger, T., Kühne, D., Schlatt, V., & Urbach, N. (2023). Designing a cross-organizational identity management system: Utilizing SSI for the certification of retailer attributes. *Electronic Markets*, *33*(1), 3. https://doi.org/10.1007/s12525-023-00620-z.

Hartwich, E., Rieger, A., Sedlmeir, J., Jurek, D., & Fridgen, G. (2023). Machine economies. *Electronic Markets*, *33*. https://doi.org/10.1007/s12525-023-00649-0.

Hoess, A., Lautenschlager, J., Sedlmeir, J., Fridgen, G., Schlatt, V., & Urbach, N. (2024). Toward seamless mobility-as-a-service. *Business & Information Systems Engineering*. https://doi.org/10.1007/s12599-024-00856-9.

Jalan, A. & Matkovskyy, R. (2023). Systemic risks in the cryptocurrency market: Evidence from the FTX collapse. *Finance Research Letters*, *53*, 103670. https://doi.org/10.1016/j.frl.2023.103670.

Jensen, T., Hedman, J., & Henningsson, S. (2019). How TradeLens delivers business value with blockchain technology. *MIS Quarterly Executive*, *18*, 221–243. https://doi.org/10.17705/2msqe.00018.

Kruzikova, A., Knapova, L., Smahel, D., Dedkova, L., & Matyas, V. (2022). Usable and secure? User perception of four authentication methods for mobile banking. *Computers & Security*, *115*, 102603. https://doi.org/10.1016/j.cose.2022.102603.

Lee, C. M., Delgado Fernandez, J., Potenciano Menci, S., Rieger, A., & Fridgen, G. (2023). Federated learning for credit risk assessment. In *Proceedings of the 56th Hawaii International Conference on System Sciences* (pp. 386–395). https://hdl.handle.net/10125/102676.

Long, G., Tan, Y., Jiang, J., & Zhang, C. (2020). Federated learning for open banking. In *Federated l: Privacy and incentive* (pp. 240–254). Springer. https://doi.org/10.1007/978-3-030-63076-8_17.

Mallat, N., Rossi, M., & Tuunainen, V. K. (2004). Mobile banking services. *Communications of the ACM*, *47*(5), 42–46. https://doi.org/10.1145/986213.986236.

Mansfield-Devine, S. (2016). Open banking: Opportunity and danger. *Computer Fraud & Security*, *2016*(10), 8–13. https://doi.org/10.1016/S1361-3723(16)30080-X.

Mattke, J., Maier, C., & Hund, A. (2019). How an enterprise blockchain application in the U.S. pharmaceuticals supply chain is saving lives. *MIS Quarterly Executive*, *18*, 246–261. https://doi.org/10.17705/2msqe.00019.

Modulus (2024). Chapter 14: The world's 1st on-chain LLM. https://medium.com/@ModulusLabs/chapter-14-the-worlds-1st-on-chain-llm-7e389189f85e.

Napirata, S., Sedlmeir, J., Rieger, A., Fridgen, G., & Zimmermann, S. (2023). The competition effect of decentralized platforms: An analytical model. In *Proceedings of the 44th International Conference on System Sciences*: AIS. https://aisel.aisnet.org/icis2023/sharing_econ/sharing_econ/16/.

Pocher, N. (2023). *Distributed ledger technologies between anonymity and transparency: AML/CFT regulation of cryptocurrency ecosystems in the EU*. PhD thesis, Alma Mater Studiorum Università di Bologna, Universitat Autònoma de Barcelona, KU Leuven. https://lirias.kuleuven.be/retrieve/706912.

Pocher, N. & Veneris, A. (2021). Privacy and transparency in CBDCs: A regulation-by-design AMC/CFT scheme. *IEEE Transactions on Network and Service Management*, *19*(2), 1776–1788. https://doi.org/10.1109/TNSM.2021.3136984.

Puschmann, T. (2017). Fintech. *Business & Information Systems Engineering*, *59*, 69–76. https://doi.org/10.1007/s12599-017-0464-6.

Richter, D. & Anke, J. (2021). Exploring potential impacts of self-sovereign identity on smart service systems: An analysis of electric vehicle charging services. In *Proceedings of the 24th International Conference on Business Information Systems* (pp. 105–116). https://doi.org/10.52825/bis.v1i.68.

Rieger, A., Roth, T., Sedlmeir, J., & Fridgen, G. (2022). We need a broader debate on the sustainability of blockchain. *Joule*, *6*(6), 1137–1141. https://doi.org/10.1016/j.joule.2022.04.013.

Sai, A. R., Buckley, J., Fitzgerald, B., & Le Gear, A. (2021). Taxonomy of centralization in public blockchain systems: A systematic literature review. *Information Processing & Management*, *58*(4), 102584. https://doi.org/10.1016/j.ipm.2021.102584.

Scharfman, J. & Scharfman, J. (2022). Decentralized finance (DeFi) compliance and operations. In *Cryptocurrency Compliance and Operations: Digital Assets, Blockchain and DeFi* (pp. 171–186). Springer. https://doi.org/10.1007/978-3-030-88000-2_9.

Schellinger, B. (2023). *The secret key to the heart of decentralized finance: Unlocking the potential of crypto assets and currencies to advance the financial sector*. PhD thesis, University of Bayreuth. https://doi.org/10.15495/EPub_UBT_00006983.

Schlatt, V., Sedlmeir, J., Feulner, S., & Urbach, N. (2022). Designing a framework for digital KYC processes built on blockchain-based self-sovereign identity. *Information & Management*, *59*. https://doi.org/10.1016/j.im.2021.103553.

Schmitt, W., Masters, B., & Chipolina, S. (2024). SEC approves first spot Bitcoin ETFs in boost to crypto advocates. Financial Times. https://www.ft.com/content/443b2589-0a4a-48ef-872e-3cd52b1b297d.

Sedlmeir, J. (2023). *Blockchain Adoption in Organizations: Technical Barriers and Potential Solutions*. PhD thesis, University of Bayreuth. https://doi.org/10.15495/EPub_UBT_00007183.

Sedlmeir, J., Barbereau, T., Huber, J., Weigl, L., & Roth, T. (2022a). Transition pathways towards design principles of self-sovereign identity. In *Proceedings of the 43rd International Conference on Information Systems*: AIS. https://aisel.aisnet.org/icis2022/is_implement/is_implement/4/.

Sedlmeir, J., Lautenschlager, J., Fridgen, G., & Urbach, N. (2022b). The transparency challenge of blockchain in organizations. *Electronic Markets, 32*, 1779–1794. https://doi.org/10.1007/s12525-022-00536-0.

Sedlmeir, J., Smethurst, R., Rieger, A., & Fridgen, G. (2021). Digital identities and verifiable credentials. *Business & Information Systems Engineering, 63*, 603–613. https://doi.org/10.1007/s12599-021-00722-y.

Sedlmeir, J., Wagner, T., Djerekarov, E., Green, R., Klepsch, J., & Rao, S. (2022c). A serverless distributed ledger for enterprises. In *Proceedings of the 55th Hawaii International Conference on System Sciences* (pp. 7382–7391). https://doi.org/10.24251/hicss.2022.886.

Srivastava, M., Arora, S., & Boneh, D. (2024). Optimistic verifiable training by controlling hardware nondeterminism. https://arxiv.org/html/2403.09603v1.

Sunyaev, A., et al. (2021). Token economy. *Business & Information Systems Engineering, 63*, 457–478. https://doi.org/10.1007/s12599-021-00684-1.

Thaler, J. et al. (2022). *Proofs, arguments, and zero-knowledge* (vol. 4). Now Publishers.

Xu, Z., Jain, S., & Kankanhalli, M. (2024). Hallucination is inevitable: An innate limitation of large language models. https://arxiv.org/abs/2401.11817.

Zavolokina, L., Dolata, M., & Schwabe, G. (2016). Fintech – what's in a name? In *Proceedings of the 36th International Conference on Information Systems*: AIS. https://aisel.aisnet.org/icis2016/DigitalInnovation/Presentations/12/.

Zetzsche, D. A. & Woxholth, J. (2022). The DLT sandbox under the Pilot-Regulation. *Capital Markets Law Journal, 17*(2), 212–236. https://doi.org/10.1093/cmlj/kmac003.

Chapter 2
Financial Regulation, Political Context, and Technology in the European Union

Tom Barbereau, Linda Weigl, and Nadia Pocher

Abstract Three decades after the establishment of the European Single Market, the ongoing digital transformation of its core socioeconomic pillars generates regulatory shifts. These shifts are also initiated by geopolitical pressures. Within its data-driven economy, innovative financial solutions and technologies strive to unfold against the backdrop of what is now a multilayered, complex regulatory environment. This chapter dismantles this complexity by outlining the main regulatory building blocks relevant to the European Union's financial industry vis-à-vis the policy goals of digital and economic sovereignty. Given the focus of this book on decentralization technologies in the financial industry, it then contextualizes the impact of such policy on these and discusses the present dynamics between regulation and innovative technology.

2.1 Introduction

In 2023, the European Union (EU) celebrated the 30th anniversary of the Single Market. This key pillar of European integration was complemented in 2014 by the Capital Markets Union, to facilitate the movement of capital (Véron & Wolff, 2016), and in 2015 by the Digital Single Market, whereby the EU set out to

T. Barbereau
Interdisciplinary Centre for Security, Reliability and Trust (SnT), University of Luxembourg, Esch-sur-Alzette, Luxembourg

Dutch Organisation for Applied Scientific Research (TNO), The Hague, Netherlands
e-mail: tom.barbereau@tno.nl

L. Weigl
Institute for Information Law, University of Amsterdam, Amsterdam, Netherlands
e-mail: l.weigl@uva.nl

N. Pocher (✉)
Interdisciplinary Centre for Security, Reliability and Trust (SnT), University of Luxembourg, Esch-sur-Alzette, Luxembourg
e-mail: nadia.pocher@uni.lu

G. Fridgen et al. (eds.), *Decentralization Technologies*, Financial Innovation and Technology, https://doi.org/10.1007/978-3-031-66047-4_2

digitize the core tenants of its fundamental freedoms. This was pursued by providing digital services with trustworthy infrastructures and an appropriate regulatory environment (e.g., standardized rules for telecommunications, copyright, and data protection) (European Commission, 2024). Early achievements included the cross-border portability of digital services, the end of roaming charges, and the end of unjustified geo-blocking (European Council, 2024).

Going forward, the protection of the data and privacy of European citizens, as well as the competitiveness of EU businesses within the digital economy, were increasingly in the limelight. With the adoption of the General Data Protection Regulation (GDPR) in 2016, EU institutions addressed a wide range of issues, including the data economy, artificial intelligence, and digital platforms. Further related legislative initiatives were put forward (European Council, 2020). While the GDPR represents a response to online scandals, breaches, and the practice of data mass aggregation without restrictions (Hoofnagle et al., 2019), the recently adopted Digital Services Act (DSA) and Digital Markets Act (DMA) respond to market dominance abuses and anticompetitive behavior by multinational companies (Larouche & de Streel, 2021).

In the aftermath of the 2008 financial crisis, the EU's regulatory approach also significantly evolved (Leonard et al., 2019). Such legislative activism in times of perceived threats or uncertainties is indeed no abnormal pattern (Codagnone & Weigl, 2023). At that time, many jurisdictions implemented preventative reforms for the sake of stability, and the previously permissive approach toward digital transformation, known as "deregulation," was replaced by a more stringent framework. In the field of digital finance, complexity was also introduced with the advent of FinTech and its new opportunities and risks (Zetzsche et al., 2017; European Commission, 2018). In particular, the emergence of financial applications on top of decentralized architectures—above all, blockchains and distributed ledger technologies (DLTs), but also technologies for digital identity management—testified to the existence of novel methods to manage data with substantial consequences in terms of sociopolitical analysis and regulatory methodology (Barbereau & Bodó, 2023; Pocher & Veneris, 2022).

Typically, information system (IS) literature focusing on information technology (IT)-enabled solutions (Benbasat & Zmud, 2003) that are characteristically decentralized or distributed by design follows a well-known 'script' (Grover & Lyytinen, 2015) of mapping regulatory requirements against technical design principles and identifying patterns of emergence, acceptance, or adoption. Notwithstanding the value of such approaches, this chapter aims to provide an overview of the regulatory 'state of play'. In addition, it contextualizes the ambitions of the EU's policy and regulatory strategy within the scope of application of these technologies in the financial domain, their impacts, and the alternative solutions they enable.

Accordingly, this chapter is structured as follows: Sect. 2.2 positions the European Single Market within the global context; Sect. 2.3 introduces regulation with direct impact on the financial industry; Sect. 2.4 discusses the interplay between decentralization and regulatory approaches; and Sect. 2.5 concludes.

2.2 The European (Digital) Single Market

The history of European integration is long and complex. It started after World War II to promote economic cooperation and prevent another deadly conflict. The first steps were taken with the establishment of European Coal and Steel Community (ECSC) in 1951. This was followed by the European Economic Community (EEC) and the European Atomic Energy Community (Euratom) in 1957. Over the years, the organization has expanded to include more Member States, and its focus has expanded beyond economic cooperation to include political and security issues.

After the 1992 Maastricht Treaty established the European Union (EU) as we know it today, the European Single Market was inaugurated in 1993 and has since expanded to additional policy areas—e.g., the single currency (the euro, €) and the Schengen Agreement which allows for the free movement of people within a designated area of the EU. The establishment and continued development of the Single Market has had a significant impact on the economic prosperity and financial integration of the EU (Underhill, 1997) (the reader can also refer to the vast literature on the history of the EU and its single market (e.g., Dedman, 2006; Laursen, 2012)). Indeed, the single market is seen to have "transformed a number of relatively closed and restricted domestic financial markets into a de-segmented, transnational financial space contiguous with global market" (Underhill, 1997, p. 101).

2.2.1 European Union's Approach Between the USA and China

The financial crisis of 2008 shocked the world, and financial turmoils offer insights into the interconnection of global markets. After the collapse of Lehman Brothers, the domino effect rapidly reached the EU, starting with the Republic of Ireland. The crisis demonstrated that the EU's financial sector was deeply interwoven with that of the United States of America (USA) and, thus, dependent on it (Navaretti et al., 2010). Meanwhile, the emergence of China as "an economic competitor in the pursuit of technological leadership, and a systemic rival promoting alternative models of governance" (European Commission, 2019, p.1) was observed in a state of shock by EU policymakers (Leonard et al., 2019). The Vice President of the European Commission (EC), Josep Borrell (2020), acknowledged that:

> "US-China strategic rivalry will probably be the dominant organizing principle for global politics, regardless who wins the next presidential US elections. In that context, we need to hold our nerve and frame our own EU approach."

On the global diplomatic stage, the EU has important ties to both the USA and China (Christiansen & Maher, 2017; Defraigne, 2017). In terms of trade and investment, the Union is one of China's largest partners, and China is the EU's second-largest partner after the USA. The EU is also a major destination for Chinese foreign direct investment (FDI), and vice versa (WITS, 2024). These indicators are the result of the EU's and China's shared and long history of cooperation on a range of issues, including climate change, energy, and sustainable development. However, the relationship is not without challenges. The EU has continuously expressed concerns on issues such as market access, intellectual property protection, and human rights (Christensen, 2015). The EU also has a close and strategic relationship with the USA—not least, through member states' memberships at the North Atlantic Treaty Organization (NATO) and the Transatlantic Economic Council. The two have a large and growing economic connection, being their respective largest trading partner. The EU and USA cooperate closely on a range of issues, including security, defense, and foreign policy (Wang & Song, 2016).

Despite these ties, since its foundation, the EU has developed a sensible position between the pressures USA and China exert on the global stage. The European think tank Bruegel argues that while "the EU does not send armies all around the world, its leaders like to believe that the EU has the collective economic size and capacity to determine its own economic destiny, to set its own rules for economic life, to negotiate on an equal footing with partner economies, to tame would-be monopolies and even to set economic standards and regulations for the rest of the world" (Leonard et al., 2019). This tendency is, for example, reflected in the EU's regulatory approach to the Digital Single Market.

2.2.2 The "EU Approach"

The way in which the "EU approach," as termed by Josep Borrell, was deployed for the Digital Single Market and contrasts the policies of the USA and China. The key notion for the EU is that of "sovereignty" (European Commission, 2020c). Sovereignty refers here to the ability to "act independently in the digital world" and is understood in terms of "protective mechanisms and offensive tools to foster digital innovation (including in cooperation with non-EU companies)" (Madiega, 2020). Several scholars have analyzed how the concept of digital sovereignty is discussed by EU institutions both in official communications, research reports, and academic literature (Roberts et al., 2021) and in legislative and nonlegislative texts (Codagnone & Weigl, 2023). Results suggest that the pursuit of technological sovereignty is a shared motivation and objective in various EU policy files. As such, sovereignty "is an idea formed not simply around practices of individual data self-care maintained through combinations of network applications and the assertion of rights, but encompasses a whole range of economic, political and social concerns and motivations" (Herian, 2020).

Admittedly, given its multiple meanings and the lack of a commonly agreed upon definition (Bellanova & Glouftsios, 2022), the concept ought to be dissected in more detail. Economic sovereignty carries a geopolitical dimension. It encompasses "the EU's ability to participate in defining the rules of the game for the global economy—what Chancellor Merkel calls *Handlungsfähigkeit* and the French call *puissance* [européenne]" (Leonard et al., 2019). Doing so underlines the provision of "value" to citizens. Here, the achievement of sovereignty is a common "belief," an objective the EU actively pursues. These values and objectives are also reflected in the contemporary meaning of digital sovereignty (see also the discussion around *value amplification* through European sovereignty (Codagnone & Weigl, 2023)). In the digital sphere, this paradigm ought to address rising user demands and increasing security risks and privacy violations by foreign governments and multinational technology corporations.

The (then) President of the European Central Bank (ECB), Mario Draghi, rightfully denotes a conflation of *independence* with *sovereignty* in beliefs around economic integration and political cooperation (Draghi, 2019). Economic sovereignty refers to "the collective capacity of EU countries working together to preserve their economic *independence*." Doing so is of strategic relevance because it "underpins the argument that the European integration process provides value" to citizens (Leonard et al., 2019). Again, parallels can be drawn to the digital sphere, where global players, like China, the USA, and ultimately also the EU, are engaging in a fierce tech rivalry. The EU decided to navigate this race (Metakides, 2022) via a constitutional approach (Floridi, 2020; Codagnone & Weigl, 2023) with a self-imposed mandate to regulate the digital in order to achieve digital sovereignty.

The exerted effects, however, are not necessarily limited to the EU. Indeed, the notion of the "Brussels Effect" was coined to describe a process of regulatory globalization by the hands of EU law. For a more extensive analysis of the "Brussels Effect" of the GDPR, see Bradford (2020); Goddard (2017).

2.3 Regulatory Developments for the European Financial Industry

EU regulatory mechanisms are strongly tied to the (perceived) need to respond to socioeconomic issues or threats. These "reactive" dynamics are defined by Rhinard (2019) as "crisisification" in EU policy-making. When it comes to the regulation of financial services and their digitization, the 2008 financial crisis represented a turning point (Leonard et al., 2019). The crisis had a substantial impact on the global economy by undermining trust in the overall stability of the financial system, leading to a decline in citizens' systemic trust in centralized institutions and their governments (Roth, 2022). Financial stability, as such, is constructed by the complex interaction between financial products, services, and the governance of financial institutions and actors through regulation. However, the emergence of decentralization technology embedded in the financial sphere was soon to be seen as an important distinctive feature and alternative to the perceived instability of traditional financial systems. Next to techno-solutionist responses, among the crisis' far-reaching and long-term effects on the regulatory side, the emerging macroprudential concerns urged regulators to balance core principles such as financial stability, consumer protection, and inclusion, with growth and

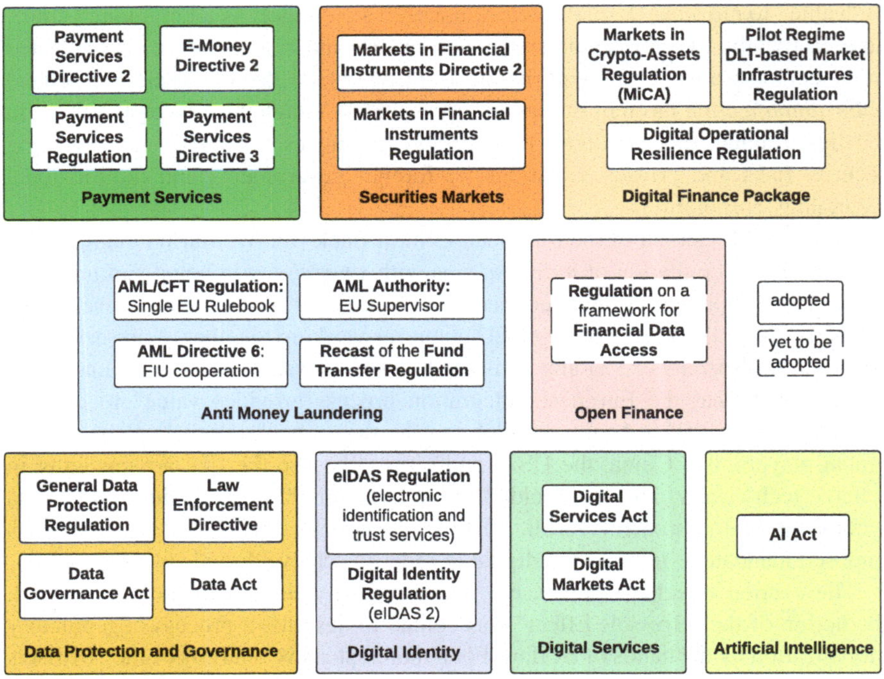

Fig. 2.1 Selected overview of the regulatory frameworks relevant to the provision of payment and financial services in the EU and of those concerning the digital space. Updated to August 2024

innovation (in financial regulation, the "macroprudential" perspective focuses on the overall impact of interrelationships between financial institutions and pinpoints those that exert systemic influence). In Sect. 2.3.1, after accounting for the interplay of international financial regulation and EU law, we dedicate a section to the general regulatory building blocks for the European data economy and the digital financial space—as testified by the FinTech Action Plan: "FinTech sits at the crossroads of financial services and the digital single market" (European Commission, 2018, p.2). Thereafter, in Sect. 2.3.2, we turn to the EU frameworks specifically regulating payment and financial services. We also provide an overview of frameworks relevant to the European Financial Industry in Fig. 2.1. Note that the list of regulatory building blocks and ongoing EU reforms does not provide an exhaustive record but a selected and context-specific overview.

2.3.1 The EU and Global Financial Regulation

Any effort to provide an overview of the EU framework for digital finance is met by two major challenges: (i) EU financial regulation is far from a singular standalone framework and is tightly interwoven with global financial regulation, and (ii) the latter is not a clear-cut legal area and consists of a compound of rules, standards, and best practices. At the global level, financial regulation largely relies on so-called "voluntary compliance" and features low levels of institutionalization (Newman & Bach, 2014). It mostly consists of global rules adopted as nonbinding agreements by regulatory agencies or institutions with undefined legal identities (Brummer, 2015). In this context, the concept of "soft law" was defined as a compendium of "instruments or agreements that are not directly enforceable like treaties, but that nevertheless create powerful expectations" (Marchant & Allenby, 2017, p.1).

The development of global financial regulation started in the late 1980s, when the increasing integration and cross-border capital flows began to urge regulatory cooperation to protect stability and consumers (Brummer, 2015). The risk of market participants escaping national supervision—so-called "regulatory/forum shopping" (Mevorach, 2013)—was mitigated by setting global standards and prudential guidelines through international forums (Brummer, 2015). While these policy forums enshrine models of technocratic cooperation, they also belong to a hierarchical system of influence and power, with sophisticated internal designs. Indeed, there are various categories of "agenda setters" (primarily, the G-20 and the Financial Stability Board (FSB)), sector-specific "standard setters" (e.g., the International Organization of Securities Commissions (IOSCO), the Basel Committee of Banking Supervision (BCBS), and the Financial Action Task Force (FATF)), and supporting organizations, such as the Bank for International Settlements (BIS) and the Committee on Payments and Markets Infrastructure (CPMI).

It is in the context of the growing distrust in these technocratic frameworks that the increasing importance of EU law must be analyzed. In particular, academic literature points out four different resources that strengthen the "Brussels Effect" in international financial regulation: first, the sheer size of the EU internal market and its resulting market power (Damro, 2012; Dür, 2011). Second, the EU's "regulatory capacity" to "formulate, monitor, and enforce a set of market rules" (Bach & Newman, 2007). Third, its external representation in international financial forums, which arguably makes a significant difference in the external influence of the EU (Mügge, 2011). Fourth, the high degree of EU cohesiveness (Quaglia, 2014) (supporters of this rationale argue that the higher the cohesiveness of the EU position (meaning that Member States' preferences are reconciled), the higher its influence in standard setting).

In parallel, it is widely acknowledged that the evolution of financial regulation tends to mirror the evolution of the industry, and the EU is no exception. In particular, there is typically a first phase in which self-regulation arises out of necessity in a situation of minimal regulation (e.g., industry members self-regulate in the form of standardization, for the sake of growth and survival) (Finck, 2019). This is followed by a second phase in which oversight regulation is generally driven by flaws of self-regulation (Johnstone, 2021). The notion of self-regulation, however, is debated, notably for what concerns the relationship between "self-regulation" and "co-regulation" (see Borrás & Edler, 2020; Hofmann et al., 2017; Pagallo et al., 2019; Trubek & Trubek, 2007). In brief, regulation requires the involvement of public institutions and regulatory actions within market systems—e.g., industry standards, if agnostically viewed by the law, are excluded (Marsden, 2012). In this sense, self-regulation consists of nonbinding norms for which formal sanctions play no part. By contrast, if there is a formal institutional involvement, there is co-regulation, which displays interactions between general legislation and a self-regulatory entity (Marsden, 2012; Pagallo et al., 2019). In these cases, self-regulatory efforts are granted legitimacy by being framed within regulation.

The interactions between these regulatory forces may occur at various intensities. Further, the institutional intervention may be indirect, as in the case of sanctions for failures to adopt standards (i.e., enforced self-regulation) (Bennett & Raab, 2020). The legislator may also lay out principles to be implemented by the private actors, under the assumption it is best positioned to give them practical application. This is the case of principles-based regulation (Bennett & Raab, 2020). This is often the case when it comes to the digitization of the financial sphere. At the EU level, examples of principle-based regulation are both the anti-money laundering (AML) and combating the financing of terrorism (CFT) regime and the GDPR.

2.3.2 *Regulatory Building Blocks*

The array of legal frameworks relevant to financial activities performed in the digital space has been under constant expansion in recent years (Codagnone & Weigl, 2023). Regarding the relevant types of EU legislation, they can primarily take the form of "regulations" or "directives." In the first case, the instrument is adopted in such a way to be binding and directly applicable at Member State level in its entirety. Indeed, as per Article 288 of the Treaty on the Functioning of the European Union (2012), "[a] *regulation* shall have general application. It shall be binding in its entirety and directly applicable in all Member States." This is because it pursues an EU-level regulatory "uniformity" in a certain (sub)field. A regulation-based regime may give rise to implementing acts or the issuance of further details for its application, but in principle, it does not require a specific transposition action at Member State level (Blom-Hansen et al., 2023).

In the case of directives, their principle-based nature pursues a "harmonization" of the various Member State approaches in a specific legal (sub)field. As per Article 288 of the Treaty on the Functioning of the European Union (2012), "[a] *directive* shall be binding, as to the result to be achieved, upon each Member State to which it is addressed, but shall leave to the national authorities the choice of form and methods." Hence, a directive sets out a goal that EU Member States must achieve, but they will decide how to reach these goals. Due to the nature of the directive instrument, Member States are required to transpose the framework into their national laws. (There are forms of "minimum" and "maximum" harmonization. In the first case, Member States can adopt higher standards if they wish. In the second case, the directive provides for minimum and maximum standards. Dougan (2000) addresses some of the issues of minimum harmonization.)

2.3.2.1 Frameworks Regulating the Digital Space

In recent years, European policy-makers and legislators have been considerably active in their attempts to regulate the digital space. Although the scope of application of these initiatives goes beyond the provisioning of payment and financial services, we select and summarize some key initiatives below to outline the context of the more targeted regulatory reforms that we address afterward.

Data Protection and Data Governance The GDPR (Regulation (EU) 2016/679) is a key regulatory building block, because it regulates the collection and processing of personal data by organizations for individuals residing in the EU (for an extensive overview, see Hoofnagle et al., 2019). Hence, the framework is also of critical importance for the proper use of data-driven financial services. The same is true for Regulation (EU) 2018/1807, establishing a framework for the free flow of nonpersonal data in the EU. The GDPR is a prime example of the mentioned "Brussels Effect," and it is hailed as the "gold standard" in data protection (Buttarelli, 2016; Cervi, 2022; Gunst & Ville, 2021). Yet, the global impact of EU legislation in the field of data protection is not new: the 1995 Privacy Directive had already inspired regulatory change outside Europe (Greenleaf, 2012; Heisenberg & Fandel, 2004). Meanwhile, the Data Protection Law Enforcement Directive (LED) (Directive (EU) 2016/680) lays out a framework that is parallel to that of the GDPR. In particular, it deals with the processing of personal data by data controllers for "law enforcement purposes"—i.e., for the purposes of the prevention, investigation, detection, or prosecution of criminal offenses or the execution of criminal penalties. Accordingly, these fall outside the scope of the GDPR.

In parallel, the Data Governance Act (DGA), adopted as Regulation EU (2022/868), is part of the "European Strategy for Data" and represents a cross-sectoral instrument that aims to enhance the availability of data by regulating the reuse of publicly held, protected data. It does so by boosting data sharing through regulating novel data intermediaries and by encouraging the sharing of data for altruistic purposes. Further, the Data Act laid out rules on fair access to and use of data, thereby complementing the DGA (Regulation (EU) 2023/2854).

Digital Identity and Trust Services The electronic Identification, Authentication and Trust Services (eIDAS) regulation Regulation (EU) 910/2014) provides the basis for trust services and remote cross-border identification within the EU (Negreiro, 2021; Tuominen & Festor, 2021). To enable electronic identity (eID)-related processes between different jurisdictions—i.e., people and businesses can use their national eIDs to access online public services in other Member States—eIDAS relies on voluntary, notified national eID schemes (Weigl et al., 2022). Hence, eIDAS creates a single market for trust services by ensuring they will work cross-border and have the same legal status as the paper-based equivalents. Importantly, for identification and authentication purposes, eIDAS is limited to public sector services (Tuominen & Festor, 2021).

The eIDAS framework was criticized for the lack of incentive for Member States and private identity providers to connect to the infrastructure due to its limitation to public sector services. For private services, individuals mainly rely on identity solutions offered by for-profit companies and intermediaries, which raise concerns about data privacy and security (Weigl et al., 2022; Negreiro, 2021). The recently adopted European Digital Identity Regulation (eIDAS2) addresses these shortcomings (Regulation (EU) 2024/1183). In particular, it aims to enhance the coverage of eID schemes, their cross-border acceptance and use, and the quality of user experience. The Regulation introduces the adoption of a free-of-charge "European Digital Identity Wallet" as a means to store, manage, and validate identity data and electronic attestations of attributes (Negreiro, 2021; Tuominen & Festor, 2021; Sedlmeir et al., 2022). It marks one step toward living up to the ideal of "user-centricity"—a design philosophy that is set out to center around users' needs and preferences, whereby it prioritizes performance-based values such as convenience, efficiency, and simplicity. In the same vein, the introduction of a digital wallet also aims at the "decentralization" of digital identity management systems by empowering individual users and disempowering centralized infrastructures and institutions (Giannopoulou, 2023; Sartor et al., 2022; Weigl et al., 2023a). Member States are required to issue at least one wallet within 24 months from the adoption of the Implementing Acts t Regulation (EU) 2024/1183.

Digital Services The DSA and DMA aim to create a safer digital space where the fundamental rights of users are protected and a level playing field for businesses is enabled. The concept of "digital services" comprises a large category of online services, from simple websites to internet infrastructure services and online platforms. The framework laid out by the DSA primarily concerns online intermediaries and platforms (Regulation (EU) 2022/2065), while the DMA specifically targets digital platforms with a systemic role that function as gatekeepers between businesses and consumers for important digital services (Regulation (EU) 2022/1925). The core ambition of both regulations is to break up the power held by centralized big platforms (Cabral et al., 2021; Weigl et al., 2023b).

Artificial Intelligence In 2021, the EC put forward a proposal for a Regulation on artificial intelligence (AI), recently adopted as Regulation (EU) 2024/1689. The approach in regulating AI is horizontal, meaning the framework will apply to all applications of AI across all domains. The framework adopts a risk-based approach and classifies AI systems into four risk categories: (1) unacceptable-risk (these AI practices are prohibited), (2) high-risk, (3) limited-risk, (4) minimal/no-risk (European Commission, 2021d; Regulation (EU) 2024/1689). For what concerns the financial sector, two use cases are considered as high-risk, namely, AI-based creditworthiness assessments, as well as pricing and risk assessments in life and health insurance. This means the relevant applications will have to comply with stricter requirements—notably in terms of risk and data management and technical documentation, but also for what concerns transparency and information to be provided to users (Chapter 2 of Regulation (EU) 2024/1689).

Overall, the contemporary technological developments have enabled governments worldwide, and the EU in particular, to produce legal approaches that aim to reshuffle the balance of power in a global economy dominated by algorithmic technologies and large centralized commercial platforms (see, e.g., also Napirata et al., 2023). The selected initiatives outlined in the previous section illustrate this dynamic. They show that EU policy-makers worked on a voluminous body of frameworks within a short and dense period of time. Although the policy areas are very diverse—ranging from data protection, digital identity, the platform economy, and much more—they share one common political narrative. This narrative appeals to the idea of "digital sovereignty" (Csernatoni, 2022; Herian, 2020; Floridi, 2020; Metakides, 2022). While terms such as "data sovereignty" still lack a broadly agreed-on definition (Ernstberger et al., 2023), the political pursuit of digital sovereignty has unfolded in two overarching ways: (1) by ensuring Europe's competitiveness in the data economy and (2) by empowering its citizens with control over their data and thereby offering users an exit strategy from the commercial mass proliferation of personal data online.

While the EU has demonstrated significant regulatory activity in the digital realm, the framing of policies around digital sovereignty has fueled this activity beyond mere policy pragmatism. This has led to a proliferation of intricate policies and regulations that exhibit a lack of coherence and consistency (Codagnone & Weigl, 2023). The pursuit of real digital sovereignty necessitates the development of capabilities and innovation across various digital sectors (ibid.). While initiatives such as the AI Act aim to regulate high-risk systems and safeguard individuals (European Commission, 2021d), they alone do not guarantee the advancement or proliferation of European AI firms to achieve a leading position. The EU's production of digital policy initiatives carries the potential downside of amplifying administrative burdens, particularly for small- and medium-sized enterprises, hampering innovation, and exacerbating uncertainty due to regulatory inconsistencies and lack of cohesion (Codagnone et al., 2022). In addition, there is also the looming concern of an "antagonistic" Brussels Effect, with both market and legal reactions, where Big Tech companies, for instance, adjust their services offered to consumers in Europe (Satariano & Mickle, 2024) or take legal action against the EC for the obligatory provisions imposed on them (Bodoni, 2024). It remains questionable whether the current wave of digital policies can thus be seen as a purely public-interventionist intention and not instead as a tool for the sake of keeping up its reputation as a standard-setter, ethical pioneer, and regulatory powerhouse.

There is undoubtedly a very reassuring spirit in the EU's approach to innovation regulation. The current array of proposals and new frameworks are commendable for establishing a stable foundation to safeguard consumers and ensure fair competition for European enterprises. Yet, rather than solely reacting to the dominance of foreign private entities, the pursuit of digital sovereignty should be viewed as a means rather than an end, in EU policy-making, aiming to attract investments, stimulate innovation, advance the Digital Single Market, and promote the adoption of standardized practices.

2.3.2.2 Frameworks Regulating Payment and Financial Services

Some of the most profound regulatory changes in the EU's modern financial history can be found in a legislative trio composed of (a) the Revised Payment Services Directive (PSD2), (b) the Electronic Money Directive 2 (EMD2), and (c) the Second Markets in Financial Instruments Directive (MiFID II) together with the Markets in Financial Instruments Regulation (MiFIR). Alongside these backbones, other legislative initiatives—in some cases adopted, in others under negotiation—pertain to (d) digital finance and crypto-assets, and (e) open finance. Further, the picture is completed by the evolving framework regarding (f) AML and CFT. We provide an overview of these dimensions below. The analysis of the PSD2 must be accompanied by the recent proposal for a Payment Services Regulation (PSR) and a Payment Services Directive 3 (PSD3).

Payment Services Addressed to the European banking and payment sector, the PSD2 is responsible for the implementation of open banking to ensure a competitive and innovative European financial ecosystem (Directive (EU) 2015/2366). Under its framework, financial institutions and providers of payment services are required to offer application programming interfaces (APIs) to be able, at the request of their customers, to share their financial data for account aggregation and initiation of payment transactions. In June 2023, the EC proposed a thorough reform of the regime through a financial data access and payments package (European Commission, 2023a). In particular, the EC proposed to amend the PSD2 into a PSD3 (European Commission, 2023b), accompanied by a PSR (European Commission, 2023d).

Electronic Money The EMD2 sets out the rules for the business practices and supervision of e-money institutions, to lay the foundations for a Single Market for e-money services in the EU. "E-money" is defined as "electronically, including magnetically, stored monetary value as represented by a claim on the issuer which is issued on receipt of funds for the purpose of making payment transactions" (Article 2, Directive 2009/110/EC). The mentioned payments package acts upon the European Banking Authority (2022), which suggested the merge of the PSD2 and the EMD2. Hence, in an effort to streamline the overall regulatory framework while leaving space for the specifics of each subfield (European Commission, 2023e), the proposed PSD3 integrates and repeals the EMD2 (European Commission, 2023b).

Financial Instruments MiFID II and MiFIR regulate the provisioning of investment services in a wide range of financial instruments on regulated trading venues and over-the-counter in the EU. MiFID II created a new framework for investment and trading activities on financial markets and enhanced investor protection (Directive 2014/65/EU). MiFIR covers aspects such as disclosure of trade data to the public, transaction reporting, derivatives trading, and the powers of national and supranational authorities (Regulation (EU) 600/2014).

Digital Finance and Crypto-Assets With the rise of digital finance triggered by a continuous evolution in service delivery due to the digital transformation, further regulatory adaptations and reforms were deemed necessary. "Digital finance" encloses a variety of novel financial information technology, including products, businesses, software, and customer communication provided by FinTech companies (Gomber et al., 2017). Although this evolution ought to improve inclusion and expand organizations' and individuals' access to financial services and products, policy-makers are confronted with the challenges and the risks entailed in the digitization process and use of data, as well as with the potential disruption and disintermediation of the traditional financial industry. In September 2020, the EC presented a "Digital Finance Package" (European Commission, 2020b) comprising an overarching strategy for a digital financial market in Europe (European Commission, 2020a), and a set of proposals for three regulations adopted in the following years and giving rise to substantial interest among industry and academics alike (Zetzsche et al., 2023).

First and foremost, the Markets in Crypto Assets Regulation (MiCAR), adopted as Regulation (EU) 2023/1114, has generated a considerable hype both in the EU and abroad and is expected to generate a significant "Brussels effect." It focuses on certain categories of crypto-assets—i.e., asset-referenced tokens, e-money tokens, and other types of tokens—which currently fall outside the scope of existing regulations. MiCAR establishes a framework for providers of certain crypto-asset services to safeguard consumers and investors, and its purpose is similar to that of MiFID II, which regulates securities, investment intermediaries, and trading venues.

Secondly, the Regulation (EU) 2022/858 established a Pilot Regime—i.e., a so-called "regulatory sandbox"—for market infrastructures based on DLT, thereby creating conditions for obtaining a license to operate, defining which instruments are tradable on these platforms. This regime applies to instruments that qualify as financial within the meaning of MiFID II and provides the possibility to develop and test DLT-based infrastructures and business models in a controlled environment under a condition of temporary (up to 6 years) exemptions from a portion of the existing, and otherwise applicable, rules (Zetzsche & Woxholth, 2022).

Lastly, Regulation (EU) 2022/2554, the Digital Operational Resilience Act (DORA), aims to strengthen the IT security of financial entities positioned in the EU by ensuring that they can withstand severe operational disruptions and information and communication technology (ICT)-related threats, thereby strengthening. Its efforts are complemented by the Directive (EU) 2022/2556, which provided for the necessary amendments to existing legislation in the area of financial services.

Open Finance In the same legislative package that included the proposals for a PSR and a PSD3, in June 2023, the EC put forward a proposal for a Regulation on Financial Data Access (FiDAR) (European Commission, 2023a). The framework aims to introduce the shift from the principles of "open banking" introduced by PSD2 to the so-called "open finance." This is done by establishing rights and obligations to manage customer (financial) data sharing beyond payment accounts, through a proposed European Commission (2023c). This framework aims to stimulate competition in the financial sector, which currently features uneven data-sharing practices and very high stakeholder reluctance in this regard, to the detriment of the creation of personalized financial services (Recital 6). In turn, open finance should drive the development of more innovative financial products and services—e.g., in the areas of insurance, savings accounts, loans, investments, and pension products. The proposed regime also introduces the new category of "financial information service providers."

Anti-money Laundering and Counter-Terrorist Financing Since 1991, the EU has drafted legislation to harmonize the responses of the Member States for what concerns AML/CFT, including know-your-customer (KYC). The process toward a common EU approach has long relied on directives of minimum harmonization, where domestic provisions can be stricter than those laid out by the EU. This is the case of the framework laid out in Directive (EU) 2015/849 as modified by Directive (EU) 2018/843. The framework largely consists of incorporating into Union law the Recommendations adopted by the AML/CFT standard-setter, the FATF (Financial Action Task Force, 2012). Also in this domain, the regime has evolved according to the increasing socioeconomic interconnections as well as to keep track of the digitization of financial services.

In 2021, the EC put forward the so-called AML Package (European Commission, 2021a), with the goal to overcome the fragmentation caused by the national transposition of a directive-based regime. The AML Package comprised four proposals. Firstly, the proposal for an AML/CFT Single Rulebook was adopted as Regulation (EU) 2024/1624. The EU AML/CFT regime is not disrupted in terms of content, but the framework becomes regulation-based and, as such, binding in its entirety. The main changes concern the expansion of regulated entities to include providers of crypto-asset services, the clarification of the specifics of the internal policies and procedures, the granularization of the measures concerning customer due diligence, and the streamlining of beneficial ownership requirements. The regulation also clarifies anomaly indicators, strengthens the measures to mitigate the misuse of bearer instruments, and includes a limit to the use of cash for large transactions (European Commission, 2021e; Regulation (EU) 2024/1624).

Secondly, Regulation (EU) 2024/1620 introduces a EU-level supervisor. The tasks attributed to the Anti-Money Laundering Authority (AMLA) include direct supervision of selected entities, assistance to financial supervisors, the coordination of information exchange and peer reviews of standards and practices of nonfinancial supervisors, and the provision of training and assistance. The AMLA will adopt regulatory technical standards, guidelines, or recommendations for regulated entities, supervisors, or financial intelligence units (FIUs) to ensure consistency with global standards and promote supervisory convergence (European Commission, 2021c; Regulation (EU) 2024/1620).

Thirdly, a portion of the new framework remains outlined in a directive, namely Directive (EU) 2024/1640. This is because it chiefly concerns activities to be performed at the national level, such as a definition of the responsibilities and tasks of FIUs. Accordingly, the proposal lays out the responsibilities and tasks of bodies involved in the supervision of obliged entities and addresses cooperation mechanisms between competent authorities and with authorities covered by the other acts (European Commission, 2021b; Directive (EU) 2024/1640).

Fourthly, the Regulation (EU) 2023/1113 recast Regulation (EU) 2015/847 to expand traceability obligations beyond wire transfers, according to which financial institutions are required to provide certain information to one another for certain electronic transfers. In brief, the regulation implements the so-called crypto travel rule, as required by the FATF recommendations. The new framework targets providers of payment services and crypto-asset services and introduces the obligation to collect and make accessible to the authorities specific data on originators and beneficiaries of crypto-asset transfers.

From our analysis of the regulatory landscape affecting the provisioning of digital financial and payment services in the EU and often beyond, several key lessons emerge. Firstly, the importance of adaptability and evolution within the individual regulatory frameworks is evident, as demonstrated by the proposed amendments such as PSD3 and PSR to keep pace with changes in financial services. In this context, a shift from closed systems to a higher degree of openness can be observed. This is realized in the implementation of open banking, facilitating the sharing of financial data through APIs to enable account aggregation and payment initiation, and by a further trend toward open finance, to promote competition and innovation. Secondly, the interplay between harmonization attempts across different directives and regulations highlights the necessity for consistency and collaboration among regulatory instruments to effectively govern complex financial ecosystems from various regulatory angles. As an example, it remains to be seen whether the FiDAR initiative will leverage possible synergies with the upcoming eIDAS2, notably in terms of user-centricity. Thirdly, the emergence of regulations targeting digital finance and crypto-assets underscores the need for policy-makers to address the challenges and opportunities presented by technological advancements in the financial sector. Finally, the focus on enhancing AML and CFT measures emphasizes the critical role of updating regulatory frameworks in safeguarding financial systems against illicit activities. However, despite these efforts, there are still a number of innovation-induced unprecedented areas and risks that are, as of now, not covered by any legislative framework.

2.4 Discussion

In this chapter, we addressed the efforts to establish the European Single Market and to regulate payment and financial services to mitigate the risks emerging from an innovation driven by a vast array of new technologies. At the same time, we outlined how the action of EU policy-makers and regulators is situated within the preexisting and multilayered framework of global financial regulation, intertwined with the macroeconomic rules governing the data economy.

In recent initiatives, one can clearly notice a shift from a long-established directive-based approach of minimum harmonization to a regulation-based law-making that aims to achieve a stricter and more uniform approach. Despite the apparent strength of such an approach, however, there are vast areas of the application of decentralization technologies that keep posing pressing questions to the EU legislator. Paradigmatic of this observation is the space of decentralized finance (DeFi) (Zetzsche et al., 2020) and the ubiquitous noncustodial software used to hold and trade crypto-asset (Barbereau & Bodó, 2023). After a discussion thereof, we shall turn to a more general discussion on the recent regulatory trends for digital finance in the European Union.

2.4.1 Introducing Decentralization Technologies to the Regulatory Mix

Decentralization can be seen as a shift from concentrated to distributed modes of production and consumption of goods and services (de Filippi & Loveluck, 2016). For technologies, the Internet serves as the most paradigmatic example of that shift—moving the distribution of information from centralized siloes to distributed nodes such that "no one is in charge, everyone is" (the consequence is increased access as price drops (Wigand, 2020)). One can observe a clear trend: building on the Internet, other decentralization technologies reached prominence in response to systematic failures and crisis.

Blockchain, and more specifically Bitcoin, emerged in response to the 2008 failures of the reserve banking system to propose a distributed system for the transfer of value on the Internet (de Filippi & Loveluck, 2016). In the first, *Genesis* block of Bitcoin, the developer added, along with normal data, the message "The Times 03/Jan/2009 Chancellor on brink of second bailout for banks" to the coinbase parameter. Bitcoin went on to inspire millions of users and developers to adopt this technology (Schneider, 2019). While regulation certainly lagged behind, the EU eventually responded with MiCAR and other packages that would see the space evolve.

Federated learning, a machine learning method developed by Google to train models locally (i.e., in a distributed manner) (Konečný et al., 2016), is seen as a paradigmatic case to break data siloes and address regulatory privacy requirements face on. In particular, it allows to reduce the amount of personal data transferred and processed by third parties. Hence, it now finds applications in sectors where applying machine learning was, until now, contentious if not impossible (Lee et al., 2023; Fernández et al., 2022). The mass adoption of AI and related risks have led the EU to respond with the AI Act.

In the field of electronic identification, digital identity wallets storing cryptographic keys and digital attestation place the holder of an identity credential at the center of digital identification, giving individuals control over their identity attributes. As such, it is more decentralized and designed to provide more autonomy and privacy to holders (Sedlmeir et al., 2021). These types of credentials are now, for better or worse, associated with notions of individual sovereignty, data control, and autonomy (Giannopoulou, 2023; Smethurst, 2023; Weigl et al., 2023a).

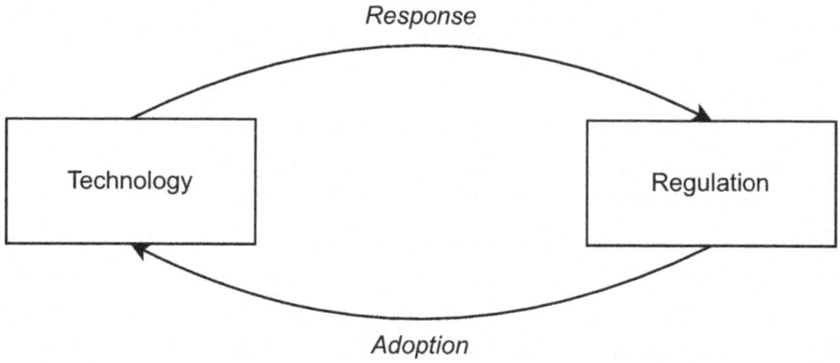

Fig. 2.2 Figurative representation of the symbiotic relationship between regulation and technology

Their emergence and regulation appear symbiotic: In response to the changing digital identity space, regulation was developed and vice versa, and with changing regulation, the adopted identity models changed (Sedlmeir et al., 2022).

While regulation is by no means the sole driver of technological trends, it would be wrong to discredit or detach it entirely. In the IS literature, repeatedly the match was made between regulatory requirements and features of decentralization technologies (Rieger et al., 2019; Schlatt et al., 2022; Roth et al., 2023). However, as wrong as it would be to generalize observations in a "scripted" manner (Grover & Lyytinen, 2015), it would seem incorrect to associate the emergence of the technologies above with regulatory developments alone. Likewise, it is certain that regulation comes as a response to technological trends. As some of the subsequent chapters of this book elaborate, the adoption of decentralization technologies is contingent on regulatory requirements. In sum, we observe that regulation drives technological trends in terms of adoption; and technological trends, in turn, drive regulation in terms of a response (see Fig. 2.2). Note that the relationship between law, regulation, and technology is more complex than figuratively represented here. Given the scope of this chapter, however, this is permissible. We wish to redirect the interested readers to the book of Brownsword et al. (2016) which unpacks that complexity with utmost accuracy.

2.4.2 Decentralized Finance and Its Regulatory Challenges

Following the "same activity, same risk, same rules" approach as per Financial Stability Board (2023), but also endorsed by Recital 9 of MiCAR, in principle DeFi would fall within the scope of application of various EU legislations for financial services on the grounds of their activities. In practice, however, they often run the risk of remaining unregulated. This is because they are offered by unregistered entities that make use of noncustodial smart contracts as "information providers," or because they operate from jurisdictions that allow them to either entirely circumvent regulation or that do not properly enforce it (Barbereau & Bodó, 2023; Pocher, 2023; Zetzsche et al., 2023).

While this "unregulated" state may align with definitions that see DeFi as representing "a whole ecosystem of financial services realized through smart contracts deployed on public distributed ledgers" (Eikmanns et al., 2023, p. 1), where "the role of the financial intermediary is taken over by the self-executing computer code" (Katona, 2021, p. 78), and the ambiguous legal status of individual DeFi projects is both a blessing and a curse. (Consider that use cases vary significantly in nature. They include stablecoin projects (e.g., DAI), lending platforms (e.g., Aave, Compound), exchanges (e.g., Bancor, Kyber, Uniswap, Sushiswap, Pancakeswap), and derivative services/DEXes (e.g., Synthetix, dYdx) (Amler et al., 2023).) Legal decentralization, or more accurately legal "disintermediation" (Becker, 2022), is to be understood as the "elusion of centralized authorities and detachment from legal legitimacy" (Barbereau et al., 2023, p. 2). Disintermediation can also be understood in economic terms and alludes to the reduction of parties involved in transactions and a consequent reduction of cost (Wigand, 2020). The value of disintermediation and the lack of compliance make these systems a libertarian dream (Lichti & Tumasjan, 2023): They are favorable to users attracted to peer-to-peer systems over trusted third parties—be they innocent advocates or criminals.

The weight and relevance of the DeFi area are represented by the total value of DeFi projects, which amounted to USD one billion in January 2020, USD 27 billion in January 2021, USD 60 billion in April 2021, and USD 40 billion in November 2022 (Chainalysis Team, 2022). Given that scale, the lack of applicable regulation is not to be underestimated. The vast scale collapses and financial turmoil caused is commonly known as "Crypto Winter." This culminated in the diversion of some USD 14 billion of crypto-asset worth and total losses amounting to almost USD 50 billion (Zetzsche et al., 2023; Woxholth et al., 2024).

Zetzsche et al. (2023) provides an overview of the current remaining challenges of regulating the DeFi space. MiCAR does not regulate the provisioning of services that are fully decentralized, but the distinction between "partially decentralized" services (in scope) and "fully decentralized platforms" (i.e., when there is no intermediary) (exempted) is far from clear. In addition, the application of many rules laid out by MiCAR will depend on implementing legislation and raises questions regarding their relation to other neighboring regulatory frameworks (van der Linden & Shirazi, 2023; Zetzsche et al., 2023). Overall, these complexities and shortcomings are likely to stifle the effectiveness of existing legislation.

Thus, while it has been demonstrated earlier that significant legislative efforts are directed toward fostering innovation and technological advancements within the financial sector, regulators often find themselves trailing behind in the complex and rapidly evolving landscape of decentralization technologies such as DeFi. This lag could be attributed to several factors, including the relative novelty of these systems, the challenges in understanding and effectively regulating emerging technologies, and the nature of DeFi as a algorithmic and protocol-driven network detached from any control by a central authority.

2.4.3 Ambitions of Proactive Regulation

As noted above, EU regulatory dynamics appear strongly "reactive" to technology and dependent on responding to socioeconomic issues or threats (see the concept of "crisisification" of EU policy-making by Rhinard, 2019). It is also widely acknowledged that "reactive" and "crisis-inspired" rules should not become a dogma (Zetzsche et al., 2017), as they show vulnerabilities to perceptive distortions and arguments backed by ideologies. Hence, the regulatory process may overlook trade-offs and empirical differences, which may possibly lead to regimes that are overfitting and structured in such a way that they are not adaptable and cannot evolve if not by breaking their own boundaries (Pocher, 2023). In this context, even if a sandbox regime such as the DLT Pilot may provide valuable insights, it cannot replace regulatory reforms (Zetzsche et al., 2017). The faith in hasty regulation of innovative technology may come with undesired outcomes (Barbereau & Bodó, 2023), some of which may even go as far as hedging regulatory loopholes.

Whenever "proactive" regulation is pursued, however, there is a substantial need for cross-disciplinary understanding and cooperation. Typically, when policy-makers and regulators are asked to focus on their broader mandate, instead of deploying an "overly rule-based approach" that can hinder innovation and "overly stretch regulatory resources" (Zetzsche et al., 2017), they are asked to develop a deep understanding of the process enabled by the given technology, which needs access to different types of expertise (Pocher, 2023). Indeed, one of the goals of establishing cross-disciplinary collaboration mechanisms is to bridge the gap between the dynamism of innovative technologies and stringent rules-based approaches.

To grasp the meaning of innovative approaches to the interplay between technology and regulation, the interested reader is referred to the literature on "regulation/compliance by/through design" (Casanovas et al., 2018; Hashmi et al., 2018; Goldbarsht & de Koker, 2022) as well as "embedded regulation, " 'embedded compliance," and "embedded supervision" (Auer, 2019; Zetzsche et al., 2020). In the face of decentralization technologies offered by unregistered parties—eponymous in DeFi—alternative regulatory frameworks may prove of greater value than those traditionally applicable (Barbereau & Bodó, 2023). These alternative regulatory frameworks may require multilayered analyses of the techno-legal specifics so as to properly situate regulatory considerations from a normative perspective (Barbereau & Bodó, 2023) or design perspective (Pocher & Veneris, 2022).

It follows that decentralization technologies inspire a new way of reasoning about legal constructs and compliance frameworks, where technology and the law can pursue joint compliance objectives going well beyond the well-known "code is/as law" approaches such as the concept advocated for by Lessig (2019). (On this topic, the reader is referred to Filippi and Wright (2018) and Werbach (2019).) It remains to be seen whether technical decentralization, equipped with suitable governance layers able to satisfy the regulatory demand for accountability (Pocher, 2023), will also display the potential to mitigate some of the current shortcomings arising from a possible overregulation tendency in the EU.

2.5 Conclusion

Situating the EU's regulatory and sociopolitical character in the field of digital finance paints a complex picture marked by deregulation, followed by the implementation of preventative reforms and more stringent legal frameworks for the sake of stability. In the field of digital finance, innovation, notably with the introduction of FinTech, decentralization technologies, and the increasing overlap between the financial sector and Big Tech companies, reshuffled the EU's regulatory approach even more.

In order to understand these dynamics, this chapter provides a historical and geopolitical context for the digital financial sector in the EU. Moreover, it summarizes the regulatory state of play, which admittedly presents a rapidly evolving environment. The EU's inclination toward intensive regulatory activity in the digital realm reflects a commitment to digital sovereignty but risks creating intricate policies lacking coherence and consistency. While commendable for consumer protection and fair competition, the pursuit of digital sovereignty should be viewed as a means to stimulate innovation and advance the Digital Single Market rather than an end in itself. An overview of the current regulatory frameworks further highlights that challenges persist, particularly in regulating emerging spaces such as that of DeFi. Despite significant legislative efforts aimed at fostering innovation, regulators often struggle to keep pace due to its novelty and complexity, highlighting the need for enhanced understanding and collaboration among regulatory bodies.

References

Amler, H., Eckey, L., Faust, S., Kaiser, M., & Schlosser, B. (2023). Defi-ning DeFi: Challenges & pathway. https://arxiv.org/abs/2101.05589.

Auer, R. (2019). Embedded supervision: How to build regulation into blockchain finance. *Federal Reserve Bank of Dallas, Globalization Institute Working Papers, 2019*. https://doi.org/10.24149/gwp371.

Bach, D., & Newman, A. L. (2007). The European regulatory state and global public policy: Micro-institutions, macro-influence. *Journal of European Public Policy, 14*(6), 827–846. https://doi.org/10.1080/13501760701497659.

Barbereau, T., & Bodó, B. (2023). Beyond financial regulation of crypto-asset wallet software: In search of secondary liability. *Computer Law & Security Review, 49*. https://doi.org/10.1016/j.clsr.2023.105829.

Barbereau, T., Smethurst, R., Papageorgiou, O., Sedlmeir, J., & Fridgen, G. (2023). Decentralised finance's timocratic governance: The distribution and exercise of tokenised voting rights. *Technology in Society, 73*, 102251. https://doi.org/10.1016/j.techsoc.2023.102251.

Becker, K. (2022). Blockchain matters – lex cryptographia and the displacement of legal symbolics and imaginaries. *Law Critique*, *33*(2), 113–130. https://doi.org/10.1007/s10978-021-09317-8.
Bellanova, R., & Glouftsios, G. (2022). Formatting European security integration through database interoperability. *European Security*, *31*(3), 454–474. https://doi.org/10.4324/9780203299722_chapter_1.
Benbasat, I., & Zmud, R. W. (2003). The identity crisis within the IS discipline: Defining and communicating the discipline's core properties. *MIS Quarterly*, *27*(2), 183–194. https://doi.org/10.2307/30036527.
Bennett, C. J., & Raab, C. D. (2020). Revisiting the governance of privacy: Contemporary policy instruments in global perspective. *Regulation and Governance*, *14*, 447–464. https://doi.org/10.1111/rego.12222.
Blom-Hansen, J., Christensen, J. G., Grøn, C. H., Jensen, M. H., & Mortensen, P. B. (2023). Transposition of EU regulations: The politics of supplementing EU regulations with national rules. *Journal of European Public Policy*, *30*(12), 2786–2806. https://doi.org/10.1080/13501763.2022.2118355.
Bodoni, S. (2024). TikTok and Meta take aim at the EU's content moderation laws. https://www.bnnbloomberg.ca/tiktok-and-meta-take-aim-at-the-eu-s-content-moderation-laws-1.2032568.
Borrás, S., & Edler, J. (2020). The roles of the state in the governance of socio-technical systems' transformation. *Research Policy*, *49*, 103971. https://doi.org/10.1016/j.respol.2020.103971.
Borrell, J. (2020). China, the United States and us. European Union External Action: The Diplomatic Service of the European Union. https://www.eeas.europa.eu/eeas/china-united-states-and-us_en.
Bradford, A. (2020). *The Brussels effect: How the European Union rules the world*. Oxford University Press. https://doi.org/10.1093/oso/9780190088583.001.0001.
Brownsword, R., Scotford, E., & Karen Yeung, K. (2016). *The Oxford handbook of law, regulation and technology*. Oxford University Press.
Brummer, C. (2015). *Soft law and the global financial crisis*. Cambridge University Press. https://doi.org/10.1017/cbo9781316423875.007.
Buttarelli, G. (2016). The EU GDPR as a clarion call for a new global digital gold standard. *International Data Privacy Law*, *6*(2), 77–78. https://doi.org/10.1093/idpl/ipw006.
Cabral, L., Haucap, J., Parker, G., Petropoulos, G., Valletti, T., & Alstyne, M. v. (2021). The EU Digital Markets Act: A report from a panel of economic experts. https://doi.org/10.2760/139337.
Casanovas, P., González-Conejero, J., & Koker, L. D. (2018). Legal compliance by design (LCbD) and through design (LCtD): Preliminary survey. *CEUR Workshop Proceedings*, *2049*, 33–49. https://ceur-ws.org/Vol-2049/05paper.pdf.
Cervi, G. V. (2022). Why and how does the EU rule global digital policy: An empirical analysis of EU regulatory influence in data protection laws. *Digital Society*, *1*(2), 18. https://doi.org/10.1007/s44206-022-00005-3.
Chainalysis Team (2022). The 2022 crypto crime report. https://go.chainalysis.com/2022-Crypto-Crime-Report.html.
Christensen, T. (2015). *The China challenge: Shaping the choices of a rising power*. W. W. Norton & Company.
Christiansen, T., & Maher, R. (2017). The rise of China — challenges and opportunities for the European Union. *Asia Europe Journal*, *15*, 121–131. https://doi.org/10.1007/s10308-017-0469-2.
Codagnone, C., Liva, G., & de las Heras Ballell, T. R. (2022). Identification and assessment of existing and draft EU legislation in the digital field. Study for the Special Committee on Artificial Intelligence in a Digital Age (AIDA). https://www.europarl.europa.eu/RegData/etudes/STUD/2022/703345/IPOL_STU(2022)703345_EN.pdf.
Codagnone, C., & Weigl, L. (2023). Leading the charge on digital regulation: The more, the better, or policy bubble? *Digital Society*, *2*(1). https://doi.org/10.1007/s44206-023-00033-7.

Csernatoni, R. (2022). The EU's hegemonic imaginaries: from European strategic autonomy in defence to technological sovereignty. *European Security*, *31*(3), 395–414. https://doi.org/10.1080/09662839.2022.2103370.

Damro, C. (2012). Market power Europe. *Journal of European Public Policy*, *19*(5), 682–699. https://doi.org/10.1080/13501763.2011.646779.

Dedman, M. (2006). *The origins and development of the European Union 1945–1995: A history of European integration*. Routledge.

de Filippi, P., & Loveluck, B. (2016). The invisible politics of Bitcoin: Governance crisis of a decentralized infrastructure. *Internet Policy Review*, *5*(4). https://doi.org/10.14763/2016.3.427.

Defraigne, J.-C. (2017). Chinese outward direct investments in Europe and the control of the global value chain. *Asia Europe Journal*, *15*, 213–228. https://doi.org/10.1007/s10308-017-0476-3.

Directive 2009/110/EC (2009). Directive 2009/110/EC of the European Parliament and of the Council of 16 September 2009 on the taking up, pursuit and prudential supervision of the business of electronic money institutions amending Directives 2005/60/EC and 2006/48/EC and repealing Directive 2000/46/EC.

Directive 2014/65/EU (2014). Directive 2014/65/EU of the European Parliament and of the Council of 15 May 2014 on markets in financial instruments and amending Directive 2002/92/EC and Directive 2011/61/EU recast Text with EEA relevance.

Directive EU 2015/2366 (2015). Directive EU 2015/2366 of the European Parliament and of the Council of 25 November 2015 on payment services in the internal market, amending Directives 2002/65/EC, 2009/110/EC and 2013/36/EU and Regulation EU No 1093/2010, and repealing Directive 2007/64/EC.

Directive EU 2015/849 (2015). Directive EU 2015/849 of the European Parliament and of the Council of 20 May 2015 on the prevention of the use of the financial system for the purposes of money laundering or terrorist financing, amending Regulation EU No 648/2012 of the European Parliament and of the Council, and repealing Directive 2005/60/EC of the European Parliament and of the Council and Commission Directive 2006/70/EC Text with EEA relevance.

Directive EU 2016/680 (2016). Directive EU 2016/680 of the European Parliament and of the Council of 27 April 2016 on the protection of natural persons with regard to the processing of personal data by competent authorities for the purposes of the prevention, investigation, detection or prosecution of criminal offences or the execution of criminal penalties, and on the free movement of such data, and repealing Council Framework Decision 2008/977/JHA.

Directive EU 2018/843 (2018). Directive EU 2018/843 of the European Parliament and of the Council of 30 May 2018 amending Directive EU 2015/849 on the prevention of the use of the financial system for the purposes of money laundering or terrorist financing, and amending Directives 2009/138/EC and 2013/36/EU.

Directive EU 2022/2556 (2022). Directive EU 2022/2556 of the European Parliament and of the Council of 14 December 2022 amending Directives 2009/65/EC, 2009/138/EC, 2011/61/EU, 2013/36/EU, 2014/59/EU, 2014/65/EU, EU 2015/2366 and EU 2016/2341 as regards digital operational resilience for the financial sector.

Directive (EU) 2024/1640 (2024). Directive EU 2024/1640 of the European Parliament and of the Council of 31 May 2024 on the mechanisms to be put in place by Member States for the prevention of the use of the financial system for the purposes of money laundering or terrorist financing, amending Directive(EU) 2019/1937, and amending and repealing Directive (EU) 2015/849.

Dougan, M. (2000). Minimum harmonization and the internal market. *Common Market Law Review*, *37*(4), 853–885. https://doi.org/10.54648/272669.

Draghi, M. (2019). Sovereignty in a globalised world Speech by Mario Draghi, President of the ECB, on the award of Laurea honoris causa in law from Università degli Studi di Bologna, Bologna, 22 February 2019. *European Central Bank*. https://www.ecb.europa.eu/press/key/date/2019/html/ecb.sp190222~fc5501c1b1.en.html.

Dür, A. (2011). Fortress Europe or open door Europe? The external impact of the EU's single market in financial services. *Journal of European Public Policy, 18*(5), 619–635. https://doi.org/10.1080/13501763.2011.586792.
Eikmanns, B. C., Mehrwald, P., Sandner, P. G., & Welpe, I. M. (2023). Decentralised finance platform ecosystems: conceptualisation and outlook. *Technology Analysis and Strategic Management*. https://doi.org/10.1080/09537325.2022.2163886.
Ernstberger, J., et al. (2023). SoK: Data sovereignty. https://eprint.iacr.org/2023/967.
European Banking Authority (2022). Opinion of the European Banking Authority on its technical advice on the review of directive EU 2015/2366 on payment services in the internal market PSD2. https://www.eba.europa.eu/sites/default/files/document_library/Publications/Opinions/2022/Opinion%20od%20PSD2%20review%20%28EBA-Op-2022-06%29/1036016/EBA%27s%20response%20to%20the%20Call%20for%20advice%20on%20the%20review%20of%20PSD2.pdf.
European Commission (2014). Proposal for a Regulation of the European Parliament and of the Council amending Regulation EU No 910/2014 as regards establishing a framework for a European Digital Identity. https://www.europarl.europa.eu/cmsdata/278103/eIDAS-4th-column-extract.pdf.
European Commission (2018). Fintech action plan: For a more competitive and innovative european financial sector. https://eur-lex.europa.eu/legal-content/EN/TXT/?uri=CELEX%3A52018DC0109.
European Commission (2019). EU - China – a strategic outlook. *European Commission and HR/VP Contribution to the European Council*. https://commission.europa.eu/system/files/2019-03/communication-eu-china-a-strategic-outlook.pdf.
European Commission (2020a). Communication from the Commission to the European Parliament, the Council, the European Economic and Social Committee and the Committee of the Regions on a Digital Finance Strategy for the EU. https://eur-lex.europa.eu/legal-content/EN/TXT/?uri=CELEX:52020DC0591.
European Commission (2020b). Digital finance package. https://finance.ec.europa.eu/publications/digital-finance-package_en.
European Commission (2020c). Shaping europe's digital future. https://commission.europa.eu/system/files/2020-02/communication-shaping-europes-digital-future-feb2020_en_4.pdf.
European Commission (2021a). Anti-money laundering and countering the financing of terrorism legislative package. https://finance.ec.europa.eu/publications/anti-money-laundering-and-countering-financing-terrorism-legislative-package_en.
European Commission (2021b). Proposal for a Directive of the European Parliament and of the Council on the mechanisms to be put in place by the Member States for the prevention of the use of the financial system for the purposes of money laundering or terrorist financing and repealing Directive EU 2015/849. Last available text during negotiations available at: https://data.consilium.europa.eu/doc/document/ST-6223-2024-INIT/en/pdf.
European Commission (2021c). Proposal for a Regulation of the European Parliament and of the Council establishing the Authority for Anti-Money Laundering and Countering the Financing of Terrorism and amending Regulations EU No 1093/2010, EU 1094/2010, EU 1095/2010.
European Commission (2021d). Proposal for a Regulation of the European Parliament and of the Council Laying Down Harmonised Rules on Artificial Intelligence Artificial Intelligence Act and Amending Certain Union Legislative Acts.
European Commission (2021e). Proposal for a Regulation of the European Parliament and of the Council on the prevention of the use of the financial system for the purposes of money laundering or terrorist financing. Last available text during negotiations available at: https://data.consilium.europa.eu/doc/document/ST-6220-2024-REV-1/en/pdf.
European Commission (2023a). Financial data access and payments package. https://finance.ec.europa.eu/publications/financial-data-access-and-payments-package_en.
European Commission (2023b). Proposal for a Directive of the European Parliament and of the Council on payment services and electronic money services in the Internal Market amending Directive 98/26/EC and repealing Directives 2015/2366/EU and 2009/110/EC.

European Commission (2023c). Proposal for a Regulation of the European Parliament and of the Council on a framework for Financial Data Access and amending Regulations EU No 1093/2010, EU No 1094/2010, EU No 1095/2010 and EU 2022/2554.

European Commission (2023d). Proposal for a Regulation of the European Parliament and of the Council on payment services in the internal market and amending Regulation EU No 1093/2010.

European Commission (2023e). Report from the Commission to the European Parliament, the Council, the European Central Bank and the European Economic and Social Committee on the review of Directive 2015/2366/EU of the European Parliament and of the Council on payment services in the internal market. https://eur-lex.europa.eu/legal-content/EN/TXT/?uri=COM%3A2023%3A365%3AFIN.

European Commission (2024). What is the Single Digital Market about? https://ec.europa.eu/eurostat/cache/infographs/ict/bloc-4.html.

European Council (2020). Shaping Europe's digital future – Council adopts conclusions. https://www.consilium.europa.eu/en/press/press-releases/2020/06/09/shaping-europe-s-digital-future-council-adopts-conclusions/.

European Council (2024). Digital Single Market for Europe. https://www.consilium.europa.eu/en/policies/digital-single-market/.

Fernández, J. D., Menci, S. P., Lee, C. M., Rieger, A., & Fridgen, G. (2022). Privacy-preserving federated learning for residential short-term load forecasting. *Applied Energy*, *326*, 119915. https://doi.org/10.1016/j.apenergy.2022.119915.

Filippi, P. D., & Wright, A. (2018). *Blockchain and the law: The Rule of Code*. Harvard University Press.

Financial Action Task Force (2012). The FATF recommendations. Last amended November 2023. https://www.fatf-gafi.org/en/publications/Fatfrecommendations/Fatf-recommendations.html.

Financial Stability Board (2023). High-level recommendations for the regulation, supervision and oversight of crypto-asset activities and markets. https://www.fsb.org/wp-content/uploads/P170723-2.pdf.

Finck, M. (2019). *Blockchain regulation and governance in Europe*. Cambridge University Press. https://doi.org/10.1017/9781108609708.

Floridi, L. (2020). The fight for digital sovereignty: What it is, and why it matters, especially for the EU. *Philosophy & Technology*, *33*(3), 369–378. https://doi.org/10.1007/s13347-020-00423-6.

Giannopoulou, A. (2023). Digital identity infrastructures: A critical approach of self-sovereign identity. *Digital Society*, *2*(2). https://doi.org/10.1007/s44206-023-00049-z.

Goddard, M. (2017). The EU general data protection regulation (GDPR): European regulation that has a global impact. *International Journal of Market Research*, *59*(6), 703–705. https://doi.org/10.2501/IJMR-2017-050.

Goldbarsht, D., & de Koker, L. (2022). *Financial technology and the law: Combating financial crime*. Springer.

Gomber, P., Koch, J.-A., & Siering, M. (2017). Digital finance and FinTech: Current research and future research directions. *Journal of Business Economics*, *87*(5), 537–580. https://doi.org/10.1007/s11573-017-0852-x.

Greenleaf, G. (2012). The influence of European data privacy standards outside Europe: Implications for globalization of Convention 108. *International Data Privacy Law*, *2*(2), 68–92. https://doi.org/10.1093/idpl/ips006.

Grover, V., & Lyytinen, K. (2015). New state of play in information systems research. *MIS Quarterly*, *39*(2), 271–296. https://doi.org/10.25300/MISQ/2015/39.2.01.

Gunst, S., & Ville, F. D. (2021). The Brussels effect: How the GDPR conquered Silicon Valley. *European Foreign Affairs Review*, *26*(3). https://doi.org/10.54648/eerr2021036.

Hashmi, M., Casanovas, P., & Koker, L. D. (2018). Legal compliance through design: Preliminary results of a literature survey. In *Proceedings of the 2nd Workshop on Technologies for Regulatory Compliance (TERECOM) Co-located with the 31st International Conference on Legal Knowledge and Information Systems (JURIX)* (Vol. 2309, pp. 59–72). https://ceur-ws.org/Vol-2309/06.pdf.

Heisenberg, D., & Fandel, M.-H. (2004). Projecting EU regimes abroad: The EU data protection directive as global standard. In S. Braman (Ed.), *The emergent global information policy regime*. International Political Economy Series (pp. 109–129). Palgrave Macmillan. https://doi.org/10.1057/9780230377684_6.

Herian, R. (2020). Blockchain, GDPR, and fantasies of data sovereignty. *Law, Innovation and Technology*, *12*(1), 156–174. https://doi.org/10.1080/17579961.2020.1727094.

Hofmann, J., Katzenbach, C., & Gollatz, K. (2017). Between coordination and regulation: Finding the governance in internet governance. *New Media and Society*, *19*, 1406–1423. https://doi.org/10.1177/1461444816639975.

Hoofnagle, C. J., van der Sloot, B., & Borgesius, F. Z. (2019). The European Union general data protection regulation: What it is and what it means. *Information & Communications Technology Law*, *28*(1), 65–98. https://doi.org/10.1080/13600834.2019.1573501.

Johnstone, S. (2021). *Rethinking the regulation of cryptoassets. Cryptographic consensus technology and the new prospect*. Elgar. https://doi.org/10.4337/9781800886797.

Katona, T. (2021). Decentralized finance: The possibilities of a blockchain "money lego" system. *Financial and Economic Review*, *20*, 74–102. https://doi.org/10.33893/fer.20.1.74102.

Konečný, J., McMahan, B., Ramage, D., & Richtárik, P. (2016). Federated optimization: Distributed machine learning for on-device intelligence. https://arxiv.org/abs/1610.02527.

Larouche, P., & de Streel, A. (2021). The European Digital Markets Act: A revolution grounded on traditions. *Journal of European Competition Law & Practice*, *12*(7), 542–560. https://doi.org/10.1093/jeclap/lpab066.

Laursen, F. (2012). *Designing the European Union: From Paris to Lisbon*. Springer. https://doi.org/10.1057/9780230367579.

Lee, C. M., Delgado Fernandez, J., Potenciano Menci, S., Rieger, A., & Fridgen, G. (2023). Federated learning for credit risk assessment. In *Proceedings of the 56th Hawaii International Conference on System Sciences* (pp. 386–395). https://hdl.handle.net/10125/102676.

Leonard, M., Pisani-Ferry, J., Ribakova, E., Shapiro, J., & Wolff, G. B. (2019). Redefining Europe's economic sovereignty. *Bruegel: Policy Contribution*, *9*. https://www.jstor.org/stable/resrep28498.

Lessig, L. (2019). *Code and other laws of cyberspace*. Basic Books.

Lichti, C., & Tumasjan, A. (2023). "My precious!": A values-affordances perspective on the adoption of Bitcoin. *Journal of the Association for Information Systems*, *24*(3), 629–663. https://doi.org/10.17705/1jais.00790.

Madiega, T. (2020). Digital sovereignty for Europe. https://www.europarl.europa.eu/RegData/etudes/BRIE/2020/651992/EPRS_BRI(2020)651992_EN.pdf.

Marchant, G. E., & Allenby, B. (2017). Soft law: New tools for governing emerging technologies. *Bulletin of the Atomic Scientists*, *73*, 108–114. https://doi.org/10.1080/00963402.2017.1288447.

Marsden, C. (2012). Internet co-regulation and constitutionalism: Towards European judicial review. *International Review of Law, Computers and Technology*, *26*. https://doi.org/10.1080/13600869.2012.698450.

Metakides, G. (2022). A crucial decade for European digital sovereignty. In H. Werthner, E. Prem, E. A. Lee, & C. Ghezzi (Eds.), *Perspectives on digital humanism* (pp. 219–225). Springer. https://doi.org/10.1007/978-3-030-86144-5_29.

Mevorach, I. (2013). Forum shopping in times of crisis: A directors' duties perspective. *European Company and Financial Law Review ECFR*, *10*, 524. https://doi.org/10.1515/ecfr-2013-0523.

Mügge, D. (2011). The European presence in global financial governance: A principal–agent perspective. *Journal of European Public Policy*, *18*(3), 383–402. https://doi.org/10.1080/13501763.2011.551075.

Napirata, S., Sedlmeir, J., Rieger, A., Fridgen, G., & Zimmermann, S. (2023). The competition effect of decentralized platforms: An analytical model. In *Proceedings of the 44th International Conference on System Sciences*. AIS. https://aisel.aisnet.org/icis2023/sharing_econ/sharing_econ/16/.

Navaretti, G. B., Calzolari, G., Pozzolo, A. F., & Levi, M. (2010). Multinational banking in Europe–financial stability and regulatory implications: Lessons from the financial crisis. *Economic Policy*, *25*(64), 703–753. https://www.jstor.org/stable/40929920.

Negreiro, M. (2021). Updating the European digital identity framework. Briefing: EU legislation in progress. European Parliamentary Research Service. https://www.europarl.europa.eu/RegData/etudes/BRIE/2021/698772/EPRS_BRI(2021)698772_EN.pdf.

Newman, A., & Bach, D. (2014). The European Union as hardening agent: Soft law and the diffusion of global financial regulation. *Journal of European Public Policy*, *21*, 430–452. https://doi.org/10.1080/13501763.2014.882968.

Pagallo, U., Casanovas, P., & Madelin, R. (2019). The middle-out approach: assessing models of legal governance in data protection, artificial intelligence, and the web of data. *Theory and Practice of Legislation*, *7*, 1–25. https://doi.org/10.1080/20508840.2019.1664543.

Pocher, N. (2023). *Distributed Ledger Technologies between Anonymity and Transparency: AML/CFT Regulation of Cryptocurrency Ecosystems in the EU*. PhD thesis, Alma Mater Studiorum Università di Bologna, Universitat Autònoma de Barcelona, KU Leuven. https://doi.org/10.48676/unibo/amsdottorato/10659.

Pocher, N., & Veneris, A. (2022). Privacy and transparency in CBDCs: A regulation-by-design AML/CFT scheme. *IEEE Transactions on Network and Service Management*, *19*(2), 1776–1788. https://doi.org/10.1109/TNSM.2021.3136984.

Quaglia, L. (2014). The sources of European Union influence in international financial regulatory fora. *Journal of European Public Policy*, *21*(3), 327–345. https://doi.org/10.1080/13501763.2014.882970.

Regulation EU 2015/847 (2015). Regulation EU 2015/847 of the European Parliament and of the Council of 20 May 2015 on information accompanying transfers of funds and repealing Regulation EC No 1781/2006 Text with EEA relevance.

Regulation EU 2016/679 (2016). Regulation EU 2016/679 of the European Parliament and of the Council of 27 April 2016 on the protection of natural persons with regard to the processing of personal data and on the free movement of such data, and repealing Directive 95/46/EC.

Regulation EU 2018/1807 (2018). Regulation EU 2018/1807 of the European Parliament and of the Council of 14 November 2018 on a framework for the free flow of non-personal data in the European Union.

Regulation EU 2022/1925 (2022). Regulation EU 2022/1925 of the European Parliament and of the Council of 14 September 2022 on contestable and fair markets in the digital sector and amending Directives EU 2019/1937 and EU 2020/1828 (Digital Markets Act).

Regulation EU 2022/2065 (2022). Regulation EU 2022/2065 of the European Parliament and of the Council of 19 October 2022 on a Single Market For Digital Services and amending Directive 2000/31/EC (Digital Services Act).

Regulation EU 2022/2554 (2022). Regulation EU 2022/2554 of the European Parliament and of the Council of 14 December 2022 on digital operational resilience for the financial sector and amending Regulations EC No 1060/2009, EU No 648/2012, EU No 600/2014, EU No 909/2014 and EU 2016/1011.

Regulation EU 2022/858 (2022). Regulation EU 2022/858 of the European Parliament and of the Council of 30 May 2022 on a pilot regime for market infrastructures based on distributed ledger technology, and amending Regulations EU No 600/2014 and EU No 909/2014 and Directive 2014/65/EU.

Regulation EU 2022/868 (2022). Regulation EU 2022/868 of the European Parliament and of the Council of 30 May 2022 on European data governance and amending Regulation EU 2018/1724 (Data Governance Act).

Regulation EU 2023/1113 (2023). Regulation EU 2023/1113 of the European Parliament and of the Council of 31 May 2023 on information accompanying transfers of funds and certain crypto-assets and amending Directive EU 2015/849 Text with EEA relevance.

Regulation EU 2023/1114 (2023). Regulation EU 2023/1114 of the European Parliament and of the Council of 31 May 2023 on markets in crypto-assets, and amending Regulations EU No 1093/2010 and EU No 1095/2010 and Directives 2013/36/EU and EU 2019/1937.

Regulation EU 2023/2854 (2023). Regulation EU 2023/2854 of the European Parliament and of the Council of 13 December 2023 on harmonised rules on fair access to and use of data and amending Regulation EU 2017/2394 and Directive EU 2020/1828 (Data Act).

Regulation EU No 600/2014 (2014). Regulation EU No 600/2014 of the European Parliament and of the Council of 15 May 2014 on markets in financial instruments and amending Regulation EU No 648/2012 Text with EEA relevance.

Regulation EU No 910/2014 (2014). Regulation EU No 910/2014 of the European Parliament and of the Council of 23 July 2014 on electronic identification and trust services for electronic transactions in the internal market and repealing Directive 1999/93/EC.

Regulation (EU) 2024/1183 (2024). Regulation EU 2024/1183 of the European Parliament and of the Council of 11 April 2024 amending Regulation (EU) No 910/2014 as regards establishing the European Digital Identity Framework.

Regulation (EU) 2024/1689 (2024). Regulation EU 2024/1689 of the European Parliament and of the Council of 13 June 2024 laying down harmonised rules on artificial intelligence and amending Regulations (EC) No 300/2008, EU No 167/2013, (EU) No 168/2013, (EU) 2018/858, (EU) 2018/1139 and (EU) 2019/2144 and Directives 2014/90/EU, (EU) 2016/797 and (EU) 2020/1828 (Artificial Intelligence Act).

Regulation (EU) 2024/1620 (2024). Regulation EU 2024/1620 of the European Parliament and of the Council of 31 May 2024 establishing the Authority for Anti-Money Laundering and Countering the Financing of Terrorism and amending Regulations (EU) No 1093/2010, (EU) No 1094/2010 and (EU) No 1095/2010.

Regulation (EU) 2024/1624 (2024). Regulation EU 2024/1624 of the European Parliament and of the Council of 31 May 2024 on the prevention of the use of the financial system for the purposes of money laundering or terrorist financing.

Rhinard, M. (2019). The crisisification of policy-making in the European Union. *Journal of Common Market Studies*, *57*(3). https://doi.org/10.1111/jcms.12838.

Rieger, A., Lockl, J., Urbach, N., Guggenmos, F., & Fridgen, G. (2019). Building a blockchain application that complies with the EU general data protection regulation. *MIS Quarterly Executive*, *18*(4), 263–279. https://doi.org/10.17705/2msqe.00020.

Roberts, H., Cowls, J., Casolari, F., Morley, J., Taddeo, M., & Floridi, L. (2021). Safeguarding european values with digital sovereignty: An analysis of statements and policies. *Internet Policy Review*. https://doi.org/10.14763/2021.3.1575.

Roth, F. (2022). The effect of the financial crisis on systemic trust. In F. Roth (Ed.), *Public support for the Euro: Essays on labor productivity, monetary economics, and political economy* (Vol. 2, pp. 219–229). Contributions to Economics. Springer. https://doi.org/10.1007/978-3-030-86024-0_11.

Roth, T., Stohr, A., Amend, J., Fridgen, G., & Rieger, A. (2023). Blockchain as a driving force for federalism: A theory of cross-organizational task-technology fit. *International Journal of Information Management*, *68*, 102476. https://doi.org/10.1016/j.ijinfomgt.2022.102476.

Sartor, S., Sedlmeir, J., Rieger, A., & Roth, T. (2022). Love at first sight? A user experience study of self-sovereign identity wallets. In *Proceedings of the 30th European Conference on Information Systems*. AIS. https://aisel.aisnet.org/ecis2022_rp/46/.

Satariano, A., & Mickle, T. (2024). Apple overhauls App Store in Europe, in response to new digital law. *The New York Times*. https://www.nytimes.com/2024/01/25/technology/apple-app-store-europe.html#:~:text=In%20Europe%2C%20customers%20will%20now,called%20the%20Digital%20Markets%20Act.

Schlatt, V., Sedlmeir, J., Feulner, S., & Urbach, N. (2022). Designing a framework for digital KYC processes built on blockchain-based self-sovereign identity. *Information & Management*, *59*(7), 103553. https://doi.org/10.1016/j.im.2021.103553.

Schneider, N. (2019). Decentralization: An incomplete ambition. *Journal of Cultural Economy*, *12*(4), 265–285. https://doi.org/10.1080/17530350.2019.1589553.

Sedlmeir, J., Barbereau, T., Huber, J., Weigl, L., & Roth, T. (2022). Transition pathways towards design principles of self-sovereign identity. In *Proceedings of the 43rd International*

Conference on Information Systems. AIS. https://aisel.aisnet.org/icis2022/is_implement/is_implement/4/.

Sedlmeir, J., Smethurst, R., Rieger, A., & Fridgen, G. (2021). Digital identities and verifiable credentials. *Business & Information Systems Engineering*, *63*(5), 603–613. https://doi.org/10.1007/s12599-021-00722-y.

Smethurst, R. (2023). Digital identity wallets and their semantic contradictions. In *Proceedings of the 31st European Conference on Information Systems*. AIS. https://aisel.aisnet.org/ecis2023_rp/288/.

Treaty on the Functioning of the European Union (2012). Consolidated version of the Treaty on the Functioning of the European Union annexed to the Final Act of the Intergovernmental Conference which adopted the Treaty of Lisbon, signed on 13 December 2007.

Trubek, D. M., & Trubek, L. G. (2007). New governance & legal regulation: Complementarity, rivalry, and transformation. *Columbia Journal of European Law*, *13*, 539–564. https://papers.ssrn.com/sol3/papers.cfm?abstract_id=988065.

Tuominen, M., & Festor, S. (2021). Establishing a framework for a European Digital Identity. Briefing: Initial appraisal of a European Commission impact assessment. European Parliamentary Research Service. http://www.europarl.europa.eu/RegData/etudes/BRIE/2021/694244/EPRS_BRI(2021)694244_EN.pdf.

Underhill, G. R. (1997). The making of the European Financial Area: Global market integration and the EU single market for financial services. In *The new world order in international finance* (pp. 101–123). Springer. https://doi.org/10.1007/978-1-349-25315-9_5.

van der Linden, T., & Shirazi, T. (2023). Markets in crypto-assets regulation: Does it provide legal certainty and increase adoption of crypto-assets? *Financial Innovation*, *9*(1), 22. https://doi.org/10.1186/s40854-022-00432-8.

Véron, N., & Wolff, G. B. (2016). Capital Markets Union: A vision for the long term. *Journal of Financial Regulation*, *2*(1), 130–153. https://doi.org/10.1093/jfr/fjw006.

Wang, J., & Song, W. (Eds.) (2016). *China, the European Union, and the international politics of global governance*. Palgrave Macmillan. https://doi.org/10.1057/9781137514004.

Weigl, L., Amard, A., Codagnone, C., & Fridgen, G. (2022). The EU's digital identity policy: Tracing policy punctuations. In *Proceedings of the 15th International Conference on Theory and Practice of Electronic Governance* (pp. 74–81). ACM. https://doi.org/10.1145/3560107.3560121.

Weigl, L., Barbereau, T., & Fridgen, G. (2023a). The construction of self-sovereign identity: Extending the interpretive flexibility of technology towards institutions. *Government Information Quarterly*, *40*(4), 101873. https://doi.org/10.1016/j.giq.2023.101873.

Weigl, L., Barbereau, T. J., Sedlmeir, J., & Zavolokina, L. (2023b). Mediating the tension between data sharing and privacy: The case of DMA and GDPR. In *Proceedings of the 31st European Conference on Information Systems*. AIS. https://aisel.aisnet.org/ecis2023_rip/49/.

Werbach, K. (2019). *The blockchain and the new architecture of trust*. MIT Press.

Wigand, R. T. (2020). Whatever happened to disintermediation? *Electronic Markets*, *30*(1), 39–47. https://doi.org/10.1007/s12525-019-00389-0.

WITS (2024). World Integrated Trade Solution. https://wits.worldbank.org/.

Woxholth, J., Zetzsche, D. A., Buckley, R. P., & Arner, D. W. (2024). Competing claims to crypto-assets. *Uniform Law Review*, *28*(2). https://doi.org/10.1093/ulr/unad018.

Zetzsche, D., Buckley, R., Arner, D., & van Ek, M. (2023). Remaining regulatory challenges in digital finance and crypto-assets after MiCA. https://ssrn.com/abstract=4487516.

Zetzsche, D. A., Arner, D. W., & Buckley, R. P. (2020). Decentralized finance. *Journal of Financial Regulation*, *6*(2), 172–203. https://doi.org/10.1093/jfr/fjaa010.

Zetzsche, D. A., Buckley, R. P., Arner, D. W., & Barberis, J. N. (2017). Regulating a revolution: From regulatory sandboxes to smart regulation. *Fordham Journal of Corporate & Financial Law*, *23*(1). https://doi.org/10.2139/ssrn.3018534.

Zetzsche, D. A., & Woxholth, J. (2022). The DLT sandbox under the Pilot-Regulation. *Capital Markets Law Journal*, *17*(2), 212–236. https://doi.org/10.1093/cmlj/kmac003.

Part II
Technical Foundations

Chapter 3
Blockchain Technology

Jan Stramm, Jonathan Lautenschlager, and Lars Keppler

Abstract This chapter summarizes a comprehensive examination of *blockchain technology* and distributed ledger technology (DLT) in the financial sector, highlighting its application in distributed systems and the significance of Byzantine fault tolerance (BFT) in ensuring secure and reliable financial transactions. In this regard, we delve deeper into the technological building blocks of blockchain, including its peer-to-peer (P2P) network, cryptographic hash functions, consensus mechanisms, and public key cryptography, emphasizing their collective role in secure data management and transaction processing. Furthermore, the versatility of blockchain in finance through the examples of *Bitcoin*, *Ethereum*, and *Hyperledger Fabric* illustrates unique characteristics and applications for digital currency transactions, decentralized finance, and enterprise solutions. The chapter also discusses the intricacies of tokens, transactions, and wallets in financial applications, including the emergence of decentralized finance (DeFi), in particular, *stablecoins*, decentralized exchanges (DEXs), and *lending protocols*. Finally, it addresses the growing role of noncore financial applications such as fair lotteries, prediction markets, and decentralized gaming, underscoring the expanding scope and potential of blockchain technology in revolutionizing the financial sector.

J. Stramm (✉) · J. Lautenschlager
Frankfurt University of Applied Sciences, Frankfurt am Main, Germany

University of Bayreuth, Bayreuth, Germany

FIM Research Center for Information Management, Bayreuth, Germany

Branch Business & Information Systems Engineering of the Fraunhofer FIT, Bayreuth, Germany
e-mail: jan.stramm@fb3.fra-uas.de; jonathan.lautenschlager@fb3.fra-uas.de

L. Keppler
Frankfurt University of Applied Sciences, Frankfurt am Main, Germany
e-mail: lars.keppler@fb3.fra-uas.de

G. Fridgen et al. (eds.), *Decentralization Technologies*, Financial Innovation and Technology, https://doi.org/10.1007/978-3-031-66047-4_3

3.1 Blockchain Terminology and Definitions

3.1.1 Distributed Systems in Finance: Understanding the Terminology of Blockchain Technology

Distributed systems have found extensive application across diverse domains, ranging from scientific computing (Armstrong et al., 1999), the World Wide Web (Berners-Lee et al., 1992), and massively multiplayer online games (Knutsson et al., 2004) to virtual reality communities (Frécon & Stenius, 1998). In essence, a distributed system refers to a system where hardware and software are situated on separated but networked computers, collaborating and cooperating by exchanging messages (Coulouris et al., 2011). The goal of these systems is typically to provide a shared service (Ghosh, 2007).

The increased application of distributed systems, as seen in organizations such as Google and Amazon Web Services (AWS), can be attributed to their notable benefits. One prominent advantage is their horizontal elastic scalability, which refers to the system's capacity to expand by incorporating extra resources in response to a surge in demand, such as additional computing power facilitating enhanced adaptability and capacity to manage higher workloads (Sedlmeir et al., 2022b). Thus, distributed systems can be structured to exhibit modularity and lose coupling, promoting flexibility and extensibility. Incorporating or removing components or functionalities can occur without disrupting the entire system, simplifying adjustments in response to evolving demands or technological advancements. Moreover, distributed systems can capitalize on existing resources and infrastructure, rendering them more cost-effective than constructing and maintaining a singular centralized system. Additionally, distributed systems may be designed to employ commodity hardware, which is generally more economical than specialized hardware. They can also be geographically distributed across multiple locations, allowing for better data locality. Data can be stored and processed closer to where it is needed, reducing network latency and improving performance for users in different geographic locations.

Distributed systems can particularly benefit global organizations or applications with geographically dispersed users. For example, banking networks mark an essential use case in that regard. While each bank must hold the balance data of their customers, they also have to communicate with each other to conduct transactions or maintain a record of fund transfers from automated teller machines, which are dispersed geographically (Coulouris et al., 2011). Lastly, distributed systems are inherently designed to withstand various types of failures, including hardware, software, or network failures. In the event of a failure in one component, the rest of the system remains functional, as other parts of the system can continue to operate. This approach helps to isolate faults, preventing them from affecting the entire system, a concept known as fault isolation. Consequently, this improves network availability and fault tolerance, enhancing overall system reliability and minimizing downtime (Coulouris et al., 2011).

In the context of services within the financial industry, elements like trust, security, and the reliability of each financial transaction are critical for the practical implementation of underlying systems. These elements are consolidated in the property of BFT and inherently manifested in the design of distributed systems, which can be used as an advantage, making those systems robust and secure. BFT refers to the ability of a system to withstand and recover from failures, including malicious or arbitrary behavior by single entities within the system. The term *"Byzantine"* originates from a classic computer science problem called *"Byzantine Generals Problem"* that deals with achieving consensus among a group of distributed entities—in this case, Byzantine generals—who have difficulties agreeing on a common course of action (Lamport et al., 1982). In the problem, the generals are attempting to coordinate a military attack on a city, and they can communicate with each other only through unreliable channels that may produce false or contradictory information. It illustrates the challenges of achieving consensus in a distributed system where some components may behave faulty or maliciously.

In distributed systems, where multiple components communicate and coordinate to achieve a common goal, failures can occur due to various reasons, such as hardware failures, network failures, software bugs, or malicious actions by adversaries. Byzantine faults are particularly challenging, because they can result in components providing inconsistent, incorrect, or conflicting information to other parts, leading to incorrect results or system failures. Therefore, the relevance of BFT in distributed systems lies in its ability to ensure system integrity, reliability, and consistency in the presence of faults, including malicious behavior (Abellán Álvarez et al., 2024). BFT techniques are designed to detect, mask, or mitigate the effects of faulty or malicious components, allowing the system to continue functioning correctly even when some parts are compromised. This is important in critical systems such as financial systems and their system of digital financial transactions. A digital financial transaction that is not Byzantine fault tolerant may be vulnerable to double-spending attacks (Crain et al., 2017). In a double-spending scenario, one system member sends two transactions relating to the same digital representation of assets to two or more other members. The other members then receive the message, confirm that the transaction's sender has the required digital representation, and accept the transaction. Without a common state, this approach allows an entity to spend a given digital representation twice or more, thereby creating conflicting information within the network (Karame et al., 2012). The need to prevent double-spending in digital currencies eventually led Nakamoto (2008) to design the first distributed system for digital financial transactions with open participation, based on a combination of technical components that became known as *blockchain technology*.

Blockchain technology is a type of DLT that enables secure, transparent, and tamper-proof data storage and transfer. Its decentralized characteristics make it highly distributed and eliminate the risk of a single point of failure by facilitating transactions without the need for a central authority (Schlatt et al., 2016; Völter et al., 2023). To achieve the desired characteristics (i.e., drawing on the advantages of a distributed system while at the same time being Byzantine fault tolerant), blockchains draw on existing technology, such as P2P networks, hash functions, consensus mechanisms, and public key cryptography to combine them in a sophisticated manner. The subsequent section elucidates the functioning of each component and how these technologies collectively operate.

Peer-to-Peer Network The traditional client-server design of distributed information systems faces challenges, primarily from an IT-security perspective, because a (non-replicated) server is a single point of failure. However, blockchain's decentralized and distributed nature makes it necessary to use P2P architectures, which allow all nodes to have equal rights and perform the same tasks, such as verifying and validating transactions. This architecture ensures the network is resilient against attacks and failures, as no single entity has total controls. Hence, public key cryptography (PKC) is often used in P2P networks to secure data identification and authentication or transfer. P2P networks can be "pure," consisting only of servants, or "hybrid," relying on a central entity to provide parts of the network service. Using a P2P architecture in blockchain networks also enables greater transparency and immutability, as all nodes have a copy of the blockchain ledger and can verify its contents (Schollmeier, 2001).

Cryptographic Hash Functions Hash functions generate a fixed-length output called a hash value or digest, which acts as a digital fingerprint of data. Blockchain implementations commonly use the *SHA-3 family* of hash algorithms introduced by National Institute of Standards and Technology (NIST) in 2015 (Dworkin, 2015). Hash functions are designed with properties such as collision resistance and preimage resistance. Collision resistance ensures that finding the same outputs with different, independent inputs is computationally infeasible. In contrast, preimage resistance ensures that finding an input for a specific hashed output is computationally infeasible. Further, second preimage resistance is similar to collision resistance, but a particular input is targeted. Preimage resistance and second preimage resistance are critical to ensuring the immutability of blockchains, and the nested use of different hash algorithms is one way to provide a higher level of (second) preimage resistance (Rogaway & Shrimpton, 2004). Finally, hashes serve as pointers that "chain" transaction blocks together. When creating the next one, this is done by referencing the previous block's hash (and, therefore, the content).

Consensus Mechanism Blockchain technology relies heavily on transactions, whether it involves calling a smart contract function or transferring crypto tokens. Blockchains employ sophisticated consensus mechanisms to validate new transactions and blocks to ensure agreement among distributed systems regarding data or network states. In contrast to centralized systems, where an authority maintains and updates the state of the database, blockchain technology operates on top of a P2P network that avoids the need for a central authority to govern the system. However, this requires that each transaction is verified and authenticated, which can be a computationally intensive process. The proof of work (PoW) consensus algorithm is currently one of the dominant approaches used by major blockchain networks but is associated with high resource consumption (Sedlmeir et al., 2020). As a result, alternatives such as practical BFT have been introduced for smaller networks. However, these consensus mechanisms have been criticized for their poor performance and scalability, prompting Hyperledger Fabric to introduce the execute-order-validate consensus logic (Pilkington, 2016; Guggenberger et al., 2022).

Public Key Cryptography Public key cryptography comprises cryptographic systems that utilize key pairs, including a secret key and a public key, to encrypt and decrypt data. The secret key is known only to the owner, while the public key is shared with other users. Digital signatures, an integral aspect of blockchains, can be implemented using PKC to verify the authenticity and origin of messages. It is crucial that the private key cannot be generated from the public key or the signature to maintain the authentication mechanism's integrity. Implementing PKC in blockchains may require a sophisticated infrastructure for key management and certificates, especially in permissioned blockchains, where user identity is known. Asymmetric encryption is computationally heavier than symmetric encryption, and transaction signing is often managed by encrypting a (shorter) hash of the transaction (Trevathan & Read, 2007).

In combination, blockchain operates on a P2P network of nodes that verify and validate transactions and then add them to the ledger as "*blocks*." Those blocks are replicated across multiple servers (*nodes*) in a fault-tolerant way. Each block contains a cryptographic and linearly connected hash pointer of the previous block, which creates a chain of transaction blocks to provide a physically distributed and organizationally decentralized yet logically synchronized data management, resulting in the corresponding terminology *blockchain technology* (Toufaily et al., 2021; Abellán Álvarez et al., 2024). Due to this cryptographic bond within an append-only structure, previous blocks cannot be altered without invalidating the entire chain, making the blockchain a secure form of data storage and resistant to malicious behavior such as tampering or censorship (Samaniego et al., 2016). In that regard, decentralization is a key feature of a blockchain providing a solution approach without a single authority or central entity—also referred to as a *single point of failure*—solely controlling the system. Instead, every node in the network has a copy of the ledger, which is constantly updated as new transactions are added. For instance, by executing transactions transparently across the P2P network, blockchains exclude subsequent data manipulation by implementing hashes linking each block to the previous one and connecting the creation and validation of blocks with a scarce resource that makes attacks costly. As a result, data cannot be altered maliciously without being detectable. In the context of decentralization technologies for finance, transactions can be processed without intermediaries like banks or financial institutions, facilitating reduced transaction costs and increasing transparency. Therefore, blockchains are highly valuable, especially in financial applications where data security and immutability are crucial for trusted financial transactions (Gramlich et al., 2022; Alt et al., 2024). In doing so, cutting out the middle man, such as banks or financial institutions, is called *disintermediation*. Disintermediation within banking processes promises to make financial transactions efficient by eliminating intermediaries and reducing transaction costs, streamlining transactions, and making them faster and more affordable.

		Access to Transaction Validation	
		Permissioned	Permissionless
Access to Transactions	Public	All nodes can read and submit transactions. Only authorized nodes can validate transactions.	All nodes can read, submit, and validate transactions.
	Private	Only authorized nodes can read, submit, and validate transactions.	Not applicable.

Fig. 3.1 Blockchain access typology following Beck et al. (2017)

Due to their inherent design, blockchains can be fine-tuned and implemented in various contexts, with their access rights and permission levels playing a pivotal role in determining their application and utility (Sedlmeir et al., 2022b). Peters and Panayi (2016) and Beck et al. (2017) conceptualized these as two primary dimensions that characterize a blockchain system: openness (public vs. private) and permissions (permissionless vs. permissioned). Figure 3.1 depicts these combinations, illustrating the spectrum of possibilities offered by the unique intersection of openness and permissions in blockchain technology.

The first dimension, openness, refers to who can participate in the network. A public blockchain is open and accessible to anyone. There are no gatekeepers or restrictions on who can join the network, read the data contained in the blockchain, or participate in the network's consensus protocol. This inclusiveness allows for high transparency and decentralization, as seen in cryptocurrencies like Bitcoin and Ethereum. On the other hand, access to a private blockchain, also known as a consortium or enterprise blockchain, is restricted. Only predefined users, typically a group of organizations or consortium members, can join the network and access the blockchain data. This kind of blockchain is often used in business contexts where privacy, speed, and efficiency are crucial, such as in supply chain management or financial transactions (Lautenschlager et al., 2023). Independent of the choice of access rights, the transparency caused by replicated transaction processing and storage is often excessive when sensitive personal or business information needs to be handled (Sedlmeir et al., 2022a).

Considering permissions, the second dimension relates to the level of authority different participants have in the network. In a permissionless blockchain, all users are on an equal footing. Every participant can validate transactions and add them to the blockchain, and no central authority can limit a user's participation. This model is followed by many cryptocurrencies, offering a high degree of decentralization but also requiring a large amount of computational resources. In contrast, a permissioned blockchain has a more controlled structure. Different entities within the network have different rights or roles. For example, only certain peers, often known as validators or trusted nodes, can validate transactions and add blocks to the chain. This model offers efficiency and scalability at the cost of some degree of centralization. It is often preferred in business environments where a certain level of trust exists among participants, and regulatory compliance is necessary. The combinations of these two dimensions yield three potential types of blockchains: *public permissionless* (like Bitcoin), *public permissioned*, and *private permissioned* (like some implementations of Hyperledger Fabric or R3's Corda).

3.1.2 Next Generation Financial Transactions: The Power of Smart Contracts for Blockchain Applications

In the context of finance as an application within the blockchain sphere, a transaction typically involves transferring funds from one address to another. However, newer types of blockchains have evolved to allow for the execution of deterministic program code, enabling a broader range of functions. These programs, commonly called smart contracts (Buterin, 2014), can run on blockchains and are essential for blockchain-based financial applications. Smart contracts represent self-executing digital programs built on blockchain technology and can be designed to automate and regulate financial transactions. Smart contracts act as computer programs that automatically execute contractual obligations when predefined conditions are met (Buterin, 2014; Szabo, 1996). The code is executed when creating a new block, and users can commit funds and input variables to a smart contract via a transaction. When the transaction is included in a new block, the block creator executes the smart contract code using the given inputs and commits any resulting state updates to the world state (Kannengieser et al., 2022). Smart contracts must be deterministic to ensure that the states of different nodes do not diverge, i.e., to maintain synchronization. Since smart contracts cannot easily query data outside the blockchain, decentralized applications (DApps) rely on Oracles to provide relevant information on-chain. In this context, the *Oracle problem* arises, because blockchain networks cannot automatically verify the accuracy of this information (Caldarelli & Ellul, 2021). One possibility to address this is by involving a consortium of incentivized entities that verify corresponding data, combining incentives and punishments for providing accurate or inaccurate data.

Smart contracts are stored on the blockchain in a distributed manner. They are executed without intermediaries or third parties verifying or enforcing the conditions of the contract. Hence, those characteristics become extremely attractive for implementing financial applications that can automate complex if-then processes (e.g., during a payment transaction) and reduce the risk of errors, fraud, or other malicious behavior. An example of smart contract automation in insurance could be the processing of claims. When a policyholder submits a claim, the smart contract automatically verifies the claim against the insurance policy terms and then executes the payment to the policyholder if the predefined conditions are met (Guggenberger et al., 2021). Without the need for manual verification by an insurance agent, the smart contract would automatically verify the details of the accident against the policy terms. If the conditions for execution of the smart contract are met, the payment to the policyholder would automatically be executed, reducing the time and cost of claims processing by a considerable margin. The risk of errors or fraudulent behavior could perhaps be reduced if one could see some truth in the highly criticized "code is law" or "code as law" paradigms (Lessig, 1999, 2006). Indeed, although they led to arguing that smart contracts could replace the law with self-executing and self-enforcing predetermined code-based rules, the (extent of the) legal qualification of (self-executing) code is far from clear-cut (Filippi & Wright, 2018; Finck, 2019; Werbach, 2018).

Overall, smart contracts offer a new way to automate processes and communicate contractual terms, reducing the need for intermediaries and increasing efficiency and transparency. As such, they are becoming an increasingly popular application of blockchain technology.

3.1.3 Exploring the Versatility of Blockchain in Finance

The blockchain landscape has witnessed substantial growth and diversification in recent years. Various blockchain technologies have emerged within the financial sector, with Bitcoin and Ethereum being noteworthy examples. While these are not the only platforms available, they offer distinctive features and cater to diverse use cases in finance, thus illustrating the adaptability of blockchain technology. This subsection presents a brief overview of these unique blockchain technologies, focusing on their essential characteristics and applications in the financial sphere.

As the pioneer of blockchain technology, the Bitcoin blockchain has provided a decentralized, transparent, and secure means for conducting P2P transactions. Its PoW consensus algorithm guarantees robust network security. In the realm of finance, the Bitcoin blockchain primarily supports digital currency transactions, cross-border remittances, micropayments, and decentralized financial services, such as lending and borrowing. For example, Bitcoin's decentralized nature offers an appealing alternative for cross-border money transfers by eliminating intermediaries and enabling direct transactions between parties, thereby reducing transfer fees and processing time (Ozili, 2022). A European user can send Bitcoins to a family member in another country using a digital wallet, after which the recipient can convert the Bitcoin to local currency through a local exchange, swiftly completing the remittance process with comparatively lower fees than traditional services (Sajter, 2022).

The Ethereum blockchain is one of the most prominent platforms in blockchain-based finance. Ethereum emerged as a versatile blockchain platform, facilitating the creation and deployment of smart contracts and DApps. With its capacity to accommodate many use cases, Ethereum is crucial in DeFi, asset tokenization, prediction markets, and initial coin offerings (ICOs) (Chen et al., 2020). Ethereum employs proof of stake (PoS) to reduce energy consumption (Sedlmeir et al., 2020), lower entrance barriers to participate, and potentially favor decentralization. Several established smart contract standards exist within this ecosystem, often specified using Ethereum request for commentss (ERCs), such as ERC-20 for fungible tokens and ERC-721 for non-fungible tokens (NFTs) (Hartwich et al., 2024). Ethereum's asset layer allows developers to create DApps that rely on the blockchain for event recording and digital asset ownership tracking, thus eliminating the need for trusted third parties (Gramlich et al., 2022). Consequently, smart contracts enable the implementation of complex DApps, including decentralized autonomous organizations (DAOs). For example, *Aave*, a leading DeFi platform, allows users to lend and borrow cryptocurrencies using Ethereum's smart contracts. Borrowers can deposit assets as collateral and obtain loans in various supported cryptocurrencies, while lenders provide liquidity to the platform and earn interest on their deposits. This decentralized lending and borrowing process operates without intermediaries, granting users enhanced control over their funds and potentially more competitive interest rates than traditional financial services (Xu & Vadgama, 2022).

Spearheaded by the Linux Foundation, Hyperledger comprises a collection of open-source, enterprise-oriented blockchain platforms. The project's modular design and support for permissioned blockchains render it appropriate for numerous financial applications, including supply chain management, trade finance, and digital identity. Hyperledger platforms like Fabric and Sawtooth offer customizable components and pluggable consensus mechanisms tailored to organizations' needs (Lautenschlager et al., 2023; Sedlmeir et al., 2021). For example, the global trade finance platform "we.trade" was built on Hyperledger Fabric and streamlined secure and efficient transactions among buyers, sellers, and banks. By harnessing blockchain's transparency and traceability, we.trade verifies the authenticity of goods and optimizes the flow of information across the supply chain. This was supposed to simplify the trade finance process, minimize paperwork, and mitigate fraud risks. By providing a unified, shared view of trade data, we.trade was expected to expedite payment processing and enhance the overall efficiency of international trade operations (Petersen, 2023).

In conclusion, the financial sector has experienced substantial advancements due to the distinctive features and potential applications of blockchain technologies such as Bitcoin, Ethereum, and Hyperledger. A comprehensive understanding of these platforms' unique characteristics and capabilities enables stakeholders to capitalize on their benefits and facilitate continued innovation within the financial domain.

3.1.4 Examining the Interplay of Tokens, Transactions, and Wallets in Financial Applications

Tokens are essential components of DeFi applications, although their design and purpose can differ considerably. Smart contracts can create new tokens with a specific supply that follows a particular logic and manage the corresponding ownership relations. At first, smart contract-based tokens were typically programmed and issued through ICOs, which were influenced by initial initial public offerings (IPOs) in traditional finance. ICOs have been employed by various projects to finance early development, marketing, or to gain initial liquidity (Arnold et al., 2018). Smart contracts can also control variables that represent control over the smart contract itself or other critical parameters. This gives the creator some leeway to modify or deactivate the smart contract in case of implementation errors or expansions. However, it also comes with a risk as the corresponding entity needs to be trusted to refrain from (mis)using this power.

Depending on the smart contract's design, tokens can act like units of a currency, equity, fractional ownership of an asset, voting rights, payments within an application, or an incentive in a network (Oliveira et al., 2018). Fungible tokens, which represent a unit of account, are the most typical type of token used in DeFi applications. Native protocol tokens like Bitcoin's "BTC" and Ethereum's "ETH" are fungible tokens that uphold their respective blockchains' consensus mechanisms by motivating honest hash rate contribution, capital, or other scarce resources, depending on the consensus mechanism. In this context, the native currency units function as "fuel" for processing transactions in the form of fees necessary to motivate block producers' activities on the network. Validators in several blockchain protocols are rewarded with newly minted native tokens upon creating a new block. Due to the pseudonymous nature of blockchain, incentive mechanisms are necessary to maintain the system's integrity by rewarding honest behavior (Bano et al., 2019).

ERC-721 tokens are unique and distinguishable NFTs that have gained attention for their use as digital assets, such as digital artworks (Barbereau et al., 2022). The ERC-1155 standard incorporates properties of both the ERC-20 and ERC-721 standards (Sunyaev et al., 2021; Whitaker & Kräussl, 2020). Transactions involving the transfer of tokens usually involve saving the sender's and receiver's addresses, the number of assets, and the unique identifier for the corresponding NFT. Digital wallets are needed to access and manage these funds, and they generate and securely store cryptographic keypairs. Hot wallets are software applications that display account balances and facilitate blockchain interaction, while cold wallets store private keys on air-gapped storage media to prevent leakage to potential attackers.

3.2 Revolutionizing Finance: The Power of Tokens, Transfers, and Wallets in Blockchain Systems

Since Ethereum has introduced the capability of programmable payments by introducing smart contracts, a more comprehensive range of financial applications has risen. Due to the decentralized structure of the Ethereum network, many of these applications fall under the umbrella of DeFi, which aims to replicate financial services without a corresponding middleman such as banks or payment providers. DeFi encompasses various application areas, including financial services or markets and gaming or gambling, but there is a high degree of interconnectedness between them (Gramlich et al., 2022). Many protocols cover multiple subcategories, and both gaming and gambling protocols and finance-related DApps may incorporate elements of the other to increase user adoption.

One of DeFi's main applications is the concept of stablecoins, which have emerged as a solution to address the issue of volatile price fluctuations in cryptocurrencies, which prohibits them as a viable option for a medium of exchange and reduces liquidity in cryptocurrency markets (Griffin & Shams, 2020; Garratt & Shin, 2023). These digital assets aim to provide a stable exchange rate to a pegged value—the collateral—such as fiat currencies, commodities, or gold (Klages-Mundt et al., 2020). Stablecoins can be categorized into fiat-backed stablecoins, seigniorage stablecoins, and crypto-backed stablecoins. Fiat-backed stablecoins are pegged directly to a certain amount of fiat currency (e.g., USD, EUR, YEN) and require a financial institution to serve as a custodian for the currency used to back the stablecoin. This makes them subject to the regulatory requirements of the jurisdiction in which they operate. On the other hand, there are two further mechanisms that try to imitate fiat currencies but cannot achieve the same stability (Buiter, 2007; Crown, 2018), as also seen in prominent collapses such as the one of TerraLuna (Briola et al., 2023): Seigniorage stablecoins are based on an algorithm that maintains the coin price close to an intended peg—similar to how central banks mint or burn money (Sams, 2015). Finally, crypto-backed stablecoins are issued using other cryptocurrencies as the underlying asset, with the peg maintained through smart contract mechanisms. Therefore, Oracles are necessary to provide pricing information for stablecoins, and several methods can be used to collateralize on-chain assets, including smart contract-based sources for exchange rates auctions, e.g., in the form of auctions, order books, or automated market makers (AMMs). All in all, stablecoins represent a crucial part of DeFi and are expected to drive the broader adoption of DeFi applications (Catalini et al., 2022).

DEXs are another emerging application DeFi. These exchanges function without a single trusted entity as the market maker, which could operate in their favor or may disappear with entrusted funds. DEXs eliminate the need for intermediaries and provide increased transparency, security, and resilience. However, they face challenges related to expensive storage space, blockchain computation, and transaction fees resulting from setting and matching orders. Extrapolating toward the future, DEXs can leverage succinct zero-knowledge proofs (ZKPs) such as (zk-SNARKs) to make order book-based DEXs a more viable, scalable, and user-friendly option. The current most popular DEXs operate based on an AMM algorithm, which creates liquidity pools holding both assets of the trading pair and acts as a counterparty to trades. Liquidity providers provide both assets of the trading pair in the current ratio to the liquidity pool and receive a share of the trading fees generated from the pool to incentivize liquidity provisioning. However, liquidity providers are exposed to "impermanent loss" due to price movements caused by arbitrage trades. At the time of writing, *Uniswap*, *Curve*, and *Bancor* are the most notable DEXs that use different interpretations of the AMM-based approach to DEXs.

Lending and borrowing protocols resemble another implementation of DeFi platforms. They enable P2P lending and the borrowing of crypto-assets using AMM, which determine interest rates based on the utilization rate of a given asset (Leshner & Hayes, 2019). Lenders earn variable interest on locked currencies, while borrowers can take out loans at fixed or variable interest rates backed by a collateral deposit of another asset. These protocols provide additional financial utility, such as decentralized margin trading for borrowers and relatively safe investment of crypto-assets for lenders (Gudgeon et al., 2020). Lending protocols are some of the most prominent Ethereum-based applications regarding total value locked.

Moreover, derivatives that receive their value from an underlying asset can be implemented using blockchain technology by issuing a new token based on a corresponding smart contract that resembles those derivatives, such as options (Juliano, 2018). Derivatives are commonly used to decrease or hedge investment risk or purposefully increase exposure to an asset without having to buy the asset itself. In DeFi, derivatives can be implemented for margin trading, similar to lending and borrowing protocols. They can function without time and price feed Oracles using Unix time stamps of blocks and decentralized pricing mechanisms of AMMs (e.g., Synthetix). DeFi allows users to hedge or leverage positions not only in crypto assets but—with further adoption—increasingly on real-world assets in a far easier way than traditional finance.

Another application of DeFi is automated asset management through smart contracts controlled by DApps that manage crypto tokens for diversification—and with that—the mitigation of certain risks (Schellinger, 2020). Yield farming protocols, such as "Yearn.finance" or "Pickle.finance" offer innovative approaches to portfolio management in DeFi. These protocols allow users to deposit their assets into "vaults" comprising different investment strategies developed, optimized, and tested off-chain by strategists and experts. However, the highly fragmented landscape of DeFi protocols and lack of standardization pose challenges for asset management. Aggregation services, such as "Zerion.io," aim to address these challenges by providing a unified interface for interacting with DeFi protocols. Nevertheless, the fluctuations in DeFi ecosystems require asset management DApps to be highly dynamic and adaptable. The management of crypto-assets in DeFi also includes taking advantage of airdrops, which are free distributions of tokens to early users and investors of blockchain projects.

The novelty and variety of DeFi applications increase the risk of smart contract vulnerabilities and corresponding exploits, requiring insurance coverage to protect against such threats. Smart-contract-based insurances in DeFi allow users to protect themselves from losses from bugs or attacks by purchasing dedicated insurance products (Guggenberger et al., 2021). Today, such insurance products are being provided, among others, by Nexus Mutual, Opium Finance, Arbol, and Etherisc. However, implementing purely smart-contract-based insurance in DeFi is challenging, because it reintroduces trusted intermediaries. A DeFi-based insurance platform could establish a competent contingency committee composed of insurance experts and advised by independent IT auditors who assess the claims. Depending on the vote, the insurance claim can be settled or declined (Guggenberger et al., 2021). To what extent the dependence on trusted intermediaries inhibits the utility of insurance products in DeFi remains to be determined; however, the settlement of insurance claims can be handled digitally and instantaneously using Oracles.

Noncore financial applications are also increasingly growing in the DeFi sector. These applications, such as fair lotteries, prediction markets, and decentralized gaming, rely on associated DeFi services and products. Fair lotteries aim to mitigate several restrictions imposed by regulators by offering cheap, accessible, and primarily fair lotteries. Prediction markets allow users to bet on the outcome of real-life events. Decentralized gaming, built on decentralization technologies such as a blockchain, offers a new paradigm for players to monetize in-game assets and benefit from earning passive income. However, due to the capacity bottlenecks of blockchains, games usually do not happen entirely on-chain and continue to build significantly on proprietary, closed-source software, making it unclear to what extent computer game manufacturers will implement blockchain-based gaming assets in a way that makes them useful across different games and versions.

To summarize, blockchain technology has been utilized in the financial sector to create DeFi applications for primary and secondary financial purposes. The success of these applications will depend on factors such as user demand, regulation, and technological progress, which will be determined over time.

References

Abellán Álvarez, I., Gramlich, V., & Sedlmeir, J. (2024). Unsealing the secrets of blockchain consensus: A systematic comparison of the formal security of proof-of-work and proof-of-stake. In *The 39th ACM/SIGAPP Symposium on Applied Computing*.

Alt, R., Fridgen, G., & Chang, Y. (2024). The future of fintech—towards ubiquitous financial services. *Electronic Markets*, *34*(1), 3. https://doi.org/10.1007/s12525-023-00687-8.

Armstrong, R., et al. (1999). Toward a common component architecture for high-performance scientific computing. In *Proceedings of the 8th International Symposium on High Performance Distributed Computing* (pp. 115–124). IEEE. https://doi.org/10.1109/hpdc.1999.805289.

Arnold, L., et al. (2018). Blockchain and initial coin offerings: Blockchain's implications for crowdfunding. In *Business transformation through blockchain* (pp. 233–272). Springer. https://doi.org/10.1007/978-3-319-98911-2_8.

Bano, S., Sonnino, A., Al-Bassam, M., Azouvi, S., McCorry, P., Meiklejohn, S., & Danezis, G. (2019). SoK: Consensus in the age of blockchains. In *Proceedings of the 1st ACM Conference on Advances in Financial Technologies*. https://doi.org/10.1145/3318041.3355458.

Barbereau, T., Sedlmeir, J., Smethurst, R., Fridgen, G., & Rieger, A. (2022). Tokenization and regulatory compliance for art and collectibles markets. In *Blockchains and the token economy: Studies in theory and practice*. Palgrave Macmillan. https://doi.org/10.1007/978-3-030-95108-5_8.

Beck, R., Avital, M., Rossi, M., & Thatcher, J. B. (2017). Blockchain technology in business and information systems research. *Business & Information Systems Engineering*, *59*(6), 381–384. https://doi.org/10.1007/s12599-017-0505-1.

Berners-Lee, T., Cailliau, R., Groff, J.-F., & Pollermann, B. (1992). World-Wide Web: The information universe. *Internet Research*, *2*(1), 52–58. https://doi.org/10.1108/eb047254.

Briola, A., Vidal-Tomás, D., Wang, Y., & Aste, T. (2023). Anatomy of a stablecoin's failure: The Terra-Luna case. *Finance Research Letters*, *51*, 103358. https://doi.org/10.1016/j.frl.2022.103358.

Buiter, W. H. (2007). Seigniorage. *Economics*, *1*(1). https://doi.org/10.5018/economics-ejournal.ja.2007-10.

Buterin, V. (2014). A next-generation smart contract and decentralized application platform. https://ethereum.org/en/whitepaper/.

Caldarelli, G., & Ellul, J. (2021). The blockchain oracle problem in decentralized finance – A multivocal approach. *Applied Sciences, 11*(16), 7572. https://doi.org/10.3390/app11167572.

Catalini, C., de Gortari, A., & Shah, N. (2022). Some simple economics of stablecoins. *Annual Review of Financial Economics, 14*. https://doi.org/10.1146/annurev-financial-111621-101151.

Chen, W., Zhang, T., Chen, Z., Zheng, Z., & Lu, Y. (2020). Traveling the token world: A graph analysis of Ethereum ERC20 token ecosystem. In *Proceedings of The Web Conference*. ACM. https://doi.org/10.1145/3366423.3380215.

Coulouris, G. F., Dollimore, J., Kindberg, T., & Blair, G. (2011). *Distributed systems* (5th edn.). Pearson.

Crain, T., Gramoli, V., Larrea, M., & Raynal, M. (2017). DBFT: Efficient Byzantine consensus with a weak coordinator and its application to consortium blockchains. https://arxiv.org/abs/1702.03068.

Crown, S. (2018). The cryptoeconomics of seigniorage shares stablecoins. https://smithandcrown.com/research/the-cryptoeconomics-of-seigniorage-shares-stablecoins-basis-and-carbon/.

Dworkin, M. J. (2015). *SHA-3 standard: Permutation-based hash and extendable-output functions*. National Institute of Standards and Technology (NIST). https://doi.org/10.6028/nist.fips.202.

Filippi, P. D., & Wright, A. (2018). *Blockchain and the law: The rule of code*. Harvard University Press.

Finck, M. (2019). *Blockchain regulation and governance in Europe*. Cambridge University Press.

Frécon, E., & Stenius, M. (1998). Dive: A scaleable network architecture for distributed virtual environments. *Distributed Systems Engineering, 5*(3), 91. https://doi.org/10.1088/0967-1846/5/3/002.

Garratt, R., & Shin, H. S. (2023). Stablecoins versus tokenised deposits: Omplications for the singleness of money. BIS Bulletin. https://www.bis.org/publ/bisbull73.htm.

Ghosh, S. (2007). *Distributed systems: An algorithmic approach*. Chapman & Hall/CRC.

Gramlich, V., et al. (2022). Decentralized finance (DeFi): Foundations, applications, potentials, and challenges. https://www.fit.fraunhofer.de/content/dam/fit/de/documents/Whitepaper__DeFi__English_Version_2022_07_15.pdf.

Griffin, J. M., & Shams, A. (2020). Is Bitcoin really untethered? *The Journal of Finance, 75*(4), 1913–1964. https://doi.org/10.1111/jofi.12903.

Gudgeon, L., Werner, S., Perez, D., & Knottenbelt, W. J. (2020). DeFi protocols for loanable funds: Interest rates, liquidity and market efficiency. In *Proceedings of the 2nd ACM Conference on Advances in Financial Technologies*. https://doi.org/10.1145/3419614.3423254.

Guggenberger, T., Kuhn, M., & Schellinger, B. (2021). Insured? Good! Designing a blockchain-based credit default insurance system for DeFi lending protocols. In *Proceedings of the 4th Middle East & North Africa Conference on Digital Information Systems*. AIS. https://aisel.aisnet.org/menacis2021/8/.

Guggenberger, T., Sedlmeir, J., Fridgen, G., & Luckow, A. (2022). An in-depth investigation of the performance characteristics of Hyperledger Fabric. *Computers and Industrial Engineering, 173*, 108716. https://doi.org/10.1016/j.cie.2022.108716.

Hartwich, E., Ollig, P., Fridgen, G., & Rieger, A. (2024). Probably something: A multi-layer taxonomy of non-fungible tokens. *Internet Research, 34*(1), 216–238. https://doi.org/10.1108/INTR-08-2022-0666.

Juliano, A. (2018). dYdX: A standard for decentralized margin trading and derivatives. https://whitepaper.dydx.exchange.

Kannengieser, N., Lins, S., Sander, C., Winter, K., Frey, H., & Sunyaev, A. (2022). Challenges and common solutions in smart contract development. *IEEE Transactions on Software Engineering, 48*(11), 4291–4318. https://doi.org/10.1109/tse.2021.3116808.

Karame, G. O., Androulaki, E., & Capkun, S. (2012). Double-spending fast payments in Bitcoin. In *Proceedings of the ACM Conference on Computer and Communications Security* (pp. 906–917). ACM. https://doi.org/10.1145/2382196.2382292.

Klages-Mundt, A., Harz, D., Gudgeon, L., Liu, J.-Y., & Minca, A. (2020). Stablecoins 2.0: Economic foundations and risk-based models. In *Proceedings of the 2nd ACM Conference on Advances in Financial Technologies*. https://doi.org/10.1145/3419614.3423261.

Knutsson, B., Lu, H., Xu, W., & Hopkins, B. (2004). Peer-to-peer support for massively multiplayer games. In *23rd Conference of the IEEE Communications Society* (Vol. 1). https://doi.org/10.1109/INFCOM.2004.1354485.

Lamport, L., Shostak, R., & Pease, M. (1982). The Byzantine generals problem. *ACM Transactions on Programming Languages and Systems*, *4*(3), 382–401. https://doi.org/10.1145/3335772.3335936.

Lautenschlager, J., Stramm, J., Guggenberger, T., Rösch, A., & Schweizer, A. (2023). Overcoming the data transparency trade-off: Designing a blockchain-based delivery invoice system for the construction industry. In *Proceeding of the 18. Internationale Tagung Wirtschaftsinformatik*. AIS. https://aisel.aisnet.org/wi2023/78/.

Leshner, R., & Hayes, G. (2019). Compound: The money market protocol. https://coincompare.eu/wp-content/uploads/2020/06/Compound-COMP-token-whitepaper-CoinCompare.pdf.

Lessig, L. (1999). *Code and other laws of cyberspace*. Basic Books.

Lessig, L. (2006). *Code v. 2.0*. Basic Books.

Nakamoto, S. (2008). A peer-to-peer electronic cash system. https://bitcoin.org/bitcoin.pdf.

Oliveira, L., Zavolokina, L., Bauer, I., & Schwabe, G. (2018). To token or not to token: Tools for understanding blockchain tokens. In *Proceedings of the 39th International Conference on Information Systems*. AIS. https://aisel.aisnet.org/icis2018/crypto/Presentations/5/.

Ozili, P. K. (2022). Decentralized finance research and developments around the world. *Journal of Banking and Financial Technology*, *6*(2), 117–133. https://doi.org/10.1007/s42786-022-00044-x.

Peters, G. W., & Panayi, E. (2016). Understanding modern banking ledgers through blockchain technologies: Future of transaction processing and smart contracts on the internet of money. In *New economic windows* (pp. 239–278). Springer. https://doi.org/10.1007/978-3-319-42448-4_13.

Petersen, D. (2023). Transforming trade finance via blockchain: The We.Trade platform. In *Blockchain in supply chain digital transformation* (pp. 74–93). CRC Press. https://www.taylorfrancis.com/chapters/edit/10.1201/9781003256755-4/transforming-trade-finance-via-blockchain-david-petersen.

Pilkington, M. (2016). Blockchain technology: Principles and applications. In *Research handbook on digital transformations* (pp. 225–253). Edward Elgar Publishing. https://ssrn.com/abstract=2662660.

Rogaway, P., & Shrimpton, T. (2004). Cryptographic hash-function basics: Definitions, implications, and separations for preimage resistance, second-preimage resistance, and collision resistance. In *International workshop on fast software encryption* (pp. 371–388). Springer. https://doi.org/10.1007/978-3-540-25937-4_24.

Sajter, D. (2022). Overseas transaction fees: Sending money via Bitcoin vs. banks. *Zagreb International Review of Economics and Business*, *25*, 65–83. https://doi.org/10.2478/zireb-2022-0025.

Samaniego, M., Jamsrandorj, U., & Deters, R. (2016). Blockchain as a service for IoT. In *IEEE International Conference on Internet of Things (iThings) and IEEE Green Computing and Communications (GreenCom) and IEEE Cyber, Physical and Social Computing (CPSCom) and IEEE Smart Data (SmartData)*. IEEE. https://doi.org/10.1109/ithings-greencom-cpscom-smartdata.2016.102.

Sams, R. (2015). A note on cryptocurrency stabilisation: Seigniorage shares. https://blog.bitmex.com/wp-content/uploads/2018/06/A-Note-on-Cryptocurrency-Stabilisation-Seigniorage-Shares.pdf.

Schellinger, B. (2020). Optimization of special cryptocurrency portfolios. *The Journal of Risk Finance*, *21*(2), 127–157. https://doi.org/10.1108/jrf-11-2019-0221.

Schlatt, V., Schweizer, A., Urbach, N., & Fridgen, G. (2016). Blockchain: Grundlagen, Anwendungen und Potenziale. https://www.fit.fraunhofer.de/content/dam/fit/de/documents/Blockchain_WhitePaper_Grundlagen-Anwendungen-Potentiale.pdf.

Schollmeier, R. (2001). A definition of peer-to-peer networking for the classification of peer-to-peer architectures and applications. In *Proceedings of the 1st International Conference on Peer-to-Peer Computing* (pp. 101–102). IEEE. https://doi.org/10.1109/p2p.2001.990434.

Sedlmeir, J., Buhl, H. U., Fridgen, G., & Keller, R. (2020). The energy consumption of blockchain technology: Beyond myth. *Business & Information Systems Engineering*, *62*, 599–608. https://doi.org/10.1007/s12599-020-00656-x.

Sedlmeir, J., Lautenschlager, J., Fridgen, G., & Urbach, N. (2022a). The transparency challenge of blockchain in organizations. *Electronic Markets*, *32*(3), 1779–1794. https://doi.org/10.1007/s12525-022-00536-0.

Sedlmeir, J., Ross, P., Luckow, A., Lockl, J., Miehle, D., & Fridgen, G. (2021). The DLPS: A new framework for benchmarking blockchains. In *Proceedings of the 54th Hawaii International Conference on System Sciences* (pp. 6855–6864). https://doi.org/10.24251/hicss.2021.822.

Sedlmeir, J., Wagner, T., Djerekarov, E., Green, R., Klepsch, J., & Rao, S. (2022b). A serverless distributed ledger for enterprises. In *Proceedings of the 55th Hawaii International Conference on System Sciences* (pp. 7382–7391). https://doi.org/10.24251/hicss.2022.886.

Sunyaev, A., et al. (2021). Token economy. *Business & Information Systems Engineering*, *63*(4), 457–478. https://doi.org/10.1007/s12599-021-00684-1.

Szabo, N. (1996). Smart contracts: Building blocks for digital markets. *EXTROPY: The Journal of Transhumanist Thought*, *18*(2), 28.

Toufaily, E., Zalan, T., & Dhaou, S. B. (2021). A framework of blockchain technology adoption: An investigation of challenges and expected value. *Information & Management*, *58*(3), 103444. https://doi.org/10.1016/j.im.2021.103444.

Trevathan, J., & Read, W. (2007). Privacy and security concerns for online share trading. In *Proceedings of the IASK International Conference E-Activity and Leading Technologies* (pp. 239–246). https://core.ac.uk/download/pdf/303714747.pdf.

Völter, F., Urbach, N., & Padget, J. (2023). Trusting the trust machine: Evaluating trust signals of blockchain applications. *International Journal of Information Management*, *68*, 102429. https://doi.org/10.1016/j.ijinfomgt.2021.102429.

Werbach, K. (2018). *The blockchain and the new architecture of trust*. MIT Press.

Whitaker, A., & Kräussl, R. (2020). Fractional equity, blockchain, and the future of creative work. *Management Science*, *66*(10), 4594–4611. https://doi.org/10.1287/mnsc.2020.3633.

Xu, J., & Vadgama, N. (2022). From banks to DeFi: The evolution of the lending market. In *Enabling the internet of value* (pp. 53–66). Springer. https://doi.org/10.1007/978-3-030-78184-2_6.

Chapter 4
Decentralized Digital Identities

Alexandre Amard, Pol Hölzmer, and Alexandra Hoess

Abstract In the financial sector, regulatory requirements impose stringent rules related to the identification of customers and the management of their identity data. Financial institutions not only need to comply with strict requirements with regard to know-your-customer (KYC) processes and customer authentication but also with legislation pertaining to the management of personal data, e.g., related to data protection and minimization. Decentralized digital identities in the form of digital identity wallets represent an alternative to the traditional identity management model, in which organizations often collect more data than necessary for the provisioning of services and struggle to verify it efficiently and effectively. Digital identity wallets enable systemic trust and give control of identity data back to the data subject. In this chapter, we outline the technical means through which such decentralized digital identities can enable high degrees of user control, identity assurance, and privacy. We cover the governance and technical aspects of digital wallet-based decentralized digital identity management and outline the challenges ahead to realize their full potential.

4.1 Introduction

With the increasing digitalization of our societies and economies, digital identity has become one of the main foci to translate trusted identity management (IdM) from the physical world to the digital world. In fact, "the Internet was built without a way to know who and what [people] are connecting to" (Cameron, 2005). Although organizations and hardware have had innate ways to identify themselves since the early days of the Internet (by different means such as the *address resolution protocol (ARP)*, *medium access control (MAC) addresses*, *domain name services (DNS)*, or

A. Amard (✉) · P. Hölzmer · A. Hoess
Interdisciplinary Centre for Security, Reliability and Trust (SnT), Luxembourg, Luxembourg
e-mail: alexandre.amard@uni.lu; pol.hoelzmer@uni.lu; alexandra.hoess@uni.lu

G. Fridgen et al. (eds.), *Decentralization Technologies*, Financial Innovation and Technology, https://doi.org/10.1007/978-3-031-66047-4_4

cryptographic certificates), end users mainly relied on ad hoc identity management (Gaedke et al., 2005).

The relevance of digital identity management is particularly exemplified in the financial sector, where regulations impose stringent requirements for customer identification (Schlatt et al., 2022). To open a bank account, KYC processes that involve the collection of identity data are considered fundamental to market integrity concerning anti-money laundering (AML) and countering the financing of terrorism objectives (Arner et al., 2019). Also, specific levels of authentication strengths are often legally required to digitally access a bank account and validate payment orders to protect customers and reduce fraud (e.g., the Revised Payment Services Directive (PSD2)) (Fabcic, 2021). On top of these requirements, financial service providers need to comply with legislation on managing and protecting personal data. These requirements are increasingly being enforced in various regions of the world (e.g., the General Data Protection Regulation (GDPR) in the European Union (EU)) (De Hert et al., 2018), imposing additional safeguards on the management of identity data.

Historically, digital identity management systems have relied on users to provide different sets of personal data to each online service they joined, and these services would store and manage this information (Sedlmeir et al., 2022). Although functional, this approach has significant drawbacks. It relies either on non-verified attributes or on certified attributes originating from physical identity documents. Transmitting these certified attributes often requires users to make copies of their identity documents and send them to the service provider. This is problematic for several reasons. First, service providers do not have a convenient way to verify that this shared information can be trusted (Lacity et al., 2023). When they do check, this verification entails a query to the identity document issuer, which leaves a trace in the trust infrastructure that can be used to track a user's interaction with a service. Furthermore, most identity documents do not allow for selective disclosure of attributes, thus leaking more data than required. Finally, identity documents are often shared via insecure communication channels, such as unencrypted email.

More recently, the federated identity management paradigm became dominant, where an identity provider collects and stores identity data and acts as an intermediary between the user and service providers (Maler & Reed, 2008; Sedlmeir et al., 2021). This approach improves convenience for users, who only need to share their data once for all the federated services, as opposed to having to do so individually for each service provider. However, this paradigm does not alleviate privacy concerns. On the contrary, it increases the amount of identity data the user shares for accessing the service, remarkably increasing the potential for aggregation of this information by identity providers. This, in turn, enables them to utilize personal data for additional purposes such as marketing, profiling, or even surveillance (Preukschat & Reed, 2021).

Decentralized digital identities were designed as a response to these shortcomings. They allow users to store their own certified identity attributes, share them through secure communication channels, and prove their integrity and authenticity without the certification authority knowing about it. Often also coined self-sovereign identity (SSI) (Allen, 2016), this concept embodies the principle that individuals should have control of the disclosure of their identity attributes without relying on any centralized authority. Instead, this user-centric model (Weigl et al., 2022) uses machine-verifiable attestations stored in users' digital identity wallets and is supplemented by a trust infrastructure. Importantly, with the incorporation of data minimization techniques such as zero-knowledge proofs (ZKPs), users can specify which information to disclose without hampering verifiability (Babel & Sedlmeir, 2023). In essence, they significantly improve on the previous paradigms from a security and data protection standpoint while granting more control to the user.

Recognizing the benefits of a more user-centric identity management system based on a privacy-respecting paradigm, in June 2021, the EU started its revision of its electronic Identification, Authentication and Trust Services (eIDAS) regulation which harmonized national electronic identity (eID) frameworks across member states in 2014. Its purpose is to massively extend the use of electronic identification from public to private services by introducing a nationally endorsed and interoperable European digital identity wallet (EUDIW) for the 450 million EU citizens, based on the paradigm of decentralized digital identities (Weigl et al., 2023).

In line with these premises, this chapter outlines the technical means through which decentralized digital identities can support user control and data minimization, marking a shift toward more user-centricity, helping to prevent tracking and identity theft while still providing high levels of assurance for identity verification (Sedlmeir et al., 2021). It also elaborates on the possibility of decoupling the relationship between attestation issuers (e.g., governmental entities) and verifiers (e.g., financial service providers), thus limiting the risk of collusion and surveillance while guaranteeing the same level of identity assurance. Finally, it outlines the key building blocks required for decentralized digital identity management and presents the challenges ahead on the way to fully transitioning to a decentralized digital identity management paradigm.

4.2 Decentralized Digital Identity Ecosystems

Decentralized digital identities represent a noteworthy advancement for digital identity management, as they grant equivalent assurance to today's physical identity management while providing data subjects with high degrees of control and privacy of their identity data. This novel identity management paradigm relies on digital attestations, which are the digital equivalent of traditional plastic cards and paper-based certificates. It combines technology with convenience (Richter et al., 2023). Decentralized digital identity ecosystems involve a set of processes and components, as well as actors. The exchange of digital attestations between issuers, holders, and verifiers happens through secure bilateral (peer-to-peer (P2P)) communication channels that rely on modern cryptography (Mühle et al., 2018). Issuers certify specific attributes and issue a digital attestation about a subject to a holder. Holders store and manage these digital attestations through a so-called

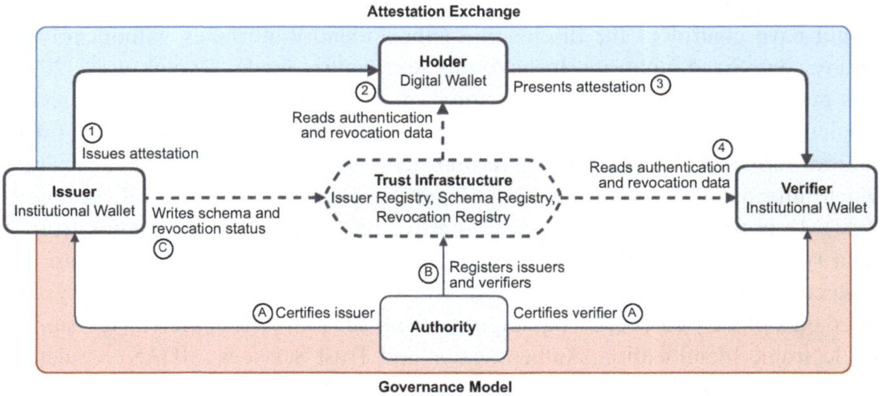

Fig. 4.1 Stakeholder roles and interactions in decentralized digital identity systems

digital identity wallet (Sartor et al., 2022; Guggenberger et al., 2023). Upon request by a verifier, they can present their digital attestation or prove specific identity attributes through a machine-verifiable presentation. To validate such a presentation, verifiers commonly check the attestation's signature, expiration date, and state of revocation (Schlatt et al., 2022; Lacity et al., 2023). In doing so, verifiers typically rely on public registries that are embedded in larger "trust infrastructures," which provide additional information that allows for verifying a digital attestation's issuer and state of revocation (Davie et al., 2019). Figure 4.1 illustrates the processes, components, and actors involved in a decentralized digital identity management system. This chapter continues by elaborating on the details of the core technical building blocks underlying such a system, namely public key cryptography, digital attestations, digital identity wallets, and trust infrastructures.

4.3 Cryptographic Foundations

In the digital age, the trustworthiness of digital identities depends on the strength of their security mechanisms. At the heart of these trust assurances are cryptographic primitives, ranging from encryption to digital signatures. The use of cryptography has profound implications in the domain of decentralized digital identities for proving ownership and correctness of attestations using digital signatures. As we move through the rest of this chapter, understanding how these cryptographic foundations build and maintain trust in digital identities is essential.

Historically, symmetric key cryptography (SKC) has been used for centuries (Luciano & Prichett, 1987). Notably, Julius Caesar already utilized a simple shift cipher to secure his messages during wartime. In general, SKC employs simple permutation (reordering bits) and substitution (replacing bits) operations in combination with a single shared secret key (k) for both encryption and decryption. Known for its efficiency, symmetric encryption is often the choice for bulk data protection at rest or in transit. However, key establishment and management present considerable challenges, especially when building trust relations with unknown entities, as identity cannot be verified, actions can be repudiated, and forward secrecy is not guaranteed.

In the realm of cryptography, one of the groundbreaking advancements that emerged in the 1970s is public key cryptography (PKC), also known as asymmetric key cryptography (Diffie & Hellman, 1976). Unlike traditional SKC, PKC employs a pair of distinct keys: a secret key (*sk* – also called a private key) and a corresponding public key (*pk*), hence the term "asymmetric." The secret key is kept securely by the individual or entity, while the public key can be openly shared with others and can function as a public identifier.

PKC has several unique applications due to its asymmetric properties rooted in discrete mathematics. The most important property is that encrypted data using a *pk* can only be decrypted using the corresponding *sk*. Thus, anybody can initiate a secure channel with the owner of the *pk*, who is the only entity able to read the corresponding messages. In doing so, the confidentiality of information can be ensured. In turn, digital signatures are created with a *sk* and can only be verified using the *pk*. In other terms, signatures can only be created by the holder of the *sk* but verified by anyone with the *pk*. That way, the integrity and authenticity of information can be ensured. Those two rather simple concepts provide the baseline security principles described by the "CIA triad" representing confidentiality, integrity, and authenticity.

Despite covering theoretical security principles, PKC lags behind in applied cryptography (BSI, 2023). Here, its limitations become evident: slow operations, suitability for small amounts of data, and the necessity for a dedicated trust infrastructure to distribute public keys. Therefore, PKC is almost explicitly limited to symmetric key establishment and digital signatures. The RSA (Rivest-Shamir-Adleman) cryptosystem (Rivest et al., 1978) is a well-established representative whose security is based on the difficulty of the integer factorization problem (IFS). Today, RSA is mostly superseded by the more efficient elliptic curve cryptography (ECC), whose security relies on the elliptic curve discrete logarithm problem (ECDLP). Noteworthy related algorithms include (EC)DH (Diffie-Hellman) derivatives for the symmetric key establishment and (EC)DSA (Digital Signature Algorithm) for digital signatures (BSI, 2023).

In modern systems, SKC and PKC go hand-in-hand to leverage each other's strengths and compensate for weaknesses. It is worth noticing that "security by obscurity" is not a robust or sustainable security strategy and that Kerckhoff's principles (Kerckhoffs, 1883) should always be applied. The core principle states that the security of a cryptographic system should not rely on the secrecy of the algorithm; instead, it must solely depend on the strength of the employed key.

Unfortunately, the IFS and discrete logarithm problem (DLP), which define the strength of many modern asymmetric keys, can be broken quickly using quantum computers, urging the transition to post-quantum cryptography (PQC) even though this vulnerability cannot be exploited yet, because current quantum computers still lack the required amount of quantum bits to leverage related attacks. This threat will nevertheless become a reality for PKC in the following years. SKC, in turn, can easily counterweight this threat by increasing the key size by a reasonable amount. In most scenarios, the impact is low, even without countermeasures. To explore similar future-proof solutions for PKC, the National Institute of Standards and Technology (NIST) launched the PQC standardization program in 2017 (NIST, 2017), which is now in the final round. Current promising candidates for post-quantum secure algorithms include Kyber for symmetric key establishment and Dilithium for digital signatures.

4.4 Digital Attestations

Whereas PKC serves as the technical basis for encryption and digital signatures, digital attestations represent the central building block in which identity information is packaged and exchanged between entities (Lacity et al., 2023). In essence, digital attestations function as the digital analogs of conventional physical identity documents and paper-based certificates, representing a convergence of traditional authentication mechanisms with contemporary cryptographic technologies (Preukschat & Reed, 2021).

Technically, these attestations are digitally signed sets of information that certify one or more identity attributes about a subject (Sedlmeir et al., 2021). Digital attestations typically consist of three main elements: metadata, a set of attributes, and cryptographic proof (W3C, 2023). The *metadata* contains a set of information that specifies when and by whom an attestation has been attested. Digital attestations can be either self-issued, which means the subject creates and signs a digital attestation about oneself, or attested and signed by a third party. The verifier has to decide if self-issued attestations are accepted. Furthermore, the metadata provides information on how an attestation can be verified, i.e., by referencing the trust infrastructure that holds information on how to interpret the information stored in an attestation or whether an attestation has been revoked or not (Glöckler et al., 2023).

Identity attributes form the core of any digital attestation. This is the part that defines the actual identity. It certifies specific characteristics about the identity subject's identity, such as the last name or date of birth. In most cases, the subject of these attributes will also act as a holder who controls the digital attestation. However, in some cases, the subject and the holder may differ. For instance, for a minor's digital ID card, a parent (holder) could act as a guardian and manage a digital attestation on behalf of their child (subject). In any case, holders store and control the digital attestations and present them to a verifier (Weigl et al., 2022). To ensure the integrity of the presented information, digital attestations contain a *cryptographic proof* in the form of a digital signature or an electronic seal. Digital signatures and electronic seals thereby serve two key features: they make digital attestations tamper-evident and allow verifiers to authenticate the attestation issuer cryptographically.

Digital attestations can be presented online and offline by a subject to a verifier (Schlatt et al., 2022). Doing so, a machine-verifiable presentation of an attestation can be created in three different ways: (1) by presenting the whole set of attributes contained within an attestation; (2) by selectively disclosing one or a subset of attributes attested in an attestation while often still exposing more information than requested by the verifier; or (3) by applying cryptographic ZKPs that allow one to prove an identity attribute to another entity without disclosing any more information than required (Babel & Sedlmeir, 2023; Goldreich & Oren, 1994). For instance, one could prove to meet a certain legal age requirement without providing any further information about one's current age or date of birth. The use of ZKPs is particularly advisable to minimize or avoid the disclosure of sensitive and correlatable data, such as unique cryptographic identifiers. Note that a holder's public keys, as well as an attestation's digital signature, are considered to be a (unique) identifier due to their characteristics and collision resistance. While creating a machine-verifiable presentation, data subjects are not limited in their information disclosure to attributes and information stored within a single digital attestation. Instead, a presentation may also combine information from multiple attestations (Preukschat & Reed, 2021). Yet, as of now, a prerequisite is that these attestations rely on the same technical standard.

Current prominent technical standards for digital attestations include the World Wide Web Consortium's (W3C) Verifiable Credentials (W3C, 2023) and the ISO/IEC 18013 (mdoc) standard for electronic attestations (ISO/IEC, 2021). Although the latter has been particularly developed for the use case of a mobile driver's license, both standards can be widely applied in different domains and use cases. Both standards will also form the technical basis for digital attestations in the EUDIW that the EU is currently developing (European Commission, 2023).

4.5 Digital Identity Wallets

Decentralized digital identity implementations emerged to empower data subjects to regain control of their digital identities (Allen, 2016; Weigl et al., 2022). Consequently, the pivotal elements of any decentralized digital identity implementation are the technologies that allow holders to store and manage digital attestations by themselves. Digital identity wallets play a central role in managing digital identities, as they integrate these technologies and make them accessible to end users (Rieger et al., 2022).

Digital identity wallets are mobile or web-based software applications that act as secure storage for that holder's digital attestations and cryptographic keys (Sartor et al., 2022). They provide features for secure communication and managing digital attestations, such as authenticating other entities based on their public keys, establishing secure connections through PKC, creating digital signatures, receiving digital attestations, and, not least, generating presentations thereof that can be shared and verified in online and offline interactions (Lacity et al., 2023). To ensure privacy-preserving digital identity management, digital identity wallets can be equipped with advanced cryptographic features that, for instance, allow users to generate a new pseudonymous cryptographic keypair for interaction with each new counterparty or to create presentations using ZKPs (Sedlmeir et al., 2022). Furthermore, digital identity wallets connect to trust infrastructures that provide relevant data for issuer and verifier authentication as well as generating proofs of attestation non-revocation (Feulner et al., 2022; Preukschat & Reed, 2021).

On par with holders' digital identity wallets, institutional wallets provide organizations with technical capabilities for decentralized digital identity management (Schlatt et al., 2022). Institutional wallets (often also referred to as enterprise wallets or agents) are software applications that can be integrated into an organization's IT infrastructure (Lacity et al., 2023; Preukschat & Reed, 2021). They allow organizations to manage their cryptographic keys and establish secure connections with holders' digital identity wallets. Furthermore, depending on the role an organization takes in the digital identity ecosystem, these institutional wallets provide dedicated features for issuing and/or verifying digital attestations. Features for issuing attestations include applications that generate templates for digital attestations, convert identity information into digital attestations, and tools for digitally signing these. OpenID's OID4VC protocol provides one emerging standard to issue digital attestations as verifiable credentials (Chadwick & Vercammen, 2022). Moreover, institutional wallets allow issuers to revoke specific digital attestations when needed and publish related trusted revocation lists (Glöckler et al., 2023). Verifier tools, in turn, allow organizations to establish secure communication channels with the holders' digital identity wallet, generate proof requests, receive presentations, and connect to trust registries to verify these presentations.

Although digital services are becoming the "new normal," the use of decentralized digital identities and digital identity wallets shall not be limited to online interactions. Instead, emerging digital identity wallet solutions, such as the EUDIW, are designed to support both sharing digital attestations online and in face-to-face interactions. Yet, depending on the underlying use case, the holder's digital identity wallets and verifier tools may implement different standards that support the sharing of digital attestations in both online and offline scenarios. Prominent standards for the online sharing of digital attestations are the Open ID Connect for verifiable presentation (OIDC4VP) (Chadwick & Vercammen, 2022) and the self-issued OpenID provider (SIOP) (Yasuda et al., 2023) protocols. However, these protocols cannot be applied in offline (often also termed as face-to-face or proximity) interactions between holder and verifier. In such scenarios, digital identity wallets typically use near-field communication (NFC) or quick response (QR) codes to establish an initial connection and transfer a proof request. Once this initial communication has been established, digital attestations can be presented using NFC or QR codes or Bluetooth low energy (BLE) (ISO/IEC, 2021).

4.6 Trust Infrastructures

While PKC and digital signatures provide technical means for authenticating attestation issuers and verifiers, their effectiveness strongly depends on the available meta-information concerning who controls the respective cryptographic keypair. To this end, systems for managing decentralized digital identities deploy trust infrastructures (often also termed verifiable data registries, trust registries, or trusted lists) that provide required certified meta-information (Sedlmeir et al., 2021; Preukschat & Reed, 2021).

In more detail, trust infrastructures are typically employed as public key infrastructure (PKI) based on certificate authorities (CAs). That is, trust infrastructures serve as a registry for legal entities that distribute verifiable information on issuers and verifiers, such as their public keys and related metadata. This data can be used to verify the digital signature and authenticity of a digital attestation (Feulner et al., 2022). The information provided by trusted registries is not only beneficial for verifiers but can also prevent holders from sharing their personal information with malicious actors and being exposed to machine-in-the-middle (MITM) attacks (Babel & Sedlmeir, 2023). To this end, digital identity wallets can connect to the registry to identify the verifier based on its public key before establishing a secure connection and sharing any personal data.

Besides implementing registries for legal entities, trust infrastructures are also important for implementing attestation revocation mechanisms. They provide a mechanism to verify the current status of a presented attestation and ensure that any communication or transaction is based on valid and trustworthy information. A well-designed revocation registry should provide issuers with the means to publish efficient, scalable, privacy-preserving, and tamper-evident revocation status (Glöckler et al., 2023). Different approaches exist for the implementation of such revocation registries. For instance, downloadable revocation lists (e.g., certificate revocation list (CRL) enlist *all* attestations that are no longer valid by providing attestation identifiers, revocation date and time, revocation reason, and the issuer's signature. In contrast, the active "phone home" (e.g., online certificate status protocol (OCSP)) approach allows active querying of the revocation registry for the revocation status of a specific attestation. Both approaches operate via unique identifiers, which can potentially allow tracking by the operator of the revocation list. As a remedy, public revocation registries paired with ZKPs of inclusion or noninclusion, as seen in Hyperledger Aries, are suggested. However, even this method encounters scalability challenges because of the necessity for extensive revocation lists, prompting the exploration of innovative, more scalable solutions.

In addition to providing cryptographic metadata for attestation verification and counterparty authentication, trust infrastructures may also be used to facilitate the standardization and interoperability of digital attestations (Preukschat & Reed, 2021). In particular, attestation issuers, governance authorities, or standardization bodies can deploy a public registry to distribute schemas that provide information on the domain-specific data model and required attributes for specific attestations.

These schemas may help verifiers to interpret digital attestations and the specific attested attributes therein. They further may act as a blueprint for other issuers that aim to issue similar attestations (Schlatt et al., 2022).

Many decentralized digital identity management implementations, such as the European self-sovereign identity framework (ESSIF) (European Blockain Services Infrastructure, 2023), or the United Kingdom (UK)'s National Health Service (NHS) staff passport (Lacity & Carmel, 2022), explore the potential of blockchain technology for their trust registries. Using blockchain for these registries is deemed particularly useful as it enables transparent, tamper-resistant, and distributed operation. Thus, in contrast to trust infrastructures that rely on centralized databases, blockchain technology enables the development of trusted registries that are not controlled by a single entity.

Concerning the implementation of trust infrastructures, particularly the role of blockchain technology within these, it is essential to note potential privacy risks that may arise when designed improperly (Rieger et al., 2021). In particular, the storage of holders' personal data, such as digital attestations and identifiers, and also their public keys, compromises holders' privacy, as it may allow for tracing and profiling (Sedlmeir et al., 2022). When using blockchain as a trust infrastructure, the tamper-resistant storage of such information may also contradict privacy regulations, such as the EU's GDPR and the therein granted right to erasure (Rieger et al., 2019). Thus, decentralized identity management systems must ensure that trust infrastructures do not store any information about natural persons (Hoess et al., 2023; Rieger et al., 2022).

4.7 Challenges

Governments and service providers are heavily investing in deploying decentralized digital identities. Yet, several technical challenges will significantly impact the adoption of decentralized digital identity and the ability to meet the related expectations of more user-controlled and privacy-preserving digital identity management.

Privacy implications are a major concern for decentralized digital identities, which require protecting personal information. ZKPs are an important privacy-enhancing technology (PET) that enables individuals to present certain (partial) information without revealing the (full) information itself. ZKPs thereby minimize vulnerability to potential breaches and undue access (Babel & Sedlmeir, 2023). Despite the promise of ZKPs, they introduce complexities in implementation and computational demands. Thus, achieving a truly robust and efficient ZKP system without sacrificing privacy or functionality remains an intricate problem.

Another challenge is the binding of identity-related data to a digital identity wallet device, which raises concerns about losing access to the digital identity. This necessitates intricate wallet recovery mechanisms, such as recovery through encrypted cloud backups (Sellung & Kubach, 2023). In this scenario, users must retain a designated recovery key created during the backup time in a secure location such as a hardware device or written note. Loss of this key results in an inability to access the wallet backup. Implementing and managing recovery mechanisms presents a multilayered challenge, balancing security, privacy, and accessibility while considering all the scenarios in which recovery may be required (Sedlmeir et al., 2022; Anderson, 2011).

While decentralized digital identities receive substantial traction, interoperability presents a significant challenge for digital identity wallets and digital attestation specifications and implementations (Rieger et al., 2022). As various solutions emerge, ensuring they can interact smoothly becomes vital. Diverse implementations can lead to friction and fragmentation, hindering user experience and broad adoption (Schlatt et al., 2022). To navigate these, challenges, regulations, and policies play a major role in shaping the adoption and standardization, necessitating a careful balance between decentralized identity principles and public interest. Moreover, there is a pressing need for maturing complementary technical standards, such as communication protocols and data formats, ensuring consistent communication across different platforms, vendors, and national borders (Sedlmeir et al., 2022).

Furthermore, the hardware components that locally protect secret keys to access the digital identity wallets pose unique challenges. Due to the immense diversity in the market, different hardware, such as smartcards (e.g., eSIM), secure elements (SE), and trusted execution environments (TEEs)), can lead to inconsistencies among implementations and their relative security level (Bastian et al., 2023). The functional inflexibility of such embedded hardware components limits the compatibility with more mature ZKPs technology and requires novel solutions for achieving data minimization (Babel & Sedlmeir, 2023). Moreover, different hardware technologies can leave the system susceptible to vulnerabilities such as side-channel attacks, posing additional challenges for hardware and firmware developers to ensure proper protection of key material storage and usage in a trusted environment. Moreover, with the growing trend by service providers (issuers and verifiers) of offloading computations to the cloud, ensuring the secure execution of sensitive operations in cloud-based TEEs becomes crucial, adding another layer of complexity to the intricate landscape of hardware security (Geppert et al., 2022).

Lastly, it is important to note that decentralized digital identity systems are not inherently secure. As they rely on common cryptographic algorithms such as Rivest-Shamir-Adleman (RSA) and ECC, decentralized digital identities are vulnerable to quantum attacks. Making such systems quantum secure requires moving to post-quantum cryptographic algorithms that are expected to resist quantum computing attacks, such as Kyber and Dilithium, which involve performances that are not fully standardized yet NIST (2017).

4.8 Conclusion

This chapter presented an introduction to the technical building blocks of a new identity management paradigm based on strong cryptographic foundations supporting trust infrastructures and digital attestations, stored in digital identity wallets controlled by the users themselves. As with any technology impacting existing ecosystems, challenges must be overcome to realize its full potential, with interoperability and recoverability of identity attestations being the most salient.

Decentralized digital identities will profoundly redefine the relationship between financial sector actors and their customers by transforming onboarding and authentication processes. New opportunities for the most innovative actors to provide new types of digital services through digital identity wallets will emerge, encompassing identity and communications capabilities. Standardized identity attribute provision mechanisms will enable them to more easily generate identity assurance for compliance purposes, while having the certainty that it is government certified, and thus reduce the administrative overhead associated with data management.

Despite the challenges ahead, powerful technology actors have already started building their identity wallets and providing services around them. For example, Apple now provides a wallet for digital driver's licenses in the United States of America (USA), and institutional actors are also currently preparing their large-scale introduction, such as the EUDIW. With these powerful institutional and economic actors committing to the technology, these challenges will eventually be solved, for decentralized digital identities to become a reality for service providers and users alike.

References

Allen, C. (2016). The path to self-sovereign identity. http://www.lifewithalacrity.com/2016/04/the-path-to-self-sovereign-identity.html.

Anderson, R. (2011). Can we fix the security economics of federated authentication? In *International Workshop on Security Protocols* (pp. 33–48). Springer. https://doi.org/10.1007/978-3-642-25867-1_5

Arner, D. W., Zetzsche, D. A., Buckley, R. P., & Barberis, J. N. (2019). The identity challenge in finance: From analogue identity to digitized identification to digital KYC utilities. *European Business Organization Law Review*, *20*(1), 55–80. https://doi.org/10.1007/s40804-019-00135-1

Babel, M., & Sedlmeir, J. (2023). Bringing data minimization to digital wallets at scale with general-purpose zero-knowledge proofs. https://arxiv.org/abs/2301.00823

Bastian, P., Kraus, M., & Fischer, J. (2023). Concepts for secure wallets in decentralized identity ecosystems. *HMD Praxis der Wirtschaftsinformatik*, *60*(2), 381–404. https://doi.org/10.1365/s40702-023-00954-4

BSI. (2023). Cryptographic mechanisms: Recommendations and key lengths. https://www.bsi.bund.de/SharedDocs/Downloads/EN/BSI/Publications/TechGuidelines/TG02102/BSI-TR-02102-1.html?nn=132646

Cameron, K. (2005). The laws of identity. https://www.identityblog.com/?p=352

Chadwick, K. N., & Vercammen, J. (2022). OpenID for verifiable credentials. https://openid.net/wordpress-content/uploads/2022/05/OIDF-Whitepaper_OpenID-for-Verifiable-Credentials_FINAL_2022-05-12.pdf

Davie, M., Gisolfi, D., Hardman, D., Jordan, J., O'Donnell, D., & Reed, D. (2019). The trust over IP stack. *IEEE Communications Standards Magazine*, *3*(4), 46–51. https://doi.org/10.1109/mcomstd.001.1900029.

De Hert, P., Papakonstantinou, V., Malgieri, G., Beslay, L., & Sanchez, I. (2018). The right to data portability in the GDPR: Towards user-centric interoperability of digital services. *Computer Law & Security Review*, *34*, 193–203. https://doi.org/10.1016/j.clsr.2017.10.003

Diffie, W., & Hellman, M. E. (1976). New directions in cryptography. *IEEE Transactions on Information Theory*. *22*(6). https://doi.org/10.1145/3549993.3550007

European Blockain Services Infrastructure. (2023). Verifiable credentials framework. https://ec.europa.eu/digital-building-blocks/wikis/display/EBSIDOC/

European Commission. (2023). The European digital identity wallet architecture and reference framework. https://digital-strategy.ec.europa.eu/en/library/european-digital-identity-wallet-architecture-and-reference-framework

Fabcic, D. (2021). Strong customer authentication in online payments under GDPR and PSD2: A case of cumulative application. In *Privacy and Identity Management: IFIP Advances in Information and Communication Technology* (pp. 78–95). Springer. https://doi.org/10.1007/978-3-030-72465-8_5

Feulner, S., Sedlmeir, J., Schlatt, V., & Urbach, N. (2022). Exploring the use of self-sovereign identity for event ticketing systems. *Electronic Markets*, *32*, 1759–1777. https://doi.org/10.1007/s12525-022-00573-9

Gaedke, M., Meinecke, J., & Nussbaumer, M. (2005). A modeling approach to federated identity and access management. In *14th International Conference on World Wide Web* (pp. 1156–1157). https://doi.org/10.1145/1062745.1062916

Geppert, T., Deml, S., Sturzenegger, D., & Ebert, N. (2022). Trusted execution environments: Applications and organizational challenges. *Frontiers in Computer Science*, *4*, 930741. https://doi.org/10.3389/fcomp.2022.930741

Glöckler, J., Sedlmeir, J., Frank, M., & Fridgen, G. (2023). A systematic review of identity and access management requirements in enterprises and potential contributions of self-sovereign identity. *Business & Information Systems Engineering*. https://doi.org/10.1007/s12599-023-00830-x

Goldreich, O., & Oren, Y. (1994). Definitions and properties of zero-knowledge proof systems. *Journal of Cryptology*, *7*(1). https://doi.org/10.1007/BF00195207

Guggenberger, T., Neubauer, L., Stramm, J., Völter, F., & Zwede, T. (2023). Accept me as I am or see me go: A qualitative analysis of user acceptance of self-sovereign identity applications. In *Proceedings of the 56th Hawaii International Conference on System Sciences* (pp. 6560–6569). https://hdl.handle.net/10125/103427

Hoess, A., Rieger, A., Roth, T., Fridgen, G., & Young, A. G. (2023). Managing fashionable organizing visions: Evidence from the European blockchain services infrastructure. In *Proceedings of the 31st European Conference on Information Systems*. AIS. https://aisel.aisnet.org/ecis2023_rp/337/

ISO/IEC. (2021). ISO/IEC 18013-5:2021 Personal identification – ISO-compliant driving licence – Part 5: Mobile driving licence (mDL) application. https://www.iso.org/standard/69084.html.

Kerckhoffs, A. (1883). La cryptographie militaire. *Journal des Sciences Militaires, 9*, 5–38.

Lacity, M., & Carmel, E. (2022). Implementing self-sovereign identity (SSI) for a digital staff passport at UK NHS. University of Arkansas. https://cpb-us-e1.wpmucdn.com/wordpressua.uark.edu/dist/5/444/files/2018/01/BCoE2022SS1FINAL.pdf

Lacity, M., Carmel, E., Young, A. G., & Roth, T. (2023). The quiet corner of Web3 that means business. *MIT Sloan Management Review*. *64*(3). https://sloanreview.mit.edu/article/the-quiet-corner-of-web3-that-means-business/

Luciano, D., & Prichett, G. (1987). Cryptology: From Caesar ciphers to public-key cryptosystems. *The College Mathematics Journal, 18*(1), 2–17. https://doi.org/10.1080/07468342.1987.11973000

Maler, E., & Reed, D. (2008). The Venn of identity: Options and issues in federated identity management. *IEEE Security & Privacy, 6*, 16–23. https://doi.org/10.1109/msp.2008.50

Mühle, A., Grüner, A., Gayvoronskaya, T., & Meinel, C. (2018). A survey on essential components of a self-sovereign identity. *Computer Science Review, 30*, 80–86. https://doi.org/10.1016/j.cosrev.2018.10.002

NIST, Computer Security Division, I. T. L. (2017). Post-quantum cryptography https://csrc.nist.gov/projects/post-quantum-cryptography.

Preukschat, A., & Reed, D. (2021). *Self-Sovereign Identity: Decentralized digital identity and verifiable credentials*. Manning Publications.

Richter, D., Praas, C. R., & Anke, J. (2023). Beyond paper and plastic: A meta-model for credential use and governance. In *Proceedings of the 31st European Conference on Information Systems*: AIS. https://aisel.aisnet.org/ecis2023_rp/371/

Rieger, A., Lockl, J., Urbach, N., Guggenmos, F., & Fridgen, G. (2019). Building a blockchain application that complies with the EU general data protection regulation. *MIS Quarterly Executive, 18*(4), 263–279. https://doi.org/10.17705/2msqe.00020

Rieger, A., Roth, T., Sedlmeir, J., & Fridgen, G. (2021). The privacy challenge in the race for digital vaccination certificates. *Med, 2*, 633–634. https://doi.org/10.1016/j.medj.2021.04.018

Rieger, A., Roth, T., Sedlmeir, J., Weigl, L., & Fridgen, G. (2022). Not yet another digital identity. *Nature Human Behaviour, 6*(1), 3. https://doi.org/10.1038/s41562-021-01243-0

Rivest, R. L., Shamir, A., & Adleman, L. (1978). A method for obtaining digital signatures and public-key cryptosystems. *Communications of the ACM, 21*(2), 120–126. https://doi.org/10.1145/359340.359342

Sartor, S., Sedlmeir, J., Rieger, A., & Roth, T. (2022). Love at first sight? A user experience study of self-sovereign identity wallets. In *Proceedings of the 30th European Conference on Information Systems*. AIS. https://aisel.aisnet.org/ecis2022_rp/46/

Schlatt, V., Sedlmeir, J., Feulner, S., & Urbach, N. (2022). Designing a framework for digital KYC processes built on blockchain-based self-sovereign identity. *Information & Management, 59*(7). https://doi.org/10.1016/j.im.2021.103553

Sedlmeir, J., Barbereau, T., Huber, J., Weigl, L., & Roth, T. (2022). Transition pathways towards design principles of self-sovereign identity. In *43rd International Conference on Information Systems*. AIS. https://aisel.aisnet.org/icis2022/is_implement/is_implement/4/

Sedlmeir, J., Smethurst, R., Rieger, A., & Fridgen, G. (2021). Digital identities and verifiable credentials. *Business & Information Systems Engineering, 63*(5), 603–613. https://doi.org/10.1007/s12599-021-00722-y

Sellung, R., & Kubach, M. (2023). Research on user experience for digital identity wallets: State-of-the-art and recommendations. In *Open Identity Summit* (pp. 39–50). Gesellschaft für Informatik eV. https://doi.org/10.18420/OID2023_03

W3C. (2023). Verifiable credentials data model 2.0. https://www.w3.org/TR/vc-data-model-2.0/

Weigl, L., Amard, A., Codagnone, C., & Fridgen, G. (2023). The EU's digital identity policy: Tracing policy punctuations. In *15th International Conference on Theory and Practice of Electronic Governance* (pp. 74–81). ACM. https://dl.acm.org/doi/10.1145/3560107.3560121

Weigl, L., Barbereau, T. J., Rieger, A., & Fridgen, G. (2022). The social construction of self-sovereign identity: An extended model of interpretive flexibility. In *Proceedings of the 55th Hawaii International Conference on System Sciences* (pp. 2543–2552). https://doi.org/10.24251/hicss.2022.316

Yasuda, K., Loddersted, T., & Jones, M. (2023). Self-issued OpenID Provider v2. https://openid.net/specs/openid-connect-self-issued-v2-1_0.html

Chapter 5
Federated Learning

Lukas Willburger

Abstract Today, machine learning (ML) sees a variety of applications in business processes, whether toward individuals or other companies. However, data privacy often comes short when vast amounts of data are to be transferred from clients participating in training processes to the ML service provider. federated learning (FL) seeks to address this issue by moving the model to the data, ensuring that data does not leave end devices. Depending on different use cases and industries, we can observe a variety of architectural patterns and algorithms to assist with the inherent requirements of FL in averaging results and ensuring stable communication. Nonetheless, maintaining privacy impels new challenges concerning algorithmic performance and fairness among participating clients. FL has the potential to revolutionize the way we train machine learning models, enabling collaboration across different devices and organizations without compromising data privacy and security. In this chapter, we portray the basic concepts of FL, discuss common architectures, address inherent challenges, and shed light on fairness aspects in conjunction with performance and privacy. We conclude by sharing considerations for implementing FL processes in practice and giving a short outlook on the potentials of FL from practice and research standpoints.

5.1 A Case for Privacy-Preserving Machine Learning

The support of a wide variety of processes with ML technologies has become an indispensable asset of today's businesses. However, traditional ML applications require vast amounts of data to be transferred, analyzed, and stored. This approach is not feasible in every context. Especially when personal data is involved, which is legally governed by regulations such as the European Union (EU) General Data Protection Regulation (GDPR) (European Commission, 2016) or the Californian Health

L. Willburger (✉)
Branch Business & Information Systems Engineering of Fraunhofer FIT, Augsburg, Germany
e-mail: lukas.willburger@fim-rc.de; lukas.willburger@fit.fraunhofer.de

G. Fridgen et al. (eds.), *Decentralization Technologies*, Financial Innovation and Technology, https://doi.org/10.1007/978-3-031-66047-4_5

Insurance Portability and Accountability Act (HIPAA) (United States Congress, 1996), data access poses a major challenge for ML projects (Mourby et al., 2021; Goldsteen et al., 2022). Although measures exist that are, among others, intended to harmonize data protection regulations with ML, such as the Artificial Intelligence Act (European Commission, 2021), uncertainty may still hamper ML applications. Also, even if processing personal data was not an issue, service users may still prefer to keep data on local devices instead of transmitting them to a central server, e.g., due to company policies regarding trade secrets or the risk of large-scale data breaches. Corporations are also motivated to withhold their valuable data from rivals for economic reasons: Access to data, which can be harnessed alongside AI models, carries strategic advantages referred to as "data network effects" (Gregory et al., 2021; Napirata et al., 2023).

FL represents a privacy-preserving approach that allows an ML model to be collaboratively trained across multiple devices on local data without requiring the exchange of training data with a central server (McMahan et al., 2017a), which can potentially solve these problems. This approach involves a central instance that coordinates the training process by sending the model to each party for training on its local data. The local model updates are then aggregated at the server to generate a new model, which is again sent to the parties for further training (Bonawitz et al., 2019; Zhang et al., 2021a). This process iteratively continues until the model converges to an acceptable accuracy. Originally introduced in 2016 (Konečný et al., 2016b,a) and used by Google to provide word suggestions for its Gboard mobile phone keyboard (McMahan & Ramage, 2017; Hard et al., 2018), FL has gained traction in different industries over the past few years (Li et al., 2020a). We see advances in the medical field, where the detection of COVID-19 (Zhang et al., 2021d) or the oxygen requirements of COVID-19 patients (Dayan et al., 2021) can be predicted anonymously, or use cases in the manufacturing industry (Kaymakci et al., 2021), like predictive maintenance (Zhang et al., 2021c). Others highlight the use of FL for autonomous driving (Li et al., 2022a; Zeng et al., 2022), for energy load forecasting Fernández et al. (2022), or for predicting loan defaults (Shingi, 2020) and credit risk (Lee et al., 2023) in the financial sector.

In this chapter, we focus on introducing FL as a privacy-oriented ML paradigm while presenting its benefits, showcasing common architecture forms, addressing challenges, and shedding light on fairness aspects.

5.2 Workflow and Architectural Patterns

5.2.1 Definition and Scope

As outlined in existing literature, we understand FL as a technique for the distributed training of an ML model, where a central entity coordinates the training process but does not perform the data processing. Instead, only the parties with access to

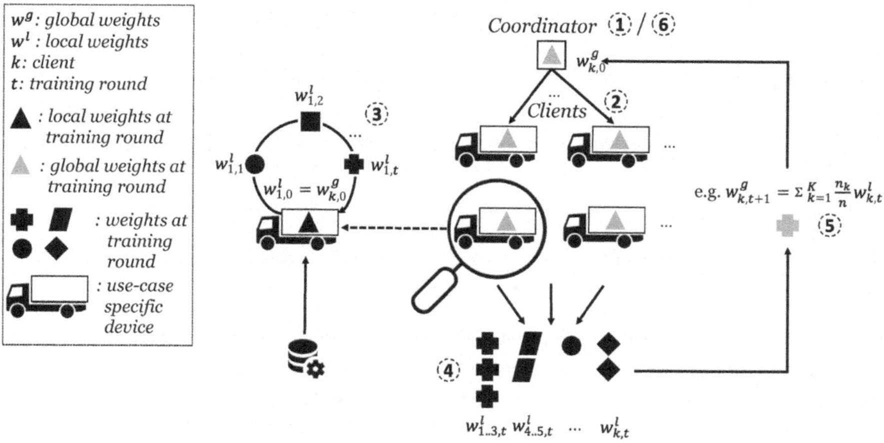

Fig. 5.1 An exemplary FL training process

the respective data sources are involved in the training process (see e.g. McMahan et al., 2017a; Li et al., 2020b). These participants or *clients* can train on a wide variety of hardware, be it mobile, battery-powered devices (Wang et al., 2020), edge devices (Lim et al., 2020), industrial machinery components (Savazzi et al., 2021; Boobalan et al., 2022), or cloud servers. The central entity, or *coordinator*, enables collaboration between the clients without needing them to know each other, while they can still benefit from each other's local training results (Bonawitz et al., 2019). The coordinator also aggregates the model updates sent by all clients, sometimes referred to as *model fusion* (Lin et al., 2020).

Figure 5.1 features an exemplary FL process for a neural network, where each client's updates represent the network weights. Depending on the ML approach used, these parameter updates may be of a different kind. First (*step 1*), a global model is introduced and initialized by the coordinator, with global weights $w^g_{k,0}$, where 0 marks the initial training round $t = 0$. This model gets then distributed to all clients $k \in K$ (*step 2*). If many clients are available, using a proper subset ($\tilde{K} \subset K$) may be useful, as this enables the selection of clients that offer the optimal conditions for a training round. In the case of mobile phones for keyboard prediction, for example, this would be those clients that have sufficient free memory and battery capacity at the time of training (Fu et al., 2023).

Each client independently performs multiple training rounds to update the parameters of its received global model using locally available data. This results in the creation of a local instance of the ML model (referred to as the local model) (*step 3*). Afterward, each client returns its parameters to the coordinator (*step 4*). The essence of FL lies in the efficient aggregation of these diverse local model parameters from various clients through an aggregation algorithm (*step 5*), which updates the global model (*step 6*). These aggregation algorithms can be simple (e.g., a weighted average) or complex. The research community is very active in this respect and continuously develops new and improved aggregation heuristics and algorithms.

Subsequently, the coordinator returns the updated global model to all clients, initiating a new round of local training. To refine the model, this FL procedure is usually repeated for a certain number of iterations or until specific criteria are met.

5.2.2 *Vertical, Horizontal, and Federated Transfer Learning*

In the context of FL processes, there are different architectures depending on the distribution of data among the clients involved in the training. According to the literature, those can be categorized into three main types: horizontal FL, vertical FL, and federated transfer learning (FTL) (Aledhari et al., 2020) (see Fig. 5.2).

Horizontal FL (Fig. 5.2a) involves clients processing the same type of data based on specific characteristics or features, while the samples may differ among different clients or participants (Konečný et al., 2016b). For instance, in the manufacturing industry, multiple companies may collect process data such as voltage or pressure, but each company's dataset represents different manufacturing scenarios or applications. This approach allows collaborative training without sharing sensitive data and can be applied to various scenarios where clients possess data with the same structure.

Vertical FL (Fig. 5.2b), also known as feature-based FL, deals with scenarios where participants possess different features or characteristics of the underlying data sources but share the same sample space (Yang et al., 2019). In the context of manufacturing, vertical FL can be applied to time-series data and corresponding

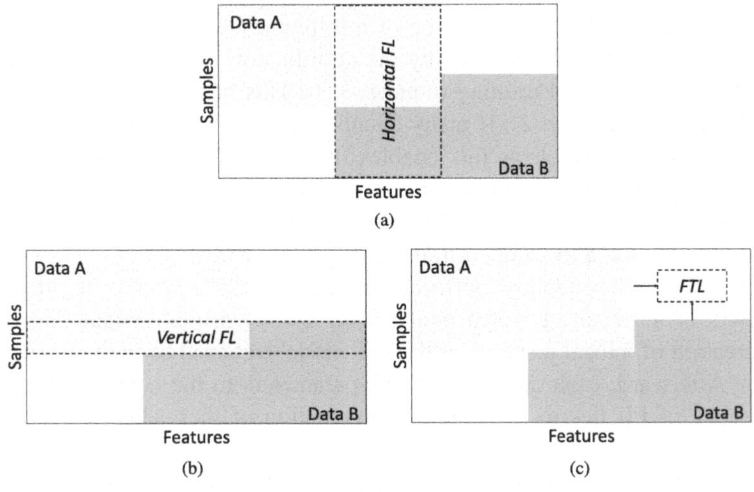

Fig. 5.2 Different FL architectures in comparison. (**a**) Horizontal FL. (**b**) Vertical FL. (**c**) FTL

feature spaces. For instance, in detecting anomalies in manufacturing processes across multiple manufacturing systems, the sample space, such as timestamps, remains the same, but the data features may differ (Zhang et al., 2021b).

FTL (Fig. 5.2c) combines FL with transfer learning techniques, allowing the transfer of knowledge from one ML model in one domain to a new ML model in a different domain (Liu et al., 2020). FTL applications involve domains with distinct characteristics and data samples. For instance, FedHealth, developed by Chen et al. (2020), uses FTL to detect activities recorded by wearable devices. Another FTL framework proposed by Ju et al. (2020) classifies different electroencephalography data sources from brain-computer interfaces. FTL has the potential to leverage knowledge learned in one domain to improve ML models in other domains, such as applying FTL techniques to different machine tools, such as milling machines or welding equipment from different manufacturers.

These three FL techniques provide flexible solutions for collaborative training on distributed data while addressing privacy concerns and utilizing knowledge transfer. By understanding each approach's characteristics and potential applications, researchers and practitioners can choose the most suitable technique for their specific domain and data requirements.

5.2.3 Advancements and Development

In the stripped-down training process, we only discussed the involvement of a central aggregator. At the same time, in practice, there may be a multitude of servers in more scaled environments to avoid a single point of failure. In addition, blockchains or other types of distributed ledgers have also been presented as a viable solution for aggregating local model updates (Nguyen et al., 2021; Shayan et al., 2021; Rückel et al., 2022). Smart contracts can assist in defining the logic for aggregation, and model updates can be deployed to the ledger to improve transparency while still maintaining the privacy guarantees of FL (Kalapaaking et al., 2023; Hua et al., 2020). However, the high degree of transparency of blockchains (Sedlmeir et al., 2022) may still expose excessive information about clients' local weights that need to be shared during the aggregation step (see also Sect. 5.3). Moreover, since many blockchain solutions don't allow for high transaction rates (Guggenberger et al., 2022; Sedlmeir et al., 2021), there may be an issue with scaling such a solution with a large number of clients. Going even one step further, an FL process might also be designed to be fully peer-to-peer (Roy et al., 2019; Wang et al., 2022), without the need for any central aggregator or distributed ledger technology (DLT) like blockchain. Instead, the clients themselves can coordinate the training with each other.

5.3 Challenges, Attack Vectors, and Mitigation Measures

FL, despite its potential to improve ML applications through improved data protection and lower bandwidth requirements, still has some characteristics that need to be investigated for challenges and potential attack vectors. In this section, we provide an overview of common scenarios and give guidance on how to approach them.

Since the local models in FL processes must train on the data of potentially very different clients, they tend to vary in terms of quality, representation, and the type of distribution (Li et al., 2020b). This heterogeneity represents a substantial barrier to building accurate and reliable models across distributed devices and organizations. Traditional ML algorithms typically assume the availability of independent and identically distributed (IID) data. Yet, in FL, the non-IID nature of the data introduces additional complexities (Kairouz et al., 2021). Researchers have developed multiple approaches on how to overcome this challenge. One of them is data preprocessing, e.g., through data normalization and feature scaling (Li et al., 2020c). Other studies highlight the potential of data augmentation, i.e., to modify existing data and produce synthetic data from it in order to enhance data diversity and reduce bias (Back de Luca et al., 2022; Hao et al., 2021; Duan et al., 2021). However, instead of homogenizing the models at a global level, the local training process can also be tailored to individual clients. This approach, called personalized FL, has thus far shown promising performance improvements for FL on non-IID data (Tan et al., 2022; Dinh et al., 2020). The already mentioned FTL architecture may also play an important role, as it focuses on different features and samples from the beginning Liu et al. (2020). Yet, heterogeneity does not only apply to data but may also reside in the underlying client systems' specifications (Karnebogen et al., 2023). Moreover, hardware and software constraints may play a vital role when designing FL applications and services. Since more data than in centralized ML needs to be (temporarily) stored and processed locally, we see higher storage requirements, which are particularly relevant for edge devices (Imteaj et al., 2022; Yang et al., 2020). Also, there are differences in connectivity capabilities (Tran et al., 2019) and power supply (Tang et al., 2021). While some FL use cases are hardware agnostic, some rely on more homogeneous or exactly the same device types (Bonawitz et al., 2019).

Another key factor when discussing FL is the communication between participants, as the efficiency of communication protocols can impact system performance (Smith et al., 2017; Chen et al., 2021b). This factor is closely coupled with the aforementioned hardware heterogeneity: Some clients may be in much more restricted environments, where only wireless communication or poor cellular connectivity is possible instead of more reliable stationary connections (Salehi & Hossain, 2021). Also, limiting the amount of data transmitted while ensuring effective model updates is an important factor, especially when dealing with resource-constrained devices (Konečný et al., 2016b; Wang et al., 2019). Researchers have identified multiple ways of minimizing communication overhead without highly impacting the overall training efficiency, such as data compression (Sattler et al., 2020; Li et al., 2022b), adapting learning rates to the computational capabilities of the clients (Ma et al., 2021; Wu et al., 2022), or prioritizing local model updates based on their relevance for the global model to reduce unnecessary updates (Ye et al., 2020; Xu et al., 2021). At the same time, however, the possible reduction in communication volume in FL systems also leads to lower energy consumption (Pham et al., 2022; Yang et al., 2021), positively impacting the environmental footprint (Savazzi et al., 2023).

Regardless of the communication speed itself, individual clients may lag behind in their computations, causing them to become stragglers in the learning process (Reisizadeh et al., 2022). As a result, the aggregation of model updates across devices may be delayed, leading to poor convergence and increased communication workloads. Since federated learning relies on aggregating updates from multiple clients, progress is slowed down by the slowest client, which undermines the overall efficiency of the learning process (Amiri & Gunduz, 2019). To address the straggler problem, researchers and practitioners have proposed several techniques. One approach is to adopt adaptive aggregation strategies that dynamically tailor the aggregation process to account for stragglers. In this process, faster and more reliable clients are weighted higher, while slow participants are penalized (Wu & Wang, 2021). Another solution is fault tolerance in the training process, allowing clients to drop out of a training iteration (Bonawitz et al., 2019). As one of the main reasons why DLT has been developed is maintaining consistency and availability in networks with potentially faulty nodes – including crashes and asynchronous networks (Abellán Álvarez et al., 2024) – the prominence of DLT in the discussion of fault-tolerant FL is not surprising (Chen et al., 2021a; Rückel et al., 2022).

Even though FL processes can enable an increased level of privacy and data security compared to classic ML architectures, they can potentially still reveal sensitive information when communicating parameter updates during the training process (McMahan et al., 2017b). Here, a distinction must be made between two points of potential privacy risks: The first one is the perspective from the client side to the server and vice versa, where local client updates should be kept private to the coordinator. Second, the global perspective is from the coordinator to the outside world, keeping global (meta-)data on the coordinator safe from malicious third parties. If the level of privacy is too low, the model updates could be reversed to draw conclusions about the raw data, via so-called model inversion or gradient inversion attacks (Geiping et al., 2020; Jere et al., 2021; Huang et al., 2021). Another attack vector is membership attacks, where a specific data point that may or may not be a part of the training set can be retraced from the model to a specific client (Hu et al., 2021; Gu et al., 2022b). Possible tactics to avoid the exposure of sensitive information include differential privacy (DP) and homomorphic encryption and secure aggregation. DP applies a certain degree of noise (e.g., Gaussian noise (Abadi et al., 2016)) to the model updates, so that the data from a particular client does not have a substantial impact on the overall model but still results in a globally correct representation of the data (Dwork, 2006). From an implementation point of view, this approach is comparatively easy to implement but inevitably results in an increasing degradation of training results the higher the degree of privacy provided by DP (Rückel et al., 2022; Fernández et al., 2022).

homomorphic encryption (HE) allows for the encryption of, e.g., model parameter updates on the client side and their subsequent use on the aggregator without decrypting them (Ma et al., 2022). Depending on the case, one can either use fully homomorphic encryption (FHE) (Gentry, 2009) (see Chap. 6) or use more leveled variants (Brakerski, 2012; Coron et al., 2014). However, a lack of privacy can also be exploited on the data flow path from server to client if malicious clients can enter a training process in this way (Jiang et al., 2021). Thus, the global learning process can also be manipulated with adversarial attacks by deliberately introducing false data to create a bias (Cao et al., 2019) or even backdoors (Bagdasaryan et al., 2020).

5.4 Fairness

Thus far, mostly the aspects of privacy and performance have been mentioned with regard to the design of FL applications. Even if these aspects seem to be the core factors to adoption at first glance, the fairness aspect also plays an important role (Karnebogen et al., 2023; Gu et al., 2022a). Fairness is not easy to grasp, because it includes different contents depending on the context. The long-standing disparity in perceptions of fairness in information systems (Joshi, 1989), which includes other complex data privacy and performance conflicts, remains present in research and is the subject of lively discussion (Haas, 2019; Dolata et al., 2022). In the context of FL, algorithmic fairness can be stated as not treating a group of individuals (personally or in the form of, e.g., machines) differently due to common properties such as gender, age, race, or even hardware specifications (Mehrabi et al., 2021; Pessach & Shmueli, 2022). An FL application could, for instance, explicitly devalue poorly performing clients or those that send parameter updates of their local models less frequently in the global model. It could also develop a bias in the case of heterogeneously distributed data. Particularly when high privacy requirements need to be met, there may be a trade-off on the side of algorithmic fairness, as identifying different client groups and resolving unfairness becomes increasingly difficult (Chang & Shokri, 2021). On the other hand, depending on the (business) context, bias may even be desirable: For clients represented by industrial machines, inequity could restore fairness for the larger group of participating clients – depending on the viewpoint. The advantage of FL is the confidentiality of clients' underlying raw data and thus a higher degree of privacy, but general knowledge of its structure may prove helpful to ensure fairness: In other contexts, one otherwise runs the risk of neglecting certain groups, e.g., in the medical field. For example, medical experts have long recognized the underrepresentation of minorities in clinical trials and medical research (Fisher & Kalbaugh, 2011; Flores et al., 2021). An FL process setup across multiple hospitals could include their demographic environments to explicitly uplift underrepresented groups in training.

The multifaceted nature of fairness can also be seen in cases in the financial industry, e.g., in federated credit scoring. Wang et al. (2024) demonstrate a federated knowledge transfer method, highlighting the improvement in model performance across diverse datasets while ensuring that there is no bias toward any demographic group. Meanwhile, Yang et al. (2023) and Djolev et al. (2024) emphasize the significance of algorithmic transparency and fairness in building trust and ensuring nondiscriminatory financial services. Lee et al. (2023) explore FL for the collaboration of smaller financial institutions, allowing them to compete with larger institutions by leveraging a collective dataset to improve credit risk models. The study demonstrates significant performance improvements in credit risk assessment models when employing FL, suggesting that collaboration through FL can lead to fairer and more equitable access to technological capabilities across financial institutions, regardless of their size. Thus, applying FL in a business use case entails an interconnection of the considered scenario and the technological foundations of FL to navigate the trade-offs between privacy, performance, and fairness.

5.5 Considerations for Federated Learning Processes in Practice

Considering the application of FL processes, there are some conditions and challenges to be met that have already been briefly discussed, whether they are technical in nature or to be understood in the overarching context of privacy, performance, and fairness. In addition, other factors are also important in practice; for instance, the choice of a suitable framework plays a crucial role. Here, there are simulative approaches as well as production-ready software that can be implemented. Both can contribute in their own way to the successful introduction of new FL processes. Simulative frameworks mimic clients from one single database without (physically) distributing the corresponding data. This approach can shed light on the basic properties of FL in the context of an application and collect base metrics. Simulative frameworks may illustrate how clients behave in their updates, how homogeneous or heterogeneous the available data on each device is, and which performance impact the shift from centralized ML to FL has on the learning process. Examples include TensorFlow Federated (TensorFlow, 2023) and FLUTE from Microsoft (Garcia et al., 2022).

On the other hand, production-ready frameworks can address different issues that are difficult to solve in the context of simulated approaches: For example, the aforementioned communication between clients and coordinators is an important issue in practice, as are general conditions from a software context, such as authentication and authorization or encryption. In addition, the model must be distributed to the clients in the first place, which requires an adjustment to the machine learning operation (MLOps) workflows used in classic ML approaches.

Known representatives of production-ready FL frameworks are FATE (Liu et al., 2021) and Flower (Beutel et al., 2020).

Technical implementation is one thing, but business decisions should be tied to business conditions. Business needs a purpose, and here, as with any other decision, it is necessary to evaluate whether FL can add appropriate value to a use case (Karnebogen et al., 2023). For example, if the protection of sensitive information as a core value proposition of FL is not relevant to the use case at hand, then other methods should be used, because FL will likely be inferior in performance to a centralized data server using ML. At the same time, a distributed system utilizing FL, with its spread across multiple clients, faces inherent complexity. Established industry processes, such as CRISP-DM, do not take effect without adaptation to the changed environment of FL, thereby potentially causing additional work. Overall, we can conclude that for the introduction of FL processes in practice, several fundamental prerequisites have to be met, and the appropriate technology needs to be selected for such a solution to be of greater value.

5.6 Summary and Outlook

FL allows a large number of distributed clients to work together on an ML problem while still keeping all training data on local devices, such as smartphones, Internet of Things (IoT) devices, or edge servers. It addresses challenges regarding data privacy, scalability, and single points of failure. FL creates the opportunity to obtain performant models even when restricted by compliance and privacy requirements. As a result, FL can also be used in sensitive areas where its use of ML was previously difficult or even unthinkable. In addition, collaboration effects between the participants become visible since, on the one hand, they are all working toward the same goal centered on themselves, and yet they are still dependent on other participants' help in the form of model updates of the other clients. Recently, there has been increased interest in both industry and practice in FL methods and applications. Large companies like Google or Apple run respective systems for productive use in highly scaled environments. At the same time, there is also continued research into new algorithms for even faster data transmission, higher performance, and reduced communication overhead while maintaining privacy guarantees.

Besides shedding light on FL's unique opportunities, this chapter on FL has also pointed to a number of challenges, including different types of heterogeneity, communication efficiency, data leakage, and a lack of robustness to certain attacks. The heterogeneity of client devices and data leads to complex training and model aggregation problems. The clients' different computational capacities and network constraints require the design of adaptive algorithms that can efficiently deal with this kind of diversity. Furthermore, ensuring fairness and mitigating potential biases in the learning process continues to be an active area of research. As FL evolves, future research should remain focused on improving privacy-preserving mechanisms, further refining communication protocols, and scaling FL to handle an ever-increasing number of clients and data sources. In addition, ensuring the security and robustness of FL against outside attacks will be of critical concern. With the potential to deliver democratized access to ML advancements and empower edge computing systems, FL can revolutionize machine learning and data-driven decision-making in a privacy-friendly and inclusive way. The fusion of collaborative intelligence and privacy that FL offers opens up exciting possibilities for disruptive applications and groundbreaking research, opening the way for a future where ML and data-driven solutions are used responsibly and ethically.

References

Abadi, M., Chu, A., Goodfellow, I., McMahan, B., Mironov, I., Talwar, K., & Zhang, L. (2016). Deep learning with differential privacy. In *Proceedings of the ACM SIGSAC Conference on Computer and Communications Security*. https://doi.org/10.1145/2976749.2978318

Abellán Álvarez, I., Gramlich, V., & Sedlmeir, J. (2024). Unsealing the secrets of blockchain consensus: A systematic comparison of the formal security of proof-of-work and proof-of-stake. In *39th ACM/SIGAPP Symposium on Applied Computing*.

Aledhari, M., Razzak, R., Parizi, R., & Saeed, F. (2020). Federated learning: A survey on enabling technologies, protocols, and applications. *IEEE Access*, *8*, 140699–140725. https://doi.org/10.1109/access.2020.3013541

Amiri, M., & Gunduz, D. (2019). Computation scheduling for distributed machine learning with straggling workers. *Transactions on Signal Processing*, *67*(24), 6270–6284. https://doi.org/10.1109/tsp.2019.2952051

Back de Luca, A., Zhang, G., Chen, X., & Yu, Y. (2022). Mitigating data heterogeneity in federated learning with data augmentation. https://arxiv.org/abs/2206.09979

Bagdasaryan, E., Veit, A., Hua, Y., Estrin, D., & Shmatikov, V. (2020). How to backdoor federated learning. In S. Chiappa & R. Calandra (Eds.), *23rd International Conference on Artificial Intelligence and Statistics* (Vol. 108, pp. 2938–2948). PMLR.

Beutel, D., et al. (2020). Flower: A friendly federated learning research framework. https://arxiv.org/abs/2007.14390

Bonawitz, K., et al. (2019). Towards federated learning at scale: System design. In A. Talwalkar, V. Smith, & M. Zaharia (Eds.), *Proceedings of Machine Learning and Systems* (Vol. 1, pp. 374–388). https://mlsys.org/Conferences/2019/doc/2019/193.pdf

Boobalan, P., et al. (2022). Fusion of federated learning and Industrial Internet of Things: A survey. *Computer Networks*, *212*, 109048. https://doi.org/10.1016/j.comnet.2022.109048

Brakerski, Z. (2012). Fully homomorphic encryption without modulus switching from classical GapSVP. In *Lecture Notes in Computer Science* (pp. 868–886). Springer. https://doi.org/10.1007/978-3-642-32009-5_50

Cao, D., Chang, S., Lin, Z., Liu, G., & Sun, D. (2019). Understanding distributed poisoning attack in federated learning. In *25th International Conference on Parallel and Distributed Systems*. IEEE. https://doi.org/10.1109/icpads47876.2019.00042.

Chang, H., & Shokri, R. (2021). On the privacy risks of algorithmic fairness. In *European Symposium on Security and Privacy* (pp. 292–303). IEEE. https://doi.org/10.1109/eurosp51992.2021.00028

Chen, J.-H., Chen, M.-R., Zeng, G.-Q., & Weng, J.-S. (2021a). BDFL: A Byzantine-fault-tolerance decentralized federated learning method for autonomous vehicle. *IEEE Transactions on Vehicular Technology*, *70*(9), 8639–8652. https://doi.org/10.1109/TVT.2021.3102121

Chen, M., Shlezinger, N., Poor, V., Eldar, Y., & Cui, S. (2021b). Communication-efficient federated learning. *Proceedings of the National Academy of Sciences, 118*(17). https://doi.org/10.1073/pnas.2024789118

Chen, Y., Qin, X., Wang, J., Yu, C., & Gao, W. (2020). FedHealth: A federated transfer learning framework for wearable healthcare. *Intelligent Systems, 35*(4), 83–93. https://doi.org/10.1109/mis.2020.2988604

Coron, J.-S., Lepoint, T., & Tibouchi, M. (2014). Scale-invariant fully homomorphic encryption over the integers. In *Public-Key Cryptography* (pp. 311–328). Springer. https://doi.org/10.1007/978-3-642-54631-0_18

Dayan, I., et al. (2021). Federated learning for predicting clinical outcomes in patients with COVID-19. *Nature Medicine, 27*(10), 1735–1743. https://doi.org/10.1038/s41591-021-01506-3

Dinh, C., Tran, N., & Nguyen, T. D. (2020). Personalized federated learning with Moreau envelopes. In *Proceedings of the 34th International Conference on Neural Information Processing Systems* (pp. 21394–21405). Curran Associates. https://proceedings.neurips.cc/paper_files/paper/2020/file/f4f1f13c8289ac1b1ee0ff176b56fc60-Paper.pdf

Djolev, D., Lazarova, M., & Nakov, O. (2024). *Federated learning for credit scoring model using blockchain* (pp. 109–122). Springer.

Dolata, M., Feuerriegel, S., & Schwabe, G. (2022). A sociotechnical view of algorithmic fairness. *Information Systems Journal, 32*(4), 754–818. https://doi.org/10.1111/isj.12370

Duan, M., Liu, D., Chen, X., Liu, R., Tan, Y., & Liang, L. (2021). Self-balancing federated learning with global imbalanced data in mobile systems. *Transactions on Parallel and Distributed Systems, 32*(1), 59–71. https://doi.org/10.1109/tpds.2020.3009406

Dwork, C. (2006). Differential privacy. In *Automata, languages and programming*. Springer. https://doi.org/10.1007/11787006_1

European Commission. (2016). Regulation (EU) 2016/679 of the European Parliament and of the Council of 27th of April 2016 on the protection of natural persons with regard to the processing of personal data and on the free movement of such data, and repealing Directive 95/46/EC (General Data Protection Regulation). https://eur-lex.europa.eu/eli/reg/2016/679/oj

European Commission. (2021). Proposal for a Regulation of the European Parliament and of the Council Laying Down Harmonised Rules on Artificial Intelligence Artificial Intelligence Act and Amending Certain Union Legislative Acts. https://eur-lex.europa.eu/legal-content/EN/TXT/?uri=celex%3A52021PC0206

Fernández, J. D., Potenciano Menci, S., Lee, C. M., Rieger, A., & Fridgen, G. (2022). Privacy-preserving federated learning for residential short-term load forecasting. *Applied Energy, 326*. https://doi.org/10.1016/j.apenergy.2022.119915

Fisher, J., & Kalbaugh, C. (2011). Challenging assumptions about minority participation in US clinical research. *American Journal of Public Health, 101*(12), 2217–2222. https://ddi.org/10.2105/AJPH.2011.300279

Flores, L., et al. (2021). Assessment of the inclusion of racial/ethnic minority, female, and older individuals in vaccine clinical trials. *JAMA Network Open, 4*(2). https://doi.org/10.1001/jamanetworkopen.2020.37640

Fu, L., Zhang, H., Gao, G., Zhang, M., & Liu, X. (2023). Client selection in federated learning: Principles, challenges, and opportunities. *Internet of Things Journal, 10*(24). https://doi.org/10.1109/jiot.2023.3299573

Garcia, M. H., Manoel, A., Diaz, D. M., Mireshghallah, F., Sim, R., & Dimitriadis, D. (2022). FLUTE: A scalable, extensible framework for high-performance federated learning simulations. https://doi.org/10.48550/ARXIV.2203.13789

Geiping, J., Bauermeister, H., Dröge, H., & Moeller, M. (2020). Inverting gradients – how easy is it to break privacy in federated learning? In *Advances in Neural Information Processing Systems* (Vol. 33, pp. 16937–16947). Curran Associates. https://proceedings.neurips.cc/paper_files/paper/2020/file/c4ede56bbd98819ae6112b20ac6bf145-Paper.pdf

Gentry, C. (2009). Fully homomorphic encryption using ideal lattices. In *41st Annual ACM Symposium on Theory of Computing*. ACM. https://doi.org/10.1145/1536414.1536440

Goldsteen, A., Ezov, G., Shmelkin, R., Moffie, M., & Farkash, A. (2022). Data minimization for GDPR compliance in machine learning models. *AI and Ethics*, *2*(3), 477–491. https://doi.org/10.1007/s43681-021-00095-8

Gregory, R. W., Henfridsson, O., Kaganer, E., & Kyriakou, H. (2021). The role of artificial intelligence and data network effects for creating user value. *Academy of Management Review*, *46*(3), 534–551. https://doi.org/10.5465/amr.2019.0178

Gu, X., Tianqing, Z., Li, J., Zhang, T., Ren, W., & Choo, K.-K. R. (2022a). Privacy, accuracy, and model fairness trade-offs in federated learning. *Computers & Security*, *122*, 102907. https://doi.org/10.1016/j.cose.2022.102907

Gu, Y., Bai, Y., & Xu, S. (2022b). CS-MIA: Membership inference attack based on prediction confidence series in federated learning. *Journal of Information Security and Applications*, *67*. https://doi.org/10.1016/j.jisa.2022.103201

Guggenberger, T., Sedlmeir, J., Fridgen, G., & Luckow, A. (2022). An in-depth investigation of the performance characteristics of Hyperledger Fabric. *Computers and Industrial Engineering*, *173*, 108716. https://doi.org/10.1016/j.cie.2022.108716

Haas, C. (2019). The price of fairness – A framework to explore trade-offs in algorithmic fairness. In *Proceedings of the 40th International Conference on Information Systems*. AIS. https://aisel.aisnet.org/icis2019/data_science/data_science/19/

Hao, W., El-Khamy, M., Lee, J., Zhang, J., Liang, K., Chen, C., & Carin, L. (2021). Towards fair federated learning with zero-shot data augmentation. In *Conference on Computer Vision and Pattern Recognition Workshops* (pp. 3305–3314). IEEE. https://doi.org/10.1109/cvprw53098.2021.00369

Hard, A., et al. (2018). Federated learning for mobile keyboard prediction. https://arxiv.org/abs/1811.03604

Hu, H., Salcic, Z., Sun, L., Dobbie, G., & Zhang, X. (2021). Source inference attacks in federated learning. In *International Conference on Data Mining* (pp. 1102–1107). IEEE. https://doi.org/10.1109/icdm51629.2021.00129

Hua, G., Zhu, L., Wu, J., Shen, C., Zhou, L., & Lin, Q. (2020). Blockchain-based federated learning for intelligent control in heavy haul railway. *IEEE Access*, *8*, 176830–176839. https://doi.org/10.1109/access.2020.3021253

Huang, Y., Gupta, S., Song, Z., Li, K., & Arora, S. (2021). Evaluating gradient inversion attacks and defenses in federated learning. In *Advances in Neural Information Processing Systems* (pp. 7232–7241). Curran Associates. https://proceedings.neurips.cc/paper_files/paper/2021/file/3b3fff6463464959dcd1b68d0320f781-Paper.pdf

Imteaj, A., Thakker, U., Wang, S., Li, J., & Amini, H. (2022). A survey on federated learning for resource-constrained IoT devices. *IEEE Internet of Things Journal*, *9*(1). https://doi.org/10.1109/jiot.2021.3095077

Jere, M., Farnan, T., & Koushanfar, F. (2021). A taxonomy of attacks on federated learning. *IEEE Security & Privacy*, *19*(2), 20–28. https://doi.org/10.1109/msec.2020.3039941

Jiang, Y., Li, Y., Zhou, Y., & Zheng, X. (2021). Sybil attacks and defense on differential privacy based federated learning. In *20th International Conference on Trust, Security and Privacy in Computing and Communications*. IEEE. https://doi.org/10.1109/trustcom53373.2021.00062

Joshi, K. (1989). The measurement of fairness or equity perceptions of management information systems users. *Management Information Systems Quarterly*, *13*(3), 343. https://doi.org/10.2307/249010

Ju, C., Gao, D., Mane, R., Tan, B., Liu, Y., & Guan, C. (2020). Federated transfer learning for EEG signal classification. In *42nd Annual International Conference of the IEEE Engineering in Medicine & Biology Society* (pp. 3040–3045). IEEE. https://doi.org/10.1109/embc44109.2020.9175344

Kairouz, P., et al. (2021). *Advances and open problems in federated learning*. Now Foundations and Trends.

Kalapaaking, A., Khalil, I., & Atiquzzaman, M. (2023). Smart policy control for securing federated learning management system. *IEEE Transactions on Network and Service Management*, *20*(2), 1600–1611. https://doi.org/10.1109/tnsm.2023.3276594

Karnebogen, P., Kaymakci, C., Willburger, L., Häckel, B., & Sauer, A. (2023). Structuring federated learning applications – a literature analysis and taxonomy. In *European Conference on Information Systems*. AIS. https://aisel.aisnet.org/ecis2023_rp/230/

Kaymakci, C., Baur, L., & Sauer, A. (2021). Federated machine learning architecture for energy-efficient industrial applications. In *Proceedings of the 2nd Conference on Production Systems and Logistics* (pp. 405–414). https://doi.org/10.15488/11237

Konečný, J., McMahan, B., Ramage, D., & Richtárik, P. (2016a). Federated optimization: Distributed machine learning for on-device intelligence. https://arxiv.org/abs/1610.02527

Konečný, J., McMahan, B., Yu, F., Richtarik, P., Suresh, A. T., & Bacon, D. (2016b). Federated learning: Strategies for improving communication efficiency. https://arxiv.org/abs/1610.05492

Lee, C. M., Delgado Fernandez, J., Potenciano Menci, S., Rieger, A., & Fridgen, G. (2023). Federated learning for credit risk assessment. In *Proceedings of the 56th Hawaii International Conference on System Sciences* (pp. 386–395). https://hdl.handle.net/10125/102676

Li, L., Fan, Y., Tse, M., & Lin, K.-Y. (2020a). A review of applications in federated learning. *Computers & Industrial Engineering*, *149*, 106854. https://doi.org/10.1016/j.cie.2020.106854

Li, T., Sahu, A. K., Talwalkar, A., & Smith, V. (2020b). Federated learning: Challenges, methods, and future directions. *Signal Processing Magazine*, *37*(3), 50–60. https://doi.org/10.1109/msp.2020.2975749

Li, X., Huang, K., Yang, W., Wang, S., & Zhang, Z. (2020c). On the convergence of FedAvg on Non-iid data. In *International Conference on Learning Representations*. https://openreview.net/forum?id=HJxNAnVtDS

Li, Y., Tao, X., Zhang, X., Liu, J., & Xu, J. (2022a). Privacy-preserved federated learning for autonomous driving. *Transactions on Intelligent Transportation Systems*, *23*(7), 8423–8434. https://doi.org/10.1109/tits.2021.3081560

Li, Z., Zhao, H., Li, B., & Chi, Y. (2022b). SoteriaFL: A unified framework for private federated learning with communication compression. In *Proceedings of the 35th Annual Conference on Advances in Neural Information Processing Systems* (pp. 4285–4300). Curran Associates. https://proceedings.neurips.cc/paper_files/paper/2022/file/1b645a77cf48821afc3ee7e5b5d42617-Paper-Conference.pdf

Lim, W. Y. B., et al. (2020). Federated learning in mobile edge networks: A comprehensive survey. *IEEE Communications Surveys & Tutorials*, *22*(3), 2031–2063. https://doi.org/10.1109/comst.2020.2986024

Lin, T., Kong, L., Stich, S., & Jaggi, M. (2020). Ensemble distillation for robust model fusion in federated learning. In *Proceedings of the 33rd Annual Conference on Advances in Neural Information Processing Systems* (pp. 2351–2363). Curran Associates. https://proceedings.neurips.cc/paper_files/paper/2020/file/18df51b97ccd68128e994804f3eccc87-Paper.pdf

Liu, Y., Fan, T., Chen, T., Xu, Q., & Yang, Q. (2021). FATE: An industrial grade platform for collaborative learning with data protection. *Journal of Machine Learning Research*. *22*(1). https://dl.acm.org/doi/abs/10.5555/3546258.3546484

Liu, Y., Kang, Y., Xing, C., Chen, T., & Yang, Q. (2020). A secure federated transfer learning framework. *Intelligent Systems*, *35*(4), 70–82. https://doi.org/10.1109/mis.2020.2988525

Ma, J., Naas, S.-A., Sigg, S., & Lyu, X. (2022). Privacy-preserving federated learning based on multi-key homomorphic encryption. *International Journal of Intelligent Systems*, *37*(9), 5880–5901. https://doi.org/10.1002/int.22818

Ma, Q., Xu, Y., Xu, H., Jiang, Z., Huang, L., & Huang, H. (2021). FedSA: A semi-asynchronous federated learning mechanism in heterogeneous edge computing. *Journal on Selected Areas in Communications*, *39*(12), 3654–3672. https://doi.org/10.1109/jsac.2021.3118435

McMahan, B., Moore, E., Ramage, D., Hampson, S., & Agüera y Arcas, B. (2017a). Communication-efficient learning of deep networks from decentralized data. In *20th International Conference on Artificial Intelligence and Statistics* (pp. 1273–1282). AISTATS. https://proceedings.mlr.press/v54/mcmahan17a/mcmahan17a.pdf

McMahan, B., & Ramage, D. (2017). Federated learning: Collaborative machine learning without centralized training data. https://ai.googleblog.com/2017/04/federated-learning-collaborative.html

McMahan, B., Ramage, D., Talwar, K., & Zhang, L. (2017b). Learning differentially private recurrent language models. In *Proceedings of the International Conference on Learning Representations*. Curran Associates. https://arxiv.org/abs/1710.06963

Mehrabi, N., Morstatter, F., Saxena, N., Lerman, K., & Galstyan, A. (2021). A survey on bias and fairness in machine learning. *ACM Computing Surveys*, *54*(6). https://doi.org/10.1145/3457607

Mourby, M., Ó Cathaoir, K., & Collin, C. B. (2021). Transparency of machine-learning in healthcare: The GDPR & European health law. *Computer Law & Security Review*, *43*, 105611. https://doi.org/10.1016/j.clsr.2021.105611

Napirata, S., Sedlmeir, J., Rieger, A., Fridgen, G., & Zimmermann, S. (2023). The competition effect of decentralized platforms: An analytical model. In *Proceedings of the 44th International Conference on Information Systems*. AIS. https://aisel.aisnet.org/icis2023/sharing_econ/sharing_econ/16/

Nguyen, D., et al. (2021). Federated learning meets blockchain in edge computing: Opportunities and challenges. *IEEE Internet of Things Journal*, *8*(16), 12806–12825. https://doi.org/10.1109/jiot.2021.3072611

Pessach, D., & Shmueli, E. (2022). A review on fairness in machine learning. *ACM Computing Surveys*, *55*(3). https://doi.org/10.1145/3494672

Pham, Q.-V., Le, M., Huynh-The, T., Han, Z., & Hwang, W.-J. (2022). Energy-efficient federated learning over UAV-enabled wireless powered communications. *Transactions on Vehicular Technology*, *71*(5), 4977–4990. https://doi.org/10.1109/tvt.2022.3150004

Reisizadeh, A., Tziotis, I., Hassani, H., Mokhtari, A., & Pedarsani, R. (2022). Straggler-resilient federated learning: Leveraging the interplay between statistical accuracy and system heterogeneity. *Journal on Selected Areas in Information Theory*, *3*(2), 197–205. https://doi.org/10.1109/jsait.2022.3205475

Roy, A. G., Siddiqui, S., Pölsterl, S., Navab, N., & Wachinger, C. (2019). BrainTorrent: A peer-to-peer environment for decentralized federated learning. https://doi.org/10.48550/ARXIV.1905.06731

Rückel, T., Sedlmeir, J., & Hofmann, P. (2022). Fairness, integrity, and privacy in a scalable blockchain-based federated learning system. *Computer Networks*, *202*, 108621. https://doi.org/10.1016/j.comnet.2021.108621

Salehi, M., & Hossain, E. (2021). Federated learning in unreliable and resource-constrained cellular wireless networks. *Transactions on Communications*, *69*(8), 5136–5151. https://doi.org/10.1109/tcomm.2021.3081746

Sattler, F., Wiedemann, S., Müller, K.-R., & Samek, W. (2020). Robust and communication-efficient federated learning from non-i.i.d. data. *Transactions on Neural Networks and Learning Systems*, *31*(9), 3400–3413. https://doi.org/10.1109/tnnls.2019.2944481

Savazzi, S., Nicoli, M., Bennis, M., Kianoush, S., & Barbieri, L. (2021). Opportunities of federated learning in connected, cooperative, and automated industrial systems. *IEEE Communications Magazine*, *59*(2), 16–21. https://doi.org/10.1109/mcom.001.2000200

Savazzi, S., Rampa, V., Kianoush, S., & Bennis, M. (2023). An energy and carbon footprint analysis of distributed and federated learning. *Transactions on Green Communications and Networking*, *7*(1), 248–264. https://doi.org/10.1109/tgcn.2022.3186439

Sedlmeir, J., Lautenschlager, J., Fridgen, G., & Urbach, N. (2022). The transparency challenge of blockchain in organizations. *Electronic Markets*, *32*, 1779–1794. https://doi.org/10.1007/s12525-022-00536-0

Sedlmeir, J., Ross, P., Luckow, A., Lockl, J., Miehle, D., & Fridgen, G. (2021). The DLPS: A new framework for benchmarking blockchains. In *Proceedings of the 54th Hawaii International Conference on System Sciences* (pp. 6855–6864). https://doi.org/10.24251/hicss.2021.822

Shayan, M., Fung, C., Yoon, C., & Beschastnikh, I. (2021). Biscotti: A blockchain system for private and secure federated learning. *Transactions on Parallel and Distributed Systems*, *32*(7), 1513–1525. https://doi.org/10.1109/tpds.2020.3044223

Shingi, G. (2020). A federated learning based approach for loan defaults prediction. In *International Conference on Data Mining Workshops*. IEEE. https://doi.org/10.1109/icdmw51313.2020.00057

Smith, V., Chiang, C.-K., Sanjabi, M., & Talwalkar, A. (2017). Federated multi-task learning. In *Proceedings of the 31st International Conference on Neural Information Processing Systems* (pp. 4427–4437). Curran Associates. https://dl.acm.org/doi/pdf/10.5555/3294996.3295196

Tan, A. Z., Yu, H., Cui, L., & Yang, Q. (2022). Towards personalized federated learning. *Transactions on Neural Networks and Learning Systems, 34*(12). https://doi.org/10.1109/tnnls.2022.3160699

Tang, S., Zhou, W., Chen, L., Lai, L., Xia, J., & Fan, L. (2021). Battery-constrained federated edge learning in UAV-enabled IoT for 5G/6G networks. *Physical Communication, 47*, 101381. https://doi.org/10.1016/j.phycom.2021.101381

TensorFlow. (2023). Tensorflow federated: Machine learning on decentralized data. https://www.tensorflow.org/federated

Tran, N., Bao, W., Zomaya, A., Nguyen, M., & Hong, C. S. (2019). Federated learning over wireless networks: Optimization model design and analysis. In *Proceedings of the Conference on Computer Communications*. IEEE. https://doi.org/10.1109/infocom.2019.8737464

United States Congress. (1996). Health Insurance Portability and Accountability Act of 1996. https://www.cdc.gov/phlp/publications/topic/hipaa.html

Wang, C., Wei, X., & Zhou, P. (2020). Optimize scheduling of federated learning on battery-powered mobile devices. In *International Parallel and Distributed Processing Symposium*. IEEE. https://doi.org/10.1109/ipdps47924.2020.00031

Wang, L., Wang, W., & Li, B. (2019). CMFL: Mitigating communication overhead for federated learning. In *39th International Conference on Distributed Computing Systems* (pp. 212–221). IEEE. https://doi.org/10.1109/icdcs.2019.00099

Wang, X., Lalitha, A., Javidi, T., & Koushanfar, F. (2022). Peer-to-peer variational federated learning over arbitrary graphs. *Journal on Selected Areas in Information Theory, 3*(2), 172–182. https://doi.org/10.1109/jsait.2022.3189051

Wang, Z., Xiao, J., Wang, L., & Yao, J. (2024). A novel federated learning approach with knowledge transfer for credit scoring. *Decision Support Systems, 177*. https://doi.org/10.1016/j.dss.2023.114084

Wu, H., & Wang, P. (2021). Fast-convergent federated learning with adaptive weighting. *Transactions on Cognitive Communications and Networking, 7*(4), 1078–1088. https://doi.org/10.1109/tccn.2021.3084406

Wu, X., Zhang, Y., Shi, M., Li, P., Li, R., & Xiong, N. (2022). An adaptive federated learning scheme with differential privacy preserving. *Future Generation Computer Systems, 127*, 362–372. https://doi.org/10.1016/j.future.2021.09.015

Xu, W., Fang, W., Ding, Y., Zou, M., & Xiong, N. (2021). Accelerating federated learning for IoT in big data analytics with pruning, quantization and selective updating. *IEEE Access, 9*, 38457–38466. https://doi.org/10.1109/access.2021.3063291

Yang, F., Abedin, M., & Hajek, P. (2023). An explainable federated learning and blockchain-based secure credit modeling method. *European Journal of Operational Research*. https://doi.org/10.1016/j.ejor.2023.08.040

Yang, K., Jiang, T., Shi, Y., & Ding, Z. (2020). Federated learning via over-the-air computation. *Transactions on Wireless Communications, 19*(3), 2022–2035. https://doi.org/10.1109/twc.2019.2961673

Yang, Q., Liu, Y., Chen, T., & Tong, Y. (2019). Federated machine learning. *ACM Transactions on Intelligent Systems and Technology, 10*(2). https://doi.org/10.1145/3298981

Yang, Z., Chen, M., Saad, W., Hong, C. S., & Shikh-Bahaei, M. (2021). Energy efficient federated learning over wireless communication networks. *Transactions on Wireless Communications, 20*(3), 1935–1949. https://doi.org/10.1109/twc.2020.3037554

Ye, D., Yu, R., Pan, M., & Han, Z. (2020). Federated learning in vehicular edge computing: A selective model aggregation approach. *IEEE Access, 8*, 23920–23935. https://doi.org/10.1109/access.2020.2968399

Zeng, T., Semiari, O., Chen, M., Saad, W., & Bennis, M. (2022). Federated learning on the road autonomous controller design for connected and autonomous vehicles. *Transactions on Wireless Communications, 21*(12), 10407–10423. https://doi.org/10.1109/twc.2022.3183996

Zhang, C., Xie, Y., Bai, H., Yu, B., Li, W., & Gao, Y. (2021a). A survey on federated learning. *Knowledge-Based Systems*, *216*, 106775. https://doi.org/10.1016/j.knosys.2021.106775

Zhang, H., Bosch, J., & Olsson, H. (2021b). Real-time end-to-end federated learning: An automotive case study. In *45th Annual Computers, Software, and Applications Conference*. IEEE. https://doi.org/10.1109/compsac51774.2021.00070

Zhang, W., Li, X., Ma, H., Luo, Z., & Li, X. (2021c). Federated learning for machinery fault diagnosis with dynamic validation and self-supervision. *Knowledge-Based Systems*, *213*. https://doi.org/10.1016/j.knosys.2020.106679

Zhang, W., et al. (2021d). Dynamic-fusion-based federated learning for COVID-19 detection. *Internet of Things Journal*, *8*(21), 15884–15891. https://doi.org/10.1109/jiot.2021.3056185

Chapter 6
Privacy-Enhancing Technologies

Iván Abellán Álvarez, Marvin Ehaus, Muriel-Larissa Frank, and Johannes Sedlmeir

Abstract In the course of the digital transformation, increasing amounts of data are exchanged digitally. Business processes and regulatory compliance requirements that demand additional degrees of verifiability of the exchanged information and the accountability of corresponding stakeholders further add to the volume and sensitivity of this data. At the same time, users' personal information calls for enhanced protection and organizations are concerned about ensuring the confidentiality of business-relevant information, as well as complying with data protection obligations. Thus, the tension between verifiability and accountability on the one hand and data minimization on the other hand has become a major concern. Maybe counterintuitively, decentralization technologies can exacerbate this issue, because they expand the number of stakeholders responsible for data processing and storage, which may increase verifiability/accountability and data minimization requirements at the same time. Privacy-enhancing technologies (PETs) provide a means to mitigate this seemingly fundamental trade-off. In this chapter, we give an overview of the technical foundations of PETs and reflect on how to leverage them in decentralized information systems to achieve verifiable and accountable results without disclosing excessive information. We particularly focus on zero-knowledge proof (ZKP)-based constructions.

I. A. Álvarez (✉) · M.-L. Frank · J. Sedlmeir
Interdisciplinary Centre for Security, Reliability and Trust (SnT), University of Luxembourg, Luxembourg, Luxembourg
e-mail: ivan.abellan@uni.lu; muriel.frank@uni.lu; johannes.sedlmeir@uni.lu

M. Ehaus
Branch Business & Information Systems Engineering of the Fraunhofer FIT, University of Bayreuth, Bayreuth, Germany
e-mail: marvin.ehaus@fim-rc.de

G. Fridgen et al. (eds.), *Decentralization Technologies*, Financial Innovation and Technology, https://doi.org/10.1007/978-3-031-66047-4_6

6.1 Introduction

Information exchange largely depends on trust relationships among the interacting parties. Businesses and users strive to communicate with entities they perceive as trustworthy. As data within existing systems can be replicated, copied, or modified with relative ease, verifiability and accountability, as well as confidentiality and data minimization need to be ensured to obtain a certain degree of trust in digital interactions (Baum et al., 2023). Data confidentiality is particularly relevant for users' personal information, but also organizations' best interest lies in protecting business- and client-related information. All these aspects are also covered by – sometimes conflicting (Codagnone & Weigl, 2023; Weigl et al., 2023) – regulatory aspects. They are particularly striking in the financial sector, as illustrated by know-your-customer (KYC) and anti-money laundering (AML) directives (European Commission, 2021) or the Basel III banking regulatory standard (Bank for International Settlements (BIS), 2024) on the one hand and the General Data Protection Regulation (GDPR) (Bernal Bernabe et al., 2019; Chatzigiannis et al., 2021; Baum et al., 2023) (see also Chap. 2) and antitrust regulation (Teece, 1993; White, 2015) on the other hand.

Blockchain (and, more generally, distributed ledger technology (DLT)) was initially considered a silver bullet to address such trust issues. It can facilitate large, neutral digital platforms that give stakeholders control over data integrity and use. Therefore, it can potentially integrate a large variety of stakeholders (Sedlmeir et al., 2022b) and improve the management of cross-organizational workflows (Fridgen et al., 2018). The consensus mechanisms that govern blockchain networks indeed ensure the verifiability and retrospective immutability of transactional data and, thus, can reduce the required trust between transaction partners such as payers and payees (Bons et al., 2020). DLT achieves data verifiability by replication, thus leading to the exposure of all information underlying transactions to all blockchain nodes (Platt et al., 2021; Sedlmeir et al., 2022b). Although this transparency may represent a desirable feature when considering auditability and accountability aspects (Barth & Schipper, 2008), it is at the same time one of its biggest challenges when it comes to the protection of sensitive information, fine-granular business information, or intellectual property rights. Such data, therefore, should not be stored on a blockchain network (Platt et al., 2021; Rieger et al., 2019), and the "control of data use" aspect of blockchain use represents a frequent misunderstanding of the technology (Sedlmeir et al., 2022b). This insight severely challenges the potential of applications of these systems, in particular, the benefits that can be expected from data processing in smart contracts (Kannengießer et al., 2020).

In general, the aspect of privacy in information system (IS) has become a significant concern in recent years, not only because of the many negative consequences associated with the disclosure of personal information but also because of strict data protection directives. The need for the confidentiality of personal information is not only apparent from economic considerations (Gross et al., 2021) but also underpinned from an ethical perspective (Rogaway, 2015). Keeping a balance between ensuring privacy and maintaining the level of transparency required for auditability is a complex and constantly evolving endeavor. Also decentralization technologies beyond blockchain, i.e., decentralized digital identities (see Chap. 4) and federated learning (FL) (see Chap. 5), can exacerbate some privacy-related requirements. Indeed, while digital identity wallets and FL may at first glance seem to effectively limit centralized data storage by design, these technologies can only create value if they vastly expand the number of stakeholders involved in information processing. In the case of self-sovereign identity (SSI), untrusted verifiers may sell sensitive or even verifiable information (Babel & Sedlmeir, 2023), and in the case of FL, participating entities may infer properties of other parties' raw data from their contributions in the weight aggregation process, leading to privacy leakage (Yin et al., 2021). This situation necessitates a reevaluation of the trust and accountability assumptions regarding the protection and sound processing of data in corresponding ISs. Depending on the system design, the extent to which the conflicting requirements in terms of auditability (i.e., transparency, accountability) on the one hand and privacy (i.e., data confidentiality, data minimization) on the other hand should be prioritized may vary significantly. In contrast to centralized IS designs with few responsible, usually broadly trusted entities who are proficient in information technology (IT)-security, decentralized networks are inherently considered less trustworthy, potentially even adversarial environments. Therefore, higher standards of data privacy and/or rigorous validation and verification processes must be placed to counteract the spread of altered or sensitive information (Baum et al., 2023).

The need for stringent verifiability and privacy measures may be less pronounced in bilateral interactions between mutually trusted entities. For instance, privacy aspects in verifiable presentations between an individual and public services by means of digital identity wallets may be considered relatively unproblematic. Nevertheless, decentralized digital identity management, with its inherent network effects, will only thrive in ecosystems with a large number of issuing and verifying organizations (Schlatt et al., 2022), and low entry barriers for such activities are desirable. As such, there is an increased need for the minimization of verifiable identity information disclosed by end users (Babel & Sedlmeir, 2023). Conversely, in a DLT-based tokenization platform, users may demand particularly high degrees of privacy when transacting because of their excessive transparency characteristics – specifically in permissionless networks in which any entity can replicate and see data processed but also in permissioned blockchains owing to the lack of fine-granular read access management when data is replicated by design (Sedlmeir et al., 2022b). As such, it is no surprise that anonymization services such as mixers have gained popularity in these systems despite their negative effects on accountability (Barbereau et al., 2023).

In this regard, PETs as a toolkit to tackle the conflicting demands of auditability, transparency, and verifiability on the one side and the protection of sensitive information on the other side emerge as particularly valuable in decentralized systems. Note that in some contexts, data minimization is not a technical but

– if any – an incentive or enforcement challenge. If the bilateral exchange of information does not require any verifiability guarantees, as in the self-attested filling of registration forms, removing some fields or reducing the level of detail may be sufficient. However, if there is a strong regulatory demand for accountability, verifiability requirements may act against such simple means of data minimization. For instance, to be verifiable, records must usually be provided in much detail, and digitally signed documents must be provided in their entirety. In this case, the tension between privacy and accountability is particularly pronounced; yet there is a need for designing privacy-by-design (Cavoukian, 2009) and compliance-by-design (Pocher, 2023) solutions. Besides anonymization techniques that are typically characterized by an accuracy – privacy trade-off, PETs (for more details, see Sect. 6.4) can serve as a foundational building block by providing secure computation techniques that allow data processing to derive useful and verifiable results without giving access to the raw data (Garrido et al., 2022; The Royal Society, 2023; Baum et al., 2023). The essence of PETs lies in their ability to empower users, consumers, and data owners with a high degree of control over their data while at the same time allowing them to leverage (verifiable) data in economic interactions.

The remainder of this chapter is structured as follows: We present an overview of the evolution of auditing in the financial sector and in decentralized systems in Sect. 6.2. We then delve into the privacy debate in Sect. 6.3. This discussion is followed by a presentation of the technical foundations of a selection of PETs that can help ensure a high degree of privacy while retaining verifiability and accountability in ISs (Sect. 6.4). The subsequent Sect. 6.5 gives two prominent examples of the construction of applications based on decentralization technologies and PETs that provide auditability while at the same time protecting sensitive information. We conclude in Sect. 6.6.

6.2 Auditability, Accountability, and Transparency

6.2.1 The Evolution of Audits

In general, auditing is characterized by three pivotal features: effectiveness, objectivity or neutrality, and transparency (Cook et al., 2016). Effectiveness refers to both the effectiveness of the internal process for performing audits and the effectiveness of the result in the form of providing a certain certification or giving legal evidence of non-fraudulent reporting. Auditing should also be neutral, unbiased, and impartial, i.e., conducted objectively without any interference or vested interest. Transparency in auditing involves maintaining a clear trail of evidence that supports the audit's findings and facilitates an understanding of the auditing process (Barth & Schipper, 2008; Byrnes et al., 2018).

In the financial sector, current regulatory frameworks and legal obligations hold stakeholders to high standards of accountability. Legal entities conduct audits of organizations to provide "certified" proofs of correct accounting and activities for informing management and shareholders as well as proving compliance to regulators. The underlying data can be, for instance, related to financial accounting, governance, environmental compliance (for environmental, social, and governance (ESG) compliance, see also Chap. 10), and the alignment with IT security standards (Cook et al., 2016). Financial platforms may need to demonstrate their liquidity and proper management of deposits to prevent funds mismanagement at a large scale, with failures having led to infamous events such as the FTX/Alameda bankruptcy (Miller & Oliver, 2023). As discussed in Chap. 2, financial institutions (FIs) also need to provide evidence for complying with AML and combating the financing of terrorism (CFT) regulation. Similarly, individuals face various accountability measures, such as tax reporting obligations.

Auditing processes have long been carried out by the manual inspection of data, potentially collected over a long period of time (Byrnes et al., 2018). Reporting has gained growing importance due to regulations on financial record keeping and the reporting of publicly traded companies. With the increasing progress in the digital transformation, real-time and fully automated electronic procedures were introduced. While this approach can improve the effectiveness and speed of audits, they are not yet broadly used on a permanent basis and, therefore, cannot do full justice to the modernization of the financial sector (Byrnes et al., 2018; Bonsón & Bednárová, 2019). However, there are already automated tools in place to control, monitor, and store timely information, e.g., log files, which represent a detailed record of events in an information system (Byrnes et al., 2018).

6.2.2 Auditing in Decentralized Systems

Both data truthfulness and confidentiality are paramount for auditing in financial markets (Baum et al., 2023). On the one hand, users require a high level of control and disclosure of their identifiable and personal data. Therefore, trustful data exchange is crucial for the interacting parties to ensure that no more user-related information than intended and necessary is disclosed. On the other hand, entities such as public institutions and financial service providers should be able to validate (i.e., verify) the trustfulness and integrity of information shared with them. Services based on centralized FIs to manage and process transactions (Qin et al., 2021) have been the dominant model in the financial sector for many years. These intermediaries act as trusted third parties that manage both customers' data and financial risks (Froomkin, 1996). Centralized finance (CeFi) has generally managed to provide accountable and auditable financial systems while safeguarding user's and businesses' sensitive information. Yet, CeFi faces several challenges, such as excessive centralized control, a lack of innovation with corresponding inefficiencies in payment processing, a lack of interoperability, and a certain degree of opacity with respect to large intermediaries' activities (Harvey et al., 2021).

Recently, a different model emerged to tackle trust issues in the financial market paradigm, namely, decentralized finance (DeFi) (Gramlich et al., 2023). These new systems mainly use peer-to-peer (P2P) transactions where two parties interact with each other, involving no trusted intermediary but instead leveraging a blockchain that publicly discloses and validates transactions (Nakamoto, 2008). Blockchains are hash-linked, distributed, immutable, and transparent ledgers that record transactions in a well-defined order, while a decentralized governance mechanism known as consensus ensures consistency (e.g., to avoid double-spending) through economic incentives (Abellán Álvarez et al., 2024). Despite the pseudonymity in the blockchains underlying cryptocurrencies, this transparency can benefit accountability activities (Cai, 2021) (see also Chap. 9). The inherent transparency of DLT as well as the deterministic and atomic transaction management, immutability or tamper-evidence, and the public trail of records resulting from replication, clearly provide potentials for improved auditing (Bonyuet, 2020). The arguably most straightforward accounting practice for DLT is what is commonly referred to as blockchain analysis. Those analyses keep a detailed history of transactions for accounting and reporting purposes. To date, companies have successfully implemented services to facilitate crypto-asset reporting for tax authorities (Dagher et al., 2015; Bonyuet, 2020) and to improve their supply-chain management (Guggenberger et al., 2022; Miehle et al., 2019). Added functionalities, such as the capability to enforce the terms of a contract (Hartwich et al., 2023), may further benefit the reliability of processes and subsequent audits.

On the other hand, many challenges beyond excessive transparency arise from the use of blockchain networks, such as scalability and cost issues (Bonsón & Bednárová, 2019; Pimentel et al., 2021) and complexity (Sedlmeir, 2023). Blockchain-based auditing also requires proper alignment among relevant stakeholders, such as auditors, regulators, and companies (Byrnes et al., 2018; Bonsón & Bednárová, 2019; Pimentel et al., 2021; Iversen et al., 2023). The new capabilities of DeFi protocols can be complex to understand from an auditing perspective (e.g., FlashLoans), particularly through their composability. Moreover, tracing assets involved in cross-chain activities (e.g., bridges or atomic swaps) can be difficult despite the transparency of the underlying blockchain networks (Iversen et al., 2023). Other challenges arise due to the system design differences between different forms of DLT governance and accessibility design objectives (Bonyuet, 2020; Bonsón & Bednárová, 2019) (see also Chap. 3). A fundamental system design consideration is defining the permissions to participate in the consensus of the DLT and the visibility of the ledger. In "private permissioned" DLTs, a consortium of designated entities holds exclusive permissions to decide on transaction inclusion and execution and to access data from the ledger, offering a higher degree of control of governance decisions and data processing (see also Sect. 13). "Permissioned" designs may face risks of maliciously performing modifications via collusion to the ledger altering financial records (Bonyuet, 2020). In contrast, "public permissionless" designs allow arbitrary stakeholders to participate in verifying transactions, which enables stronger verifiability guarantees but also gives any entity read access to all data (Rossi et al., 2019; Baldacci & Frade, 2021). In both cases, there is also a need for integrating "external/off-chain" systems that facilitate the reporting, classification, and management of secondary data for an adequate auditing process (e.g., exchange rate). In sum, even when considering different design choices, decentralized financial markets create a strong tension between auditability and accountability requirements on the one side and the protection of sensitive data on the other side. Note that transparency and auditability are close terms, but not the same. While transparency entails audibility, the exclusion of transparency does not necessarily prevent the latter. Intuitively, we can say that transparent data allows for audits, because the data can be seen, traced, and cross-checked; however, keeping certain data confidential does not prevent its auditability when using, for instance, certain types of PETs (see Sect. 6.4).

6.3 The Privacy Debate

Given the increasing use of IT and the corresponding progress of the digital transformation, the issue of (data) privacy has become a central topic for our society. In the past, mass surveillance was identified as a major threat to individuals' privacy (Clarke, 1988). Nowadays, in highly digital environments where leaving traces is almost inevitable, traditional means of privacy protection are insufficient (Enserink & Chin, 2015). As a result, the concept of privacy has attracted the attention of researchers from various disciplines, but there is still no consensus on an overarching definition that can be applied to all research fields (Zwick & Dholakia, 2004; Smith et al., 2011). Complicating things further, related concepts such as data protection and minimization, confidentiality, secrecy, anonymity, security, and ethics make it more difficult to develop a universally accepted definition of privacy.

In general, privacy can be considered a right, a commodity, a state, or a control. Privacy as control over a certain matter, e.g., information, is a concept that is widely used in various research areas. The reasoning behind this is that control shapes general privacy and, thus, enables this concept (Smith et al., 2011; Laufer & Wolfe, 1977). While the concept of privacy is often associated only with natural persons, in this chapter, we also consider juridical persons or – even more generally – organizations. As such, we define privacy as control over the ability to control information disclosure, providing information at will while protecting and concealing information when desired or deemed necessary (Hughes, 1993; Smith et al., 2011). As such, it corresponds to the concept of what is sometimes called "data sovereignty" (Ernstberger et al., 2023). Technical or organizational measures to achieve this goal, such as privacy-by-design architectures or the PETs we introduce in Sect. 6.4, should be interpreted in the same general sense, expanding their utility far beyond individuals' personally identifiable information (PII) and including sensitive information in the context of organizations. For FIs, such sensitive nonpersonal data may comprise, among others, portfolio compositions and corresponding risk exposure or liquidity-related metrics.

For instance, to augment privacy for web-based communications, the transport layer security (TLS) protocol was introduced in 1999 to provide a layer of encryption and, thus, confidentiality for bilateral communication between authenticated parties. The widespread adoption of TLS in standards such as the hypertext transfer protocol secure (HTTPS) has been made possible by its user-friendly design and mass deployment. As such, cryptography has emerged as an essential tool for protecting individual and collective privacy (Rogaway, 2015). Yet, while encrypted communication has become the default in online interactions, and many messaging apps now even offer end-to-end (E2E) encryption capabilities that prevent the operators of messaging services from getting access to their users' data, applications in the realm of email or payment systems that ensure privacy also with respect to the service provider or FI are less frequent (Gross et al., 2021). Besides operational (e.g., ensuring that a payment is properly authorized and does not change total supply) and regulatory transparency requirements in payment systems (Gross et al., 2021), there are also economic reasons for data collection. In particular, data network effects (Gregory et al., 2021) contribute to the development of large data silos controlled by FIs or Big Tech (Zuboff, 2015). Nevertheless, the protection of sensitive customer information has become a core priority for organizations in many jurisdictions owing to strict regulations, such as the GDPR in the European Union (EU). In verifiable business processes and communications associated with cross-organizational workflows, privacy-by-design is also less frequent. We trace this limited widespread adoption back to the complexity of applications and the challenge of designing systems with well-defined security and privacy-preserving mechanisms while accommodating regulation and ensuring accountability.

In the traditional financial sector, privacy is centrally guaranteed through the implementation of security and privacy standards for data management. Audits are conducted by manual verification of data integrity in a way that external entities examine internal processes and data records to verify its origin. The data is made available to the auditors who diligently perform verification and cross-checking procedures (Cook et al., 2016; Bonyuet, 2020). While CeFi institutions typically offer their customers a decent level of privacy by means of confidentiality (except for data sharing with regulators to comply with AML / CFT regulation or enforcing sanctions), the transparency of DeFi implies a lower degree of privacy, because it allows governments, other authorities, and in fact any entity that can link pseudonymous blockchain addresses to a particular user (e.g., via a previous transaction in account-based models) to track and analyze all their historical financial transactions (Qin et al., 2021; Sedlmeir et al., 2022b).

6.4 Technical Foundations of Privacy-Enhancing Technologies

PETs refer to a set of cryptographic solutions, including primitives, protocols, and system designs, that aim to protect data privacy and security by preventing the unauthorized or unintended disclosure of data while nevertheless facilitating data utilization (Garrido et al., 2022). Recent advancements in cryptography now enable increasingly generic solutions for practical use, which may help ease the aforementioned tension between auditability and accountability on the one side and data privacy on the other side. Consequently, PETs have frequently been explored or used in the context of decentralization technologies. However, particularly general-purpose variants of PETs are often complex to use or come with trade-offs, such as being computationally demanding. Finding the right balance between efficiency and flexibility in implementations and between the amount of input data that can be hidden and the utility obtained from processing remains a challenge that must be considered when developing corresponding solutions.

6.4.1 Verifiable Computation and Zero-Knowledge Proofs

ZKPs, first introduced by Goldwasser et al. (1989), represent a cryptographic technique that can be used to prove that a particular statement is true without conveying any other information that would shed light on why it is true. In other words, ZKPs allow two parties, often referred to as "prover" and "verifier," to engage in an interaction in which the "prover" can (probabilistically) convince a "verifier" of the truthfulness of a statement (Evans & Angeris, 2024), without sharing any other useful information beyond what can be interred easily from the statement itself.

To be regarded as ZKP, the following three properties must be met: *soundness*, *completeness*, and *zero knowledge*. A proof system is complete when the prover is able to convince the verifier of a true statement with high probability. Soundness refers to the fact that the prover can convince the verifier of a wrong statement with only small probability. Zero-knowledge means that no (typically sensitive) information about the reason for the truthfulness of the statement is disclosed or can be extracted from the transcript of the interaction (Goldwasser et al., 1989; Gailly et al., 2022). Even though it is up to the verifier to define which data is needed for verification and, therefore, directly exposed as a part of the statement, it can still be considered a privacy-oriented construction, because the disclosed data can be minimized given the restrictions posed by the involved entities while maintaining verifiability (Babel & Sedlmeir, 2023).

As such, ZKPs allow for "verifiable computation" in the sense that the statement under consideration can be the correct execution of some program with given outputs, without the need for sharing any inputs or intermediary results with the verifier. Nevertheless, there are some limitations that must be taken into account (Ernstberger et al., 2024). First and foremost, some forms of ZKPs are interactive protocols, which means that both participants must be connected through a communication channel and that observers or third parties seeing the transcript will not be convinced of the truthfulness of the statement. While this property can be very useful for privacy as it allows the implementation of targeted ("designated verifier") verifiability guarantees and, therefore, can prevent the unauthorized resharing of verifiable data (Babel & Sedlmeir, 2023), it can also be disadvantageous for recordkeeping and auditability or on blockchains where all nodes would have to be convinced when verifying a ZKP in a smart contract. To counteract this limitation, a specific type of ZKPs is often used, namely, non-interactive zero-knowledge proofs (NIZKPs). First introduced by Blum et al. (1988), NIZKPs involve only a single message ("proof") from the prover to the verifier and, therefore, convince any observer or third party. Generally speaking, NIZKP constructions usually leverage the Fiat-Shamir transformation, which eliminates the interactive process by obtaining the cryptographic randomness from a hash function (Fiat & Shamir, 1986).

A common trade-off for NIZKPs is between security (soundness) guarantees and proving time. The higher the soundness guarantee, the more computationally expensive it will be to generate the proofs, and the larger proof sizes and verification time. Furthermore, NIZKPs require an initial setup, which can be either trusted or transparent. In trusted setups, malicious behavior leads to soundness violations, i.e., the ability to efficiently prove wrong statements. Therefore, honest behavior in this setup process is critical, and decentralized proposals such as those by Ben-Sasson et al. (2015) and Bowe et al. (2017) (which, in turn, are based on multi-party computation (MPC), see below) are used to greatly reduce the trust required in the execution of this phase. Another disadvantage is that the general-purpose ZKPs that facilitate verifiable computation for any program require a large computational effort on the prover side, with the multiplicative overhead being on the order of a million (Thaler, 2020). This can be a substantial obstacle, particularly to the adoption of mobile phone applications (Babel & Sedlmeir, 2023), even though rapid improvements are being observed in the research community, and viable solutions, such as outsourcing to an untrusted, high-performance prover (Chiesa et al., 2023), are emerging. In the following, we will present two very different ways of constructing NIZKPs that are both highly relevant in practical applications.

CL and BBS+ Short Signatures Early on, practical ZKPs could only serve very specific purposes by means of highly efficient constructions that do not face the abovementioned performance challenges. Among the first usages of NIZKPs in practice are Camenisch-Lysyanskaya (CL) signatures. They allow the implementation of an unlinkable and anonymous system of digital attestations (Camenisch & Lysyanskaya, 2001, 2003). Anonymous credentials are a conceptual design for the granular and privacy-preserving, verifiable revelation of attested attributes (e.g., from a digital ID card or diploma). The user or "holder" only proves knowledge of the issuer's (e.g., government's or university's) digital signature but does not reveal anything about the original signature, which could be linked upon repeated presentations of the attestation (Babel & Sedlmeir, 2023). CL signatures have been widely used in pilots for privacy-oriented decentralized digital identity systems (Sedlmeir et al., 2022a) (see also Chap. 4) and are currently being replaced by a scheme with similar capabilities yet faster proof generation and shorter proofs, known as BBS (Boneh et al., 2004) and Boneh-Boyen-Shacham (BBS)+ signatures (Au et al., 2006). In particular, these anonymous credential schemes support the "selective disclosure" of attributes requested by the relying party, as well as unlinkable proofs of non-revocation and range proofs (e.g., to prove that an account balance recorded on the digitally signed attestation exceeds a given threshold, without sharing the account balance) (Glöckler et al., 2023; Kaaniche et al., 2020).

zk-SNARKs A zero-knowledge succinct non-interactive argument of knowledge (zk-SNARK) allows to prove an arbitrary statement (i.e., it is a general-purpose, non-interactive ZKPs) where additionally, proofs are short in size and verification is short in time ("succinctness") relative to the complexity and size of verifying the original statement. Note that zk-SNARKs are a subset of (SNARKs), which are broadly used for blockchain scaling projects for their succinctness. Intuitively, it is relatively easy to make a zk-SNARK from a SNARK, because a succinct proof can no longer contain a lot of detailed information about why a statement is true. Additionally, SNARKs guarantee that the prover indeed knows the reason why the statement being proven is true (Bitansky et al., 2017). Zk-SNARKs address the limitations of special-purpose NIZKPs, such as CL and BBS+ signatures, yet at the cost of substantially larger proving time. It is worth noting that the main drawback of some zk-SNARK – particularly those with very short proofs – is that they require a trusted setup. Nevertheless, trusted setups enable faster proof systems than transparent setups. Note that efficient, thus scalable solutions of general-purpose zk-SNARK positively affect the digital space as more complex statements, including composable statements, can be proven without revealing sensitive information.

One effort concerning SNARKs in general is to achieve transparent setups where no trust is needed in the entity or group that generates common reference strings. Ben-Sasson et al. (2018a) introduced a construction called fast Reed-Solomon interactive oracle proofs of proximity (FRI) that for the first time enabled the design of transparent and succinct general-purpose SNARKs that can easily be converted into zk-SNARKs. Moreover, this construction is plausibly post-quantum secure. Note that the zero-knowledge property for common zk-SNARKs holds unconditionally, but quantum computers can break the soundness guarantees of many SNARK constructions. One implementation of such a design is known as (zk-STARKs) (Ben-Sasson et al., 2018b). zk-STARKs are therefore transparent and post-quantum resistant SNARKs but suffer from the disadvantage that the proofs are generally larger (though still only on the order of tens or hundreds of kilobytes) than the shortest SNARKs. Another somewhat efficient construction of transparent NIZKPs that trades larger proof sizes for higher proving speed is Spartan (Setty, 2020). Emergent solutions that reduce the trade-off between related proving and verification efforts are typically leveraging composability techniques for SNARKs, namely, *compression*, *recursion*, and *aggregation*. Compression uses two different SNARK systems, where one provides a faster prover but produces a larger (but still relatively small) proof, and the second compresses this proof further by verifying it in another SNARKs with longer proving time but shorter proof size. More generally, recursion makes it possible to prove the correct verification of one or more previously computed proofs, thus allowing for constructions such as incrementally verifiable computation (Valiant, 2008). For instance, protocols such as Mina leverage SNARK recursion for compressing the blockchain state. Aggregation, on the other hand, represents a type of composable proof system that enables the combination of a set of different SNARK proofs to be verified all at once in a single SNARK proof only (Gailly et al., 2022). It is particularly useful to save costs when verifying zk-SNARKs on blockchains, where any operation is expensive.

There are some constructions of zk-SNARKs that do not require their implementation in a domain-specific language or a preprocessing step that depends on the computations to be supported. Examples for these zero-knowledge virtual machines (zkVMs) are the zkEVM and RISC-0. ZkVMs run a set of instructions and output verifiable attestations of the correct execution of the program. Thus, they provide a general-purpose, programmable, and privacy-preserving computing environment. However, limitations do exist to the extent that these environments rely on their associated (trusted or transparent) setup phases for instruction sets.

6.4.2 Multiparty Computation

MPC allows a set of N entities to perform computing tasks on their collection of data without revealing each entity's data to any other entity or a third party. MPC designs come in many forms (Kamara et al., 2011): One common construction assumes "honest-but-curious" participants. In this model, for a computation task to be successful, the parties involved should behave honestly, otherwise, the computation will be interrupted or may not lead to a valid result. By contrast, in the malicious attacker model, deviation from the protocol and any dishonest behavior is possible. MPC protocols that guarantee the correctness of results even in this model tend to be more computationally intensive and require more bandwidth.

MPC protocols are primarily built upon cryptographic primitives such as garbled circuits (Yao, 1982), special-purpose ZKPs, and oblivious transfers (Jarecki & Liu, 2009). One can also create malicious attacker-secure MPC from honest-but-curious MPC by using ZKPs to "force" the parties to prove their correct behavior while protecting their sensitive inputs, intermediary results, and outputs in the MPC (Ozdemir & Boneh, 2022). Similar to the case of ZKPs, general-purpose MPC protocols are inefficient. Therefore, many have proposed optimized MPC protocols for particular tasks, such as intrusion detection or statistical analysis (Du & Atallah, 2001; Corrigan-Gibbs & Boneh, 2017). The limits of these protocols usually concern the size of the messages that must be exchanged between the parties (Damgård & Nielsen, 2007). An example of special-purpose MPC applications is the decentralized approach for signature schemes such as the elliptic curve digital signature algorithm (ECDSA) (Aumasson et al., 2020), where a "shared" key pair is generated such that the private key can only be recovered by a certain threshold of parties cooperating, and message signing is possible without exposing or even reconstructing the private key, provided a certain threshold of parties to participate.

Other applications could be envisioned, such as cross-bank average interest rate, as well as performing due diligence or fraud detection checks (The Royal Society, 2023) and suspicious transaction identification where each FI does not share their transaction sub-graph.

6.4.3 Homomorphic Encryption

Encrypted data at rest has many advantages from an information security perspective; however, processing data is commonly done in the clear. Homomorphic encryption (HE) systems allow performing computations on encrypted data without the need to decrypt it first. Simply put, HE allows us to get the same result whether we perform a computation task with raw inputs and then encrypt the result, or first encrypt the raw inputs and perform another operation on the encrypted values (Paillier, 1999).

HE comes in different forms depending on their capabilities, that is, the number and type of operations they can perform (Garrido et al., 2022): partially HE systems support only either addition or multiplication, while fully HE systems support all types of operations (Martins et al., 2017). It is worth noting that while some encryption systems are partially homomorphic (e.g., Rivest-Shamir-Adleman (RSA)), this is not true for all encryption schemes. HE gives some guarantees on the correctness of computations because manipulating the computation would likely produce inconsistent results after decryption. Yet, oftentimes stronger guarantees are required or the correctness of the encryption process ("well-formedness") must be verified. NIZKPs can be helpful here, too. In general, partially HE schemes can be highly efficient, whole fully homomorphic encryption (FHE) is computationally expensive and requires large storage and also bandwidth for sharing results. Thus, this kind of encryption scheme is still largely impractical for general-purpose computation, although substantial advances have been made recently. Some specifically tailored approaches, such as a faster fully HE system for operations in machine learning (Chillotti et al., 2016), can be used in various applications as diverse as image filtering and deep learning neuronal network training (Meyre et al., 2022). A common limitation that makes HE to be considered a subset of MPC protocols is that it often needs to be combined with threshold encryption schemes to achieve the desired goal, e.g., when multiple parties contribute data for joint processing and also should obtain the result.

6.4.4 Trusted Execution Environments

In general, the execution of code on a remote server or device cannot be fully trusted because the device operators or unauthorized users could always try to change or manipulate the behavior of the code during execution by gaining physical or root access. Unforeseen access can also compromise confidentiality and data integrity guarantees at rest. To tackle this problem, one can resort to secure hardware, the most prominent example being trusted execution environments (TEEs) (Fotiadis et al., 2021). They can protect cryptographic keys within the secure hardware and attest to correct processing while ensuring no external access is allowed (Garrido et al., 2022). There are also less general-purpose, but more secure alternatives, such as secure elements – self-contained physical environment with standalone capabilities that can perform a limited range of cryptographic operations, including key management and the generation of digital signatures (Michalopoulos et al., 2024).

TEEs enable "remote attestation", i.e., guarantees of the correct execution of code inside them (Fotiadis et al., 2021). As the trusted and secure environment can generate and securely store cryptographic keys, they support verification procedures (e.g., in the form of electronic passports), where the "remote" verifier can accept or reject the received information based on whether or not they trust the manufacturer of the corresponding chip (Birkholz et al., 2023), representing an alternative to the certificate-based paradigm of decentralized digital identities (see Chap. 4). Moreover, as data can be asymmetrically encrypted for a keypair generated in the secure hardware, TEEs can be used for confidential computing, as the decrypted data does not leak outside the secure processing environment. As such, it represents a powerful and highly efficient alternative to ZKPs and MPC. However, due to numerous vulnerabilities in TEEs, as well as the required trust in manufacturers and their future support for such functionalities, research communities, practitioners and companies are often hesitant to adopt TEEs (Garrido et al., 2022).

6.4.5 Differential Privacy

Differential privacy (DP) is a privacy-enhancing technique that aims to obfuscate statistical queries resulting from a set of fine-granular data in such a way that no meaningful insights about individual records can be extracted from the query result (Dwork, 2006). This technique adds a certain amount of random noise to the output of any statistical analysis in order to protect privacy (Garrido et al., 2022). All computations based on these randomized inputs introduce plausible deniability and, therefore, do not allow any inferences or extractions of sensitive information about specific individuals. The main limitation of such an approach is the loss of accuracy. Therefore, when using DP, there is a strict trade-off between the degree of accuracy of the results and the privacy guarantees against de-anonymization (Fernández et al., 2022). One decentralization technology where DP can be useful is FL (see Chap. 5), where DP noise imposed during the local training can help protect the local models that are shared in the FL process against the extraction of sensitive raw training data. Yet, the adequacy of using DP in FL is still debated (Domingo-Ferrer et al., 2021).

6.5 Foundational Private and Verifiable Applications

6.5.1 Privacy Coins

The introduction of the digital currency and payment network Bitcoin, which can fully function without trusted third parties, has opened the door for decentralized asset transfers. Soon, the research community has broadened its focus beyond payments. Smart contracts are a natural evolution in this permissionless environment. Smart contracts are programs or protocols that automatically execute transactions between different parties on decentralized platforms (Szabo, 1996). The public Ethereum blockchain is a prominent example of a public ledger that integrates such smart contracts, allowing the execution of any deterministic program (Buterin, 2014). As such, Ethereum enables programmable asset transfers that unlock alternative electronic payments, e.g., non-fungible tokens (NFTs). NFTs denote digital tokens that can be held in single or shared ownership and represent unique data such as text, images, or documents (Hartwich et al., 2022).

However, the aforementioned systems, i.e., public blockchains, were not designed with privacy in mind. They only guarantee a certain degree of privacy as long as the real identities behind pseudonymous blockchain addresses are not revealed. To provide higher privacy guarantees, some approaches rely on PETs. The cryptocurrency Zcash, for instance, aims to protect the privacy of senders and recipients by masking sensitive data during the payment process, facilitating unlinkable P2Ps payments using zk-SNARKs (Ben-Sasson et al., 2014). Like most blockchains, it leverages a Merkle tree as the principal data structure. A Merkle tree is a cryptographic data structure represented as a binary tree. It provides an efficient way to store and reference data by fingerprinting each value to its parent node. The parent nodes contain the hash values of their corresponding two children nodes (Merkle, 1987). This construction ensures that any alteration to the original data would result in a complete change in the entire trail of fingerprints. Merkle trees offer various benefits, including efficient proofs of inclusion and non-inclusion, as well as the quick verification of data integrity (Bernal Bernabe et al., 2019).

In Zcash, instead of recording raw transactions (including the sender, receiver, and amount) on a blockchain, only the hash thereof is revealed. A public database stores all transactions hashes and "nullifiers" that have ever existed. A nullifier also corresponds to a transaction hash. Its purpose is to invalidate previously created coins without disclosing which coin. For efficiency, the public database is based on a Merkle tree that (1) serves as an append-only database and (2) enables efficient proofs of inclusion of previously appended hashed transactions (Ben-Sasson et al., 2014). To adequately check whether the rightful owner is spending coins, Zcash uses zk-SNARKs. With zk-SNARKs, the sender can prove that only he/she is the owner of a certain coin—represented by a previously received transaction that has not been spent. To prove that it has indeed not yet been spent, the zk-SNARK also outputs another deterministic hash of the transaction (its corresponding nullifier), so that the smart contract can check whether this nullifier has already been revealed.

Additional accountability measures can be implemented based on this approach, such as demonstrating that a sender is not included in a sanctions list (Barbereau et al., 2023; Nadler & Schär, 2023).

6.5.2 Private Smart Contracts

Blockchain-based applications are often more complex than simple asset transfers, requiring also more general smart contracts (Sedlmeir et al., 2022b). There have been various proposals for such frameworks, and designs for smart contracts that provide different levels of privacy. We outline a few in the following paragraphs.

Ekiden provides a platform that outsources smart contract functions and blockchain consensus to external TEEs (Cheng et al., 2019). This makes it possible to keep the input data private and thus ensures confidentiality while offloading computation to external servers, which also helps improve the throughput of the overall system. However, trusted vendors are necessary to build and distribute TEEs, which may falter decentralization.

Eagle offers privacy-preserving smart contracts leveraging MPC and NIZKPs (Baum et al., 2022). The computation is outsourced to a group of servers running an MPC protocol and information is shared blindly. Nobody but the owner has access to input data unless the MPCs servers collude. The integrity of each server's contribution in the MPC protocol is achieved with NIZKPs, facilitating the verifability of the result in a smart contract.

Zether is a privacy-preserving payment mechanism built to be compatible with existing account-based blockchains in the form of a smart contract (Bünz et al., 2020). The information about the transactions is kept confidential except between the parties conducting the transactions. Nonetheless, Zether may also provide anonymity sets, allowing a group of participants to make transactions without revealing which of them is doing the transactions.

Zero-Knowledge EXEcution (ZEXE) Beyond contributing a formalized crypto-asset transaction model, ZEXE introduces a new building block to offload computation from the ledger for privacy and scalability reasons by embedding a proof of correct computation in the blockchain. Confidential transactions keep information private while short verifiable proofs improves transaction verification's costs. The system enables fully decentralized and private computation on arbitrary assets. One novelty provided by ZEXE is that it can hide which smart contract was executed, providing privacy beyond the realm of an isolated application. Using zk-SNARK ensures that the executed contract exists and is executed correctly (Bowe et al., 2020). ZEXE has been implemented as the core of the smart contract cryptocurrency Aleo.

6.6 Discussion and Conclusion

Driven by regulatory and market forces, sensitive data processing has been increasingly abundant and centralized. Emerging digital ecosystems aim to provide ubiquitous, secure, private, accountable, and practical mechanisms and a full range of digital artifacts that meet both technical and societal needs. It seems that, thus far, there is no one-size-fits-all solution for achieving strong privacy guarantees in decentralized information systems, including blockchains. Accountability is traditionally addressed by providing transparent documentation to auditing and certifying entities. This approach relies on a trusted third party and may violate users' privacy expectations. A corrupted auditor also poses a risk as the resulting certification could be manipulated and/or reveal insider information.

The foundations for building privacy-oriented solutions at a larger scale seem to be already in place. The combination of the above PETs, such as ZKPs and MPC, with decentralized information system can ensure the minimization of information that needs to be disclosed in accountable and verifiable digital interactions. Processing data using PETs helps to use information about the processed data for demonstrating regulatory compliance or value capture in businesses but still guarantees that the specified requirements or limits of the system are met. Privacy-oriented digital identities (Camenisch & Herreweghen, 2003; Garman et al., 2014; Rosenberg et al., 2023; Babel & Sedlmeir, 2023), blockchain-based solutions (Buterin, 2014; Ben-Sasson et al., 2014; Bünz et al., 2020; Bowe et al., 2020; Jaroucheh & Abellán, 2021; Baum et al., 2022), and federated learning architectures (Jäschke & Armknecht, 2019; Ziller et al., 2021; Fernández et al., 2022; Rückel et al., 2022) are just a few examples of the rich yet complex design space of privacy-preserving artifacts based on decentralization technologies and their different tradeoffs. In combination or alone, these concepts may guide the path of decentralized financial markets toward a more successful and scalable future. Yet, finding the right combination of technologies and use cases, as well as the right tradeoff between verifiability/accountability and data minimization once the potential of PETs is fully leveraged, remains crucial.

References

Abellán Álvarez, I., Gramlich, V., & Sedlmeir, J. (2024). Unsealing the secrets of blockchain consensus: A systematic comparison of the formal security of proof-of-work and proof-of-stake. In *Proceedings of the 39th Symposium on Applied Computing*. ACM. https://doi.org/10.1145/3605098.3635970

Au, M. H., Susilo, W., & Mu, Y. (2006). Constant-Size dynamic k-TAA. In *Security and Cryptography for Networks* (pp. 111–125). Springer. https://doi.org/10.1007/11832072_8

Aumasson, J.-P., Hamelink, A., & Shlomovits, O. (2020). A survey of ECDSA threshold signing. https://eprint.iacr.org/2020/1390

Babel, M., & Sedlmeir, J. (2023). Bringing data minimization to digital wallets at scale with general-purpose zero-knowledge proofs. https://arxiv.org/abs/2301.00823

Baldacci, E., & Frade, J. R. (2021). Advancing digital transformation in the public sector with blockchain: A view from the European Union. In *Disintermediation Economics* (pp. 281–295). Springer. https://link.springer.com/10.1007/978-3-030-65781-9_13

Bank for International Settlements (BIS). (2024). The Basel framework. https://www.bis.org/baselframework/BaselFramework.pdf

Barbereau, T., Ermolaev, E., Brennecke, M., Hartwich, E., & Sedlmeir, J. (2023). Beyond a fistful of tumblers: Toward a multi-layered taxonomy of Ethereum-based crypto-asset mixers. In *Proceedings of the 44th International Conference on Information Systems*. AIS. https://aisel.aisnet.org/icis2023/cyber_security/cyber_security/13/

Barth, M. E., & Schipper, K. (2008). Financial reporting transparency. *Journal of Accounting, Auditing & Finance*, *23*, 173–190. https://doi.org/10.1177/0148558X0802300203

Baum, C., Chiang, J. H.-y., David, B., & Frederiksen, T. K. (2022). Eagle: Efficient privacy preserving smart contracts. In *Financial Cryptography and Data Security: 27th International Conference* (pp. 270–288). Springer. https://doi.org/10.1007/978-3-031-47754-6_16

Baum, C., Chiang, J. H.-y., David, B., & Frederiksen, T. K. (2023). SoK: Privacy-enhancing technologies in finance. In *5th Conference on Advances in Financial Technologies*. https://doi.org/10.4230/LIPIcs.AFT.2023.12

Ben-Sasson, E., Bentov, I., Horesh, Y., & Riabzev, M. (2018a). Fast Reed-Solomon interactive oracle proofs of proximity. In *45th International Colloquium on Automata, Languages, and Programming*. https://doi.org/10.4230/LIPIcs.ICALP.2018.14

Ben-Sasson, E., Bentov, I., Horesh, Y., & Riabzev, M. (2018b). Scalable, transparent, and post-quantum secure computational integrity. https://eprint.iacr.org/2018/046.pdf

Ben-Sasson, E., Chiesa, A., Garman, C., Green, M., Miers, I., Tromer, E., & Virza, M. (2014). Zerocash: Decentralized anonymous payments from Bitcoin. In *Symposium on Security and Privacy* (pp. 459–474). IEEE. https://doi.org/10.1109/SP.2014.36

Ben-Sasson, E., Chiesa, A., Green, M., Tromer, E., & Virza, M. (2015). Secure sampling of public parameters for succinct zero knowledge proofs. In *Symposium on Security and Privacy* (pp. 287–304). IEEE. https://doi.org/10.1109/SP.2015.25

Bernal Bernabe, J., Canovas, J. L., Hernandez-Ramos, J. L., Torres Moreno, R., & Skarmeta, A. (2019). Privacy-preserving solutions for blockchain: Review and challenges. *IEEE Access*, *7*, 164908–164940. https://doi.org/10.1109/ACCESS.2019.2950872

Birkholz, H., Thaler, D., Richardson, M., Smith, N., & Pan, W. (2023). *Remote ATtestation procedureS (RATS) Architecture*. RFC 9334. IETF. https://www.rfc-editor.org/rfc/rfc9334

Bitansky, N., Canetti, R., Chiesa, A., Goldwasser, S., Lin, H., Rubinstein, A., & Tromer, E. (2017). The hunting of the SNARK. *Journal of Cryptology*, *30*(4), 989–1066. https://doi.org/10.1007/s00145-016-9241-9

Blum, M., Feldman, P., & Micali, S. (1988). Non-interactive zero-knowledge and its applications. In *Proceedings of the 20th Annual Symposium on Theory of Computing* (pp. 103–112). ACM. https://doi.org/10.1145/62212.62222

Boneh, D., Boyen, X., & Shacham, H. (2004). Short group signatures. In *Annual International Cryptology Conference* (pp. 41–55). Springer. https://doi.org/10.1007/978-3-540-28628-8_3

Bons, R. W., Versendaal, J., Zavolokina, L., & Shi, W. L. (2020). Potential and limits of blockchain technology for networked businesses. *Electronic Markets*, *30*(2), 189–194. https://doi.org/10.1007/s12525-020-00421-8

Bonsón, E., & Bednárová, M. (2019). Blockchain and its implications for accounting and auditing. *Meditari Accountancy Research*, *27*(5), 725–740. https://doi.org/10.1108/MEDAR-11-2018-0406

Bonyuet, D. (2020). Overview and impact of blockchain on auditing. *The International Journal of Digital Accounting Research* (pp. 31–43). https://doi.org/10.4192/1577-8517-v20_2

Bowe, S., Chiesa, A., Green, M., Miers, I., Mishra, P., & Wu, H. (2020). ZEXE: Enabling decentralized private computation. In *Symposium on Security and Privacy* (pp. 947–964). IEEE. https://doi.org/10.1109/SP40000.2020.00050

Bowe, S., Gabizon, A., & Miers, I. (2017). Scalable multi-party computation for zk-SNARK parameters in the random beacon model. https://eprint.iacr.org/2017/1050.pdf

Buterin, V. (2014). A next-generation smart contract and decentralized application platform. https://ethereum.org/en/whitepaper

Byrnes, P. E., Al-Awadhi, A., Gullvist, B., Brown-Liburd, H., Teeter, R., Warren, J. D., & Vasarhelyi, M. (2018). Evolution of auditing: From the traditional approach to the future audit. In *Continuous Auditing* (pp. 285–297). Emerald. https://doi.org/10.1108/978-1-78743-413-420181014

Búnz, B., Agrawal, S., Zamani, M., & Boneh, D. (2020). Zether: Towards privacy in a smart contract world. In *International Conference on Financial Cryptography and Data Security* (pp. 423–443). Springer. https://doi.org/10.1007/978-3-030-51280-4_23

Cai, C. W. (2021). Triple-entry accounting with blockchain: How far have we come? *Accounting & Finance*, *61*(1), 71–93. https://doi.org/https://doi.org/10.1111/acfi.12556

Camenisch, J., & Herreweghen, E. (2003). Design and implementation of the Idemix anonymous credential system. In *Proceedings of the ACM Conference on Computer and Communications Security* (pp. 21–30). https://doi.org/10.1145/586110.586114

Camenisch, J., & Lysyanskaya, A. (2001). An efficient system for non-transferable anonymous credentials with optional anonymity revocation. In *International Conference on the Theory and Applications of Cryptographic Techniques* (pp. 93–118). Springer. https://doi.org/10.1007/3-540-44987-6_7

Camenisch, J., & Lysyanskaya, A. (2003). A signature scheme with efficient protocols. In *International Conference on Security in Communication Networks* (pp. 268–289). Springer. https://doi.org/10.1007/3-540-36413-7_20

Cavoukian, A. (2009). Privacy by design: The 7 foundational principles. Information and privacy commissioner of Ontario, Canada. https://www.ipc.on.ca/wp-content/uploads/2018/01/pbd.pdf

Chatzigiannis, P., Baldimtsi, F., & Chalkias, K. (2021). SoK: Auditability and accountability in distributed payment systems. In *International Conference on Applied Cryptography and Network Security* (pp. 311–337). Springer. https://doi.org/10.1007/978-3-030-78375-4_13

Cheng, R., et al. (2019). Ekiden: A platform for confidentiality-preserving, trustworthy, and performant smart contracts. In *European Symposium on Security and Privacy* (pp. 185–200). IEEE. https://doi.org/10.1109/EuroSP.2019.00023

Chiesa, A., Lehmkuhl, R., Mishra, P., & Zhang, Y. (2023). EOS: Efficient private delegation of zkSNARK provers. In *32nd USENIX Security Symposium*. USENIX Association. https://www.usenix.org/system/files/sec23fall-prepub-492-chiesa.pdf

Chillotti, I., Gama, N., Georgieva, M., & Izabachene, M. (2016). Faster fully homomorphic encryption: Bootstrapping in less than 0.1 seconds. In *22nd International Conference on the Theory and Application of Cryptology and Information Security* (pp. 3–33). Springer. https://doi.org/10.1007/978-3-662-53887-6_1

Clarke, R. (1988). Information technology and dataveillance. *Communications of the ACM*, *31*(5), 498–512. https://doi.org/10.1145/42411.42413

Codagnone, C., & Weigl, L. (2023). Leading the charge on digital regulation: The more, the better, or policy bubble? *Digital Society*, *2*(1). https://doi.org/10.1007/s44206-023-00033-7

Cook, W., van Bommel, S., & Turnhout, E. (2016). Inside environmental auditing: Effectiveness, objectivity, and transparency. *Current Opinion in Environmental Sustainability*, *18*, 33–39. https://doi.org/10.1016/j.cosust.2015.07.016

Corrigan-Gibbs, H., & Boneh, D. (2017). Prio: Private, robust, and scalable computation of aggregate statistics. In *14th USENIX Symposium on Networked Systems Design and Implementation* (pp. 259–282). USENIX Association. https://www.usenix.org/system/files/conference/nsdi17/nsdi17-corrigan-gibbs.pdf

Dagher, G. G., Bunz, B., Bonneau, J., Clark, J., & Boneh, D. (2015). Provisions: Privacy-preserving proofs of solvency for Bitcoin exchanges. In *Proceedings of the 22nd ACM SIGSAC Conference on Computer and Communications Security* (pp. 720–731). https://doi.org/10.1145/2810103.2813674

Damgård, I., & Nielsen, J. B. (2007). Scalable and unconditionally secure multiparty computation. In *Annual International Cryptology Conference* (pp. 572–590). Springer. https://doi.org/10.1007/978-3-540-74143-5_32

Domingo-Ferrer, J., Sánchez, D., & Blanco-Justicia, A. (2021). The limits of differential privacy (and its misuse in data release and machine learning). *Communications of the ACM*, *64*(7), 33–35. https://doi.org/10.1145/3433638

Du, W., & Atallah, M. J. (2001). Secure multi-party computation problems and their applications: A review and open problems. In *Proceedings of the Workshop on New Security Paradigms* (pp. 13–22). ACM. https://doi.org/10.1145/508171.508174

Dwork, C. (2006). Differential privacy. In *Proceedings of the 33rd International Conference on Automata, Languages and Programming*. Springer. https://doi.org/10.1007/11787006_1

Enserink, M., & Chin, G. (2015). The end of privacy. *Science*, *347*, 490–491. https://doi.org/10.1126/science.347.6221.490

Ernstberger, J., Chaliasos, S., Zhou, L., Jovanovic, P., & Gervais, A. (2024). Do you need a zero knowledge proof? In *CfC St. Moritz Academic Research Track*. https://eprint.iacr.org/2024/050

Ernstberger, J., et al. (2023). SoK: Data sovereignty. In *8th European Symposium on Security and Privacy* (pp. 122–143). IEEE.

European Commission. (2021). Anti-money laundering and countering the financing of terrorism legislative package. https://finance.ec.europa.eu/publications/anti-money-laundering-and-countering-financing-terrorism-legislative-package_en

Evans, A., & Angeris, G. (2024). Succinct proofs and linear algebra. https://eprint.iacr.org/2023/1478

Fernández, J. D., Menci, S. P., Lee, C. M., Rieger, A., & Fridgen, G. (2022). Privacy-preserving federated learning for residential short-term load forecasting. *Applied Energy*, *326*, 119915. https://doi.org/10.1016/j.apenergy.2022.119915

Fiat, A., & Shamir, A. (1986). How to prove yourself: Practical solutions to identification and signature problems. In *Conference on the Theory and Application of Cryptographic Techniques* (pp. 186–194). Springer. https://link.springer.com/content/pdf/10.1007/3-540-47721-7_12.pdf

Fotiadis, G., Moreira, J., Giannetsos, T., Chen, L., Rønne, P. B., Ryan, M. D., & Ryan, P. Y. A. (2021). Root-of-Trust abstractions for symbolic analysis: Application to attestation protocols. In *Security and Trust Management* (pp. 163–184). Springer. https://link.springer.com/10.1007/978-3-030-91859-0_9

Fridgen, G., Radszuwill, S., Urbach, N., & Utz, L. (2018). Cross-organizational workflow management using blockchain technology – towards applicability, auditability, and automation. In *Proceedings of the 51st Hawaii International Conference on System Sciences* (pp. 3507–3516). https://doi.org/10.24251/hicss.2018.444

Froomkin, A. M. (1996). The essential role of trusted third parties in electronic commerce. *75 Oregon Law Review*, *49*, 119–176. https://papers.ssrn.com/sol3/papers.cfm?abstract_id=11450

Gailly, N., Maller, M., & Nitulescu, A. (2022). SnarkPack: Practical SNARK aggregation. In *Financial Cryptography and Data Security* (pp. 203–229). Springer. https://doi.org/10.1007/978-3-031-18283-9_10

Garman, C., Green, M., & Miers, I. (2014). Decentralized anonymous credentials. In *Network and Distributed System Security Symposium*. Internet Society. https://doi.org/10.14722/ndss.2014.23253

Garrido, G. M., Sedlmeir, J., Uludağ, O., Alaoui, I. S., Luckow, A., & Matthes, F. (2022). Revealing the landscape of privacy-enhancing technologies in the context of data markets for the IoT: A systematic literature review. *Journal of Network and Computer Applications*, *207*. https://doi.org/10.1016/j.jnca.2022.103465

Glöckler, J., Sedlmeir, J., Frank, M., & Fridgen, G. (2023). A systematic review of identity and access management requirements in enterprises and potential contributions of self-sovereign identity. *Business & Information Systems Engineering*. https://doi.org/10.1007/s12599-023-00830-x

Goldwasser, S., Micali, S., & Rackoff, C. (1989). The knowledge complexity of interactive proof systems. *SIAM Journal on Computing*, *18*(1), 186–208. https://doi.org/10.1145/22145.22178

Gramlich, V., Guggenberger, T., Principato, M., Schellinger, B., & Urbach, N. (2023). A multivocal literature review of decentralized finance: Current knowledge and future research avenues. *Electronic Markets*, *33*. https://doi.org/10.1007/s12525-023-00637-4

Gregory, R. W., Henfridsson, O., Kaganer, E., & Kyriakou, H. (2021). The role of artificial intelligence and data network effects for creating user value. *Academy of Management Review, 46*(3), 534–551. https://doi.org/10.5465/amr.2019.0178

Gross, J., Sedlmeir, J., Babel, M., Babel, M., Bechtel, A., Schellinger, B., & Schellinger, B. (2021). Designing a central bank digital currency with support for cash-like privacy. https://papers.ssrn.com/sol3/papers.cfm?abstract_id=3891121

Guggenberger, T., Sedlmeir, J., Fridgen, G., & Luckow, A. (2022). An in-depth investigation of the performance characteristics of Hyperledger Fabric. *Computers and Industrial Engineering, 173*, 108716. https://doi.org/10.1016/j.cie.2022.108716

Hartwich, E., Ollig, P., Fridgen, G., & Rieger, A. (2022). Probably something: A multi-layer taxonomy of non-fungible tokens. *Internet Research*. https://doi.org/10.1108/INTR-08-2022-0666

Hartwich, E., Rieger, A., Sedlmeir, J., Jurek, D., & Fridgen, G. (2023). Machine economies. *Electronic Markets, 33*. https://doi.org/10.1007/s12525-023-00649-0

Harvey, C. R., Ramachandran, A., & Santoro, J. (2021). *DeFi and the future of finance*. Wiley.

Hughes, E. (1993). A cypherpunk's manifesto. https://www.activism.net/cypherpunk/manifesto.html

Iversen, H. M. W., Schmidt, T. A., Pedersen, A. B., & Beck, R. (2023). How to cross the bridge: Interoperability among blockchain systems. In *Proceedings of the 44th International Conference on Information Systems*. AIS. https://aisel.aisnet.org/icis2023/blockchain/blockchain/4

Jarecki, S., & Liu, X. (2009). Efficient oblivious pseudorandom function with applications to adaptive OT and secure computation of set intersection. In *Theory of Cryptography Conference* (pp. 577–594). Springer. https://doi.org/10.1007/978-3-642-00457-5_34

Jaroucheh, Z., & Abellán, I. (2021). Secretation: Toward a decentralised identity and verifiable credentials based scalable and decentralised secret management solution. In *International Conference on Blockchain and Cryptocurrency*. IEEE. https://doi.org/10.1109/ICBC51069.2021.9461144

Jäschke, A., & Armknecht, F. (2019). Unsupervised machine learning on encrypted data. In *International Conference on Selected Areas in Cryptography* (pp. 453–478). Springer. https://doi.org/10.1007/978-3-030-10970-7_21

Kaaniche, N., Laurent, M., & Belguith, S. (2020). Privacy enhancing technologies for solving the privacy-personalization paradox: Taxonomy and survey. *Journal of Network and Computer Applications, 171*, 102807. https://doi.org/j.jnca.2020.102807

Kamara, S., Mohassel, P., & Raykova, M. (2011). Outsourcing multi-party computation. https://eprint.iacr.org/2011/272

Kannengießer, N., Lins, S., Dehling, T., & Sunyaev, A. (2020). Trade-offs between distributed ledger technology characteristics. *ACM Computing Surveys, 53*. https://doi.org/10.1145/3379463

Laufer, R. S., & Wolfe, M. (1977). Privacy as a concept and a social issue: A multidimensional developmental theory. *Journal of Social Issues, 33*, 22–42. https://doi.org/10.1111/j.1540-4560.1977.tb01880.x

Martins, P., Sousa, L., & Mariano, A. (2017). A survey on fully homomorphic encryption: An engineering perspective. *ACM Computing Surveys, 50*. https://doi.org/10.1145/3124441

Merkle, R. C. (1987). A digital signature based on a conventional encryption function. In *Conference on the Theory and Application of Cryptographic Techniques* (pp. 369–378)

Meyre, A., Chevallier-Mames, B., Frery, J., Stoian, A., Bredehoft, R., Montero, L., & Kherfallah, C. (2022). Concrete-ML: A privacy-preserving machine learning library using fully homomorphic encryption for data scientists. https://github.com/zama-ai/concrete-ml

Michalopoulos, P., Olowookere, O., Pocher, N., Sedlmeir, J., Veneris, A., & Puri, P. (2024). Compliance design options for offline CBDCs: Balancing privacy and AML/CFT. In *Proceedings on the 6th International Conference on Blockchain and Cryptocurrency*. IEEE.

Miehle, D., Henze, D., Seitz, A., Luckow, A., & Bruegge, B. (2019). PartChain: A decentralized traceability application for multi-tier supply chain networks in the automotive industry. In

International Conference on Decentralized Applications and Infrastructure (pp. 140–145). IEEE. https://doi.org/10.1109/dappcon.2019.00027

Miller, J., & Oliver, J. (2023). Sam Bankman-Fried convicted of fraud over FTX collapse. Financial Times. https://www.ft.com/content/24d153b0-0c28-4946-acbe-2e93329bca52

Nadler, M., & Schär, F. (2023). Tornado Cash and blockchain privacy: A primer for economists and policymakers. *Federal Reserve Bank of St. Louis Review, 105*(2), 122–136. https://doi.org/10.20955/r.105.122-136

Nakamoto, S. (2008). A peer-to-peer electronic cash system. https://bitcoin.org/bitcoin.pdf

Ozdemir, A., & Boneh, D. (2022). Experimenting with collaborative zk-SNARKs: Zero-knowledge proofs for distributed secrets. In *31st USENIX Security Symposium* (pp. 4291–4308). USENIX Association. https://www.usenix.org/system/files/usenixsecurity22-ozdemir.pdf

Paillier, P. (1999). Public-key cryptosystems based on composite degree residuosity classes. In *International Conference on the Theory and Applications of Cryptographic Techniques* (pp. 223–238). Springer. https://doi.org/10.1007/3-540-48910-X_16

Pimentel, E., Boulianne, E., Eskandari, S., & Clark, J. (2021). Systemizing the challenges of auditing blockchain-based assets. *Journal of Information Systems, 35*(2), 61–75. https://doi.org/10.2308/ISYS-19-007

Platt, M., Bandara, R. J., Drăgnoiu, A.-E., & Krishnamoorthy, S. (2021). Information privacy in decentralized applications. In *Trust Models for Next-Generation Blockchain Ecosystems* (pp. 85–104). Springer. https://doi.org/10.1007/978-3-030-75107-4_4

Pocher, N. (2023). *Distributed Ledger Technologies between Anonymity and Transparency: AML/CFT Regulation of Cryptocurrency Ecosystems in the EU*. PhD thesis, Alma Mater Studiorum Università di Bologna, Universitat Autònoma de Barcelona, KU Leuven. https://doi.org/10.48676/unibo/amsdottorato/10659

Qin, K., Zhou, L., Afonin, Y., Lazzaretti, L., & Gervais, A. (2021). CeFi vs. DeFi – comparing centralized to decentralized finance. https://arxiv.org/abs/2106.08157

Rieger, A., Guggenmos, F., Lockl, J., Fridgen, G., & Urbach, N. (2019). Building a blockchain application that complies with the EU general data protection regulation. *MIS Quarterly Executive, 18*, 263–279. https://doi.org/10.17705/2msqe.00020

Rogaway, P. (2015). The moral character of cryptographic work. https://web.cs.ucdavis.edu/~rogaway/papers/moral-fn.pdf

Rosenberg, M., White, J., Garman, C., & Miers, I. (2023). zk-creds: Flexible anonymous credentials from zkSNARKs and existing identity infrastructure. In *Symposium on Security and Privacy* (pp. 790–808). IEEE. https://doi.org/10.1109/SP46215.2023.10179430

Rossi, M., Mueller-Bloch, C., Thatcher, J. B., & Beck, R. (2019). Blockchain research in information systems: Current trends and an inclusive future research agenda. *Journal of the Association for Information Systems, 20*(9), 1388–1403. https://doi.org/10.17705/1jais.00571

Rückel, T., Sedlmeir, J., & Hofmann, P. (2022). Fairness, integrity, and privacy in a scalable blockchain-based federated learning system. *Computer Networks, 202*, 108621. https://doi.org/10.1016/j.comnet.2021.108621

Schlatt, V., Sedlmeir, J., Feulner, S., & Urbach, N. (2022). Designing a framework for digital KYC processes built on blockchain-based self-sovereign identity. *Information & Management, 59*(7). https://doi.org/10.1016/j.im.2021.103553

Sedlmeir, J. (2023). *Blockchain Adoption in Organizations: Technical Barriers and Potential Solutions*. PhD thesis, University of Bayreuth. https://doi.org/10.15495/EPub_UBT_00007183

Sedlmeir, J., Barbereau, T., Huber, J., Weigl, L., & Roth, T. (2022a). Transition pathways towards design principles of self-sovereign identity. In *Proceedings of the 43rd International Conference on Information Systems*. AIS. https://aisel.aisnet.org/icis2022/is_implement/is_implement/4/

Sedlmeir, J., Lautenschlager, J., Fridgen, G., & Urbach, N. (2022b). The transparency challenge of blockchain in organizations. *Electronic Markets, 32*, 1779–1794. https://doi.org/10.1007/s12525-022-00536-0

Setty, S. (2020). Spartan: Efficient and general-purpose zkSNARKs without trusted setup. In *Annual International Cryptology Conference* (pp. 704–737). Springer. 10.1007/978-3-030-56877-1_25

Smith, H. J., Dinev, T., & Xu, H. (2011). Information privacy research: An interdisciplinary review. *MIS Quarterly, 35*(4), 989–1016. https://doi.org/10.2307/41409970

Szabo, N. (1996). Smart contracts: building blocks for digital markets. *EXTROPY: The Journal of Transhumanist Thought, 18*(2), 28. https://www.fon.hum.uva.nl/rob/Courses/InformationInSpeech/CDROM/Literature/LOTwinterschool2006/szabo.best.vwh.net/smart_contracts_2.html

Teece, D. J. (1993). Information sharing, innovation, and antitrust. *Antitrust Law Journal, 62*(4), 465–481. https://www.jstor.org/stable/40844123

Thaler, J. (2020). *Proofs, arguments, and zero-knowledge*. Foundations and trends in privacy and security. Now Publishers. https://people.cs.georgetown.edu/jthaler/ProofsArgsAndZK.pdf

The Royal Society. (2023). From privacy to partnership: The role of privacy enhancing technologies in data governance and collaborative analysis. https://royalsociety.org/news-resources/projects/privacy-enhancing-technologies/

Valiant, P. (2008). Incrementally verifiable computation or proofs of knowledge imply time/space efficiency. In *Theory of cryptography*. Springer. https://doi.org/10.1007/978-3-540-78524-8_1

Weigl, L., Barbereau, T. J., Sedlmeir, J., & Zavolokina, L. (2023). Mediating the tension between data sharing and privacy: The case of DMA and GDPR. In *Proceedings of the 31st European Conference on Information Systems*. AIS. https://aisel.aisnet.org/ecis2023_rip/49/

White, L. J. (2015). Antitrust and financial regulation in the wake of Philadelphia National Bank: Complements, not substitutes. *Antitrust Law Journal, 80*, 413. https://www.jstor.org/stable/26411543

Yao, A. C. (1982). Protocols for secure computations. In *23rd Annual Symposium on Foundations of Computer Science* (pp. 160–164). IEEE. https://doi.org/10.1109/SFCS.1982.38

Yin, X., Zhu, Y., & Hu, J. (2021). A comprehensive survey of privacy-preserving federated learning: A taxonomy, review, and future directions. *ACM Computing Surveys, 54*(6). https://doi.org/10.1145/3460427

Ziller, A., et al. (2021). ySyft: A library for easy federated learning. In *Federated Learning Systems: Towards Next-Generation AI* (pp. 111–139). Springer. https://doi.org/10.1007/978-3-030-70604-3_5

Zuboff, S. (2015). Big other: Surveillance capitalism and the prospects of an information civilization. *Journal of Information Technology, 30*, 75–89. https://doi.org/10.1057/jit.2015.5

Zwick, D., & Dholakia, N. (2004). Whose identity is it anyway? Consumer representation in the age of database marketing. *Journal of Macromarketing, 24*, 31–43. https://doi.org/10.1177/0276146704263920

Part III
Applications

Chapter 7
Self-Sovereign Identity for Digital KYC

Simon Feulner, Vincent Schlatt, Tobias Guggenberger, Fabiane Völter, and Jens-Christian Stoetzer

Abstract Current know-your-customer (KYC) processes at financial institutions are inefficient, costly, and – in many cases – inconvenient for customers. Among the often-mentioned solutions to improve KYC processes are blockchains and self-sovereign identity (SSI). However, the literature provides little guidance on those technologies with regard to regulatory compliance and efficiency. Hence, we propose a framework for blockchain-based SSI in KYC processes, which can mitigate some of the current challenges of KYC. Our framework provides guidance for practitioners and academia on how to design blockchain-based SSI processes in KYC.

7.1 Motivation

Besides financial inclusion and stability, financial regulation also primarily aims to achieve market integrity (Zetzsche et al., 2018), thus avoiding fraudulent behavior such as insider dealing, the unlawful disclosure of inside information, and market manipulation. In order to ensure the latter, regulators have implemented various regulatory measures within the financial sector, including the Financial Action Task Force (FATF) recommendations, which aim to prevent money laundering and the financing of international terrorism, as well as Basel III, which defines

S. Feulner
Frankfurt University of Applied Sciences, Frankfurt am Main, Germany
e-mail: simon.feulner@fim-rc.de

V. Schlatt · T. Guggenberger
Branch Business & Information Systems Engineering of the Fraunhofer FIT, Sankt Augustin, Germany

FIM Research Center, University of Bayreuth, Bayreuth, Germany
e-mail: tobias.guggenberger@fim-rc.de

F. Völter · J.-C. Stoetzer (✉)
FIM Research Center, University of Bayreuth, Bayreuth, Germany
e-mail: fabiane.voelter@fim-rc.de; jens.stoetzer@fim-rc.de

G. Fridgen et al. (eds.), *Decentralization Technologies*, Financial Innovation and Technology, https://doi.org/10.1007/978-3-031-66047-4_7

equity requirements in response to the 2008 global financial crisis (Arner et al., 2016). These measures are considered international standards (Ruce, 2011). A crucial component of these measures is the KYC process, which requires financial institutions to avoid opening anonymous accounts or accounts with blatantly fictitious names. In this context, due diligence is recommended to verify customer identities using independent, reliable documents (Arasa & Ottichilo, 2015).

The KYC process represents challenges for financial institutions, as it is time-consuming, inconvenient for customers, and resulting in estimated €12 billion operating costs for banks in Europe alone (Zetzsche et al., 2018; Pratz & Weiss, 2024). Several attempts at improvement have been made, primarily involving the digitization or outsourcing of specific process steps. For example, some banks utilize customers' analog identification documents, like passports, to create digital customer identities for internal use and streamline the process. However, this approach still suffers from inefficiencies, being error-prone, time-consuming (Jessel et al., 2018), and highly repetitive (Zetzsche et al., 2018). The absence of shared standards and banks' reluctance to share customer information with competitors also restrict the reusability of a customer's KYC data across different banks (Arner et al., 2019).

A centralized utility that gathers and supplies identity-related data for an electronic KYC (eKYC) process, as implemented in India or Australia, is often suggested as a solution to these issues (Zetzsche et al., 2018; Arner et al., 2019; Perlman & Gurung, 2019). Such a utility can reduce costs and significantly expedite KYC onboarding processes (Rajput & Gopinath, 2017). However, recent instances of leaks and misuse of personal data have diminished both banks' and customers' confidence in solutions that create central data repositories (Swinhoe, 2020). Generally, the apprehension of significant market or political power concentration in a distinct service provider can hinder the establishment of a widely accepted centralized provider (Zavolokina et al., 2020; Sedlmeir et al., 2022). From a regulatory perspective, the evaluation of the electronic Identification, Authentication and Trust Services (eIDAS) regulation lays the foundation for a neutral and General Data Protection Regulation (GDPR)-compliant identity management systems. In this context, KYC-processes serve as a primary use-case for eIDAS (European Commission, 2023).

This alternative approach involves depositing KYC information with customers in a standardized format. Therefore, SSI is a promising solution, which aspires to create a comprehensive digital identity management system based on the paradigm that users control all their data, similar to current analog identity management using plastic cards in physical wallets (Sedlmeir et al., 2021; Weigl et al., 2022). However, SSI remains closely tied to blockchain technology, because it requires a neutral platform that offers governance, standards, and essential public information for verifying the validity of attestations (Guggenberger et al., 2020). Due to the abovementioned disadvantages of central authorities, its promise of an interoperable digital identity management system without a central authority in control makes SSI particularly appealing for digitizing the KYC process. Initial studies have illustrated the potential of SSI-based KYC and concluded that an SSI-based "portable identity significantly improves both consumer experience and protection while accelerating customer onboarding and reducing KYC and compliance-related costs for financial institutions" (Ledger Insights, 2020). Thus, both research and practice require a generic and validated framework to guide the design of SSI solutions for comprehensive eKYC processes, as well as an overview of the resulting implications to evaluate potential benefits and learn how to leverage them. In this chapter, we present an eKYC framework built on blockchain-based SSI. We thereby focus on the European jurisdiction.

7.1.1 The KYC Process and Centralized Attempts to eKYC

KYC processes may differ owing to countries' different regulatory requirements and the banks' specific requirements. However, some repeating patterns of the KYC process can be identified (see Fig. 7.1). We will describe these patterns in the following. The process begins with the collection of data about potential customers to identify them. Government-issued documents are preferred but can be complemented by documents, such as telephone or gas invoices issued by companies (Mugarura, 2014).

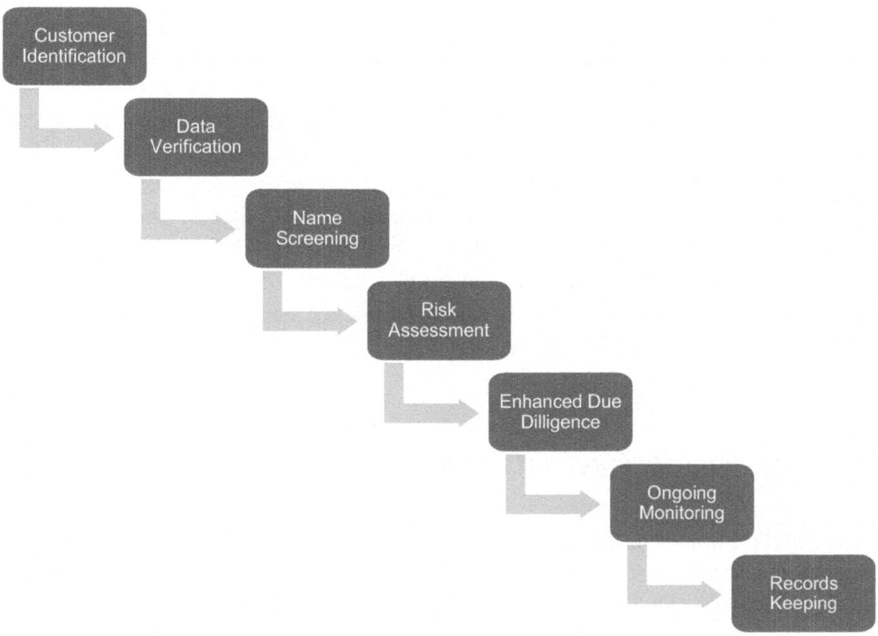

Fig. 7.1 The KYC process

After customer identification and the verification of identity data claims, the bank checks whether the person represents a risk to the financial institution. This audit includes a matching against a list of known terrorists, criminals, and politically exposed persons (Arasa & Ottichilo, 2015). Further initial and ongoing measures follow to allow the bank to perform permanent risk monitoring.

Thus, the KYC process is very time-intensive and inconvenient for both customers and banks, leading to poor customer experiences and a limited number of account openings (Thomson Reuters, 2016), and resulting in the need for financial institutions to make essential improvements. Further, the estimated operative KYC costs amount to about €200 million to €400 million for a typical larger bank. An improved process could significantly reduce these costs (Pratz & Weiss, 2024). The digitization and automation of processes and the resulting opportunities for data processing and analysis can simultaneously reduce compliance costs, prevent regulatory penalties, and harness new potential (Lootsma, 2017).

Thereby, the term eKYC describes the digitization of analog documents altogether (Christie, 2018). A sector-wide eKYC utility could avoid the repeated execution of the KYC process at different banks. These systems typically use biometrics such as fingerprints, iris scans, or facial recognition. The data is then stored on a smart ID card and supplemented by online information deposited in a central database, together with personally identifiable information such as the customer's name, age, or place of residence. During the eKYC process, the customer's biometric data are captured and matched against the data in the central online database.

An example of such a sector-wide eKYC utility is India's centralized Aadhaar system (Zetzsche et al., 2018). The system has led to faster onboarding times and fewer losses from fraud and corruption (The Economist, 2016). However, several data breaches have raised questions regarding the privacy and security of the system (Zetzsche et al., 2018). While it is a key step toward increasing process efficiency, the design of the used identity systems is critical for their success and acceptance, because they process highly sensitive data in the context of KYC applications. Thus, applying digital identity systems to the KYC procedure not only requires benefits regarding the system's efficiency and user experience but also concerning privacy and security (Perlman & Gurung, 2019).

7.1.2 SSI and Its Potential Application to eKYC

Owing to the limitations and downsides of centralized platforms, banks have started exploring technical alternatives to the existing KYC processes, one being distributed ledger technology (DLT). Considering the generic properties of DLT, a blockchain-based, neutral platform on which banks could collaborate on eKYC seems very appealing, since this approach can eliminate the threat of monopolies. However, it aggravates the privacy-related problems due to the immutability and transparency of stored data (Rieger et al., 2019; Kolb et al., 2020; Sedlmeir et al., 2022), which complicates the integration of a DLT into the KYC process.

Today, identification and authentication are usually carried out against a service provider using a username and password, a so-called *centralized* identity model, which is related to several disadvantages, such as poor user experiences and security issues (Rajput & Gopinath, 2017; Sedlmeir et al., 2021). A novel approach for identities, thus, puts the users in full control of their data. This approach has been called *self-sovereign* (Allen, 2016).

Since the concept places users in full control, some challenges arise in SSI. First, user-friendliness must be ensured. Second, a governance framework is required to establish the possibility of gaining trust in a large variety of issuers. Third, the users' authenticity must be guaranteed (Camenisch & Lysyanskaya, 2001). However, various concepts, such as the use of user-friendly interfaces, biometric authentication on mobile phones in combination with secure hardware for cryptographic key management, as well as zero-knowledge proof (ZKP) and trust registries, allow to address these issues (Davie et al., 2019; Hardman et al., 2019; Hardman, 2020; Glöckler et al., 2023). In sum, SSI allows for highly decentralized management of personal identifiers and electronic attestations that are reusable across different contexts to be managed by the user from a single app. We investigate how this approach may help solve the challenges of the eKYC process.

7.2 Consideration for an Improved KYC System

To address the challenges of the KYC process comprehensively, we propose five main objectives for an effective SSI-based eKYC framework from the literature. The current KYC process is often costly and labor-intensive, presenting challenges for financial institutions. Fast and convenient identity verification can reduce costs, enhance customer appeal, and provide a competitive advantage. To achieve greater efficiency, we find three requirements: *end-to-end digital processing of relevant documents*, *automation of manual processes*, and *interbank collaboration*.

Objective 1: Regulatory Compliance Compliance with regulations is a crucial aspect of the KYC process (Ostern & Riedel, 2020). The *money laundering act (MLA)* sets requirements for customer identification and risk record storage. The *GDPR* governs the processing of data concerning natural persons but not legal entities, imposing several requirements. Moreover, the 5th European Union (EU) anti-money laundering (AML) Directive accepts electronic ID systems that comply with eIDAS as legitimate means of identification for KYC procedures (Arner et al., 2019). *eIDAS* imposes requirements on electronic means of identification, such as compliance with specific levels of assurance and the cross-border interoperability of systems.

Objective 2: Decentralization Centralized customer data silos are attractive targets for attackers, and securing such information is costly and not a core business of banks. Mistakes can have severe consequences for reputation, fines, or both (Rajput & Gopinath, 2017). To avoid similar data breaches, an improved eKYC process should *avoid central storage of customer data* and *prevent lock-in effects*, which could result in the aggregation of market power. Decentralization of both data storage and workflows is a key objective of the new eKYC architecture.

Objective 3: Trust A primary goal for banks is to make eKYC documents reusable in customer registrations at different banks, which necessitates trust in the KYC process at other banks. Thus, *acceptance of KYC documents attested by other banks* is required. The documents must be tamper-proof, meaning that *validity checks* of these documents are feasible (Moyano & Ross, 2017). Additionally, sharing or selling KYC documents among customers must be prevented. The requirement for *authenticity checks* ensures a high level of assurance for the customer's identity and their connection with the documents.

Objective 4: Privacy Protecting customer privacy is key to an eKYC process. Customers are increasingly aware of privacy issues, and a privacy-preserving solution may increase acceptance (Kokolakis, 2017). A requirement in this context is *compliance with the "need to know" principle*: only customers themselves and entities relevant to the KYC process should have access to customers' personal data (Moor, 1997). Furthermore, not only the parties involved in the KYC process, but also the de facto data exchanged should be restricted to what is necessary (Arner et al., 2019). We call this requirement *data minimization*.

Objective 5: User Experience From the user's perspective, the most important objective is a seamless user experience (Kokolakis, 2017). A high level of security and acceptance can be achieved only if the eKYC process is fast and simple for the customer. Thus, *low complexity* is a key requirement in the eKYC process. Additionally, the availability of *different user interfaces* is essential. The user experience should also be satisfactory concerning exception handling, such as when a device storing customer data is lost or stolen. In these cases, either a built-in recovery mechanism or fast customer support needs to be available. This can be challenging if no central entity owns the process. Thus, *backup, recovery, and support* features are also required.

7.3 A Framework for eKYC Processes Built on Blockchain-Based SSI

7.3.1 The SSI-Based eKYC Architecture

The eKYC framework we propose is inspired by blockchain-based SSI principles and involves three key stakeholders (see also Chap. 4): the customer (holder), a bank (verifier) and an issuer (which can be the same bank, another bank, or any third party trusted by the verifying bank, such as a government agency). It is important to note that credentials from different issuers can be conjugated, as attributes attested in various verifiable credentials (VCs) can be combined in a verifiable presentation (VP) (Sporny et al., 2019; Glöckler et al., 2023).

For the purpose of our discussion, we will assume a single issuer. In this architecture, the customer is at the center of all interactions and serves as the subject of the KYC process (see Fig. 7.2). Customers manage their digital identities using user agents, which help create and store decentralized identifiers (DIDs) and cryptographic keys in digital wallets. User agents also assist customers in collecting credentials, creating backups, and managing permissions. Customers can interact with agents on a range of devices, such as smartphones or laptops, and maintain full control over their data, especially their KYC-related documents represented by VCs.

Traditional certificate-based approaches, such as X.509 certificates, require full disclosure to the verifier in order to validate the signature Sedlmeir et al. (2021). In contrast, the VC standard and respective implementations like Hyperledger Aries AnonCreds enable the creation of ZKPs from the VC. These proofs allow the verifier to derive the authenticity and validity of certain claims extracted from the VC without having to process the entire VC (Glöckler et al., 2023). This approach is enabled by cryptographic constructions introduced by Camenisch and Lysyanskaya (2001). In the context of our eKYC architecture, the VP contains proofs of the validity of the attributes that need to be disclosed during the KYC process.

One essential aspect of our proposed architecture is the integration of cloud agents and wallets, which facilitate redundant storage of credentials and provide users with easy access to their SSI documents. These cloud components also enable secure communication with other entities in the network. It is crucial to note that permissions for identification activities differ between edge and cloud instances. Edge agents and wallets typically have full access to an individual's data, while cloud agents and wallets are primarily used for redundant storage and communication with other entities. A blockchain can serve as a neutral infrastructure for storing publicly verifiable information, such as the public signing keys of VC issuers and other institutional data (Sedlmeir et al., 2021). Additionally, the blockchain can hold KYC VC schemas, enabling public verification. Publicly accessible revocation registries are also stored on the blockchain, allowing for public checks of privacy-preserving revocation information (Glöckler et al., 2023). Each bank can determine which credentials are accepted in the KYC process based on its requirements and trust relationships. By combining eIDAS and DIDs, it is possible to create qualified digital signatures that comply with eIDAS regulations (European Commission, 2019). Credential issuers utilize institutional agents explicitly designed for creating credentials. Beyond issuing credentials, these agents conduct identification activities, such as verifying credential integrity and facilitating direct communication with customers during and after the KYC process. They also interface with name screening services, the bank's risk engine, and customer monitoring systems. Financial institutions are required to store customer data, for which they utilize separate storage systems. This storage is an integral part

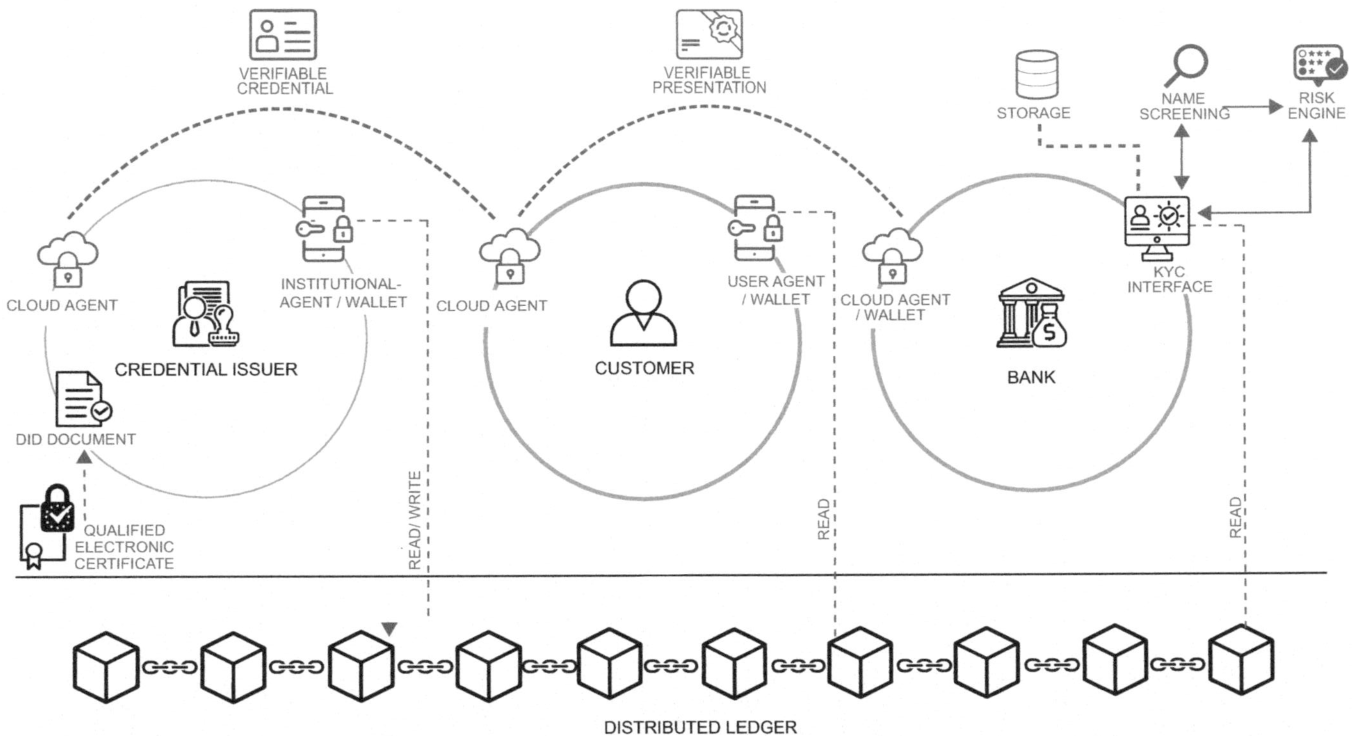

Fig. 7.2 SSI-based KYC architecture (based on European Commission, 2019; Moyano & Ross, 2017; Soltani et al., 2018; Reed et al., 2020; Sporny et al., 2019)

of the overall eKYC framework, ensuring compliance with regulatory requirements while leveraging the benefits of decentralization technologies.

7.3.2 *The Redefined KYC Process*

The KYC process begins with customer onboarding, where three cases can be distinguished (see Fig. 7.3). We have termed the first case *completely new onboarding*, which occurs when the customer has neither an SSI wallet nor a VCs that confirms a previously completed KYC process. The second case, *fast onboarding*, is possible if the customer already has an SSI wallet with corresponding VCs that attest to the prior completion of a KYC process. This scenario allows for a streamlined onboarding process, since the verifying institution can rely on the previously verified information to complete the KYC process. Lastly, we discuss a simplified case called *new to KYC*. In this case, customers already have an SSI wallet and a VCs that contains their basic identity information trusted by the verifying bank (or is allowed to trust from a legal perspective) but don't yet have VCs that demonstrate the completion of the KYC process at some institution.

7.3.2.1 Completely New Onboarding

We first present the case of completely new onboarding in an UML sequence diagram (see Fig. 7.4). To enable SSI-based onboarding, banks must undertake a one-time bootstrapping process (Soltani et al., 2018). This involves storing a public DID and its associated DID document on a distributed ledger. The DID document may contain the bank's service endpoints, such as those used for providing customer services or conducting eKYC procedures. Furthermore, the bank publishes a credential definition, which is typically derived from a schema that outlines the attributes to be attested in a credential. Besides, a revocation registry is

	WITHOUT SSI USER AGENT	WITH SSI USER AGENT
WITHOUT KYC CREDENTIALS	Completely new Onboarding	New to KYC
WITH KYC CREDENTIALS		Fast Onboarding

Fig. 7.3 Case distinction for SSI-based customer onboarding during the KYC process

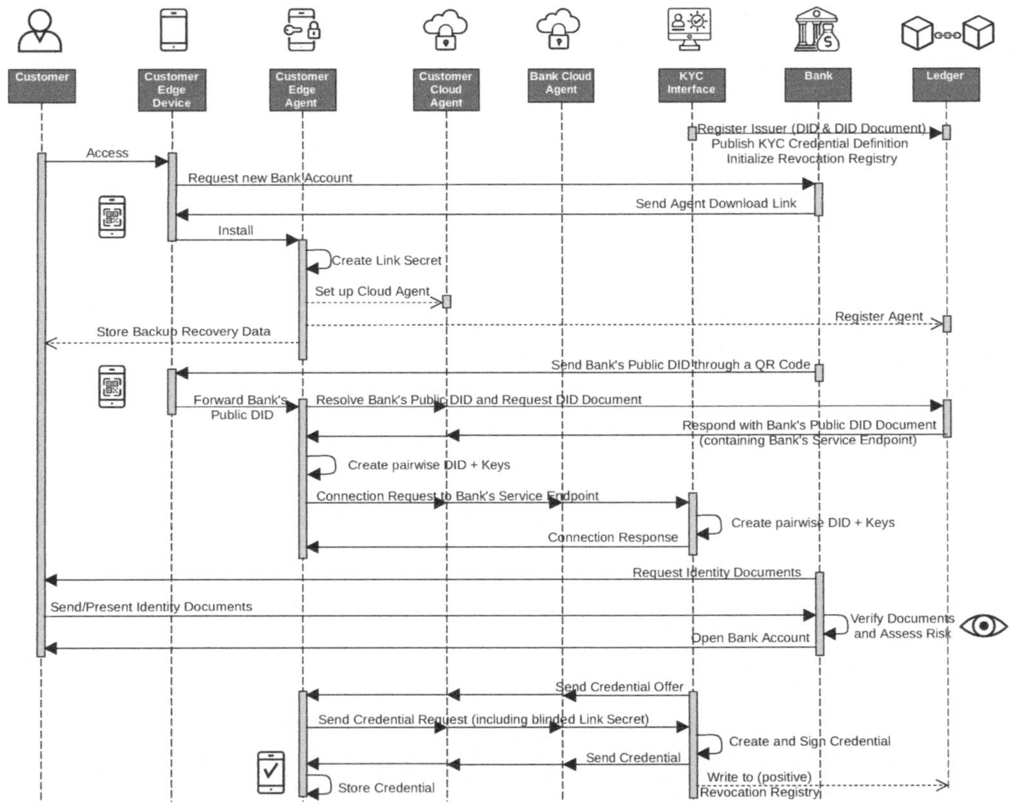

Fig. 7.4 UML diagram: *Completely new onboarding*

also published. All this information is meant to be publicly readable and contains cryptographic information that allows banks (acting as verifiers) to verify the validity of VPs associated with VC. Additionally, it enables customers (as holders) to provide proofs of non-revocation. All this information is publicly readable and does not contain any personally identifiable information. Thus, potential privacy concerns related to the GDPR when storing KYC-related information on a public blockchain can be mitigated (Rieger et al., 2019).

Once the initial setup is complete, the bank is ready to perform customer onboarding processes. The process of completely new onboarding begins when a customer visits the bank's website using their mobile phone or laptop or physically visits a local bank branch to open a new account. Since the customer lacks an SSI user wallet and the required KYC credentials, the bank recommends a wallet by a third party or provides a wallet itself, offering a corresponding download link to the customer. Customers have the option to download any digital wallet that supports public DID, peer DID, and VC standards. These wallets store credentials and keys, secured by a password or biometrics. The bank may also offer an edge agent in encrypted form in the cloud, enabling backup and recovery capabilities. Upon installation, the user wallet generates a new DID and associated keys for encryption, which are stored in the wallet. Initially, the user also creates a "link secret" to later connect different credentials within a VC, helping prevent selective credential sharing (Glöckler et al., 2023). However, if all credentials contain the customer's name or another strongly binding attribute that must be revealed in the VP, it is easy to prove that they belong together also without a link secret.

With the customer's newly generated DID, they can now establish an end-to-end encrypted, secure connection with the bank's eKYC endpoint. The bank may provide this information by sending a quick response (QR) code to the customer, for example, via email. Upon scanning the QR code with their wallet app, the customer connects to the bank's public service endpoint. The bank's service then creates a new pairwise DID, along with a key pair exclusively for this relationship, and sends a connection request to the customer's service endpoint or cloud agent. This agent forwards the connection request to the customer's wallet app. The connection request includes the bank's pairwise DID, the bank's public key, and the service endpoint where the customer can contact the bank. It may also contain proof that the pairwise DID has been authorized by the bank, such as a VPs revealing the bank's legal identifier certified by a reputable public institution. The customer's digital wallet verifies the connection's authenticity, creating a pairwise DID and keys for its relationship with the bank. It then sends a connection response to the bank's cloud agent or wallet, which forwards it to the bank's KYC interface. At this point, an end-to-end encrypted connection is established between the bank and the customer, allowing them to securely exchange messages, public keys, and VPs. Since the customer does not yet possess VCs, their identity must first be verified. The customer submits the necessary identity documents to the bank, either through traditional physical means or, if feasible, in scanned form via email or the established connection. If the customer opens an account at a bank branch, the documents can also be verified in person.

Once the customer's identity has been verified and confirmed, the bank sends a credential offer to the customer's edge user agent via the established connection. This offer includes a preview of the attested data, credential issuer information, an expiration date for the VC, and details about credential revocation. The customer accepts the credential offer and sends it back to the bank, containing the link secret in blinded form. This link secret is created only once and can be reused for other VCs. The bank incorporates the blinded link secret into the VCs attested attributes and sends the VC to the customer. The credential may support selective disclosure, allowing the customer to include only the necessary attributes attested by the VC in any VP and combine claims from different VCs into a VP. If the issuer wants to support revocation and has bootstrapped a revocation registry, the VC will also contain information on how to check its revocation status. The credential issuer can then revoke credentials by updating a revocation registry on the distributed ledger. For example, the bank can use this mechanism to invalidate a credential that was wrongly issued. Importantly, it is through the additional information about revocation in the credential that the customer can make sense of the public revocation registry's data and create a proof of non-revocation within a VP containing attributes from the VC. As the credential is never revealed in its entirety and only proofs are derived from it, public revocation registries are likely to be compliant with the GDPR.

7.3.2.2 Fast Onboarding

Compared to the previously described completely new onboarding case, the process of fast onboarding enables a quick and secure onboarding experience for customers who already have an SSI user agent and VCs in place. The fast onboarding process also starts when a bank customer visits the bank's website or a local branch to open a new account. In the case of online account opening, the bank sends the customer its bank public DID, for instance, via a QR code that the customer scans with their wallet app. The channel through which the customer receives this information must be trusted, as the customer does not know the bank's DID in advance. By utilizing an identity infrastructure like eIDAS, the customer can verify they are communicating with the correct bank by checking the eIDAS certification on the bank's public key in the DID document or other means, such as qualified website authentication certificates (QWACs). The customer's user agent identifies the distributed ledger storing the DID document associated with the DID and queries the ledger for the document. It then uses the DID document to locate the bank's eKYC-related service endpoint. The customer's user agent creates a pairwise DID for this relationship, along with the corresponding keys, and sends a connection request to the bank. This request contains the customer's pairwise DID and the public key used. In response, the bank generates a pairwise DID and corresponding cryptographic keys and sends the customer a connection response, which includes the pairwise DID and public key.

Once the secure connection is established between the bank and the customer, the bank sends a proof request for the fast onboarding KYC. This request contains a random nonce to prevent replay attacks and specifies the data the customer must transmit, along with any restrictions on accepting the verifiable presentation. The request includes accepted issuers, credential definitions, schemas for the VCs used, and whether there is a need for proof of non-revocation. If required, the request specifies a timestamp of the revocation registry that the customer should refer to when creating this proof. The customer's edge agent automatically searches for VCs that match these requirements in their digital wallet, updates their local revocation registry through a query if not cached before, and creates a VP that is sent to the bank (Sartor et al., 2022). The bank can then cryptographically verify the claims, possibly involving reading from revocation registries and other information regarding credential definitions unless sufficiently timely local data from previous queries are cached.

After cryptographically verifying the proof, the bank checks the digital signatures of issuers for all attributes involved in the VP, ensures none of the attested attributes come from a revoked VC, and confirms that all VCs involved were issued to a commitment of the same common link secret. Once the proof is verified, the bank account is opened. This entire process can be highly automated and completed in just a few seconds. The secure channel established between the bank and the customer, based on pairwise DIDs, can be used in the future to exchange further documents and communicate securely and reliably. The exchanged keys enable the unique authentication of the involved entities, which is crucial when dealing with digital identities, as the bank must ensure it communicates with the same person over time.

7.3.2.3 New to KYC

The third case is *new to KYC*, where the customer already has an SSI user agent and maybe also identity-related VCs but not yet a VC that is accepted by the banks during the KYC process. Thus, *new to KYC* is a combination of *completely new onboarding* (Fig. 7.4) and *fast onboarding* (Fig. 7.5). While constructing a pairwise DID relationship between the bank and the customer corresponds to the fast onboarding process, the transmission of analog ID documents and obtaining a KYC credential from the bank aligns with the completely new onboarding process. Customers can first check, through a proof request, whether a subset of ID documents is necessary, because they already have some digital identity proofs in their wallet. In addition to online account opening, customers can also open an account directly at a bank branch by using a QR code to receive the bank's service endpoint and have their analog ID documents checked in person.

Once the identity data is exchanged and cryptographically verified, the bank's name screening service runs in the background to check the data against public blacklists related to terrorism, illegal money laundering activities, politically exposed persons, and negative press. The screening results are fed directly into the

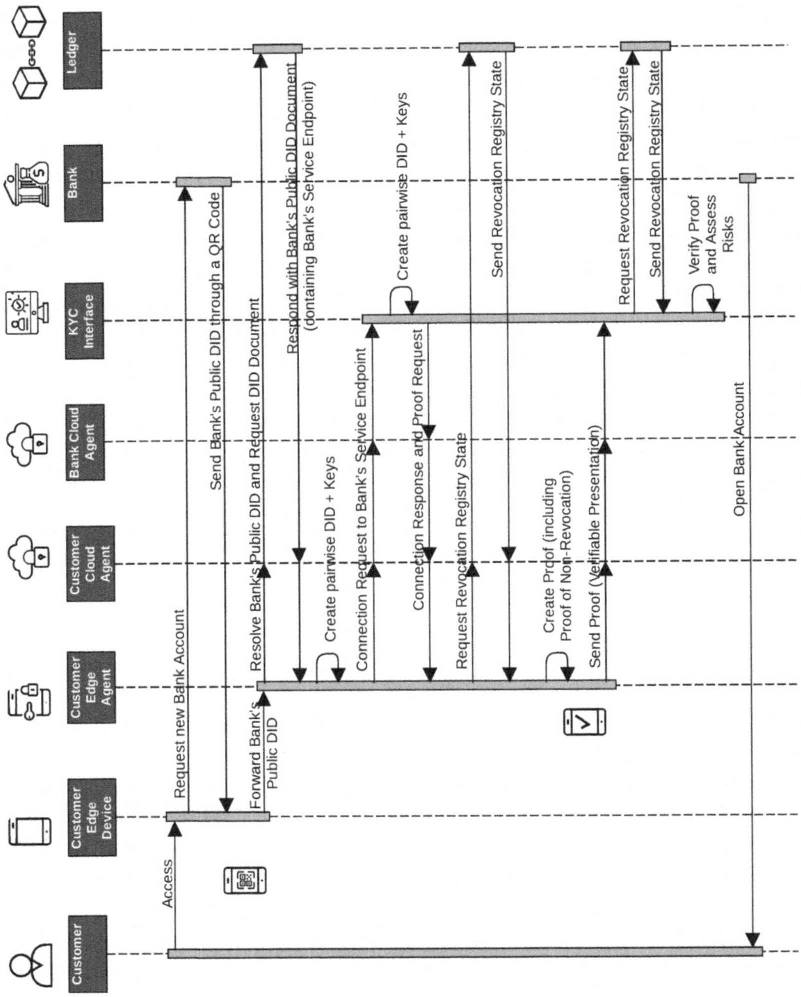

Fig. 7.5 UML diagram: *Fast onboarding*

risk engine, which uses this and other information to classify the customer into a risk class. Depending on the results, further checks may be necessary before the bank opens the account. To mitigate risks, the bank can use the previously established secure communication channel to request additional documents and information, such as an income statement or the reason for opening the account. Such documentation can be provided in analog form or through VCs already in the customer's wallet, like an income statement issued by a trusted employer, and delivered as an associated VP. Once the customer's verification is successfully completed, the bank can open the account.

7.4 Opportunities of SSI for eKYC

SSI Improves the Efficiency of KYC Processes The KYC process efficiency can be improved through the use of SSI-based solutions. This is achieved through the use of fully digital cryptographic proofs in the form of VCs, which can eliminate the need for face-to-face verification, manual data processing, and repeated KYC processes. Digital data processing reduces friction in the onboarding process for both the customer and the bank. The use of reusable VCs and revocation registries on the blockchain can save costs for manual and repeated process steps. Through the bilateral and secure communication channel, the customer can easily provide VPs to the bank, reducing the effort required for updates or the periodic confirmation of data.

The use of SSIs-based solutions can also lead to savings in personnel costs, improve authentication with a high level of security, and reduce the risk of noncompliance with due diligence regulations and standards. However, the benefits of *fast onboarding*, where a prior eKYC process has taken place at another bank or official document issuer, only apply where there is an existing ecosystem of official, identity-related documents. To facilitate standardization, KYC credential templates can be created and stored on a public blockchain, making them accessible to a range of institutions and avoiding the verification of unknown, foreign documents. However, questions remain about governance, such as who defines standards. A governance framework is needed to provide clear guidelines for defining which institutions are suitable as credential issuers.

SSI Provides Regulatory Compliance The design of the framework is not expected to pose significant challenges to compliance with the MLA. However, compliance with the GDPR may be more complicated. Although it is unclear how encrypted and hashed personal data will be treated under this regulation (Rieger et al., 2019; Sedlmeir et al., 2022), it is assumed that such data will be subject to the right of erasure. In addition, public DIDs and public keys may also be considered personal data and must be deleted upon request. Therefore, storing such data on a distributed ledger for KYCs purposes is not feasible. However, our framework has the potential to address these issues by using pairwise DIDs and exchanging information bilaterally, thus avoiding the need to store personal data on a distributed ledger. The selective disclosure capabilities of the VCs also address the data minimization requirements of the GDPRs. More in-depth legal analysis will be required in the future to account for changing legislation.

Compliance with the eIDAS regulation is also necessary for the effective use of the system. The SSI concept could take a central role in the user-centric eIDAS infrastructure. The EU has started to build the eIDAS bridge to provide digital identities which might also include use-cases for KYC using the VC standard. Still, many aspects of the future eIDAS remain uncertain, and the implementation is not yet complete.

SSI Improves Resilience with Decentralization Our eKYC framework stores identity-related data in the customer's digital wallet, which is located on their mobile phone or laptop. This approach eliminates the need for central storage, except for the regulatory compliance requirements that necessitate the storage of customer information for a certain period of time. While user agents may be viewed as a form of centralized storage, they store encrypted data under user-managed keys. Due to the heavy standardization associated with SSI, it is unlikely that user agents hosted by third parties will encounter the same network effects that lead to centralization in federated systems, thus preventing data silos that are highly attractive to hackers.

Our framework has the potential to avoid the introduction of new central parties into the KYC process. The use of blockchain technology ensures that no single entity controls the infrastructure involved in checking credential schemas or revocation registries. Still, institutions will be included in the process in some form in the future as well, even though they do not act as single entities overseeing the whole process. For instance, banks may provide cloud agents and wallets due to their position of trust with their customers. Some experts further suggest banks as potential service providers for backups of credentials (Soltani et al., 2018).

SSI Ensures Trust Among All Parties Involved Our framework relies on VCs as the basis for KYC documents. VCs are a more advanced form of digital certificates, offering additional capabilities such as selective disclosure and privacy-preserving revocation mechanisms, potentially based on a blockchain to improve availability and transparency. They provide a natural digital equivalent of physical KYC documents that customers can fully control and take with them to other banks. The validity of a VC can be verified by checking the integrity of its digital signature, with the signing keys of issuing institutions (such as other banks) being publicly available on a blockchain. It is not possible to create fake credentials, as they are not valid without the signature of the credential issuer. In addition, the ownership of credentials can be cryptographically proven, and the binding of multiple credentials through a strongly correlated attribute, such as the holder's name or biometric characteristics, or cryptographically through secure hardware, makes it difficult and unattractive to share or sell VCs.

From the perspective of banks and regulators, the all-digital verification of VCs offers significant advantages over previously used analog documents. It improves data accuracy and eliminates manual errors in data processing. However, governance mechanisms for the legal acceptance of such VCs and other aspects of interbank cooperation remain open. The blockchain infrastructure used to store information on VC issuers (e.g., other banks or government institutions) and revocation registries for VCs allow banks to verify VCs issued by other banks. However, there is a need to clarify which credentials banks accept and who they accept as credential issuers.

SSI Embraces Privacy-by-Design In our eKYC framework, users can manage their identity data independently, without relying on a third party. Communication is bilateral between a VC owner and a verifier and only requires occasional read queries to a random node on a public blockchain to update information. This approach prevents third parties from accessing users' comprehensive data and improves scalability. Users can have different digital identities for different contexts and only disclose necessary information. In this approach, customers have complete control over their data and can decide whom to share their data with. This selective disclosure of information can be achieved through novel cryptographic approaches like ZKPs (see Chap. 6). The goal of SSI is not anonymity but privacy in each scenario. However, the possibility of connecting KYC data with transactional data raises concerns about customer privacy and conflicts with SSI principles. Once personally identifiable information is received in plain text, it can be connected to other data.

SSI Improves User Experience Through Streamlined Processes The use of SSI in eKYC has the potential to improve the customer experience greatly. Many of the current hurdles, such as filling out online forms, visiting a bank branch or having a video call with a bank employee for identification purposes (Moyano & Ross, 2017), can be eliminated. Instead, customers can complete the onboarding process on their smartphones in just a few steps, including scanning QR codes and accepting invitation links and verification requests through simple interfaces. The framework is based on generic and open standards, with reference implementations available for mobile and computer operating systems, allowing different user interfaces to be realized.

Customers also have a comprehensive overview of what data they have shared with whom at which time. However, the full responsibility for storing and managing their data rests with the customers themselves. This could be a potential problem as customers need to be aware of their responsibilities and take appropriate measures to back up and recover their data to mitigate the consequences of loss or theft of the device.

7.5 Bridging the Gap: Implementing Blockchain-Based SSI in KYC and Beyond

Innovations should yield practical benefits, but their successful implementation calls for suitable strategies. Even when innovations are crafted to address specific issues, their deployment can be intricate, as it demands a comprehensive understanding of the underlying problem and a fitting approach that considers the context of the implementation (Baskerville et al., 2018).

One of the ways to ensure successful implementation is by considering the adoption of the SSI-based eKYC (Moore & McKenna, 1999). The general adoption of SSI in the public and private sectors can help bridge the gap between early adopters and widespread use. Currently, the low number of VC issuers creates a *chicken and egg* problem. Users are reluctant to adopt SSI-based solutions due to the lack of available credentials (Guggenberger et al., 2023b), while organizations are not incentivized to become VC issuers as long as there are only a few users. However, network effects can help overcome this challenge. By offering the technology in the isolated KYC use case, banks can issue VCs to contribute to its spread in the mass market. The more banks accept these credentials, the more attractive the system becomes for customers. In turn, higher usage by customers leads to a higher attractiveness for further organizations to accept VCs. Furthermore, the anticipated revision of the eIDAS regulation by the EU might help to further disseminate SSI-based digital identities.

Thereby, the cooperation of banks and the creation of shared standards are crucial for the adoption of the eKYC solution to become possible. The development of shared standards is important to ensure interoperability and facilitate the integration of SSI-based solutions into existing systems (Guggenberger et al., 2023a). Moreover, the cooperation of banks is important to ensure the availability of VCs and to provide the necessary infrastructure for their issuance.

The principles of the GDPR include privacy by design, portability, right to erasure, transparency, purpose limitation, data minimization, accuracy, storage limitation, and information integrity. SSI holds the potential to address some of these principles as users keep control over their data. With SSI, users can keep track of who they have shared their data with through a comprehensive overview, which can assist in the facilitation of the right to erasure. This feature may lead to wider adoption of the technology, as the strict requirements of the GDPR have been seen as a barrier to blockchain-related innovation in Europe (Rieger et al., 2019). Ultimately, however, these requirements may encourage innovation and allow for the benefits of blockchain-based interoperability while avoiding typical privacy and scalability-related challenges (Sedlmeir et al., 2022).

The relationship between SSI and regulation also reveals several interesting dimensions. Our research suggests that the eIDAS regulation can positively influence the SSI concept, and SSI can increase the practicality and value of the underutilized eIDAS infrastructure (European Commission, 2019). In addition, SSI can technically provide even greater privacy than is required by regulation. However, the MLA requires banks to retain customer data for 5 years, creating tension between the goals of user control and preventing data silos versus data protection regulations. As such, SSI may spark new discussions about the balance between market integrity and privacy.

Acknowledgments This chapter is based on the following journal article: Schlatt et al. (2022).

References

Allen, C. (2016). The path to self-sovereign identity. http://www.lifewithalacrity.com/previous/2016/04/the-path-to-self-soverereign-identity.html

Arasa, R., & Ottichilo, L. (2015). Determinants of know your customer (KYC) compliance among commercial banks in Kenya. *Journal of Economics and Behavioral Studies*, *2*, 162–175. https://doi.org/10.22610/jebs.v7i2(J).574

Arner, D. W., Barberis, J. N., & Buckley, R. P. (2016). The emergence of RegTech 2.0: From know your customer to know your data. https://papers.ssrn.com/sol3/papers.cfm?abstract_id=3044280

Arner, D. W., Zetzsche, D. A., Buckley, R. P., & Barberis, J. N. (2019). The identity challenge in finance: From analogue identity to digitized identification to digital KYC utilities. *European Business Organization Law Review*, *20*(1), 55–80. https://doi.org/10.2139/ssrn.3224115

Baskerville, R., Baiyere, A., Gregor, S., Hevner, A., & Rossi, M. (2018). Design science research contributions: Finding a balance between artifact and theory. *Journal of the Association for Information Systems*, *19*(5), 358–376. https://doi.org/10.17705/1jais.00495

Camenisch, J., & Lysyanskaya, A. (2001). An efficient system for non-transferable anonymous credentials with optional anonymity revocation. In *International Conference on the Theory and Applications of Cryptographic Techniques* (pp. 93–118). Springer. https://doi.org/10.1007/3-540-44987-6_7

Christie, R. (2018). Setting a standard path forward for KYC. *Journal of Financial Transformation*, *47*, 155–164. https://www.capco.com/-/media/CapcoMedia/CAPCO/Capco-Institute/Journal-47/CapcoJournal47ChristiePrintv11.ashx

Davie, M., Gisolfi, D., Hardman, D., Jordan, J., O'Donnell, D., & Reed, D. (2019). The trust over IP stack. *IEEE Communications Standards Magazine*, *3*(4), 46–51. https://doi.org/10.1109/MCOMSTD.001.1900029

European Commission. (2019). eIDAS supported self-sovereign identity. https://ec.europa.eu/futurium/en/system/files/ged/eidas_supported_ssi_may_2019_0.pdf

European Commission. (2023). Discover eIDAS. https://digital-strategy.ec.europa.eu/en/policies/discover-eidas

Glöckler, J., Sedlmeir, J., Frank, M., & Fridgen, G. (2023). A systematic review of identity and access management requirements in enterprises and potential contributions of self-sovereign identity. *Business & Information Systems Engineering*. https://doi.org/10.1007/s12599-023-00830-x

Guggenberger, T., Kühne, D., Schlatt, V., & Urbach, N. (2023a). Designing a cross-organizational identity management system: Utilizing SSI for the certification of retailer attributes. *Electronic Markets*, *33*(1), 3. https://doi.org/10.1007/s12525-023-00620-z

Guggenberger, T., Neubauer, L., Stramm, J., Völter, F., & Zwede, T. (2023b). Accept me as I am or see me go: A qualitative analysis of user acceptance of self-sovereign identity applications. In *Proceedings of the 56th Hawaii International Conference on System Sciences* (pp. 6560–6569). https://hdl.handle.net/10125/103427

Guggenberger, T., Schweizer, A., & Urbach, N. (2020). Improving interorganizational information sharing for vendor managed inventory: Toward a decentralized information hub using blockchain technology. *IEEE Transactions on Engineering Management*, *67*(4), 1074–1085. https://doi.org/10.1109/TEM.2020.2978628

Hardman, D. (2020). No paradox here: ZKPs deliver savvy trust. https://www.evernym.com/blog/no-paradox-here-zkps-deliver-savvy-trust/

Hardman, D., Harchandani, L., Othman, A., & Callahan, J. (2019). Using biometrics to fight credential fraud. *IEEE Communications Standards Magazine*, *3*(4), 39–45. https://doi.org/10.1109/MCOMSTD.001.1900033

Jessel, B., Lowmaster, K., Hughes, N., et al. (2018). Digital identity: The foundation for trusted transactions in financial services. *Journal of Financial Transformation*, *47*, 143–150. https://ideas.repec.org/a/ris/jofitr/1607.html

Kokolakis, S. (2017). Privacy attitudes and privacy behaviour: A review of current research on the privacy paradox phenomenon. *Computers & Security*, *64*, 122–134. https://doi.org/10.1016/j.cose.2015.07.002

Kolb, J., AbdelBaky, M., Katz, R. H., & Culler, D. E. (2020). Core concepts, challenges, and future directions in blockchain: A centralized tutorial. *ACM Computing Surveys*, *53*(1). https://doi.org/10.1145/3366370

Ledger Insights. (2020). Self-sovereign identity successfully trialed for KYC in UK regulatory sandbox. https://www.ledgerinsights.com/self-sovereign-identity-successfully-trialed-for-kyc-in-uk-regulatory-sandbox/

Lootsma, Y. (2017). Blockchain as the newest RegTech application – the opportunity to reduce the burden of KYC for financial institutions. *Banking & Financial Services Policy Report*, *36*(8), 16–21. https://www.academia.edu/39393562/Blockchain_as_the_Newest_Regtech_Application_the_Opportunity_to_Reduce_the_Burden_of_KYC_for_Financial_Institutions

Moor, J. H. (1997). Towards a theory of privacy in the information age. *ACM SIGCAS Computers and Society*, *27*(3), 27–32. https://doi.org/10.1145/270858.270866

Moore, G. A., & McKenna, R. (1999). *Crossing the chasm*. Harper Business Essentials.

Moyano, J. P., & Ross, O. (2017). KYC optimization using distributed ledger technology. *Business & Information Systems Engineering*, *59*(6), 411–423. https://doi.org/10.1007/s12599-017-0504-2

Mugarura, N. (2014). Customer due diligence (CDD) mandate and the propensity of its application as a global AML paradigm. *Journal of Money Laundering Control*, *17*(1), 75–96. https://doi.org/10.1108/JMLC-07-2013-0024

Ostern, N. K., & Riedel, J. (2020). Know-your-customer (KYC) requirements for initial coin offerings. *Business & Information Systems Engineering*, *63*, 551–567. https://doi.org/10.1007/s12599-020-00677-6

Perlman, L., & Gurung, N. (2019). Focus note: The use of eKYC for customer identity and verification and AML. https://papers.ssrn.com/sol3/papers.cfm?abstract_id=3370665

Pratz, A., & Weiss, M. (2024). Capturing the value in 'knowing your customer'. https://www.strategyand.pwc.com/de/en/industries/financial-services/kyc.html

Rajput, A., & Gopinath, K. (2017). Towards a more secure Aadhaar. In *International Conference on Information Systems Security* (pp. 283–300). Springer. https://doi.org/10.1007/978-3-319-72598-7_17

Reed, D., Sporny, M., Longley, D., Allen, C., Grant, R., & Sabadello, M. (2020). Decentralized identifiers (DIDs) v1.0. https://w3c.github.io/did-core

Rieger, A., Lockl, J., Urbach, N., Guggenmos, F., & Fridgen, G. (2019). Building a blockchain application that complies with the EU general data protection regulation. *MIS Quarterly Executive*, *18*(4), 263–279. https://doi.org/10.17705/2msqe.00020

Ruce, P. J. (2011). Anti-money laundering: The challenges of know your customer legislation for private bankers and the hidden benefits for relationship management (the bright side of knowing your customer). *The Banking Law Journal*, *128*(6), 548–564. https://papers.ssrn.com/sol3/papers.cfm?abstract_id=1852743

Sartor, S., Sedlmeir, J., Rieger, A., & Roth, T. (2022). Love at first sight? A user experience study of self-sovereign identity wallets. In *Proceedings of the 30th European Conference on Information Systems*. AIS. https://aisel.aisnet.org/ecis2022_rp/46/

Schlatt, V., Sedlmeir, J., Feulner, S., & Urbach, N. (2022). Designing a framework for digital KYC processes built on blockchain-based self-sovereign identity. *Information & Management*, *59*. https://doi.org/10.1016/j.im.2021.103553

Sedlmeir, J., Lautenschlager, J., Fridgen, G., & Urbach, N. (2022). The transparency challenge of blockchain in organizations. *Electronic Markets*, *32*, 1779–1794. https://doi.org/10.1007/s12525-022-00536-0

Sedlmeir, J., Smethurst, R., Rieger, A., & Fridgen, G. (2021). Digital identities and verifiable credentials. *Business & Information Systems Engineering*, *63*(5), 603–613. https://doi.org/10.1007/s12599-021-00722-y

Soltani, R., Nguyen, U. T., & An, A. (2018). A new approach to client onboarding using self-sovereign identity and distributed ledger. In *International Conference on Internet of Things and Green Computing and Communications and Cyber, Physical and Social Computing and Smart Data* (pp. 1129–1136). IEEE. https://doi.org/10.1109/Cybermatics_2018.2018.00205.

Sporny, M., Longley, D., & Chadwick, D. (2019). Verifiable credentials data model 1.0. https://www.w3.org/TR/vc-data-model/

Swinhoe, D. (2020). The 15 biggest data breaches of the 21st century. https://www.csoonline.com/article/2130877/the-biggest-data-breaches-of-the-21st-century.html

The Economist. (2016). Indian business prepares to tap into Aadhaar, a state-owned fingerprint-identification system https://www.economist.com/business/2016/12/24/indian-business-prepares-to-tap-into-aadhaar-a-state-owned-fingerprint-identification-system

Thomson Reuters. (2016). Know your customer surveys reveal escalating costs and complexity. https://www.thomsonreuters.com/en/press-releases/2016/may/thomson-reuters-2016-know-your-customer-surveys.html

Weigl, L., Barbereau, T. J., Rieger, A., & Fridgen, G. (2022). The social construction of self-sovereign identity: An extended model of interpretive flexibility. In *Proceedings of the 55th Hawaii International Conference on System Sciences* (pp. 2543–2552). https://doi.org/10.24251/hicss.2022.316

Zavolokina, L., Ziolkowski, R., Bauer, I., & Schwabe, G. (2020). Management, governance and value creation in a blockchain consortium. *MIS Quarterly Executive*, *19*(1). https://doi.org/10.17705/2msqe.00022

Zetzsche, D. A., Buckley, R. P., & Arner, D. W. (2018). Digital ID and AML/CDD/KYC utilities for financial inclusion, integrity and competition. *Journal of Financial Transformation* (pp. 133–142). https://hdl.handle.net/10993/38943

Chapter 8
Decentralized Finance and Blockchain in Traditional Finance: Economic Opportunities and Adoption Challenges

Eduard Hartwich and Tom Barbereau

Abstract This chapter positions the increasingly mature space of decentralized finance (DeFi) in terms of its technological foundations and economic opportunities in the context of adoption by the "traditional" financial sector. It presents applications of DeFi and cooperative ventures initiated by well-known financial institutions. At last, we introduce and contextualize socioeconomic and regulatory challenges in terms of market dynamics and news.

8.1 Introduction

Financial institutions (FIs) traditionally fulfill many vital functions in our economy. These include – among others – regulating the monetary supply, facilitating monetary flows, ensuring financial stability, as well as arranging and settling transactions between interacting parties domestically and internationally. Because FIs – such as banks, brokers, and exchanges – connect and mediate between these parties, they often function as what is called trusted third parties (TTP) (Allen & Santomero, 2001). In this role, they act as intermediaries and strive to reduce information asymmetries while providing regulated access to financial markets (Bons & Alt, 2015; Allen & Santomero, 2001). While these are essential functions, they inherently place significant trust in the TTP, giving them power as they can act as gatekeepers. However, this trust can also be corrupted or abused, as seen in the 2008/2009 financial crisis and the resulting ripple effects. With the

E. Hartwich (✉)
Interdisciplinary Centre for Security, Reliability and Trust (SnT), University of Luxembourg, Luxembourg, Luxembourg
e-mail: eduard.hartwich@uni.lu

T. Barbereau
Interdisciplinary Centre for Security, Reliability and Trust (SnT), University of Luxembourg, Luxembourg, Luxembourg

Dutch Organisation for Applied Scientific Research, The Hague, The Netherlands
e-mail: tom.barbereau@tno.nl

G. Fridgen et al. (eds.), *Decentralization Technologies*, Financial Innovation and Technology, https://doi.org/10.1007/978-3-031-66047-4_8

ambition of finding solutions to prevent such a generational crisis from repeating, Satoshi Nakamoto developed and implemented the first permissionless blockchain application, the Bitcoin network (Nakamoto, 2008). Not only did Bitcoin launch the perhaps most significant financial revolution in recent decades and become the best-performing asset following its inception in 2009 (Sriram, 2021), but it also triggered the development of what we know today as the blockchain industry.

Blockchains are distributed databases (see also Chap. 3), which enable multilayered DeFi applications that promise significant advantages. DeFi inherently represents an open, transparent, and immutable financial infrastructure and consequently brings a number of opportunities (Schär, 2021). Many, though not all, DeFi applications do not require a TTP to function. As such, they have the potential to significantly reduce transaction costs, which most FIs, like any enterprise, naturally aim for as they strive to improve efficiencies, reduce expenses, and thereby maximize revenue and profits. These advantages of DeFi, however, present a double-edged sword for traditional finance (TradFi). On the one hand, they are believed to entail opportunities to increase operating speed, cut costs, and improve overall efficiency (Gramlich et al., 2023). On the other hand, as many DeFi solutions do not require TTPs, they raise questions about the necessity for centralized FIs or at least challenge their position of power and influence. Under these circumstances, along with other factors that hinder adoption, FIs have hesitated to implement blockchain solutions on a broad scale (Prewett et al., 2020; Hartwich et al., 2024).

To unpack how DeFi blockchain applications fit into the TradFi landscape, we structure this chapter as follows. In Sect. 8.2, we introduce DeFi and its core technological tenets before discussing economic and financial opportunities for TradFi. In Sect. 8.3, we debate applications and implementations between notable TradFi and DeFi organizations. We continue with socioeconomic and regulatory adoption challenges in Sect. 8.4, before closing this chapter in Sect. 8.5 with a brief outlook.

8.2 On Decentralized Finance

To fully acknowledge DeFi and its potential, it is crucial to understand its core components and main building blocks. This chapter presents the technical foundations of DeFi – blockchain, smart contracts, and tokens – before discussing how these come together to form what is known today as DeFi. On this basis, we then explore the economic opportunities – efficiency, transparency, accessibility, and composability – that arise for FIs.

8.2.1 Technical Building Blocks

Blockchain In its most basic form, a blockchain is a replicated, distributed database and ledger that is owned and run by the members of its network, so-called nodes (Christidis & Devetsikiotis, 2016). Figuratively speaking, each block represents a page in the ledger containing a running list of transactions. These are linked through cryptographic hashes, which represent the content of each block by a fix-sized value. Each block starts with the hash of the previous block and ends with a new hash comprised of the previous hash and the content of the current block. This ending hash, in turn, starts the new block, thus forming a chain that links all blocks together (Hartwich et al., 2023b). Consequently, if any content of an older block is changed, it would automatically alter its hash and require a distortion of all following hashes to maintain consistency (Nakamoto, 2008). Accordingly, a malicious actor in the network would need to "recalculate" blocks to "re-align" the hashes. Through this, blockchains become unidirectional, tamper-proof, and probabilistically final (Abellán Álvarez et al., 2024). The latter describes that with each new block, transactions become more final as the probability of an attacker successfully changing entries in the earlier blocks decreases (Anceaume et al., 2020). Once a block is filled with a predefined maximum number of transactions, it is distributed to all nodes in the network for verification and replicated storage – or in other words, to settle the transaction (Butijn et al., 2020).

Smart Contracts While Bitcoin, the first blockchain, supported only simple cryptocurrency transfers on its ledger (Nakamoto, 2008), other projects incorporated smart contracts – most prominently, the Ethereum blockchain – which facilitate more complex multistep processes and applications (Wood et al., 2014). Smart contracts are algorithms deployed on the blockchain, which automatically execute protocols if users or devices trigger specific commands (Szabo, 1997). Additionally, smart contracts are deterministic in nature, which means that the same set of input parameters will always produce the same output. Further, due to the tamper-proof nature of blockchains, smart contracts are permanently inscribed on the blockchain and execute every time they are called and predefined conditions are met, which can help reduce the need for TTPs in financial applications significantly (Sunyaev et al., 2021; Hartwich et al., 2023a). This can be demonstrated through a simple example: Alice asks Bob to lend her 1000 €, which she would pay back in installments. Bob agrees to lend Alice the money under the condition that she transfers him 100 € every time she receives 500 € or more into her account. Alice is willing to accept these conditions. To avoid tensions between the two, and to reduce the effort of chasing each other, Alice and Bob decide to deploy a smart contract connected to Alice's account that captures these conditions. By choosing this approach, they have created a financial relationship that does not require a TTP and cannot be tampered with. Due to the abovementioned characteristics of blockchains, neither Bob nor Alice can control the smart contract execution and, thus, can rest assured that it will be executed.

For such applications and agreements to occur, both parties naturally first need access to the blockchain network. Motivated by the reduced trust toward financial TTPs resulting from the financial crisis of 2008/2009, Bitcoin was founded as a fully transparent and open network that everyone who fulfills minimal software and hardware requirements can join (De Filippi & Loveluck, 2016) – a so-called public permissionless blockchain. Consequently, without formal identification, users can join the network and read all information stored on the blockchain or add new data without requiring specific permission rights. Private permissioned blockchains are the polar opposite as they demand users to identify themselves and only allow authorized nodes to write and read data (Beck et al., 2018). Lastly, public permissioned blockchains describe a compromise between the two as they allow every user to read information without specific authorization. Adding new data to the blockchain, however, remains reserved for a select, preapproved group of users. In conclusion, blockchains and smart contracts allow for the design and development of a wide variety of applications while providing fine-granular differentiation in write access control while only providing a very coarse level of read access control (Sedlmeir et al., 2022).

Tokens Given that blockchains operate as their own, independent networks, they are independent of the monetary systems used for fiat transactions (i.e., the € used in the example of Alice and Bob). In fact, many blockchains try to feature their own monetary system on the basis of what is called tokens. The use of tokens started as fungible payment tokens in the form of Bitcoins. Smart contracts on Ethereum later enabled the standardized development of different token types that allowed them to fulfill various functions and enable non-fungibility in the digital realm (Hartwich et al., 2024). Effectively, tokens can be described as digital assets on a blockchain that can be traded between its users.

8.2.2 Foundations of Decentralized Finance

DeFi is an umbrella term that describes multilayered decentralized financial applications or services combining and using the abovementioned technologies (see also Chap. 3). To describe how DeFi operates, we need to first introduce its architectural layers. Here, we rely on the definition of Schär (2021):

1. The first fundamental layer consists of the underlying blockchain and its native token, i.e., Bitcoin (BTC) on the Bitcoin or Ether (ETH) on the Ethereum blockchain. This layer determines the ground rules that each following layer has to conform to. It is also the layer upon which all transactions are settled.
2. The second layer is formed by the tokens built on top of the first layer. These can be either native or follow specific token standards. Ethereum, most prominently, provides token standards such as ERC-20 or ERC-721 that developers can follow to issue tokens with their own characteristics on the Ethereum chain.

3. The third layer is composed of protocols and smart contracts that enable specific use cases such as automated market makers (AMMs) or decentralized exchanges (DEXs).
4. The fourth layer complements the third one by providing front ends that users can interact with, i.e., in the form of websites or mobile applications.
5. The fifth and last layer connects various applications from the fourth layer and bundles them into one service. This allows users to utilize the functionalities of different applications simultaneously and provides them with information aggregated across applications. This layered approach creates a composable environment where services can be facilitated and utilized across layers, applications, and protocols.

Liquidity Pools In "traditional" finance, liquidity pools (LPs) describe a "claim structure" in which banks are connected through funds held in a commonly shared pool (Sáez & Shi, 2004). Examples include monetary organizations such as the International Monetary Fund (IMF) or the World Trade Organization (WTO). In DeFi, LPs follow similar principles (see Fig. 8.1). Liquidity providers need to lock two or more assets into a smart contract (step 1), adding to the pool's reserves. In return, the smart contract mints new tokens (step 2), so-called liquidity pool tokens (LPTs), that represent the deposited share (Werner et al., 2022). The LP is then used as capital to provide financial services to users. As users interact with these financial services, they are charged transaction fees or commissions (steps 3 and 4), which in turn get passed on to the liquidity providers in proportion to their share in the overall pool, represented by said LPTs (step 5) (Aigner & Dhaliwal, 2021).

By engaging in existing or creating their own LPs, enterprises can build financial protocols and products that yield new revenue streams in the form of (trading) fees. Further, the deterministic nature of smart contracts (Christidis & Devetsikiotis, 2016) mitigates the risk exposure for enterprises as it reduces the uncertainty of outcomes; "the same input will always produce the same output" (Christidis and Devetsikiotis, 2016, p. 2297). Paired with oracles (trusted entities that bring outside data onto the blockchain) (Adler et al., 2018), this allows enterprises to automate their processes and reduce headcount-heavy tasks.

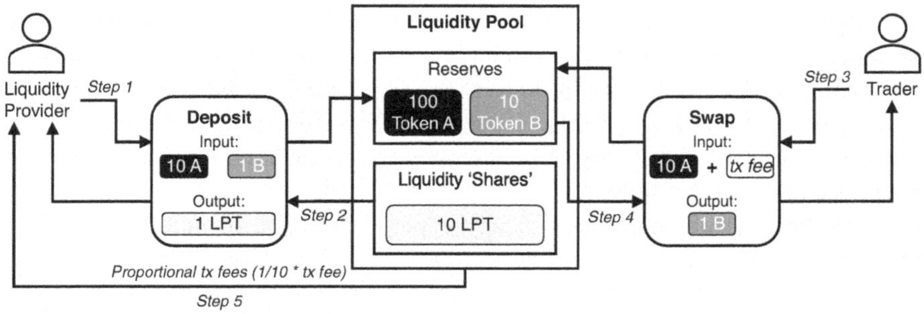

Fig. 8.1 Simplified graphical representation of liquidity pools in decentralized exchanges

Automated Market Makers One essential protocol that builds the backbone of many DeFi applications is the AMM. In TradFi, market makers describe entities that match buy and sell orders for specific assets (Rust & Hall, 2003). By providing the necessary trading volume, a market maker is able to set the price of the underlying asset and turn a profit from the spread – the difference between the buy and sell price (Menkveld, 2013). Consequently, for this system to work, there need to be individual parties willing to make a trade. AMMs, on the other hand, neither require a counterparty to a trade nor do they require a middleman to match and execute orders. Instead, AMMs allow traders to place orders directly with the protocol, which then automatically executes the trade following an algorithmically calculated price (Aigner & Dhaliwal, 2021; Mohan, 2022). This allows 365/24/7 operation of DeFi services built on top of that protocol since trades occur between humans and smart contracts. These properties provide notable economic opportunities, which we discuss in the next section.

8.2.3 Economic Opportunities

Due to the characteristics described in the previous section, DeFi opens up multiple economic opportunities for TradFi, mainly attributable to its efficiency, transparency, accessibility, and composability.

Efficiency gains are among the most impactful benefits that DeFi can provide. Cutting out the intermediary opens up the opportunity to settle transactions directly between peers. Additionally, as smart contracts are transparent and deterministic, their outcome is predictable (Alharby et al., 2018), which allows tech-savvy users to inspect the code and determine whether a smart contract is trustworthy enough to interact with (Kannengiesser et al., 2021). This combination of eliminating third parties and smart contracts creates an environment for trustless interactions where rules are automatically enforced, and the need and cost of an entity that audits the third party are reduced (Schär, 2021). In essence, avoiding an intermediary can lower the costs and transaction times that come with it.

Transparency in DeFi refers to two aspects. First, as mentioned above, users have the opportunity to scrutinize the underlying code of a protocol to ensure that fraudulent transactions and one-sided abuse are averted. Second, the public nature of the DeFi ecosystem allows users to inspect if an application has enough funds to operate in the magnitude that it promises (e.g., the liquidity pool of a decentralized exchange) (Carter & Jeng, 2021). These distinct properties have the potential to reduce the number of disputes and consequently decrease the time and costs that need to be allocated to alignment.

Accessibility DeFi applications can be permissionless. In other words, they allow anyone, anywhere, to participate in the network and get access to financial services – given that the necessary technical requirements are met (e.g., access to a mobile phone and internet connection) and sufficient degrees of digital literacy are achieved. Further, the default pseudonymity in most DeFi applications can ensure that users are not discriminated against (Schär, 2021) and have the same rights and access as every other market participant. Hence, an argument can be made that the unbanked may get the chance to participate in these financial markets (Schuetz & Venkatesh, 2020). This phenomenon of accessibility continues that of previous blockchain-based systems that are public and permissionless, starting from the cryptocurrency Bitcoin.

Composability in itself describes that components within a system can operate with one another. In the case of DeFi, this translates to assets that can be used across applications (Carter & Jeng, 2021), opening up possibilities for countless new applications and use cases. To say it in the words of Schär (2021, p. 169): "[A]nything that has been created before can be used by an individual or by other smart contracts. This flexibility allows for an ever-expanding range of possibilities and unprecedented interest in open financial engineering."

8.3 Applications in the Financial Sector

Subsequently, we introduce notable partnerships and collaborations between DeFi and TradFi. These were selected based on the profile of the organizations involved.[1] Note that these merely act as illustrative applications and should not be generalized per se. Given the degree of secrecy around the projects, we are limited to a high-level description of these applications. We chose the projects based on available documentation and their reputation/successes at the time of writing.

8.3.1 Cross-Border Payments: IBM and Stellar

Financial institutions use costly systems that were designed decades ago to transfer trillions of dollars globally on a daily basis. These financial structures are inefficient, overengineered, and prone to human error. In response, IBM partnered with stellar to redefine cross-border payments by allowing for the quick, safe, and cheap clearing and settlement of international transactions (Stellar Development Foundation, 2019; Rugg & Gaur, 2021).

Stellar is an open-source, decentralized network launched in 2014 by the Stellar Development Foundation with the purpose of facilitating payments and asset issuance. The platform is optimized to move financial resources across borders quickly and safely while keeping low transaction fees to enable smooth interactions between financial actors. This can be achieved by creating and exchanging digital representations (tokens) of real-world assets, such as currencies and real estate, while using blockchain technology to systematically keep track of all the network

[1] The authors declare no competing interests.

activity. Stellar is powered by its native cryptocurrency Lumen, which is mainly used to pay for transaction fees.

The partnership between IBM and Stellar gave birth to World Wire – an application programming interface (API)-based payments product that links financial institutions to the Stellar blockchain. By connecting their existing front-end interfaces to World Wire APIs, the transactions are processed in accordance with the Stellar Consensus Protocol, which relies on the proof-of-agreement consensus mechanism. Apart from money transfer operations, in the long term, this network is designed to handle larger business-to-business (B2B) and corporate payments (Stellar Development Foundation, 2019; Rugg & Gaur, 2021). The role of IBM in the project is to select and approve the applications of regulated financial actors that would like to benefit from World Wire. It also carries the functions of a network operator and hosts validator nodes. In particular, IBM creates accounts for the network participants, which in turn are used to exchange information and transfer value.

8.3.2 *Wholesale Funding Markets: DBS Bank, JP Morgan, and Aave Arc*

DBS Bank, JP Morgan, and SBI Digital Asset Holdings executed their first real-time trades using the permissioned Aave Arc protocol (Monetary Authority of Singapore, 2022b). Aave is a decentralized lending platform built on Ethereum. It allows users to borrow and lend a wide variety of assets as well as to build applications. The protocol is open-source, and the AAVE token is used to govern the network. Aave moved away from the common peer-to-peer (P2P) lending concept when borrowers and lenders are directly connected to a pool-based strategy where no direct connection between the two parties exists. Instead, lenders deposit liquidity into a pool contract and earn interest on it while borrowers take funds from that same contract by offering a collateral and paying an interest rate. The latter is determined algorithmically.

The trades happened under the umbrella of the first pilot of Project Guardian, organized by the Monetary Authority of Singapore (MAS) (Monetary Authority of Singapore, 2022a). The aim was to identify DeFi opportunities in wholesale funding markets. In particular, the pilot project explored whether tokenized asset transactions and deposits can be conducted on a public blockchain while relying on DeFi protocols to maintain regulatory compliance. The pilot consisted of two parts:

1. Foreign exchange transactions using tokenized Singapore Dollars (SGD) issued by J.P. Morgan and tokenized Japanese Yen (JPY) issued by SBI Digital Asset Holdings.

2. Buying and selling of foreign exchange and government bonds by means of tokenized deposits and tokenized securities of DBS and SBI Digital Asset Holdings.

The successful trades demonstrate that wholesale transactions can be conducted directly between stakeholders through a DeFi protocol, eliminating the need for intermediary involvement and effectively demonstrating that the deployment of the new infrastructure could yield potential cost savings in the clearing and execution of trades.

8.3.3 Digital Bonds: European Investment Bank, BNP Paribas, HSBC, and RBC Capital Markets

The European Investment Bank, in collaboration with BNP Paribas, HSBC, and RBC Capital Markets, successfully issued its first digital bond on a combination of private and public blockchains (European Investment Bank, 2023). In total, the $50 million digital bonds with a floating interest rate were registered in an optimized and efficient private blockchain provided by HSBC Orion. The blockchain records were mirrored on a public blockchain to ensure transparency. The goal of this partnership is to decrease expenses, enhance productivity, and facilitate real-time data synchronization among all the stakeholders.

The digital bonds are stored in digital securities accounts maintained on the HSBC Orion platform. BNP Paribas Securities Services in Luxembourg, along with RBC and HSBC, will serve as custodians for their current clients who choose to invest in this digital bond. The underlying infrastructure is shared among the three actors, while HSBC is responsible for recording transactions related to digital bonds on its HSBC Orion platform as a central account keeper.

8.3.4 Debt Securities: Société Générale and Tezos

Société Générale issued a euro medium-term note – flexible debt security that matures in 5–10 years – as a security token on the Tezos blockchain (Société Générale, 2021). This issuance of the first structured product on the blockchain signals the rising relevance of Société Générale Forge – an innovative subsidiary of Société Générale Group dedicated to offering services around crypto-assets. This project indicates that European legal and operational frameworks allow for the issuance of complex financial products on public blockchains. The benefits of exploring and adopting this technology include an abundance of tools for creating tailor-made and complex structural products, reduced time-to-market, as well as faster transactions and settlements. Moreover, by eliminating redundant intermediaries, the transparency of the issuance process increases, while operational costs decrease.

8.4 Challenges to Adoption

Despite the economic opportunities and the emergence of first partnerships between TradFi and DeFi, FIs still seem to be hesitant to adopt blockchain solutions on a broader scale. The reasons for this hesitancy are manifold, principally consisting of a variety of socioeconomic challenges and technical risks, as well as regulatory challenges. In this chapter, we discuss a selection of those challenges.

8.4.1 Composability Versus Market Volatility

One of the unique selling propositions of DeFi also poses one of its greater challenges – composability. DeFi, just like traditional asset markets, are subject to volatility. Unlike regular markets, however, DeFi protocols and assets are strongly interconnected. As such, they seem particularly vulnerable to systemic risks (Gramlich et al., 2022). If one asset is subject to high price volatility, it impacts all the protocols it is interconnected with. This manifested, among others, in the case of LUNA/Terra USD (UST): in 2022, a downward cascade for the broader market occurred. UST was a so-called *algorithmic stablecoin* whose design was pegging its value to fiat currencies such as the US Dollar. The LUNA token, in turn, was used to stabilize the value of Terra by arbitraging between LUNA and UST pools to ensure that UST demand and supply were in equilibrium (Briola et al., 2023). Since both tokens were freely tradable, this coupling led to a situation where strong sell pressure for the LUNA token created fear in the market that UST would lose its peg. This fear, in turn, led to a bank run, in which investors traded their UST for fiat currency, triggering an adjustment of the LUNA supply. More specifically, LUNA was minted to be sold on the market to reestablish the UST peg. Naturally, this created an even higher sell pressure for LUNA, causing more fear and more UST sell orders, eventually leading to a downward price spiral that resulted in the price collapse of both tokens. This affected not only all protocols in the Terra LUNA ecosystem but also protocols that had a bridge to Terra (Kitzler et al., 2023). For more details on the complexity of the LUNA/UST case, we point to Briola et al. (2023) and Liu et al. (2023).

In essence, and as an overarching challenge, we denote that if TradFi players are exposed to one of those assets or protocols, their investment is affected accordingly. This risk, however, is only prevalent when TradFis are exposed to assets that are utilized in public-permissionless blockchains. In cases where private permissioned protocols with proprietary tokens are utilized, these risks are reduced.

8.4.2 *Immutability Versus Transaction Reversibility*

Another challenge that may cause hesitancy to adopt DeFi solutions on a broad scale is yet again linked to one of its main propositions – its immutability, or, more specifically, its probabilistic finality. That is, with every new block added to the ledger, it becomes increasingly more difficult for potential attackers to alter transactions already recorded on the ledger (Butijn et al., 2020; Abellán Álvarez et al., 2024). If attackers intended to change transactions of older blocks, they would need to change the hash values of the block the transaction resides in as well as every following block. Hence, the more blocks are added, the more effort it would require attackers to calculate and alter hash values and convince all other nodes in the network that their blocks are legitimate. Since the probability to do so shrinks with every new block, transactions are considered "final" or "finalized" when a certain probabilistic threshold is met (Zhang & Lee, 2020).

While immutability is one of the foundations of the security of permissionless blockchain networks, it also stands in stark contrast to one of many value propositions that characterize TradFi intuitions, namely, to unburden their customers (Bravo et al., 2009). Moreover, while immutable transactions are beneficial for the transparency and traceability of funds, they do not allow for any post hoc correction. Hence, everyday issues and mishaps, such as transferring funds to wrong addresses or sending incorrect amounts, cannot be easily corrected. In the case of blockchain, there are only a few means to make corrections and "wind back time" without the help of the involved transaction parties, i.e., allowing short, temporary reversibility defined in token standards (Wang et al., 2022). In general, however, there are not many resolutions to potential disputes other than being at the mercy of the recipient for a potential refund. As such, taking on these risks is not for everyone, be it customers or banks.

8.4.3 *Distributed Governance Versus Oligarchy*

Developers in the field of DeFi have aimed to create formal governance structures that align with the goal of sociopolitical decentralization. To achieve this goal, first advancements were made for the DEX Uniswap. The developers of Uniswap introduced tokens that grant voting power, known as *governance tokens* or *voting rights tokens*. These tokens are tradable and can be purchased on centralized and decentralized exchanges before being used to cast votes on specific platforms. However, despite the efforts made to achieve decentralization, the tradability of voting rights tokens means that power can still become highly concentrated over time, because single individuals can amass large amounts of these tokens (Barbereau et al., 2023b; Fernandez et al., 2024). This concentration of power is risky, as it can lead to centralization and predatory behavior that manipulates markets (rekt.news, 2024).

In Bancor, for instance, the power of single voting rights token holders was repeatedly abused, as they managed to tip the election balance in their favor. At the Snapshot proposal[2] 12.516.455, on an electorate of 142 voters, four parties cast 91% of the votes "against." Similarly, at Snapshot proposal 12.516.466, on an electorate of 156 voters, four parties cast 92% of the "against" votes. This problem is one that enterprises must be aware of, as it can lead to a loss of agency (Barbereau et al., 2022b).

8.4.4 Disintermediation Versus Liability

The United States (US) Infrastructure Investment and Jobs Act (2021) and the European Union (EU)'s Fifth Anti-Money Laundering Act (2021) – both of which represent considerable efforts on regulating anti-money laundering (AML)/know-your-customer (KYC) in the institutional crypto space (Salami, 2021) – require service providers to perform KYC checks on users prior to issuing a centralized and custodial wallet (as is typically done on registered platforms such as Binance and Coinbase). DeFi platforms, on the other hand, operate without intermediaries; in other words, they are by nature non-custodial and unregistered. Conversely, they pose considerable challenges to find vectors upon which (financial) regulation can uphold its purpose (Aramonte et al., 2021; Barbereau & Bodó, 2023). In reality, regulation can technically only target the *on-ramp* (conversion of fiat currency to cryptocurrency) and *off-ramp* (conversion of cryptocurrency to fiat currency) of DeFi platforms, leaving regulators in a deadlock (Zetzsche et al., 2020). This challenge was also denoted in response to the developments of the EU's Markets in Crypto Assets Regulation (MiCAR), where the interpretation of Art. 3 (6) (an "issuer of crypto-assets") is contentious for DAOs (Hansen, 2021). Likewise, the legal implications should a DeFi project face insolvency or misappropriate user funds are unclear at most. Claims of liability or cases of consumer protection are qua null. The same holds for issues of taxation, as well as issues related to asset ownership and custody, should the project fail (Kokorin et al., 2020).

There are now legal regimes that address the legal status of DAOs and define clear(er) boundaries. Notably, the United Kingdom (UK) Financial Conduct Authority (FCA) granted an Electronic Money Institution license to a DeFi entity (Aave) (Madeira, 2021), and the State of Wyoming provided the first legal basis for the operation, management, and liability of (financial) DAOs (Committee on Blockchain and of the State of Wyoming, 2021). However, we foresee these, at least in the short term, to be ambiguous. One argument for the use of DeFi is the very legal nature that puts it at odds with financial regulation: the lack of (legal)

---

[2] Snapshot is a decentralized voting system for off-chain elections. It is popular among many decentralized autonomous organizations (DAOs), including Uniswap, Aave, and SushiSwap.

TTPs can be considered both a blessing and curse. This means that both contracting and compliance will remain fuzzy, putting at risk the legal reputation of TradFi enterprises that wish to engage in these systems.

It is worth noting that the DeFi space is also looking for its own "solutions." The platform Aave is a notable project that aims to provide (decentralized) financial services and products to institutional investors (Wintermeyer, 2022), de facto operating within a legal sandbox. Aave developed and launched a separate platform (Aave Arc) for lending and liquidity services specifically designed to serve institutional investors while ensuring regulatory compliance. Aave Arc will require enterprises to undergo a KYC or know-your-business (KYB) process, ensuring AML and combating the financing of terrorism (CFT) compliance. On the on-ramp, it requires customers to undergo verification processes in adherence with the Financial Action Task Force (FATF) (so-called wallet *whitelisting*), thereby obtaining opportunities to invest in DeFi. The off-ramps, then, are operated securely by a TTP, who provide financial transparency for auditors (Aave Protocol, 2021). As such, Aave is spearheading a system that allows institutional investors to benefit from DeFi while adhering to regulatory standards – notably, by allowing them to combat money laundering and terrorist financing practices more effectively. Arguably, this may further spark greater adoption of DeFi services, as pointed out by Senator Lummis: "We certainly want to comply with things like the anti-money laundering laws [and] the Bank Secrecy Act, but we also want to make sure that we're not stifling innovation in the way it's implemented" (CNBC, 2021).

8.4.5 Privacy Versus Transparency

Beyond the sometimes ambiguous legal status, one primary concern of public ledgers is to find an appropriate balance between users' demands for privacy and regulators' demands for transparency. This concern is well known, and technological solutions were proposed in the literature (Barbereau et al., 2022a; Nadler & Schär, 2023; Barbereau et al., 2023a). From a technical perspective, it would be possible to save information of market participants on a public ledger – not least, using Ethereum's ERC-725 identity claims. However, this would conflict with some norms of discretion and Europe's General Data Protection Regulation (GDPR) as well as potentially standing in conflict with confidentiality requirements in business interactions (Sedlmeir et al., 2022; Rieger et al., 2019; Platt et al., 2021). Therefore, an off-chain method is needed to store the identity information of natural persons. Common options such as paper-based documents or PDF files are not machine-readable and not efficient. Instead, X.509 certificates or verifiable credentials (VCs) (see Chap. 4) can be used to store machine-readable identity information off-chain (Chadwick et al., 2019). VCs can be combined with crypto-asset wallets, allowing investors to control the exchange of tokenized claims and off-chain identity information. For tokenization in the art market, this approach was proposed by Barbereau et al. (2022a).

8.5 Conclusion

In this chapter, we introduced the core advantages posed by DeFi to the TradFi sector and its stakeholders. To this end, the technological building blocks and economic opportunities were introduced and contextualized by means of exemplification with concrete applications. To our knowledge, these applications are not exclusive and were merely selected to serve as an introduction. We closed this chapter by highlighting some challenges of adoption.

As the space evolves to address critical technical issues and regulatory frameworks designed to clarify possibilities and curb systematic failures (such as MiCAR), we foresee greater adoption. The latest demonstration, aside from the cited examples, is PayPal's stablecoin that takes another step furthering DeFi adoption in TradFi. Hence, it is possible that DeFi is here to stay and that its opportunities will be leveraged and its benefits reaped at a greater scale.

References

Aave Protocol. (2021). AAVE protocol V2 whitepaper. https://github.com/aave/protocol-v2

Abellán Álvarez, I., Gramlich, V., & Sedlmeir, J. (2024). Unsealing the secrets of blockchain consensus: A systematic comparison of the formal security of proof-of-work and proof-of-stake. In *39th ACM/SIGAPP Symposium on Applied Computing*. https://doi.org/10.1145/3605098.3635970

Adler, J., Berryhill, R., Veneris, A., Poulos, Z., Veira, N., & Kastania, A. (2018). Astraea: A decentralized blockchain oracle. In *International Conference on Internet of Things (IThings) and IEEE Green Computing and Communications (GreenCom) and IEEE Cyber, Physical and Social Computing (CPSCom) and IEEE Smart Data (SmartData)* (pp. 1145–1152). IEEE. https://doi.org/10.1109/Cybermatics_2018.2018.00207

Aigner, A. A., & Dhaliwal, G. (2021). Uniswap: Impermanent loss and risk profile of a liquidity provider.

Alharby, M., Aldweesh, A., & Van Moorsel, A. (2018). Blockchain-based smart contracts: A systematic mapping study of academic research (2018). In *International Conference on Cloud Computing, Big Data and Blockchain*. IEEE. https://doi.org/10.1109/ICCBB.2018.8756390.

Allen, F., & Santomero, A. M. (2001). What do financial intermediaries do? *Journal of Banking & Finance*, *25*(2), 271–294. https://doi.org/10.1016/S0378-4266(99)00129-6

Anceaume, E., Pozzo, A., Rieutord, T., & Tucci-Piergiovanni, S. (2020). On finality in blockchains.

Aramonte, S., Huang, W., & Schrimpf, A. (2021). DeFi risks and the decentralisation illusion. *BIS Quarterly Review*. https://www.bis.org/publ/qtrpdf/r_qt2112b.htm?utm_campaign=This%20week%20in%20fintech&utm_medium=email&utm_source=Revue%20newsletter

Barbereau, T., & Bodó, B. (2023). Beyond financial regulation of crypto-asset wallet software: In search of secondary liability. *Computer Law & Security Review*, *49*, 105829. https://doi.org/10.1016/j.clsr.2023.105829

Barbereau, T., Ermolaev, E., Brennecke, M., Hartwich, E., & Sedlmeir, J. (2023a). Beyond a fistful of tumblers: Toward a taxonomy of Ethereum-based mixers. In *Proceedings of the 44th International Conference on System Sciences*. AIS. https://aisel.aisnet.org/icis2023/cyber_security/cyber_security/13/

Barbereau, T., Sedlmeir, J., Smethurst, R., Fridgen, G., & Rieger, A. (2022a). Tokenization and regulatory compliance for art and collectibles markets: From regulators' demands for transparency to investors' demands for privacy. In *Blockchains and the Token Economy* (pp. 213–236). Palgrave Macmillan. https://doi.org/10.1007/978-3-030-95108-5_8

Barbereau, T., Smethurst, R., Papageorgiou, O., Rieger, A., & Fridgen, G. (2022b). DeFi, not so decentralized: The measured distribution of voting rights. *Proceedings of the 55th Annual Hawaii International Conference on System Sciences*. https://doi.org/10.24251/HICSS.2022.734

Barbereau, T., Smethurst, R., Papageorgiou, O., Sedlmeir, J., & Fridgen, G. (2023b). Decentralised finance's timocratic governance: The distribution and exercise of tokenised voting rights. *Technology in Society, 73*, 102251. https://doi.org/10.1016/j.techsoc.2023.102251

Beck, R., Müller-Bloch, C., & King, J. L. (2018). Governance in the blockchain economy: A framework and research agenda. *Journal of the Association for Information Systems, 19*(10), 1020–1034. https://doi.org/10.17705/1jais.00518

Bons, R. W., & Alt, R. (2015). E-commerce online payments. *The International Encyclopedia of Digital Communication and Society*. https://doi.org/10.1002/9781118767771.wbiedcs062

Bravo, R., Montaner, T., & Pina, J. M. (2009). The role of bank image for customers versus non-customers. *International Journal of Bank Marketing, 27*(4), 315–334. https://doi.org/10.1108/02652320910968377

Briola, A., Vidal-Tomás, D., Wang, Y., & Aste, T. (2023). Anatomy of a stablecoin's failure: The Terra-Luna case. *Finance Research Letters, 51*, 103358. https://doi.org/10.1016/j.frl.2022.103358

Butijn, B.-J., Tamburri, D. A., & Heuvel, W.-J. V. D. (2020). Blockchains: A systematic multivocal literature review. *ACM Computing Surveys, 53*(3). https://doi.org/10.1145/3369052.

Carter, N., & Jeng, L. (2021). DeFi protocol risks: The paradox of DeFi. *Regtech, Suptech and Beyond: Innovation and Technology in Financial Services" RiskBooks–Forthcoming Q, 3*. https://doi.org/10.2139/ssrn.3866699

Chadwick, D. W., Laborde, R., Oglaza, A., Venant, R., Wazan, S., & Nijjar, M. (2019). Improved identity management with verifiable credentials and FIDO. *IEEE Communications Standards Magazine, 3*(4), 14–20. https://doi.org/10.1109/MCOMSTD.001.1900020

Christidis, K., & Devetsikiotis, M. (2016). Blockchains and smart contracts for the Internet of Things. *IEEE Access, 4*, 2292–2303. https://doi.org/10.1109/ACCESS.2016.2566339

CNBC. (2021). CNBC transcript: Senator Cynthia Lummis speaks with Ylan Mui from the CNBC financial advisor summit. https://www.cnbc.com/2021/06/29/cnbc-transcript-senator-cynthia-lummis-speaks-with-ylan-mui-from-the-cnbc-financial-advisor-summit.html

Committee on Blockchain, F. T. & of the State of Wyoming, D. I. T. (2021). Decentralized autonomous organizations. *66th Legislature of the State of Wyoming* https://www.wyoleg.gov/Legislation/2021/SF0038

De Filippi, P., & Loveluck, B. (2016). The invisible politics of Bitcoin: Governance crisis of a decentralised infrastructure. *Internet Policy Review, 5*(3). https://doi.org/10.14763/2016.3.427

European Investment Bank. (2023). EIB issues its first ever digital bond in pound sterling. https://www.eib.org/en/press/all/2023-030-eib-issues-its-first-ever-digital-bond-in-british-pounds

Fernandez, J. D., Barbereau, T., & Papageorgiou, O. (2024). Agent-based model of initial token allocations: Simulating distributions post fair launch. *ACM Transactions on Management Information Systems*. https://doi.org/10.1145/3649318

Gramlich, V., Guggenberger, T., Principato, M., Schellinger, B., & Urbach, N. (2023). A multivocal literature review of decentralized finance: Current knowledge and future research avenues. *Electronic Markets, 33*(1), 11. https://doi.org/10.1007/s12525-023-00637-4

Gramlich, V., et al. (2022). Decentralized finance (DeFi): Foundations, applications, potentials, and challenges. https://www.fit.fraunhofer.de/content/dam/fit/de/documents/Whitepaper__DeFi__English_Version_2022_07_15.pdf

Hansen, P. (2021). New crypto rules in the European Union – gateway for mass adoption, or excessive regulation? *Stanford Law School*. https://law.stanford.edu/2021/01/12/new-crypto-rules-in-the-eu-gateway-for-mass-adoption-or-excessive-regulation/

Hartwich, E., Hoess, A., Rieger, A., Roth, T., Fridgen, G., & Young, A. G. (2023a). How organizations sustain and navigate between (de) centralization equilibria: A process model.

In *Proceedings of the 44th International Conference on Information Systems*. AIS. https://aisel.aisnet.org/icis2023/itadopt/itadopt/10.

Hartwich, E., Ollig, P., Fridgen, G., & Rieger, A. (2024). Probably something: A multi-layer taxonomy of non-fungible tokens. *Internet Research*, *34*(1), 216–238. https://doi.org/10.1108/INTR-08-2022-0666

Hartwich, E., Rieger, A., Sedlmeir, J., Jurek, D., & Fridgen, G. (2023b). Machine economies. *Electronic Markets*, *33*(1). https://doi.org/10.1007/s12525-023-00649-0

Hartwich, E., Roth, T. H., Rieger, A., Zavolokina, L., & Fridgen, G. (2024). Negotiation and Translation Between Discursive Fields: A Study on the Diffusion of Decentralized Finance. In *Proceedings of the European Conference of Information Systems*. AIS Electronic Library, 1228. https://aisel.aisnet.org/ecis2024/track20_adoption/track20_adoption/4.

Kannengiesser, N., Lins, S., Sander, C., Winter, K., Frey, H., & Sunyaev, A. (2021). Challenges and common solutions in smart contract development. *IEEE Transactions on Software Engineering*, *48*(11), 4291–4318. https://doi.org/10.1109/TSE.2021.3116808

Kitzler, S., Victor, F., Saggese, P., & Haslhofer, B. (2023). Disentangling decentralized finance (DeFi) compositions. *ACM Transactions on the Web*, *17*(2). https://doi.org/10.1145/3532857

Kokorin, I., De Graaf, T., & Haentjens, M. (2020). The failed hopes of disintermediation: Crypto-custodian insolvency, legal risks and howto avoid them. *Singapore Journal of Legal Studies* (pp. 526–563). https://search.informit.org/doi/10.3316/informit.622490322420398

Liu, J., Makarov, I., & Schoar, A. (2023). Anatomy of a run: The Terra Luna crash. *National Bureau of Economic Research*. https://doi.org/10.3386/w31160

Madeira, A. (2021). DeFi giant Aave (LEND) rallies 40% after receiving UK FCA approval. *Coin-Telegraph*. https://cointelegraph.com/news/defi-giant-aave-lend-rallies-40-after-receiving-uk-fca-approval

Menkveld, A. J. (2013). High frequency trading and the new market makers. *Journal of financial Markets*, *16*(4), 712–740. https://doi.org/10.1016/j.finmar.2013.06.006

Mohan, V. (2022). Automated market makers and decentralized exchanges: A DeFi primer. *Financial Innovation*, *8*(1). https://doi.org/10.1186/s40854-021-00314-5

Monetary Authority of Singapore. (2022a). First industry pilot for digital asset and decentralised finance goes live. https://www.mas.gov.sg/news/media-releases/2022/first-industry-pilot-for-digital-asset-and-decentralised-finance-goes-live

Monetary Authority of Singapore. (2022b). MAS partners the industry to pilot use cases in digital assets. https://www.mas.gov.sg/news/media-releases/2022/mas-partners-the-industry-to-pilot-use-cases-in-digital-assets

Nadler, M., & Schär, F. (2023). Tornado Cash and blockchain privacy: A primer for economists and policymakers. *Federal Reserve Bank of St. Louis Review*, *105*(2), 122–136. https://doi.org/10.20955/r.105.122-36

Nakamoto, S. (2008). Bitcoin: A peer-to-peer electronic cash system. https://bitcoin.org/bitcoin.pdf

Platt, M., Bandara, R. J., Drăgnoiu, A.-E., & Krishnamoorthy, S. (2021). Information privacy in decentralized applications. In *Trust models for next-generation blockchain ecosystems* (pp. 85–104). Springer. https://doi.org/10.1007/978-3-030-75107-4_4

Prewett, K. W., Prescott, G. L., & Phillips, K. (2020). Blockchain adoption is inevitable – barriers and risks remain. *Journal of Corporate Accounting & Finance*, *31*(2), 21–28. https://doi.org/10.1002/jcaf.22415

rekt.news. (2024). Rekt - Leaderboard — rekt.news. https://rekt.news/leaderboard/

Rieger, A., Lockl, J., Urbach, N., Guggenmos, F., & Fridgen, G. (2019). Building a blockchain application that complies with the EU general data protection regulation. *MIS Quarterly Executive*, *18*(4), 263–279. https://doi.org/10.17705/2msqe.00020

Rugg, R., & Gaur, N. (2021). Fueling the financial industry with open source cross-border payments IBM supply chain and blockchain blog. https://www.ibm.com/blogs/blockchain/2021/10/fueling-the-financial-industry-with-open-source-cross-border-payments

Rust, J., & Hall, G. (2003). Middlemen versus market makers: A theory of competitive exchange. *Journal of Political Economy*, *111*(2), 353–403. https://doi.org/10.1086/367684

Sáez, L., & Shi, X. (2004). Liquidity pools, risk sharing, and financial contagion. *Journal of Financial Services Research*, *25*(1), 5–23. https://doi.org/10.1023/B:FINA.0000008662.59653.33

Salami, I. (2021). Challenges and approaches to regulating decentralized finance. *American Journal of International Law Ubound*, *115*, 425–429. https://doi.org/10.1017/aju.2021.66. https://www.cambridge.org/core/product/identifier/S2398772321000660/type/journal_article

Schär, F. (2021). Decentralized finance: On blockchain-and smart contract-based financial markets. *Federal Reserve Bank of St. Louis Review*. https://doi.org/10.20955/r.103.153-74

Schuetz, S., & Venkatesh, V. (2020). Blockchain, adoption, and financial inclusion in India: Research opportunities. *International Journal of Information Management*, *52*, 101936. https://doi.org/10.1016/j.ijinfomgt.2019.04.009

Sedlmeir, J., Lautenschlager, J., Fridgen, G., & Urbach, N. (2022). The transparency challenge of blockchain in organizations. *Electronic Markets*, *32*, 1779–1794. https://doi.org/10.1007/s12525-022-00536-0

Société Générale (2021). Societe Generale issues the first structured product on public blockchain. https://www.societegenerale.com/en/news/press-release/first-structured-product-public-blockchain

Sriram, S. (2021). Bitcoin becomes best performing asset of the decade, returning ten times more than NASDAQ 100. https://finance.yahoo.com/news/bitcoin-becomes-best-performing-asset-132208120.html

Stellar Development Foundation. (2019). Why IBM built World Wire on Stellar. https://www.stellar.org/blog/why-ibm-built-world-wire-on-stellar

Sunyaev, A., et al. (2021). Token economy. *Business & Information Systems Engineering*, *63*, 457–478. https://doi.org/10.1007/s12599-021-00684-1

Szabo, N. (1997). Formalizing and securing relationships on public networks. *First Monday*, *2*(9). https://doi.org/10.5210/fm.v2i9.548

Wang, K., Wang, Q., & Boneh, D. (2022). ERC-20R and ERC-721R: Reversible transactions on Ethereum. https://arxiv.org/abs/2208.00543

Werner, S. M., Perez, D., Gudgeon, L., Klages-Mundt, A., Harz, D., & Knottenbelt, W. J. (2022). SoK: Decentralized finance (DeFi). In *Proceedings of the 4th ACM Conference on Advances in Financial Technologies* (pp. 30–46). https://doi.org/10.1145/3558535.3559780

Wintermeyer, L. (2022). DeFi is on the move to the institutional market: More a marathon than a sprint. https://www.forbes.com/sites/lawrencewintermeyer/2022/02/17/defi-is-on-the-move-to-the-institutional-market-more-a-marathon-than-a-sprint

Wood, G. et al. (2014). Ethereum: A secure decentralised generalised transaction ledger. https://gavwood.com/paper.pdf

Zetzsche, D. A., Arner, D. W., & Buckley, R. P. (2020). Decentralized finance. *Journal of Financial Regulation*, *6*(2), 172–203. https://doi.org/10.1093/jfr/fjaa010

Zhang, S., & Lee, J.-H. (2020). Analysis of the main consensus protocols of blockchain. *ICT express*, *6*(2), 93–97. https://doi.org/10.1016/j.icte.2019.08.001

Chapter 9
Decentralized Finance and Decentralized Digital Identities: Opportunities and Challenges of Identity Solutions

Vincent Gramlich, Tobias Guggenberger, Sarah Lichtmannecker, Marc Principato, Benjamin Schellinger, and Jens Strüker

Abstract Decentralized finance (DeFi) presents individuals with financial autonomy and opens numerous avenues within the financial services sector. However, there are obstacles that impede its broader adoption. Many of these hurdles cannot be exclusively addressed through technical means and stem from issues related to the absence of a consistent, enduring identity framework. This chapter delves into these issues faced by DeFi, examines possible identity solutions, discusses their potentials and challenges, and ultimately outlines pathways for progression.

9.1 Motivation

Since the launch of the *cryptocurrency* Bitcoin in 2008 (Nakamoto, 2008), the market capitalization of various blockchain-based assets has grown significantly. In addition, developments in crypto finance over the past few years have contributed to the emergence of a decentralized financial ecosystem, commonly referred to as *DeFi* (Schär, 2021). DeFi comprises various financial applications that enable trustless and decentralized financial activities (Gramlich et al., 2022). Its popularity is, among other figures, emphasized by the total value of assets, which peaked at approx. 180 billion USD in December 2021 (DeFi Llama, 2022). As DeFi contains significant funds and opportunities for business operations, a rich financial service sector has formed around DeFi services. Besides crypto-native businesses like centralized exchanges (CEXs) (e.g., Binance), institutions from the existing

V. Gramlich (✉)
Frankfurt University of Applied Sciences, Frankfurt am Main, Germany
e-mail: vincent.gramlich@fim-rc.de

T. Guggenberger · S. Lichtmannecker · M. Principato · B. Schellinger · J. Strüker
FIM Research Center for Information Management (FIM), Bayreuth, Germany
e-mail: tobias.guggenberger@fim-rc.de; sarah.lichtmannecker@fim-rc.de;
marc.principato@fim-rc.de; benjamin.schellinger@web.de; jens.strueker@fim-rc.de

G. Fridgen et al. (eds.), *Decentralization Technologies*, Financial Innovation and Technology, https://doi.org/10.1007/978-3-031-66047-4_9

financial system such as traditional banks (e.g., J.P. Morgan) show increasing interest and involvement in this upcoming ecosystem, too (Qin et al., 2022).

Advocates of DeFi-based services argue that these applications can promote financial inclusion, reduce poverty and inequality, and enhance global economic growth (Schär, 2021). Furthermore, the fundamental protocols of DeFi applications offer the potential to automate processes across multiple organizations, which can result in faster transaction speeds and improved overall efficiency (Fridgen et al., 2018). Owing to the inherent open-source characteristic of the code and its unalterable state subsequent to deployment, there is a diminished necessity to trust the integrity and functionality of DeFi applications blindly. Moreover, the modular elements of DeFi protocols strive to simplify the creation and incorporation of financial applications without requiring bank-specific application programming interfaces (APIs).

Despite the potential advantages DeFi offers to the economy and society, significant challenges must be addressed. By default, the identity of a user on a public blockchain only comprises a blockchain address. This missing linkage between DeFi users and their real-world identity limits its functionality and adoption (Voskobojnikov et al., 2021). The security and efficiency of DeFi applications are impaired, because the absence of identity trust and reputation-based models inhibits financial products like undercollateralized loans or the design of secure governance mechanisms (Schär, 2021; Werner et al., 2021; Barbereau et al., 2023b). Furthermore, the pseudonymity of DeFi users attracts and enables scams and other illicit activities (Gramlich et al., 2023; Meyer et al., 2022). Moreover, the adoption of DeFi, especially from financial institutions, is hindered, as they have to integrate know-your-customer (KYC) processes to comply with anti-money laundering (AML) and combating the financing of terrorism (CFT) regulation (Gramlich et al., 2022; Qin et al., 2022; Barbereau et al., 2023a).

There are continuous advancements in technologies that could potentially interact with DeFi applications in the future, including digital identities based on asymmetric cryptography that allow for machine-verifiable information (Sedlmeir et al., 2021; Strüker et al., 2021) (see also Chap. 4). These technologies could serve as a bridge between regulated domains and the DeFi ecosystem and remedy aforementioned issues (Sedlmeir et al., 2022).

Consequently, the purpose of this chapter is to deliver a thorough comprehension of the technological underpinnings of DeFi, encompassing identities, along with an exploration of challenges and prospects related to identities within the realm of DeFi. We discuss the technology stack that powers DeFi, including *blockchains*, *smart contracts*, *tokens*, and *digital wallets*. Subsequently, we cover the conceptualization of identities in DeFi and then analyze opportunities, evaluate related promises, and discuss potential solutions to overcome current obstacles in DeFi.

9.2 Foundations of DeFi

According to Gramlich et al. (2023), DeFi can be defined as *"a decentralized financial system that enables financial services and instruments to be offered and used without the need for intermediaries."* This innovative system aims to replicate traditional financial services and instruments while reducing reliance on trusted centralized institutions (Buterin et al., 2014; Schueffel, 2021; Zetzsche et al., 2020). DeFi has the potential to not only bring the benefits of blockchain and smart contracts to traditional finance but also to enhance existing infrastructures, markets, services, and instruments (Gramlich et al., 2022; Nadler & Schär, 2020; Schär, 2021).

As illustrated in Fig. 9.1, DeFi consists of multiple layers (Schär, 2021). The foundation of DeFi are blockchains that store programming code. In this regard, non-native assets are often implemented as tokens using smart contracts facilitated through standardized templates covering a wide range of use cases (Buterin et al., 2014; Schär, 2021). The protocol layer comprises smart contracts that define the fundamental building blocks of DeFi, such as exchanges, money markets, derivatives, and asset management (Schär, 2021). DeFi applications modify and combine these building blocks to create sophisticated financial services and instruments with accessible front ends and back ends. Aggregators in the top layer combine applications to build platforms by integrating multiple services into a portfolio with a single entry point for users (Schär, 2021). To provide easy access to these services, web-based interfaces are often used by DeFi applications and aggregators to visualize their front end (Jensen et al., 2021; Schär, 2021). Due to their standardization and modularity, DeFi-based protocols are highly interoperable and composable, earning them the moniker of "Money Lego" (Grigo et al., 2020).

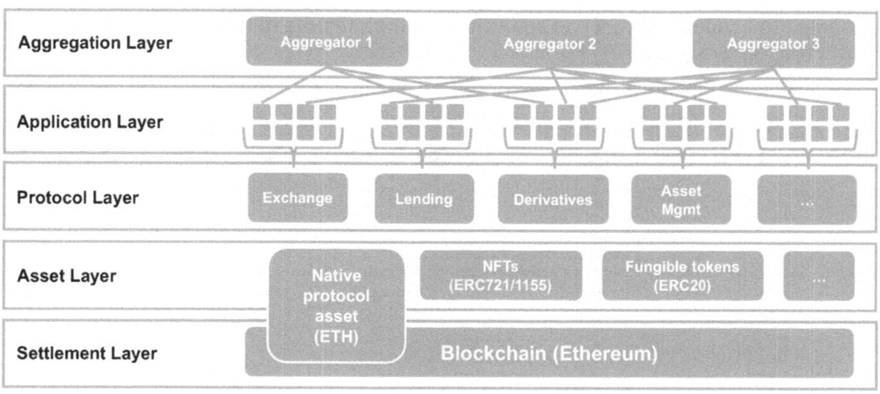

Fig. 9.1 DeFi stack following Schär (2021)

9.3 Digital Identities in DeFi

The concept of identities in DeFi is comprised of three main aspects. Figure 9.2 displays these three aspects: entities, identities and attributes, as well as their different variations, and their respective relationships. Every entity possesses attributes, while different identities of an entity can be expressed as different subsets of the set that contains all its attributes (Beres et al., 2021).

In DeFi, entities can be differentiated into external and internal entities. Internal entities in DeFi exist organically within the system (i.e., on-chain), including transactions (Victor, 2020), smart contract-based entities such as tokens (Cernera et al., 2023), and decentralized applications (DApps) (Saengchote et al., 2022). Internal entities in DeFi have only one identity that is stored on-chain and whose attributes are known to everyone in the system. For example, all the attributes of a transaction have to be known in order to process it and prevent double spending (Wu et al., 2021). The same applies to smart contract-based entities such as tokens and DApps whose bytecode needs to be public, so that the computations can be distributed and verified decentrally (Das et al., 2022).

External entities in DeFi refer to every entity that exists off-chain, such as CEXs (Jabotinsky & Lavi, 2021), tokenized artworks (Barbereau et al., 2022), or the human user (Brennecke et al., 2022). External entities are represented by externally-owned accounts (EOAs) in the blockchain system (Chang et al., 2022) and are characterized by their transaction history and blockchain address (Linoy et al., 2019). Transactions play an essential role in DeFi as they represent the interplay between on-chain identities (Weyl et al., 2022; Beres et al., 2021). Important transaction attributes are the unique transaction identifier (i.e., transaction hash) as well as the sender and receiver addresses (Linoy et al., 2019). Because transactions have to be publicly verifiable to achieve consensus in DeFi, they enable the transaction history attribute of on-chain identities by linking transaction attributes to sender and receiver identifiers, which results in transparency benefits in DeFi (Wright & Meier, 2021).

External entities have off-chain identities, for instance, the legal identity of users, i.e., the "real-world" identity, consisting of attributes that are personally identifiable information (PII) (see also Chap. 4) (Bansod & Ragha, 2022; Gao et al., 2021). The

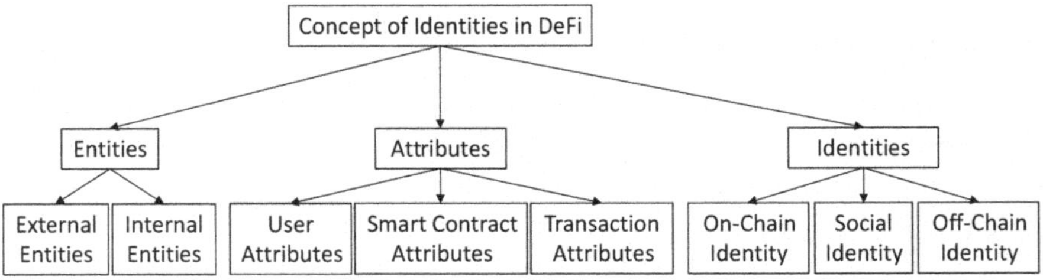

Fig. 9.2 Digital identities in DeFi

social identity refers to interactions between users and is two-sided. It can be on-chain, expressed through users transacting with each other (Kuśmierz & Overko, 2022; Pauwels et al., 2022), and off-chain, expressed via social media or in-person interactions of DeFi users (e.g., in conventions) (Beres et al., 2021; Weyl et al., 2022). The on-chain identity only contains on-chain attributes, is natively cost-free, and requires no linkage of other identities, such as the real-world identity or a user's previous on-chain identities for verification purposes or other measures to restrict access (Jensen et al., 2021). This circumstance is often subsumed under the permissionless, decentralization, and openness features of DeFi.

The identity concept we have outlined here is based on a specific blockchain system; i.e., for other blockchain systems, on-chain identities are perceived off-chain and cannot be transferred seamlessly. An internal processing of off-chain data is not possible in this context, because it requires external integration with identities of other blockchain systems (Barbereau et al., 2022; Harwick & Caton, 2022). This circumstance also explains the need for oracles in DeFi, which are, in essence, identity verifiers and curators between blockchains to bridge these hermetically separated data spaces and on-chain external entities by creating and managing trusted identities for them (Avrilionis & Hardjono, 2021).

9.4 Potentials of Digital Identities in DeFi

DeFi is an inherently transparent system that uses the public visibility of on-chain identity attributes to execute and verify transactions (Gramlich et al., 2023; Liu et al., 2020). However, the public on-chain identity is not directly linked to a real-world, i.e., external, identity. This results in the absence of a clear authority in such a system but also the nonexistence of effective accountability measures (Jabotinsky & Lavi, 2021). This situation, in turn, leads to significant drawbacks and hurdles for the current DeFi system that could be alleviated by a proper identity system, as displayed in Fig. 9.3.

The lack of accountability comes with two main drawbacks that manifest in the design of DeFi applications. The first is a security and complexity issue in DeFi's governance. As a replacement for accountability, incentive mechanisms are commonly put in place to enforce the benevolent behavior of participants via game-theoretic means (Harwick & Caton, 2022; Qin et al., 2022). However, relying on incentives significantly limits DeFi's ability to become a secure and efficient financial system (Kroon et al., 2021). The degree of security can be impaired by centralization in DeFi application governance, i.e., in the form of token ownership (Guggenberger et al., 2023; Sun et al., 2022) and the creation of an authority structure for the management of *DApps* (Brennecke et al., 2022). Accumulating power in a system that is supposed to be decentralized and therefore does not ensure a clear accountability structure from the outset leads to security gaps in the system, e.g., attacks on parts of its governance (Gramlich et al., 2022; Weyl et al., 2022).

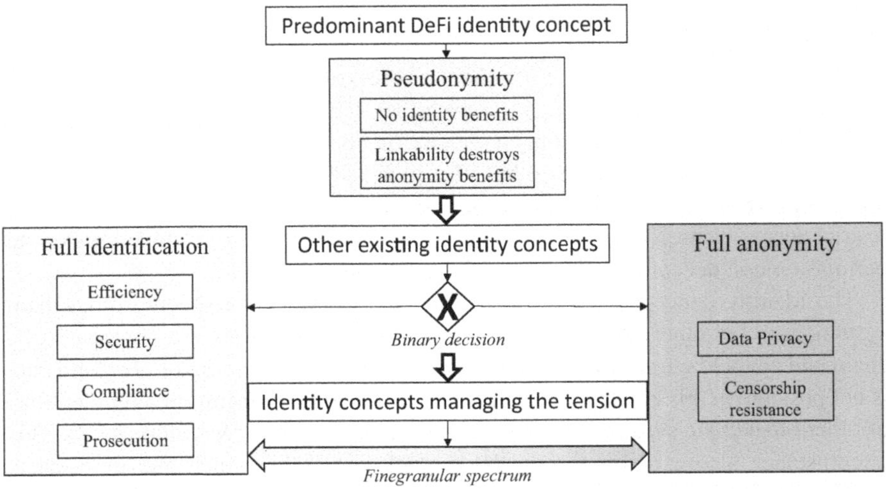

Fig. 9.3 The DeFi identity trade-off

The nonexistence of identities also impairs DeFi's efficiency, for example, DeFi loans need to be overcollateralized because a reputation score (e.g., a credit score) can easily be discarded by creating a new identity that is detached from the one with the credit score (Gramlich et al., 2023; Kroon et al., 2021). In general, on-chain governance mechanisms as a substitute for accountability structures limit DeFi's efficiency at the very moment when external information from off-chain would be required (Avrilionis & Hardjono, 2021; Zhao et al., 2022). Furthermore, it severely limits DeFi's adoption of off-chain assets, such as the tokenization of digital artworks and even physical assets in *non-fungible tokens (NFTs)* (Barbereau et al., 2022), as one cannot be entirely sure whether that asset is an authentic on-chain representation of its off-chain version or whether it is a case of "asset identity theft" (Das et al., 2022). Similarly, oracles suffer from nonpersistent identities and require some degree of trust (Harwick & Caton, 2022).

In addition to the inherent challenges due to the lack of an identity system, DeFi also faces obstacles and limitations related to regulatory compliance and widespread adoption. Financial institutions in traditional financial systems are subject to specific regulations and laws to prevent illicit behavior, as they are responsible for the transfer and custody of assets and money (Jabotinsky & Lavi, 2021). Thus, compliance with financial regulation is a prerequisite for the market entry of these financial institutions and critical for the adoption of DeFi in general (Barbereau et al., 2022). Most noticeably, the effectiveness and enforcement of AML regulation are critical, in particular, for regulators (Jabotinsky & Lavi, 2021; Mell, 2019). Because of the absence of a persistent identity layer in DeFi, individual institutions that are subject to these regulations need to integrate KYC checks to ensure that the transaction parties are known to authorities, i.e., all institutions individually need to create a link between an on-chain and the real-world identity of an entity (Biryukov et al., 2018; Pauwels et al., 2022). However, following standard KYC processes to collect PII to link off-chain identity to on-chain identities for use in monitoring activities or accountability processes comes with several limitations. Firstly, it exposes the entire financial history of a user to all institutions that are required to collect this information, which introduces privacy issues (Hickey & Harrigan, 2022) and centralized points that represent a single point of failure and attract cyberattacks (Das et al., 2022). Secondly, the isolated and thus redundant implementation by all the individual institutions introduces inefficiency and hinders the scalability of a large-spread adoption of DeFi (Gramlich et al., 2022). Moreover, it can often be bypassed by malicious actors, for example, by using multiple on-chain identities (Wright & Meier, 2021). Such issues could be addressed by concepts such as all-or-nothing nontransferability based on a strongly bound government identity (Feulner et al., 2022) or "soulbound" assets (Weyl et al., 2022). Lastly, the question arises of how these could be technically implemented in smart contract-based entities since storing PII on-chain must be avoided to comply with data protection regulations, for example, with the European Union (EU)'s General Data Protection Regulation (GDPR) (Bansod & Ragha, 2022). Zero-knowledge proofs (ZKPs) seem to be a promising technology to address this issue (Barbereau et al., 2023a; Sedlmeir et al., 2022).

Besides the compliance issues, the separation of real-world and DeFi identities also enables illicit activities, such as scams or market manipulation, because it impedes accountability in the form of tracing misbehavior and prosecuting malicious actors (Perdana et al., 2023; von Wachter et al., 2022). Thus, an identity system would come with a multitude of benefits, as displayed in Fig. 9.3. In particular, reintroducing trust through a persistent identity for users and assets could facilitate representation and reputation and would improve the security of DeFi and open up new design options for more efficient applications (Weyl et al., 2022; Zhao et al., 2022). Furthermore, establishing comprehensive and verifiable identities in DeFi is a prerequisite for compliance with financial regulation, would help combat illicit activities, and could overall increase the adoption of DeFi (Gramlich et al., 2023).

9.5 Challenges of Digital Identities in DeFi

Privacy is an important aspect in DeFi, as the protection of sensitive financial data is important not only for compliance with data protection laws such as the EU's GDPR but also for user adoption in general (Bansod & Ragha, 2022). When it comes to data privacy, a critical differentiation must be made between pseudonymity and anonymity that denote different degrees of linkability between an entity and its identities. While anonymity refers to the complete absence of linkability, pseudonymity allows assigning specific identity aspects, e.g., DeFi transactions, to one pseudonym with no direct linkage to the entity behind it (Linoy et al., 2019; Qin et al., 2022).

As displayed in Fig. 9.3, the predominant concept of DeFi is a pseudonymous system based on transparent and public blockchains that make transaction data accessible to everyone (Gramlich et al., 2023). With the combination of pseudonymity and transparency, however, additional external data can enable certain stakeholders to associate a pseudonym to an entity. Thus, these stakeholders can de-anonymize all the information associated with the pseudonym (Wu et al., 2021). As a result, a pseudonymous system with linkability also loses the benefits of an anonymous system in the form of privacy and censorship resistance. Moreover, if it is possible to map tokens' ownership history to the identities of their past owners, different coins of the same currencies might be treated differently, which impairs the fungibility of the currency itself.

The arguably simplest case of linkability is represented by users publicly sharing their blockchain address (i.e., on-chain identity), e.g., via social media (Babu & Abraham, 2021; Chang et al., 2022). However, even without this direct way of de-anonymization, it is possible to establish connections between pseudonyms and entities with forensic analyses that can be categorized into three different layers: network layer, application layer, and transaction layer (Gao et al., 2021; Wu et al., 2021).

The analysis of the network layer is performed by connecting a full node to the blockchain's peer-to-peer (P2P) network, monitoring the transaction packages sent between other nodes and inferring the original sender. When successful, one can link the IP address of a source node to its blockchain address. If users themselves run their nodes, stakeholder such as Internet service providers (ISPs) can then potentially link off-chain identities to on-chain identities (Gao et al., 2021). The application layer analysis targets DApps at the application front end (Wang et al., 2021). On the other hand, backend analyses of DApps can be conducted by monitoring the code properties of smart contracts (Beres et al., 2021). It is also possible to extract information from end devices, such as Web2 credentials (e.g., HTTP cookies), blockchain addresses, and transaction identifiers to provide attribution (Chang et al., 2022). The most widely used analyses happen on the transaction layer, where connections between different on-chain entities can be established by clustering addresses that show commonalities like similar behavior or strong transactional connections (Hickey & Harrigan, 2022; Victor, 2020).

All these methods allow for entity recognition. When additional side-channel information (e.g., IP addresses or meta information on a centralized exchange) is available, full de-anonymization can be achieved (Gao et al., 2021; Hickey & Harrigan, 2022). This scenario not only violates users' privacy but also makes them vulnerable to censorship by the providers of these different layers (Gramlich et al., 2022).

In sum, an identity system for DeFi needs to consider the benefits of an anonymous system and the various techniques that create linkability and de-anonymization to enable users to make intentional decisions regarding their identity usage and data privacy and protect them from censorship (Biryukov et al., 2018; Pauwels et al., 2022). ZKPs provide many means of maintaining accountability and verifiable compliance with regulatory or application-level rules while minimizing the amount of information that needs to be publicly disclosed in this context (Babel & Sedlmeir, 2023).

9.6 Outlook

As outlined above and displayed in Fig. 9.3, DeFi is predominantly a pseudonymous ecosystem that has none of the benefits of a persistent identity but also misses the benefits of anonymity due to linkability. Most of the other existing identity concepts form a binary decision between full identification or full anonymity, with the respective benefits. However, the literature identifies a need for a more differentiated decision between these two poles and proposes concepts to manage the tension between potentials and challenges of an identity system (Pauwels et al., 2022; Barbereau et al., 2022). Only a few proposals center around centralized identity management, such as using permissioned blockchains that link off-chain to on-chain identity by requiring PII at the infrastructure level before granting entry (Jabotinsky & Lavi, 2021; Mell, 2019) or using third parties that manage the identity and access management (IAM) process and then post the result on-chain (Harwick & Caton, 2022). For public blockchain governance, more decentralized options could be feasible.

Most proposals for managing identity potentials while minimizing drawbacks focus on *self-sovereign identity (SSI)* approaches with identity proofs in the form of *verifiable credentials (VCs)* and *verifiable presentations (VPs)*. In an SSI-based DeFi ecosystem, an identity issuer (a trusted third party for the application at hand) hereby issues a cryptographic identity proof (i.e., a VC) to an entity that can use the VC to generate VPs to authenticate arbitrary claims that are made about attributes of the VC to a verifier, e.g., a smart contract related to a DeFi service (Bansod & Ragha, 2022; Kroon et al., 2021). As this paradigm allows for the user-controlled and seamless transfer of attributes between identities, it is commonly used to port attributes from a real-world identity over to the on-chain identity for usage in compliance processes, such as KYC checks to prevent money laundering by encapsulating PII (Barbereau et al., 2022; Biryukov et al., 2018).

In addition, SSI can enable trust in an uncollateralized loan setting (Kroon et al., 2021) or the creation of verified digital identities for off-chain assets (Avrilionis & Hardjono, 2021), levering DeFi-based services. To comply with privacy requirements, ZKPs can be used for the VP, so that only the minimal requested identity information is shared with the verifier, a feature commonly called "selective disclosure" (Barbereau et al., 2022; Pauwels et al., 2022) and "predicate proofs" (Babel & Sedlmeir, 2023). Combined with the use of multiple identities, one can also enable a feature that we will call "selective privacy": VC holders can create identities that are used for purposes with differing degrees of identification and thus avoid that a verifier can link different revealed identity attributes to the same entity (Pauwels et al., 2022). The implementation of SSI in DeFi is commonly envisioned by IAM smart contracts that are used as a layer prior to accessing the financial functions of other smart contracts (Biryukov et al., 2018; Kroon et al., 2021). A significant limitation is that the standard SSI paradigm based on ZKPs is unilateral for two reasons: It fails to account for (I) a way to persistently share relevant attributes to every participant at once instead of only one verifier at a time (note that this could be circumvented by using a specific family of ZKPs called (zk-SNARKs), see, e.g., Babel & Sedlmeir, 2023 and also Chap. 6), and (II) "multi-party control" over the sharing of credentials that comprise attributes concerning more than one party (Weyl et al., 2022).

We find that the concept of identities commonly used in information system (IS) research can be extended to the domain of DeFi. Our findings highlight that DeFi natively does not require the newly created identity in one of its blockchains to be linked to other identities of its users. Hence, not a single DeFi identity exists but individual on-chain identities for different DeFi blockchains. The nonexistence of a persistent identity comes with several drawbacks for DeFi in terms of security and efficiency. Furthermore, it hinders regulatory compliance and the combatting of illicit activities, which ultimately inhibits DeFi adoption. On the other hand, we also reveal the challenges faced by an identity system that tries to leverage these potentials. Here, the literature is mainly concerned with privacy issues that can arise from the transparency or traceability of financial transactions. These de-anonymization methods also expose users to the risk of censorship.

Based on our illustrations of potentials and challenges of identities in DeFi, we showcase the concepts that manage this tension. To achieve an efficient, secure, regulatory compliant, and widely adopted DeFi ecosystem, an identity concept is required that allows for the privacy-preserving sharing of identity attributes, with multiparty control over attributes that concern multiple entities. A potential solution provides the concept of SSI in combination with identity-representing tokens (e.g., ERC-725 or ERC-721). We highlight the challenge of designing various identity-representing tokens and the SSI paradigm to support omnidirectional proofs and functionalities for multiparty-controlled credentials. We advocate for transdisciplinary research between academia and practice that includes DeFi experts, cryptographers, software engineers, regulators, and IAM researchers.

We envision that a consistent and secure identity system can improve DeFi's security, efficiency, regulatory compliance, and, ultimately, adoption. However, data privacy and the risk of censorship – two fundamental values of DeFi – also need to be taken into account. Thus, future research should focus on and extend concepts that manage the tension in between and allow for a more fine-granular and self-determined decision between identification and anonymity.

Acknowledgments This chapter is based on the following conference article: Gramlich et al. (2024).

References

Avrilionis, D., & Hardjono, T. (2021). Towards blockchain-enabled open architectures for scalable digital asset platforms. https://arxiv.org/abs/2110.12553

Babel, M., & Sedlmeir, J. (2023). Bringing data minimization to digital wallets at scale with general-purpose zero-knowledge proofs. https://arxiv.org/abs/2301.00823

Babu, S., & Abraham, K. M. (2021). Central bank digital currencies: policy and operational perspectives for India. *CSI Transactions on ICT*, *9*(2), 85–94. https://doi.org/10.1007/s40012-021-00327-6

Bansod, S., & Ragha, L. (2022). Challenges in making blockchain privacy compliant for the digital world: Some measures. *Sādhanā*, *47*(168). https://doi.org/10.1007/s12046-022-01931-1

Barbereau, T., Ermolaev, E., Brennecke, M., Hartwich, E., & Sedlmeir, J. (2023a). Beyond a fistful of tumblers: Toward a taxonomy of Ethereum-based mixers. In *Proceedings of the 44th International Conference on System Sciences*. AIS. https://aisel.aisnet.org/icis2023/cyber_security/cyber_security/13/

Barbereau, T., Sedlmeir, J., Smethurst, R., Fridgen, G., & Rieger, A. (2022). Tokenization and regulatory compliance for art and collectibles markets: From regulators' demands for transparency to investors' demands for privacy. In *Blockchains and the token economy* (pp. 213–236). Springer. https://doi.org/10.1007/978-3-030-95108-5_8

Barbereau, T., Smethurst, R., Papageorgiou, O., Sedlmeir, J., & Fridgen, G. (2023b). Decentralised finance's timocratic governance: The distribution and exercise of tokenised voting rights. *Technology in Society*, *73*, 102251. https://doi.org/10.1016/j.techsoc.2023.102251

Beres, F., Seres, I. A., Benczur, A. A., & Quintyne-Collins, M. (2021). Blockchain is watching you: Profiling and deanonymizing Ethereum users. In *Proceedings of the International Conference on Decentralized Applications and Infrastructures* (pp. 69–78). IEEE. https://doi.org/10.1109/DAPPS52256.2021.00013

Biryukov, A., Khovratovich, D., & Tikhomirov, S. (2018). Privacy-preserving KYC on Ethereum. In *Proceedings of the 1st ERCIM Blockchain Workshop*. European Society for Socially Embedded Technologies. https://doi.org/10.18420/blockchain2018_09

Brennecke, M., Guggenberger, T., Schellinger, B., & Urbach, N. (2022). The de-central bank in decentralized finance: A case study of MakerDAO. In *Proceedings of the 55th Hawaii International Conference on System Sciences* (pp. 6073–6082). AIS. http://hdl.handle.net/10125/80077

Buterin, V. et al. (2014). A next-generation smart contract and decentralized application platform. https://github.com/ethereum/wiki/wiki/White-Paper

Cernera, F., La Morgia, M., Mei, A., & Sassi, F. (2023). Token spammers, rug and otherspulls, and sniperbots: An analysis of the ecosystem of tokens in Ethereum and the Binance Smart Chain (BNB). In *Prodeedings of the USENIX 32nd Security Symposium* (pp. 3349–3366). ACM. https://dl.acm.org/doi/10.5555/3620237.3620425

Chang, E., Darcy, P., Choo, K.-K. R., & Le-Khac, N.-A. (2022). Forensic artefact discovery and attribution from Android cryptocurrency wallet applications. https://arxiv.org/abs/2205.14611

Das, D., Bose, P., Ruaro, N., Kruegel, C., & Vigna, G. (2022). Understanding security issues in the NFT ecosystem. In *Proceedings of the ACM SIGSAC Conference on Computer and Communications Security* (pp. 667–681). https://doi.org/10.1145/3548606.3559342

DeFi Llama. (2022). Total value locked (TVL) in DeFi. https://defillama.com/

Feulner, S., Sedlmeir, J., Schlatt, V., & Urbach, N. (2022). Exploring the use of self-sovereign identity for event ticketing systems. *Electronic Markets*, *32*(3), 1759–1777. https://doi.org/10.1007/s12525-022-00573-9

Fridgen, G., Radszuwill, S., Urbach, N., & Utz, L. (2018). Cross-organizational workflow management using blockchain technology – towards applicability, auditability, and automation. In *Proceedings of the 51st Hawaii International Conference on System Sciences* (pp. 3507–3517). AIS. https://doi.org/10.24251/hicss.2018.444

Gao, Y., Shi, J., Wang, X., Shi, R., Yin, Z., & Yang, Y. (2021). Practical deanonymization attack in Ethereum based on P2P network analysis. In *Prooceedings of the IEEE International Conference on Parallel & Distributed Processing with Applications, Big Data & Cloud Computing, Sustainable Computing & Communications, Social Computing & Networking (ISPA/BDCloud/SocialCom/SustainCom)* (pp. 1402–1409). https://doi.org/10.1109/ISPA-BDCloud-SocialCom-SustainCom52081.2021.00191

Gramlich, V., Guggenberger, T., Principato, M., Schellinger, B., Duda, S., & Stoetzer, J. (2024). In decentralized finance nobody knows you are a dog. In *Proceedings of the 57th Hawaiin International Conference on Information Systems* (pp. 4558–4567). https://hdl.handle.net/10125/106932

Gramlich, V., Guggenberger, T., Principato, M., Schellinger, B., & Urbach, N. (2023). A multivocal literature review of decentralized finance: Current knowledge and future research avenues. *Electronic Markets, 33*. https://doi.org/10.1007/s12525-023-00637-4

Gramlich, V., et al. (2022). Decentralized finance (DeFi): Foundations, applications, potentials, and challenges. https://www.fit.fraunhofer.de/content/dam/fit/de/documents/Whitepaper__DeFi__English_Version_2022_07_15.pdf

Grigo, J., Hansen, P., Patz, D., & von Wachter, V. (2020). Decentralized finance (DeFi) – a new fintech revolution? https://www.bitkom.org/sites/default/files/2020-07/200729_whitepaper_decentralized-finance.pdf

Guggenberger, T., Kühne, D., Schlatt, V., & Urbach, N. (2023). Designing a cross-organizational identity management system: Utilizing ssi for the certification of retailer attributes. *Electronic Markets, 33*(3). https://doi.org/10.1007/s12525-023-00620-z

Harwick, C., & Caton, J. (2022). What's holding back blockchain finance? On the possibility of decentralized autonomous finance. *The Quarterly Review of Economics and Finance, 84*, 420–429. https://doi.org/10.1016/j.qref.2020.09.006

Hickey, L., & Harrigan, M. (2022). The Bisq decentralised exchange: on the privacy cost of participation. *Blockchain: Research and Applications, 3*(1), 100029. https://doi.org/10.1016/j.bcra.2021.100029

Jabotinsky, H. Y., & Lavi, M. (2021). Speak out: Verifying and unmasking cryptocurrency user identity. *Fordham Intellectual Property Media & Entertainment Law Journal, 32*(3), 518–591. https://ir.lawnet.fordham.edu/iplj/vol32/iss3/1/

Jensen, J. R., von Wachter, V., & Ross, O. (2021). How decentralized is the governance of blockchain-based finance: Empirical evidence from four governance token distributions. https://arxiv.org/abs/2102.10096

Kroon, H., de Vos, M., & Pouwelse, J. (2021). Introducing self-sovereign identity and identity as collateral in decentralized finance. https://repository.tudelft.nl/islandora/object/uuid:5728bcf1-265a-49d0-b3f5-b6653c315b1d/datastream/OBJ/download

Kuśmierz, B., & Overko, R. (2022). How centralized is decentralized? Comparison of wealth distribution in coins and tokens. In *Proceedings of the IEEE International Conference on Omni-Layer Intelligent Systems*. https://doi.org/10.1109/COINS54846.2022.9854972

Linoy, S., Stakhanova, N., & Matyukhina, A. (2019). Exploring Ethereum's blockchain anonymity using smart contract code attribution. In *Proceedings of the 15th International Conference on Network and Service Management*. IEEE. https://doi.org/10.23919/CNSM46954.2019.9012681

Liu, Q., Yu, L., & Jia, C. (2020). MovER: Stabilize decentralized finance system with practical risk management. In *Proceedings of the 2nd Conference on Blockchain Research & Applications for Innovative Networks and Services* (pp. 55–56). IEEE. https://doi.org/10.1109/BRAINS49436.2020.9223274

Mell, P. (2019). Augmenting fiat currency with an integrated managed cryptocurrency. https://arxiv.org/abs/1912.06487

Meyer, E., Welpe, I. M., & Sandner, P. G. (2022). Decentralized finance—a systematic literature review and research directions. In *Proceedings of the 30th European Conference on Information Systems*. AIS. https://aisel.aisnet.org/ecis2022_rp/25

Nadler, M., & Schär, F. (2020). Decentralized finance, centralized ownership? An iterative mapping process to measure protocol token distribution. *Journal of Blockchain Research, 1*(1), 29–36. https://doi.org/10.4310/JBR.2022.v1.n1.a3

Nakamoto, S. (2008). Bitcoin: A peer-to-peer electronic cash system. https://bitcoin.org/bitcoin.pdf

Pauwels, P., Pirovich, J., Braunz, P., & Deeb, J. (2022). zkKYC in DeFi: An approach for implementing the zkKYC solution concept in decentralized finance. https://eprint.iacr.org/2022/321

Perdana, A., Hu, E. I., & Rianto (2023). Decentralized finance (DeFi), strengths become weaknesses: A literature survey. *Jurnal RESTI (Rekayasa Sistem dan Teknologi Informasi), 7*(2), 397–404. https://doi.org/10.29207/resti.v7i2.4806

Qin, K., Zhou, L., & Gervais, A. (2022). Quantifying blockchain extractable value: How dark is the forest? In *IEEE Symposium on Security and Privacy* (pp. 198–214). https://doi.org/10.1109/SP46214.2022.9833734.

Saengchote, K., Putniņš, T., & Samphantharak, K. (2022). Does DeFi remove the need for trust? Evidence from a natural experiment in stablecoin lending. *Journal of Behavioral and Experimental Finance, 40*, 100858. https://doi.org/10.1016/j.jbef.2023.100858

Schueffel, P. (2021). DeFi: Decentralized finance – an introduction and overview. *Journal of Innovation Management, 9*(3). https://doi.org/10.24840/2183-0606_009.003_0001

Schär, F. (2021). Decentralized finance: On blockchain- and smart contract-based financial markets. *Federal Reserve Bank of St. Louis Review, 103*(2), 153–174. https://doi.org/10.20955/r.103.153-74

Sedlmeir, J., Lautenschlager, J., Fridgen, G., & Urbach, N. (2022). The transparency challenge of blockchain in organizations. *Electronic Markets, 32*, 1779–1794. https://doi.org/10.1007/s12525-022-00536-0

Sedlmeir, J., Smethurst, R., Rieger, A., & Fridgen, G. (2021). Digital identities and verifiable credentials. *Business & Information Systems Engineering, 63*(5), 603–613. https://doi.org/10.1007/s12599-021-00722-y

Strüker, J., et al. (2021). Self-sovereign identity: Foundations, applications, and potentials of portable digital identities. https://www.fit.fraunhofer.de/content/dam/fit/de/documents/Fraunhofer%20FIT_SSI_Whitepaper_EN.pdf

Sun, X., Stasinakis, C., & Sermpinis, G. (2022). Decentralization illusion in decentralized finance: Evidence from tokenized voting in MakerDAO polls. https://arxiv.org/abs/2203.16612

Victor, F. (2020). Address clustering heuristics for Ethereum. In *Financial Cryptography and Data Security* (pp. 617–633). Springer. https://doi.org/10.1007/978-3-030-51280-4_33

von Wachter, V., Jensen, J. R., Regner, F., & Ross, O. (2022). NFT wash trading: Quantifying suspicious behaviour in NFT markets. https://arxiv.org/abs/2202.03866

Voskobojnikov, A., Abramova, S., Beznosov, K., & Böhme, R. (2021). Non-adoption of crypto-assets: Exploring the role of trust, self-efficacy, and risk. In *Proceedings of the 29th European Conference on Information Systems*. AIS. https://aisel.aisnet.org/ecis2021_rp/9/

Wang, Z., Jiang, G., & Ye, Q. (2021). On fair designs of cross-chain exchange for cryptocurrencies via Monte Carlo simulation. *Naval Research Logistics, 69*, 144–162. https://doi.org/10.1002/nav.21989

Werner, S. M., Perez, D., Gudgeon, L., Klages-Mundt, A., Harz, D., & Knottenbelt, W. J. (2021). SoK: Decentralized finance (DeFi). In *Proceedings of the 4th ACM Conference on Advances in Financial Technologies* (pp. 30–46). https://doi.org/10.1145/3558535.3559780

Weyl, E. G., Ohlhaver, P., & Buterin, V. (2022). Decentralized society: Finding Web3's soul. https://papers.ssrn.com/sol3/papers.cfm?abstract_id=4105763

Wright, A., & Meier, S. (2021). Analyzing FinCEN's proposed regulation relating to AML and KYC laws. In *International Conference on Financial Cryptography and Data Security* (pp. 54–62). Springer. https://doi.org/10.1007/978-3-662-63958-0_5

Wu, J., Liu, J., Zhao, Y., & Zheng, Z. (2021). Analysis of cryptocurrency transactions from a network perspective: An overview. *Journal of Network and Computer Applications*, *190*, 103139. https://doi.org/10.1016/j.jnca.2021.103139

Zetzsche, D. A., Arner, D. W., & Buckley, R. P. (2020). Decentralized finance. *Journal of Financial Regulation*, *6*(2), 172–203. https://doi.org/10.1093/jfr/fjaa010

Zhao, Y., Kang, X., Li, T., Chu, C.-K., & Wang, H. (2022). Toward trustworthy DeFi oracles: Past, present, and future. *IEEE Access*, *10*, 60914–60928. https://doi.org/10.1109/ACCESS.2022.3179374

Chapter 10
Decentralization Technologies in the Context of ESG Accounting and Reporting

Vincent Gramlich, Marc-Fabian Körner, Tobias Ströher, Jens Strüker, and Maximilian Volland

Abstract Sustainable finance, driven by the goal of addressing global climate change and societal concerns, has recently increased in prominence. Correspondingly, environmental, social, and governance (ESG) considerations have become integral to financial decision-making, necessitating robust accounting and reporting mechanisms. However, current ESG reporting faces challenges such as greenwashing and data aggregation issues, which hinder transparency and accuracy. This chapter examines ESG accounting and reporting from an information system (IS) perspective by highlighting the potential of decentralization technologies in addressing its challenges. It aims to provide insights for stakeholders in the financial sector who seek to navigate the evolving landscape of digital ESG accounting and reporting. Starting with an overview of recent practices and challenges, we delve into the requirements for future-proof ESG reporting and accounting systems. After emphasizing the importance of digitalization, particularly using decentralization technologies, we explore how they can enhance transparency and reliability in ESG accounting and reporting. By discussing existing technological concepts, we illustrate how decentralization technologies could add significant value to ESG reporting practices. We conclude with an outlook on the future prospects and unresolved questions about the integration of decentralization technologies in accounting and reporting systems.

V. Gramlich (✉)
Frankfurt University of Applied Sciences, Frankfurt am Main, Germany
e-mail: vincent.gramlich@fim-rc.de

M.-F. Körner · T. Ströher · J. Strüker
FIM Research Center, University of Bayreuth, Bayreuth, Germany
e-mail: marc.koerner@fim-rc.de; tobias.stroeher@fim-rc.de; jens.strueker@fim-rc.de

M. Volland
University of Bayreuth, Bayreuth, Germany
e-mail: maximilian.volland@fim-rc.de

G. Fridgen et al. (eds.), *Decentralization Technologies*, Financial Innovation and Technology, https://doi.org/10.1007/978-3-031-66047-4_10

10.1 Introduction

Due to a plethora of reasons, such as the increasingly noticeable effects of global climate change, sustainable finance has become a highly relevant topic in literature and practice in recent years (Friede et al., 2015). According to the Global Sustainable Investment Alliance (GSIA), sustainable investments accounted for 35.3 trillion US Dollars worldwide in 2020, roughly 15 % more than in 2018 (Global Sustainable Investment Alliance, 2020). Sustainable finance represents a paradigm that is – unlike the classical shareholder wealth maximization model – classified by a recognition (i.e., accounting) of environmental and social impacts of companies' decisions (Fatemi & Fooladi, 2013). Therefore, ESG aspects became a major topic for research from the finance community (Braasch & Velte, 2022; Friede et al., 2015; Gillan et al., 2021). According to the European Banking Authority (EBA), ESG represents a framework that considers environmental, social, and governance sustainability factors and is often associated with corporate social responsibility (CSR) (European Banking Authority, 2021a; Gillan et al., 2021; Vysochan et al., 2022). Currently, there is an intensive public discourse about sustainable finance and ESG across various media. On the one hand, they are widely seen as a necessity for reaching net-zero emissions due to the importance of the financial sector (e.g., for the financing and insurance of companies). On the other hand, the current realization of ESG faces large challenges, especially greenwashing, which denotes the concept of deceptively accounting and reporting ESG factors to conceal negative aspects and create an overly positive company image (Toucan, 2023; Sutcliffe & Lofts, 2021).

ESG factors can have positive or negative impacts on the financial performance of entities, sovereigns, or individuals (European Banking Authority, 2021a). Friede et al. (2015), for example, showed by combining findings of more than 2200 academic studies that ESG performance may be positively correlated with the financial performance of companies. As a result, ESG factors increasingly represent key points to consider during the investment analysis, decision-making, and measurement of the social and sustainability impact of business activities (European Banking Authority, 2021b).

For ESG factors to represent a sound basis for decisions, companies have to properly and verifiably account and report their respective ESG data (Müller et al., 2023; Sedlmeir et al., 2021). Currently, there are different standards and norms for ESG accounting and reporting, depending on the legal frameworks of the specific countries and whether reporting is voluntary or mandatory. Hence, it is difficult to compare different companies in terms of their ESG performance. This recently resulted in various revealed cases of greenwashing and misconduct; see, for example, the recent scandal on the carbon offsets issued by one of the largest certifiers, Verra (Greenfield, 2023). The manual gathering and processing of data, as well as the usage of average values or even estimates, enables this kind of fraud. Furthermore, ESG data is typically published in annual reports. This large time gap between reports and the strong aggregation of data leads to a lack of transparency. The lack of spatial or temporal granularity in ESG accounting can also lead to wrong incentives, e.g., in the context of green electricity (Sedlmeir et al., 2021). Consequently, digital technologies are necessary to automate and verify data flows (Körner et al., 2023a). Industry 4.0. brings the potential and the need to redefine the accounting system by adapting to and integrating the technologies, and especially the information systems, that underlie Industry 4.0. This renewal of the accounting system is also denoted as accounting 4.0 (Aslanertik and Yardımcı, 2019). As we will outline in this chapter, digital – and especially decentralized – technologies have a major potential for addressing these and related issues of current ESG accounting and reporting.

In this chapter, we provide an overview of current practices and challenges of ESG accounting and reporting from an IS perspective as well as why decentralization technologies can represent an enabler for appropriate accounting and reporting systems. To achieve this, we first explain what ESG accounting and reporting is, why actors in the financial sector should gain a deeper understanding of it, and which requirements a future-proof ESG accounting and reporting has to fulfill. Addressing these requirements, we illustrate the affordances of digitalization with a focus on decentralization technologies and discuss existing technological concepts that could realize a significant added value for the practice of ESG accounting and reporting. We conclude with an outlook on future prospects and open questions for the application of decentralization technologies in accounting and reporting systems.

10.2 ESG Accounting and Reporting: Why, How, and What?

In the following, we provide an overview of what ESG accounting and reporting is and why it is necessary for companies and organizations to engage in these activities. Furthermore, we show which current challenges and limitations exist in this area and which requirements have to be fulfilled for a functioning and meaningful ESG accounting and reporting system.

10.2.1 What Is ESG Accounting and Reporting?

Over 70 years ago, the American Institute of Certified Public Accountants (AICPA) provided the following general definition of accounting that still holds today: "Accounting is the art of recording, classifying and summarizing in a significant manner and in terms of money, transactions and events which are, in part at least, of a financial character, and interpreting the results thereof" (American Institute of Certified Public Accountants. Committee on Terminology, 1953, p. 9). According to the International Accounting Standards Board (IASB), financial reporting – which is often associated with disclosure – aims to provide financial information about an entity that can help investors, lenders, and other creditors to make decisions about providing resources to this entity (IFRS Foundation, 2018). These definitions

– which we will use for the terms accounting and reporting hereafter – illustrate that accounting and reporting represent very closely related concepts. Nevertheless, accounting focuses on the collecting of information while reporting refers to sharing this information with third parties (e.g., for investment decisions). Typically, entities follow widely used standards for their financial accounting and reporting (e.g., the conceptual framework for financial reporting of the IFRS Foundation (2018)).

In contrast to "traditional" approaches, which are based on financial indicators, ESG accounting and reporting refer to nonfinancial information, are typically voluntary, and utilize less well-defined practices (Darnall et al., 2022; Erkens et al., 2015; Vysochan et al., 2022). Particularly the latter two characteristics leave room for various possible standards and interpretations, which ultimately results in a reporting that is opaque, inconsistent, and thus often difficult to compare. As outlined in Sect. 10.1, this situation leads to a lack of comparability and opportunities for greenwashing. For instance, Nestlé, the world's largest food and beverage company manages to get high ESG ratings despite various allegations and scandals – especially concerning environmental topics, such as plastic waste (Bernardo, 2023; Watson, 2016). The financial service provider MSCI Inc. rated Nestlé with AA in 2020, classifying them as an ESG "leader" (Nestlé, 2023a). Nestlé's sustainability reporting is – according to their own statement – aligned with the Global Reporting Initiative (GRI) and Sustainability Accounting Standards Board (SASB) standards (Nestlé, 2023b). The discrepancy between good external ratings and own reports on the one side and accusations and scandals on the other side illustrates that current ESG accounting and reporting – even if it is based on renowned international standards – falls short of providing a timely, transparent, and verifiable picture of companies' ESG situation.

10.2.2 Why Is ESG Accounting and Reporting Important for the Financial Sector?

The reasons why financial actors attempt to gain a deeper understanding of the relevance of ESG accounting and reporting are manifold. Consequently, the need for ESG accounting and reporting has to be considered from multiple perspectives. In the following, we give an overview of potential reasons for stakeholders to consider ESG accounting and reporting.

Compliance: Regulation and State Requirements One reason for aspiring ESG accounting in finance is that it can help companies comply with regulatory requirements related to ESG issues (Pollman, 2019). In recent years, there has been a growing trend toward mandatory reporting requirements for ESG, with many countries and regions introducing regulations.

For instance, from 2018 onward, companies in the European Union (EU) are required by the Non-Financial Reporting Directive (European Commission, 2014) to include nonfinancial information in their annual reports or a separate filing. This information may include details on environmental protection, social responsibility, employee treatment, human rights, anti-corruption, bribery, and board diversity. The directive applies to companies in the EU with more than 500 employees, which amounts to around 6000 companies, and groups such as banks, listed companies, insurance companies, and other public-interest entities (European Commission, 2014). The prudential directive recommends the use of international standards such as ISO 26000, UN Global Compact, Organisation for Economic Co-operation and Development (OECD) Guidelines, or GRI. In the United States (US), the Securities and Exchange Commission (SEC) has issued guidance on ESG disclosure and proposed several ESG-related rules. Likewise, several states have introduced laws that require certain companies to report on their ESG impact.

Companies that fail to comply with these requirements may face legal consequences resulting in financial loss or reputational risks. By implementing ESG accounting practices and reporting on their ESG impact, companies can ensure that they are complying with regulatory requirements and meeting the expectations of regulations. As a result, purposeful accounting and reporting should not be seen as a voluntary commitment but rather as a progressively increasing obligation (Arvidsson & Dumay, 2021).

An illustrative example of increasing regulation in this area is the Supply Chain Due Diligence Act, which was introduced in Germany on the 1 January 2023. The law will initially apply to companies with at least 3000 employees in Germany from 2023 and to companies with at least 1000 employees from 2024. The law aims to strengthen human rights and environmental protection in global supply chains. It obliges companies in Germany to respect human rights by implementing defined due diligence obligations. These obligations apply to the company's own business operations, to the actions of a contractual partner, and to the actions of other (indirect) suppliers. As a result, companies' responsibilities no longer end at their own factory gates but exist along their entire supply chain. First, companies must identify, assess, and prioritize the ESG-related risks in their supply chains. Building on the results, a policy statement is published. Other obligations also include establishing grievance channels for workers in supply chains and mandatory annual reporting on the company's compliance with its due diligence obligations. The sanctions for violating the obligations can be far-reaching: exclusion from public funding, entry into a pillory register, as well as high coercive and administrative fines.

Access to Capital: Investments and Funding Most companies and organizations depend on the capital of investors or public funding. The aspiration of ESG-related investing strategies has been established as the term socially responsible investing (SRI). We outline the numerous reasons for a rising interest in SRI below.

On the one hand, in recent years, there has been growing awareness of social and environmental issues such as climate change, human rights, and social justice. As a result, investors are increasingly interested in investing in companies that are taking a proactive approach to addressing these issues (Hoang, 2018). Moreover, even large investment firms must adhere to mandatory ESG reports. To meet these regulatory standards set by state actors or international boards, they have to – even if involuntarily – invest a certain share in ESG-related companies. Demographic change also works to the advantage of ESG investing. Younger investors, in particular, are more likely to prioritize social and environmental issues when making investment decisions. As Millennials and Generation Z represent an increasingly large share of the population, there is a growing demand for investments that align with their values (Zumente & Bistrova, 2021).

Furthermore, there are progressively more regulatory incentives. Governments around the world are introducing policies and regulations that encourage companies to address social and environmental issues. A recent example is the legislative measure, namely, the Inflation Reduction Act (IRA), that has been enforced in the US since August 2022 (US Congress, 2022). The IRA provides federal funding of approximately $400 billion to promote clean energy with the objective of substantially decreasing the country's carbon emissions by the end of this decade. The allocation of funds will be in the form of a combination of tax incentives, grants, and loan guarantees (European Parliament, 2023). A significant proportion of the funding will be directed toward promoting clean power generation and transmission, followed by clean transportation, which includes incentives for electric vehicles (EVs). To receive funding, precise record-taking is mandatory. As such, there is a strong need for companies to establish transparent and trusted ESG accounting and reporting systems.

At the same time, it becomes apparent that the need for a standardized definition of sustainability is growing. The EU has launched an attempt in the form of an EU taxonomy for sustainable activities (European Commission, 2020). In order to meet the EU's climate and energy targets for 2030 and reach the objectives of the European green deal, the EU noticed that is inevitable to find a common language and a clear definition of what can be classified as "sustainable." Such a classification of sustainability, of course, has far-reaching consequences for the labeling of, for instance, "sustainable funds" or "sustainable products." As a result, many different interest groups and stakeholders were involved in the finding of a definition, resulting in highly controversial decisions, e.g., the classification of gas and nuclear as sustainable energy sources (European Parliament, 2022). This experience illustrates how difficult it is to find uniform definitions and how unstable they can be. Consequently, systems that measure sustainability must always be dynamic to some extent.

Another aspect of why a meaningful ESG accounting and reporting is important for a company's access to capital is the improved accessibility of companies' data. As more companies report on their social and environmental impact, investors have better access to data and can make more informed investment decisions. This has led to an increase in demand for companies that report on ESG factors and demonstrate a commitment to sustainability (Rook et al., 2019).

Competition: Consumers and Markets Today's consumers are increasingly interested in the social and environmental impact of the products and services they buy. By implementing ESG accounting and reporting practices, companies can provide transparency and demonstrate their commitment to sustainability, which can help attract and retain customers (Koh et al., 2022). Furthermore, companies that are ahead of the curve on ESG issues may be able to gain a competitive advantage in the market and add price premiums to their products.

Similarly, a company's reputation is closely linked to its social and environmental impact. By reporting ESG issues, companies can improve transparency and accountability, which can help them protect their reputation and appear more trustworthy toward (potential) customers. At the same time, it affects a company's risk management. ESG issues can pose significant risks to companies, including reputational, legal, and operational risks. By identifying and reporting these risks, companies can take steps to mitigate them, which may help to protect the company and its stakeholders in a competitive market. As alluded to above, a recent case in which the reporting of carbon offsets ESG caused a widely discussed scandal is the example of Verra, the world's top certifier of carbon credits (Greenfield, 2023). Verra was accused of significantly exaggerating the emissions reductions associated with its "avoided deforestation" credits. It is claimed that only 6 % of these credits represented real emissions reductions. Verra has denied the allegations, but the legitimacy of this form of carbon offsetting has been called into question. Not only Verra but also companies such as Gucci, Disney, and Shell have taken advantage of the certificates and recently come under negative media scrutiny.

Overall, ESG accounting provides valuable information for finance professionals, investors, and other stakeholders, supporting them in their decision-making and in achieving their sustainability goals.

10.2.3 What Are the Requirements for a Future-Proof ESG Accounting and Reporting?

As illustrated above, scholars as well as practitioners acknowledge the need for a standardized, efficient, and precise ESG accounting as well as reporting to integrate ESG information in a meaningful way. To achieve this, several requirements have to be fulfilled.

First, scholars outline the need for more transparent reporting to provide trustworthy information for stakeholders like customers (see., e.g., Vasilyeva and Makarenko, 2016). Companies with shorter accounting and audit cycles appear more transparent, which – aside from potential cost reductions – drives the desire for a fast way of ESG accounting and reporting. Hence, researchers have identified (near) real-time reporting (RTR) as an important feature in this context. RTR is characterized by sharing company information continuously, while the periods of time (e.g., every minute or every hour) are typically not specified (Vasilyeva & Makarenko, 2016). Vasarhelyi and Alles (2008) emphasize that a real-time economy can provide such information but also has the need for real-time accounting and reporting. Only RTR can provide a steering effect on stakeholders in a way that they make CO_2-adaptive decisions. For example, companies could shift their energy-intensive production processes toward times when the energy has a low CO_2-intensity to gain competitive advantages through lower prices or better ESG ratings (van Stiphoudt et al., 2023).

Second, related work addresses a lack of data quality (Körner et al., 2023b; Vasilyeva & Makarenko, 2016). Currently, ESG data is mainly based on average values or even only estimates; see, for example, emission factors in company reports based on the greenhouse gas (GHG) protocol (WRI and WBCSD, 2023). This approach does not allow for a transparent and precise measurement of the ESG performance of companies or other organizations. Hence, the use of fine-granular primary data instead of generic values is necessary to enable investors and other stakeholders to get trustworthy and comparable information about different entities.

Third, ESG accounting and reporting require individual solutions for each entity. Currently, while the data used in ESG-related reports is often specific to a particular entity, the characteristics of the reports are not customized to the needs of stakeholders (Alles et al., 2021). Progress in the digitalization of reporting – also referred to as "Reporting 4.0" – may allow for mass customization (i.e., individually customized goods and services with mass production efficiency) (Piller & Stotko, 2002). This efficiency is especially needed in the light of ESG data that is rapidly increasing in volume and variety. Furthermore, it would enable a comprehensive analysis of reporting indicators, which is necessary for an appropriate ESG accounting and reporting (Vasilyeva & Makarenko, 2016). Therefore, an automated, customizable, and flexible communication instead of paperwork and digital analogs (e.g., PDF files, Excel Sheets, and XBRL, a global reporting framework) – which are currently predominantly used – is necessary to satisfy end users and other stakeholders (Alles et al., 2021). An interoperable system that allows for such communication would facilitate the handling of data within company departments, which is currently characterized by manual and, hence, error-prone collection inside and between companies. Digital solutions offer a variety of potentials to address this topic, as we will outline in the next section.

Last, ESG accounting and reporting need to be comparable. Despite the fact that there are national and international standards (cf. Sect. 10.2.2), comparing companies that follow different ones is hardly possible due to a lack of standardization (Shaikh, 2022). Additionally, various companies have international supply chains, which mean that different regulations and standards may apply to a single company. Consequently, future solutions for ESG accounting and reporting have to address the lack of data quality, transparency, and steering effect of current solutions and should consider digital technologies to enable – mainly through automation – RTR and mass customization.

10.3 Decentralization Technologies: Enabler for Digital ESG Accounting and Reporting

As stated in Sect. 10.2, ESG accounting and reporting currently face multiple challenges that future approaches have to overcome. Digitalization offers a variety of tools and ideas that address these challenges. In general, the application of digital technologies in this area can provide a higher degree of automation in accounting, reporting, and verification by replacing manual processes and, hence, enables the efficient and scalable handling of increasing amounts of data without human errors. This provides a sound basis for more fine-granular accounting and RTR. In addition to these general potentials of digitalization, particularly decentralization technologies can be valuable for ESG accounting and reporting in the light of growing globalization: As discussed in Sect. 10.2, many – especially large – companies nowadays have international supply chains, which make ESG accounting and reporting a cross-border system. While for national information systems there is a central trusted entity (e.g., a governmental authority that is responsible for the respective sector), cross-border systems often lack such a central trusted entity due to a variety of reasons, such as challenges regarding the practical implementation (Körner et al., 2022) (e.g., regarding technical, regulatory, and logistics topics) and the implications of a central entity (e.g., the World Trade Organization (WTO)) with access to such an enormous amount of data (e.g., the possibility of creating a "data octopus" that can exploit personal or competition-relevant information on a large scale or pass it on to third parties, thereby violating data protection regulations and/or personal rights). Decentralization technologies do not depend on a single trusted entity and can, therefore, bypass these and related challenges, providing "neutral platforms" for cross-organizational workflows and data streams (Sedlmeir et al., 2022). Furthermore, as outlined above, an appropriate ESG accounting and reporting requires transparency and automation. Enterprises may, however, not voluntarily disclose ESG data, since it makes them vulnerable to losing their competitive advantages, and they may harm the privacy of their customers (Agahari et al., 2022). Scholars outline the potentials of decentralization technologies in combination with privacy-enhancing technologies (see Chap. 6) to address this issue(see, e.g., Babel et al., 2022; Sedlmeir et al., 2022). Therefore, in this section, we outline the specific advantages and challenges regarding the implementation of decentralization technologies in ESG accounting and reporting.

10.3.1 Affordances of Different Decentralization Technologies for Accounting and Reporting

As discussed before, a key benefit of decentralization technologies in accounting and reporting is that they can grant independence from central, globally trusted institutions, which are absent in many important industries and their accounting and reporting systems in today's world. Besides this advantage, the different decentralization technologies that have already been introduced throughout the book bring their own individual benefits but also challenges in the context of reporting and accounting.

Blockchain technology has often been proposed by academic literature as a reliable data infrastructure for reporting and accounting systems; see, e.g., Bonson and Bednarova (2019) or Schmitz and Leoni (2019). This is due to the fact that some of the key features and merits of blockchain technology match the requirements and challenges of an accounting and reporting system. Especially the explicit chronological ordering of transactions, the immutability of this ordering and the transactions and data itself, and the ability to clearly define and enforce rules on the recorded transactions by means of smart contracts are essential benefits of blockchain technology (see also Chap. 3). However, applying blockchain in the accounting and reporting context also entails many challenges, which are especially centered around the pseudonymity that typically exists on blockchains and that can be disadvantageous in two ways. On the one hand, the absence of a clear linkability between legal entities and the digital pseudonym of a blockchain address can be hindering for participants who want to verifiably present accounting and reporting information that is only linked to their blockchain address. On the other hand, a pseudonymous system, unlike an anonymous system, still allows for the detection of interrelationships and connections (Sedlmeir et al., 2022). If such a connection between a "real-world" entity and a pseudonymous blockchain address can be established, the transaction data becomes fully visible to all network participants, which can be seen as a feature in many reporting scenarios but in the cases where, for instance, accounting is done on a more fine-granular level than the reporting, e.g., in order to protect person-related data or corporate secrets, might exclude the blockchain as a possible data infrastructure.

Identifying businesses and machines that a company interacts with within its supply chain is an important task in accounting and reporting, especially as most of the measurements that are to be reported are not solely bound to the company itself but encompass the whole supply chain that the company is involved in. **Decentralized digital identities**, also known as self-sovereign identity (SSI), could also play an essential role in the identification of counterparties and verification of their data (Körner et al., 2023b). More precisely, the main perks of SSI (see Chap. 4) for accounting and reporting, besides its decentralized nature that enables trust without a centralized trusted institution, are public keys or decentralized identifier (DID), which can act as a globally unique identifier for machines and entities, and digital attestations (e.g., in the form of verifiable credentials (VCs)) that can attest additional, verifiable information to an identity (Hamilton-Duffy et al., 2021; Guggenberger et al., 2023). Especially companies and practitioners are actively looking into how SSI can be used to improve business and machine identification, thereby increasing the reliability and verifiability of supply chain data and improving the accounting and reporting of that data (DB Systel GmbH, 2020; Mueller, 2019; Körner et al., 2022). Additionally, SSI can also be used in blockchain-based applications to eliminate some of the drawbacks of pseudonymity, by facilitating accountability despite anonymity (Sedlmeir et al., 2022) or equipping blockchain addresses with their owners' digital identities, thus creating a direct and verifiable connection between pseudonymous blockchain addresses and real-world identities (see also Chap. 9).

Besides the aforementioned decentralization technologies blockchain and SSI, there are some other concepts from applied cryptography, especially privacy enhancing technologies (PETs), specifically applied cryptography, that have been introduced earlier in this book and can be advantageous in accounting and reporting applications (see Chap. 6). Zero-knowledge proofs (ZKPs) can be useful in the reporting context, as they allow proving the correctness of a statement without the need to reveal more detailed information. Thus, ZKPs enable a reporting system in which, for example, compliance with certain regulations can be proven without revealing sensitive data (Sahai et al., 2020; Wang & Kogan, 2018). Furthermore, while SSI can compensate for some of the drawbacks related to the pseudonymity of blockchains by creating digital identities for pseudonymous blockchain addresses, ZKPs can compensate for the other drawback of the blockchain pseudonymity, i.e., data-privacy issues (Babel & Sedlmeir, 2023). Just as ZKPs can be used in general to prove compliance with a rule-set without revealing more information, they can be used in the blockchain context to prove compliance with the blockchain rules, e.g., no double spending or only sending funds that belong to an address that you control with your private key, without the need to reveal the detailed transaction data. For instance, using a ZKP, companies can prove on a common, neutral blockchain infrastructure that they did not use more materials in their processes than they previously obtained from certified sources, without revealing the underlying quantities that may constitute sensitive business information (Sedlmeir et al., 2022). ZKPs in combination with blockchain technology also seem promising to achieve the verifiable accounting for carbon in electricity (Sedlmeir et al., 2021) or industry supply chains (Heiss et al., 2023). Besides ZKPs, other concepts from applied cryptography can also be useful in accounting and reporting systems, oftentimes in more specific applications. For example, multi-party computation (MPC) can be beneficial in applications where cumulative reports have to be created on data that is held by multiple parties that do not want to share their data (Bogdanov et al., 2015; Agahari et al., 2022).

10.3.2 Exemplary Concepts and Applications

As pointed out above, different decentralization technologies have many properties that are important for accounting and reporting systems. In the following, we present a cross-section of the field of decentralization technologies for accounting and reporting by presenting one specific technological concept that leverages different technologies, one basic building block of ESG accounting and reporting, and a higher-level ecosystem where different technologies and application areas converge.

10.3.2.1 Shielded NFTs

As illustrated above, blockchains represent a good option to record various forms of transactions in an immutable and comprehensible way, especially in settings without a single trusted entity. Academics and practitioners have conceptualized many different approaches, one of which we will present in the following (Babel et al., 2022). Assets, products, or their components relevant for reporting and verification can be represented by tokens on a blockchain, which can store various forms of information to facilitate the representation and transfer of ownership Sedlmeir et al. (2021). This can be especially useful when there are certificates bound to a product, e.g., the attestation of a green product carbon footprint (Sedlmeir et al., 2021). By tokenizing the product with the respective certificate, it can be ensured that a single certificate cannot be used for multiple products, i.e., the blockchain prevents the double-spending of the certificate. Tokens can be fungible token (FT) when there are multiple identical tokens or non-fungible token (NFT) when every token is unique, e.g., because the token represents a very specific product, produced at a certain location at a certain time. Furthermore, tokens can also be fractionalized to make them divisible into small fractions and, thus, are able to map more complex supply-chain processes, e.g., the splitting or merging of products and their certificates. With these properties, FTs and NFTs can facilitate all forms of transactions on any level of granularity. While this specificity and fine-granularity provide advantages in the context of the previously highlighted challenges, these amounts of fine-granular and verifiable data are also extremely sensitive. If they are business-related, they can be the key to competitive advantages, and if they are person-related, they are subject to data protection laws (Sedlmeir et al., 2021).

Consequently, a system like a blockchain that stores this data and makes it accessible to a consortium (in the case of a private blockchain) or the public (in the case of a public blockchain) would be damaging for the participating corporations or even violate data protection laws (Sedlmeir et al., 2022). Thus, using blockchain technology alone is not sufficient in this case but needs to be supplemented with PETs, for example, ZKPs. Corresponding system designs provide the abovementioned benefits, yet without the need to publicly display transaction data or further fine-granular information associated with the tokens and the products they represent. The combination of NFTs that can display arbitrary information and transaction data of assets and products with ZKPs to shield this information to the public is denoted as shielded NFT. Babel et al. (2022) present this concept in the application of carbon emission tracing in the electricity grid. NFTs on a blockchain represent units of electric energy that were produced by an asset in a certain time frame and can store information like the time frame, the location, and the type of the asset, as well as the amount of carbon that was emitted during electricity production. These tokens can then be forwarded along the electricity supply chain. End customers obtain the tokens when they purchase certain goods and, therefore, can verify the origin and carbon intensity of the electricity they use on a fine-granular level in real time. This information can then be used in accounting and reporting systems to verifiably calculate precise carbon footprints associated with companies or specific products or even enable the steering of processes to optimize for low carbon intensity.

The concept of tracing products and product-related information through supply chains with shielded NFTs is not bound to the energy sector but could apply to arbitrary supply chains. Additionally, the concepts might be supplemented with the usage of digital identities to enable a direct binding between the parties transacting tokens on a blockchain and real-world entities like end consumers of businesses (Gramlich et al., 2024). Furthermore, machine identities can be leveraged to establish a traceable and verifiable connection between metering data and the respective device (Babel et al., 2023; Sedlmeir et al., 2021). Thus, leveraging digital identities can bring additional verifiability, especially if the information is used for reporting purposes.

10.3.2.2 Digital Product Passports

A digital product passport (DPP) is a concept for a standardized digital document that provides comprehensive information about a product's environmental, social, and economic impact throughout its entire life cycle (Heeß et al., 2024). The idea is to create a single, accessible source of information about a product that can be used by various stakeholders, such as manufacturers, retailers, consumers, and regulators. DPPs are widely discussed in academic literature and practice, which can also be seen in the recent proposal for a new Ecodesign for Sustainable Products Regulation by the European Commission (European Commission, 2022). Essentially, DPPs serve as a data carrier for master data (e.g., manufacturer and composition) as well as transaction data (e.g., use and maintenance) and represent a basic building block for a future-proof ESG accounting and reporting by providing an automated and more transparent collection and processing of ESG data (Götz et al., 2022). In contrast to the shielded NFT approach outlined above – which represents a promising technological solution for a specific use case – product passports are rather a tool for enabling more sustainable supply chains in general (Berger et al., 2022). This tool can be used for a variety of applications across multiple sectors. Berg et al. (2022), for example, illustrate the benefits of DPPs in the plastics value chain and Walden et al. (2021) in the battery supply chain, both promoting a circular economy in their respective fields. Just as DPPs can be used in many different application areas, they can also be implemented in different ways. DPPs come with the same challenges as general accounting and reporting systems, i.e., a multitude of different stakeholders, the lack of a central trusted entity, and the need for processing large quantities of sensitive data. To address these challenges, scholars have suggested the use of different decentralization technologies. Berg et al. (2022), for instance, leverage a decentralized public key infrastructure (PKI) to create digital identities for companies and products and to enable the exchange of trustful and digital product passport data among all entities related to the respective industry. In general, the concept of SSI bears a lot of potential in the context of DPPs, since it allows providing an identity to products via cryptographic identifiers and verifiable product information via digital attestations like VCs, while the product data owner keeps the control over the respective information (Berg et al., 2022; Hamilton-Duffy et al., 2021). The concept of shielded NFTs as introduced above could also be expanded to DPPs, which would enable DPPs that leverage blockchain technology for data integrity and availability, while ZKPs ensure a high degree of data protection.

A more high-level concept that – among other things – could also facilitate the data aggregation and exchange that is required for DPPs are **data spaces**. Data spaces are a trusted and decentralized infrastructure for data sharing, where data providers retain control over their data, while data users can access and process the data in a secure and transparent way (Otto, 2022). From a technical perspective, data spaces can be seen as a decentralized concept that leverages several of the decentralization technologies we have discussed throughout this chapter and book. Especially digital identities play an important role in verifying the identities of the different data space participants and managing their access and governance rights. Other cryptographic primitives like MPCs can be utilized for precise and sensitive data sharing, while ZKPs allow for the verifiability of results of in situ data processing (Weigl et al., 2023). The goal of data spaces, i.e., to facilitate secure and trustworthy data sharing and exchange between different stakeholders, matches the needs for DPPs and accounting and reporting systems in general. For example, a DPP could be created and continuously updated with the master and transaction data that the different stakeholders collectively aggregated in a data space. Furthermore, the aggregated data of the DPPs could be securely exchanged with third parties, e.g., potential consumers of a product.

10.4 Conclusion

In this chapter, we emphasize that ESG accounting and reporting in general is a major challenge for many companies, while the field is becoming increasingly important and unavoidable. Awareness of the topic is therefore urgently needed. We argue that the requirements for a comprehensive and effective ESG accounting and reporting system are progressively increasing and that it is not possible to achieve the desired quality, speed, and increasing global interconnectedness of ESG accounting and reporting without digitalization. However, the mere use of digital technologies does not pose a suitable solution, as many digital systems come with data privacy issues or require centralized coordination that is not achievable in the globalized setting of ESG accounting and reporting. In contrast, decentralization technologies like blockchain and SSI can enable a trustworthy and reliable system without the need for a centralized entity. Furthermore, PETs, specifically based on concepts from applied cryptography like ZKPs, can facilitate data privacy and solve the tension between traceability and transparency on the one hand and the protection of business secrets on the other. Thus, decentralization technologies may play an essential role in building systems that fulfill the current and future demands of ESG accounting and reporting.

At the same time, it is clear that there is still a long way to go before the theoretically proposed concepts can be put into practice. Not only will the technical infrastructure and digitization of companies have to be expanded, but traditional accounting and reporting systems will also have to be rethought. Further research on all aspects, i.e., on the technical, regulatory, and economic levels, is necessary for a successful implementation of decentralization technologies for ESG accounting and reporting.

References

Agahari, W., Ofe, H., & de Reuver, M. (2022). It is not (only) about privacy: How multi-party computation redefines control, trust, and risk in data sharing. *Electronic Markets*, *32*, 1577–1602. https://doi.org/10.1007/s12525-022-00572-w

Alles, M. G., Dai, J., & Vasarhelyi, M. A. (2021). Reporting 4.0: Business reporting for the age of mass customization. *Journal of Emerging Technologies in Accounting*, *18*(1). https://doi.org/10.2308/jeta-10764

American Institute of Certified Public Accountants. Committee on Terminology. (1953). Review and resume; accounting terminology bulletins, no. 1. https://egrove.olemiss.edu/cgi/viewcontent.cgi?article=1355&context=dl_aia

Arvidsson, S., & Dumay, J. (2021). Corporate ESG reporting quantity, quality and performance: Where to now for environmental policy and practice? *Business Strategy and the Environment*, *31*, 1091–1110. https://doi.org/10.1002/bse.2937

Aslanertik, B. E. & Yardımcı, Bs. (2019). A comprehensive framework for accounting 4.0: Implications of industry 4.0 in digital era. In *Blockchain Economics and Financial Market Innovation: Financial Innovations in the Digital Age* (pp. 549–563). Springer. https://doi.org/10.1007/978-3-030-25275-5_27

Babel, M., Gramlich, V., Guthmann, C., Schober, M., Körner, M.-F., & Strüker, J. (2023). Trust through digital identification: On SSI's contribution to the integration of decentralized oracles in information systems. *HMD Praxis der Wirtschaftsinformatik*, *60*(2), 478–493. https://doi.org/10.1365/s40702-023-00955-3

Babel, M., Gramlich, V., Körner, M.-F., Sedlmeir, J., Strüker, J., & Zwede, T. (2022). Enabling end-to-end digital carbon emission tracing with shielded NFTs. *Energy Informatics*, *5*. https://doi.org/10.1186/s42162-022-00199-3

Babel, M., & Sedlmeir, J. (2023). Bringing data minimization to digital wallets at scale with general-purpose zero-knowledge proofs. https://arxiv.org/abs/2301.00823

Berg, H., Kulinna, R., Stöcker, C., Guth-Orlowski, S., Thiermann, R., & Porepp, N. (2022). Overcoming information asymmetry in the plastics value chain with digital product passports. https://epub.wupperinst.org/files/7940/WP197.pdf

Berger, K., Schöggl, J.-P., & Baumgartner, R. J. (2022). Digital battery passports to enable circular and sustainable value chains: Conceptualization and use cases. *Journal of Cleaner Production*, *353*. https://doi.org/10.1016/j.jclepro.2022.131492

Bernardo, S. (2023). What is greenwashing? A Nestlé case study. https://measurepnw.com/blog/what-is-greenwashing-a-nestle-case-study

Bogdanov, D., Jõemets, M., Siim, S., & Vaht, M. (2015). How the Estonian tax and customs board evaluated a tax fraud detection system based on secure multi-party computation. In *Financial Cryptography and Data Security* (pp. 227–234). Springer. https://doi.org/10.1007/978-3-662-47854-7_14

Bonson, E., & Bednarova, M. (2019). Blockchain and its implications for accounting and auditing. *Meditari Accountancy Research*, *27*(5), 725–740. https://doi.org/10.1108/MEDAR-11-2018-0406

Braasch, A., & Velte, P. (2022). Climate reporting quality following the recommendations of the task force on climate-related financial disclosures: A focus on the German capital market. *Sustainable Development*, *31*(2), 926–940. https://doi.org/10.1002/sd.2430

Darnall, N., Ji, H., Iwata, K., & Arimura, T. H. (2022). Do ESG reporting guidelines and verifications enhance firms' information disclosure? *Corporate Social Responsibility and Environmental Management*, *29*(5), 1214–1230. https://doi.org/10.1002/csr.2265

DB Systel GmbH. (2020). The new face of identity management. https://www.dbsystel.de/dbsystel-en/about-us/Digital-Stories-en/The-new-face-of-identity-management-6180352?

Erkens, M., Paugam, L., & Stolowy, H. (2015). Non-financial information: State of the art and research perspectives based on a bibliometric study. *Comptabilité Contrôle Audit*, *21*(3), 15–92. https://doi.org/10.3917/cca.213.0015

European Banking Authority. (2021a). EBA report on management and supervision of ESG risks for credit institutions and investment firms. https://www.eba.europa.eu/sites/default/documents/files/document_library/Publications/Reports/2021/1015656/EBA%20Report%20on%20ESG%20risks%20management%20and%20supervision.pdf

European Banking Authority. (2021b). Environmental, social and governance disclosures. https://www.eba.europa.eu/sites/default/documents/files/document_library/Publications/Consultations/2021/Consultation%20on%20draft%20ITS%20on%20Pillar%20disclosures%20on%20ESG%20risk/963626/Factsheet%20-%20ESG%20disclosures.pdf

European Commission. (2014). Directive 2014/95/EU of the European Parliament and of the Council of 22 October 2014 amending Directive 2013/34/EU as regards disclosure of non-financial and diversity information by certain large undertakings and groups Text with EEA relevance. https://eur-lex.europa.eu/eli/dir/2014/95/oj

European Commission. (2020). EU taxonomy for sustainable activities. https://finance.ec.europa.eu/system/files/2020-03/200309-sustainable-finance-teg-final-report-taxonomy_en.pdf

European Commission. (2022). Proposal for a Regulation of the European Parliament and of the Council, establishing a framework for setting ecodesign requirements for sustainable products and repealing Directive 2009/125/EC. https://environment.ec.europa.eu/system/files/2022-03/COM_2022_142_1_EN_ACT_part1_v6.pdf

European Parliament. (2022). Taxonomy: MEPs do not object to inclusion of gas and nuclear activities. https://www.europarl.europa.eu/news/en/press-room/20220701IPR34365/taxonomy-meps-do-not-object-to-inclusion-of-gas-and-nuclear-activities

European Parliament. (2023). EU-US climate and energy relations in light of the Inflation Reduction Act. https://www.europarl.europa.eu/RegData/etudes/BRIE/2023/739300/EPRS_BRI(2023)739300_EN.pdf

Fatemi, A. M., & Fooladi, I. J. (2013). Sustainable finance: A new paradigm. *Global Finance Journal*, *24*(2), 101–113. https://doi.org/10.1016/j.gfj.2013.07.006

Friede, G., Busch, T., & Bassen, A. (2015). ESG and financial performance: aggregated evidence from more than 2000 empirical studies. *Journal of Sustainable Finance & Investment*, *5*(4), 210–233. https://doi.org/10.1080/20430795.2015.1118917

Gillan, S. L., Koch, A., & Starks, L. T. (2021). Firms and social responsibility: A review of ESG and CSR research in corporate finance. *Journal of Corporate Finance*, *66*. https://doi.org/10.1016/j.jcorpfin.2021.101889

Global Sustainable Investment Alliance. (2020). Global sustainable investment review 2020. https://www.gsi-alliance.org/wp-content/uploads/2021/08/GSIR-20201.pdf

Götz, T., Berg, H., Jansen, M., Adisorn, T., Cembrero, D., Markkanen, S., & Chowdhury, T. (2022). Digital product passport: the ticket to achieving a climate neutral and circular European economy? https://www.corporateleadersgroup.com/files/cisl_digital_products_passport_report_v6.pdf

Gramlich, V., Guggenberger, T., Principato, M., Schellinger, B., Duda, S., & Stoetzer, J. (2024). In decentralized finance nobody knows you are a dog. In *Proceedings of the 57th Hawaiin*

International Conference on Information Systems. (pp. 4558–4567). https://hdl.handle.net/10125/106932

Greenfield, P. (2023). Revealed: more than 90% of rainforest carbon offsets by biggest certifier are worthless, analysis shows. https://www.theguardian.com/environment/2023/jan/18/revealed-forest-carbon-offsets-biggest-provider-worthless-verra-aoe

Guggenberger, T., Kühne, D., Schlatt, V., & Urbach, N. (2023). Designing a cross-organizational identity management system: Utilizing SSI for the certification of retailer attributes. *Electronic Markets*, *33*(1). https://doi.org/10.1007/s12525-023-00620-z

Hamilton-Duffy, K., Grant, R., & Adrian, G. (2021). Use cases and requirements for decentralized identifiers: Enterprise identifiers. https://www.w3.org/TR/did-use-cases/#didEnterprise

Heeß, P., Rockstuhl, J., Körner, M.-F., & Strüker, J. (2024). Enhancing trust in global supply chains: Conceptualizing digital product passports for a low-carbon hydrogen market. *Electronic Markets*, *34*. https://doi.org/10.1007/s12525-024-00690-7

Heiss, J., Oegel, T., Shakeri, M., & Tai, S. (2023). Verifiable carbon accounting in supply chains. *IEEE Transactions on Services Computing*. https://doi.org/10.1109/TSC.2023.3332831

Hoang, T. (2018). The role of the integrated reporting in raising awareness of environmental, social and corporate governance (ESG) performance. *Stakeholders, Governance and Responsibility*, *14*, 1091–1110. https://doi.org/10.1108/S2043-052320180000014003

IFRS Foundation. (2018). Conceptual framework for financial reporting. https://www.ifrs.org/issued-standards/list-of-standards/conceptual-framework/

Koh, H.-K., Burnasheva, R., & Gu Suh, Y. (2022). Perceived ESG (environmental, social, governance) and consumers' responses: The mediating role of brand credibility, brand image, and perceived quality. *Sustainability*, *14*(8). https://doi.org/10.3390/su14084515

Körner, M.-F., Michaelis, A., Spazierer, S., & Strüker, J. (2023a). Accelerating sustainability in companies: A taxonomy of information systems for corporate carbon risk management. In *Proceedings of the 31st European Conference on Information Systems*. https://aisel.aisnet.org/ecis2023_rp/248/

Körner, M.-F., Schober, M., Ströher, T., & Strüker, J. (2023b). Digital carbon accounting for accelerating decarbonization: Characteristics of IS-enabled system architectures. In *Proceedings of the 29th Americas Conference on Information Systems*. AIS. https://aisel.aisnet.org/amcis2023/sig_green/sig_green/2/

Körner, M.-F., Sedlmeir, J., Weibelzahl, M., Fridgen, G., Heine, M., & Neumann, C. (2022). Systemic risks in electricity systems: A perspective on the potential of digital technologies. *Energy Policy*, *164*, 112901. https://doi.org/10.1016/j.enpol.2022.112901

Mueller, T. (2019). Know your supplier: Digital identities in the interconnected supply chain management. https://medium.com/evan-network/know-your-supplier-digital-identities-in-the-interconnected-supply-chain-management-a5a2a65f43e8

Müller, F., Leinauer, C., Hofmann, P., Körner, M.-F., & Strüker, J. (2023). Digital decarbonization: Design principles for an enterprise-wide emissions data architecture. In *Proceedings of the 56th Hawaii International Conference on System Sciences* (pp. 5822–5831). https://hdl.handle.net/10125/103342

Nestlé (2023a). External recognition. https://www.nestle.com/sustainability/performance-reporting/external-recognition

Nestlé (2023b). Performance and reporting. https://www.nestle.com/sustainability/performance-reporting

Otto, B. (2022). The evolution of data spaces. In *Designing data spaces*, (pp. 3–15). https://doi.org/10.1007/978-3-030-93975-5_1

Piller, F., & Stotko, C. (2002). Mass customization: four approaches to deliver customized products and services with mass production efficiency. In *Engineering management conference* (Vol. 2, pp. 773–778). https://doi.org/10.1109/IEMC.2002.1038535

Pollman, E. (2019). Corporate social responsibility, ESG, and compliance. *Cambridge Handbook of Compliance*, *20*. https://doi.org/10.2139/ssrn.3479723

Rook, D., In, S. Y., & Monk, A. (2019). Integrating alternative data (also known as ESG data) in investment decision making. *Global Economic Review*, *48*, 237–260. https://doi.org/10.1080/1226508X.2019.1643059

Sahai, S., Singh, N., & Dayama, P. (2020). Enabling privacy and traceability in supply chains using blockchain and zero knowledge proofs. In *Proceedings of the International Conference on Blockchain* (pp. 134–143). IEEE. https://doi.org/10.1109/Blockchain50366.2020.00024

Schmitz, J., & Leoni, G. (2019). Accounting and auditing at the time of blockchain technology: A research agenda. *Australian Accounting Review*, *29*(2), 331–342. https://doi.org/10.1111/auar.12286

Sedlmeir, J., Lautenschlager, J., Fridgen, G., & Urbach, N. (2022). The transparency challenge of blockchain in organizations. *Electronic Markets*, *32*, 1779–1794. https://doi.org/10.1007/s12525-022-00536-0

Sedlmeir, J., Völter, F., & Strüker, J. (2021). The next stage of green electricity labeling: Using zero-knowledge proofs for blockchain-based certificates of origin and use. *ACM SIGENERGY Energy Informatics Review*, *1*(1), 20–31. https://doi.org/10.1145/3508467.3508470

Shaikh, I. (2022). Environmental, social, and governance (ESG) practice and firm performance: an international evidence. *Journal of Business Economics and Management*, *23*(1), 218–237. https://doi.org/10.1111/auar.12286

Sutcliffe, B., & Lofts, G. (2021). Sustainable finance has become an urgent priority across financial services – thanks to the goal of net-zero carbon emissions by 2050. https://www.ey.com/en_gl/financial-services/how-can-sustainable-finance-support-the-road-to-net-zero

Toucan. (2023). Carbon has evolved. https://toucan.earth/

US Congress. (2022). Inflation Reduction Act of 2022. *Public Law*, (pp. 117–169). https://www.congress.gov/117/plaws/publ169/PLAW-117publ169.pdf

van Stiphoudt, C., et al. (2023). Energy synchronization platform concept to enable and streamline automated industrial demand response. In *Proceedings of the 15th International Conference on Applied Energy (ICAE)*. https://www.researchgate.net/publication/376910178_Energy_Synchronization_Platform_Concept_to_Enable_and_Streamline_Automated_Industrial_Demand_Response

Vasarhelyi, M. A., & Alles, M. G. (2008). The "now"' economy and the traditional accounting reporting model: Opportunities and challenges for AIS research. *International Journal of Accounting Information Systems*, *9*(4), 227–239. https://doi.org/10.1016/j.accinf.2008.09.002

Vasilyeva, T., & Makarenko, I. (2016). *The role of innovation in corporate reporting in the transformation of accounting method's elements*, (pp. 171–179). Prague Institute for Qualification Enhancement. https://core.ac.uk/download/pdf/324245241.pdf#page=171

Vysochan, O., Hyk, V., Vysochan, O., & Olshanska, M. (2022). Sustainability accounting: A systematic literature review and bibliometric analysis. *Quality - Access to Success*, *22*, 95–102. https://doi.org/10.47750/QAS/22.185.14

Walden, J., Steinbrecher, A., & Marinkovic, M. (2021). Digital product passports as enabler of the circular economy. *Chemie Ingenieur Technik*, *93*(11), 1717–1727. https://doi.org/10.1002/cite.202100121

Wang, Y., & Kogan, A. (2018). Designing confidentiality-preserving blockchain-based transaction processing systems. *International Journal of Accounting Information Systems*, *30*. https://doi.org/10.1016/j.accinf.2018.06.001

Watson, B. (2016). The troubling evolution of corporate greenwashing. https://www.theguardian.com/sustainable-business/2016/aug/20/greenwashing-environmentalism-lies-companies

Weigl, L., Barbereau, T., Sedlmeir, J., & Zavolokina, L. (2023). Mediating the tension between data sharing and privacy: The case of DMA and GDPR. In *Proceedings of the 31st European Conference on Information Systems*. AIS. https://aisel.aisnet.org/ecis2023_rip/49/

WRI and WBCSD. (2023). Calculation tools. https://ghgprotocol.org/calculation-tools

Zumente, I., & Bistrova, J. (2021). SESG importance for long-term shareholder value creation: Literature vs. practice author links open overlay panel. *Journal of Open Innovation: Technology, Market, and Complexity*, *7*, 127. https://doi.org/10.3390/joitmc7020127

Chapter 11
Opportunities and Applications of Federated Learning in the Financial Services Industry

Joaquin Delgado Fernandez, Renan Lima Baima, Tom Barbereau, and Alexander Rieger

Abstract Federated learning is an innovative machine learning technique that gained significant attention in the financial sector for its potential to address privacy concerns while maintaining the accuracy of predictive models. This technology enables financial institutions to train machine learning models in a decentralized manner from multiple devices without sharing raw data with a central server. This approach ensures data privacy and security while enabling financial institutions to make more informed decisions regarding, for example, credit risk, systemic risk, portfolio overlap, fraud detection systems, personalized investment advice, and open banking. Overall, this chapter explains how federated learning can be applied in the financial services industry and what considerations financial institutions must address to adopt federated learning.

11.1 Introduction

> With federated learning technology, we can harness data while protecting customer privacy. That gives us an advantage over our peers. (WeBank CFO Arthur Wang in McKinsey & Company (2022).)

J. D. Fernandez (✉) · R. L. Baima
Interdisciplinary Centre for Security, Reliability and Trust (SnT), University of Luxembourg, Luxembourg, Luxembourg
e-mail: joaquin.delgadofernandez@uni.lu; renan.limabaima@uni.lu

T. Barbereau
Interdisciplinary Centre for Security, Reliability and Trust (SnT), University of Luxembourg, Luxembourg, Luxembourg

Dutch Organisation for Applied Scientific Research (TNO), The Hague, Netherlands
e-mail: tom.barbereau@tno.nl

A. Rieger
Sam M. Walton College of Business, University of Arkansas, Fayetteville, AR, USA
e-mail: arieger@walton.uark.ear

G. Fridgen et al. (eds.), *Decentralization Technologies*, Financial Innovation and Technology, https://doi.org/10.1007/978-3-031-66047-4_11

Techniques such as machine learning (ML) and deep learning (DL) – under the wider umbrella of artificial intelligence (AI) – have become common methods for the data-driven prediction of outcomes and finding solutions to complex problems (Janiesch et al., 2021). Recent breakthroughs in AI, such as DeepMind's AlphaFold and OpenAI's GPT4 and DALL-E 2, have captured mainstream attention and led some to believe that humanity is in a "golden age of progress in artificial intelligence" (Roose, 2022).

While the implications of these advancements are profound, a fundamental challenge for businesses remains: data availability. The challenge of data availability is apparent when understanding the ideal scenario in which ML/DL techniques can produce effective results. ML/DL techniques are frequently attributed as "data-hungry" (Adadi, 2021), because the main concept of these techniques is to automate the extraction of complex representations or abstractions manifested in data (Najafabadi et al., 2015). In fact, a large body of empirical evidence suggests that more data does improve the performance of ML/DL techniques (Campbell et al., 2003; Chen et al., 2019b; Gibbons et al., 2017). Therefore, the success of ML/DL is contingent not only on the selection of the technique and corresponding parameters but also on the availability of data. However, data of sufficient quantity and quality is not always available. This is because data is costly, requires advanced information technology (IT) capabilities (Aral & Weill, 2007), and is often restricted to organizational boundaries for competitive, regulatory, and ethical reasons (Jordan & Mitchell, 2015; Adadi, 2021). For instance, companies have strong incentives against sharing their valuable data with competitors as access to data that can be leveraged with AI models has strategic benefits with winner-takes-all dynamics, called "data network effects" (Gregory et al., 2021; Napirata et al., 2023). The bottleneck of data availability can potentially be addressed by applying federated learning (FL) (see also Chap. 5).

FL allows multiple decentralized clients to train a global model using their own local training datasets without sharing access to these datasets (Konečný et al., 2016; McMahan et al., 2017). In short, it presents an opportunity to increase the quantity of available training data while meeting privacy and confidentiality requirements. FL enables individual clients to train their models using their own data, allowing them to leverage the unique insights present in their respective datasets. Subsequently, the models are aggregated to create a shared model that encompasses the collective knowledge from the different datasets, all while ensuring that the data remains inaccessible to the central model.

This chapter focuses on the potential applications of FL in the financial industry, discussing its core opportunities and five specific applications: credit risk, systemic risk and portfolio overlap, fraud detection, personalized investment advice, and open banking. By leveraging FL, financial institutions can collaborate amid competition and increase the utility of training datasets without exposing or disclosing them (Banabilah et al., 2022). We conclude with an outlook on the future of FL in the financial services industry.

11.2 Opportunities of Federated Learning

ML typically requires a significant amount of data in order to produce robust and accurate results. In competitive environments such as the financial services industry, obtaining this critical mass of data can be both costly and difficult (Walczak, 2001). Additionally, given the sensitive nature of most financial data, the endeavor of gaining great accessibility to data proves challenging.

Introduced in 2016, FL allows distributed entities to train a global model between multiple decentralized clients using each client's own local training dataset without access to each other's training dataset (Konečný et al., 2016; McMahan et al., 2017). Collaboration is coordinated by a central server that should act as a trusted messenger and prevents collusion or Byzantine behavior (see Lamport et al., 1982). Neither the coordinator nor other clients have access to a client's original dataset. What makes FL a powerful ML technique is that information derived from datasets can be shared between participants without providing access or moving them. In effect, the utility of training datasets can be extracted without these being exposed or disclosed to any party (Wang et al., 2020). As such, FL presents an opportunity to create a new type of environment for collaboration amid competition as data quantity is increased, all while enhancing privacy by exchanging aggregated information rather than raw data (Banabilah et al., 2022).

Rooted in the existing literature and our own experiences developing FL-based solutions, FL offers two key advantages: data privacy and increased model accuracy based on cross-silo accessibility to resources.

11.2.1 Data Privacy

FL offers a unique proposition: It is a ML technique that allows participants to share information derived from datasets without giving access to or transferring the raw data. In other words, FL enables the extraction of patterns from training datasets without exposing or disclosing the raw training data. However, because of the architectural need for a central server for coordination, both the model and the communication channels still require solutions that improve privacy. Promising avenues are the addition of privacy-preserving techniques to the FL architecture, notably, differential privacy (DP) (McMahan et al., 2018) and secure aggregation (SecAgg) (Bonawitz et al., 2017). In principle, when combined with these privacy-preserving techniques, FL is protective of privacy *by design*.

11.2.2 Model Accuracy Based on Cross-Silo Accessibility

FL encourages collaboration between different stakeholders, allowing them to pool their resources and expertise to train better models while maintaining the privacy and security of their data. Ensuring high model accuracy in today's data-driven landscape necessitates collaborative efforts across organizational boundaries. FL revolutionizes the traditional approach by decentralizing model training, allowing for the aggregation of data from diverse stakeholders across silos. This collaborative framework not only enhances the quantity of data available for model training but also promotes the inclusion of diverse perspectives and insights, thereby potentially improving accuracy (Thiebes et al., 2021). This is especially useful in scenarios where data is distributed across multiple locations and cannot be easily pooled, such as in the financial services sector. Moreover, FL acknowledges the significance of factors beyond data quantity, such as dataset variability, in the pursuit of accuracy improvement (Xiong et al., 2021; Shin et al., 2022). By facilitating cross-silo collaboration while safeguarding data privacy and security, FL emerges as a promising solution to both the challenges of data availability and accuracy enhancement in machine learning applications.

11.3 Applications in the Financial Industry

In the following, we present examples of FL applications in the financial industry. These are illustrative and serve the purpose of demonstrating how FL could solve or help address specific problems in the financial services industry.

11.3.1 Credit Risk

In a fractional banking system, financial institutions (FIs) play a key role in allocating capital between savers and spenders. They make profits by lending money to clients and waiting for a larger payout in the future. This process creates a unique form of risk – called *credit risk* – which arises when borrowers fail to make required payments. To navigate through the complexities of credit risk, FIs rely on data; that is, they employ data-driven strategies for the quantification of credit risk. In doing so, they cluster borrowers with similar risk profiles and manage the overarching risk across various commodities such as financial products (Altman & Saunders, 1997; Basel Committee on Banking Supervision, 1999). While FIs have typically used traditional or static methods (i.e., non-data-driven statistical models) for this purpose (Chen et al., 2016; Galindo & Tamayo, 2000), with increased availability of related data, intelligent or AI-powered methods are now more common. Although these methods show a substantial increase in performance for small institutions, they still face limitations. Specifically, the performance of these credit risk models depends not only on the methodology used but also on data inputs – i.e., data availability and quality (Heitfield, 2009; Tarashev, 2010). While centralized models outperform decentralized ones under the same conditions, the amount of data within reach of decentralized architectures is sufficient to outperform centralized ones (Almanifi et al., 2023; Walczak, 2001; Bansal et al., 1993).

One potential solution to these limitations is FL. It has shown promise in improving the performance of credit risk models as, through collaboration, FIs can increase the quantity and quality of data (Lee et al., 2023). In doing so, FIs can potentially improve the accuracy and effectiveness of their credit. In this process, FL facilitates the local data analysis either on the user's device or within a specific department, negating the need for centralized data collection. This analysis could involve data related to users' app usage, behavior, and transfer patterns. The localized data processing model ensures a minimum of aggregated insights to be stored on end-user devices, keeping sensitive individual data points within the originating domain. This approach mitigates the risk of data breaches and strengthens the security framework of the credit risk assessment process.

However, the adoption of FL in credit risk assessment is not without its challenges. Because it is a relatively new technology, standardized best practices and industry benchmarks are yet to be established, potentially leading to inconsistencies in data analysis methodologies and complicating comparative analyses across different FIs (Kairouz et al., 2021; Li et al., 2020b; Zhang et al., 2021; Li et al., 2020a). Moreover, the inherent complexity of FL algorithms may pose interpretative challenges for those not well-versed in the technology, complicating the understanding and application of FL-derived insights in credit risk management (Nilsson et al., 2018; Almanifi et al., 2023). A particular case in point is the reluctance among some FIs to engage in data-sharing models, especially when the data-sharing framework could inadvertently benefit competitors. Despite these concerns, FL models are designed to share only model updates or aggregated insights rather than raw data, thereby preserving the competitive edge of participating FIs while still leveraging collective intelligence for enhanced credit risk assessment. Financial institutions, including smaller entities like FinTech startups and neobanks, can harness the power of FL to collectively develop credit risk models without compromising data privacy. By processing data without disclosing sensitive information, institutions can derive mutual benefit, tapping into shared knowledge to expand the breadth of their models. This collaborative approach enables smaller players to mitigate biases, better cater to new clientele, and access untapped markets, ultimately fostering increased competitiveness and growth in the financial landscape.

11.3.2 Systemic Risk and Portfolio Overlap

Systemic risk is broadly defined "as the risk of an event that destabilizes or adversely affects systemically essential financial intermediaries or markets, compromising the proper functioning of a more extensive financial system and/or the real economy" (European Central Bank, 2009). One example of such systemic risk is the likelihood of *portfolio overlap* (Gualdi et al., 2016). It is defined as the degree to which the investment portfolios of two or more banks hold the same securities or assets (Inhoffen et al., 2019). If banks have a significant overlap in their portfolios, they may be exposed to similar risks and vulnerabilities in the event of a market downturn or other economic shocks (Garnier et al., 2013).

Regulators and policy-makers recognize that systemic risk can cause extensive damage and are taking measures to address it (Basel Committee on Banking Supervision, 2018). They are promoting disclosure requirements for FIs and have created platforms to facilitate voluntary sharing of credit risk information at the national level (European Central Bank, 2010; Israël et al., 2017). However, concerns about the protection of confidential information such as trade secrets, intellectual property, and financial data arise (Philip Chen & Zhang, 2014; Chen et al., 2014). Loss of data ownership could lead to a loss of market presence, which would be harmful to FIs' operations.

FL – coupled with privacy-preserving mechanisms – can alleviate many of the stressors found when it comes to detecting and mitigating systemic risk (Byrd & Polychroniadou, 2021). For instance, a federated approach can be implemented where the regulator can act as a central coordinator and the banks under its jurisdiction build their models to estimate their exposure to specific risk events such as loan defaults (Bessis, 2011; Riccetti et al., 2022). In addition, risk exposure contains sensitive information that can be mitigated using FL. In this way, the regulator will have an overview of the portfolios of the different FIs without having access to the data and respecting their privacy. This model will thus be able to estimate the probability of systemic risk caused by portfolio overlap under uncertain conditions.

Other existing solutions, such as multi-party computation (MPC), can also be used for this purpose (see also Chap. 6). However, they are limited by their deterministic formulation and do not account for future changes in systemic risk patterns. By contrast, due to their *intelligent* nature, FL models can adapt to unforeseen events to some extent.

Implementing these new methods still faces significant obstacles. On the one hand, interorganizational deployments may give central banks an overwhelming amount of power over other FIs. Balancing the power dynamics between individual banks and central banks will require complex agreements, and implementing such agreements coupled with the inherent complexity of FL can make it difficult to hold decision-makers accountable. One solution to alleviate these tensions could be blockchain-based coordination (Rückel et al., 2022), where decision-making power is not held by central banks. Central banks will also need to play a crucial role in the models that each bank trains to ensure the final model's quality. This model will have significant responsibility as it guides the regulator toward less risky situations through their decisions, making the issue of liabilities an essential consideration. Questions such as who is responsible for such behaviors need to be thoroughly studied to achieve these goals.

11.3.3 Fraud Detection Systems

In the financial industry, detecting fraud is challenging: Traditional methods are susceptible to human error and do not detect fraud in real time (Leite et al., 2015). With fraudsters and hackers becoming more innovative, AI and outlier detection approaches are becoming increasingly crucial in the fight against fraud. In response, the industry has developed fraud detection systems (FDS). These systems focus on fraud prevention through inconvenient authorization techniques – including signatures, credit card numbers, identification numbers, cardholder addresses, and expiration dates (Yang et al., 2019c). Yet, as these methods are often insufficient in curbing fraudulent activities, there is an urgent need to adopt detection approaches that systematically analyze data and address fraud in real time.

Detecting fraudulent transactions is a significant challenge for individual smaller banks due to the data imbalance between ordinary and fraudulent transactions. This makes it challenging to train a classifier and learn from different transaction data (Myalil et al., 2021). Collaborating with other institutions that provide data is, therefore, essential to develop a more accurate FDS (Lopez-Rojas & Axelsson, 2016; Paruchuri, 2017). However, sharing such transactional data is difficult due to high developmental costs or legal limitations such as the General Data Protection Regulation (GDPR) (Mathews & Assefa, 2022).

FLs enables institutions to collaborate on developing FDS models without revealing transaction data, solving data privacy and security issues (Mathews & Assefa, 2022). Recent research by Yang et al. (2019c) indicates that FL can detect suspicious transactions across multiple data sources, improving the accuracy of FDS models and reducing false positives. According to Mohammed et al. (2018), FLs also improves scalability when working with highly imbalanced big datasets, such as those of big credit card market players. Governmental institutions and Treasury representatives have hailed FLs technology as a crucial "building block" in safeguarding the financial system and financial service applications against criminal activities, such as illicit finance (Vanderford, 2022). By sharing insights learned from transaction data but not the raw data using FLs, FIs can collaborate to develop more robust FDS algorithms while maintaining the confidentiality of sensitive data.

One issue that arises in FL systems for fraud detection is competitive distrust. In a cross-silo context, data held by various participants may have different distributions, creating a non-independent and identically distributed (non-IID) scenario where certain institutions may operate as malevolent adversaries. These participants, referred to as rogue nodes, can act maliciously and compromise the integrity of the trained global FL model. This is a problem for all participants, because the model's accuracy is compromised, and there is a risk of exposing sensitive data. Experimental works have attempted to address this issue. For instance, Myalil et al. (2021) have demonstrated a method for improving FDS accuracy while preserving data privacy and security by preventing rogue nodes from contributing to the trained global FL model. However, this approach remains to be evaluated in practice. Secure computing techniques (Garrido et al., 2022) such as trusted execution environments (TEEs) or zero-knowledge proofs (ZKPs) could also be used in combination with FL to provide correctness guarantees for the contributed locally trained models (Rückel et al., 2022).

11.3.4 Personalized Investment Advice

The financial industry constantly seeks ways to improve its products and services, particularly in light of systematic changes and demographic trends (Schmähl, 1999). This is particularly evident in the provision of *personalized investment advice*. Traditional methods of providing such advice have typically relied on a combination of manual analysis, risk assessments, and asset allocation strategies (Capponi et al., 2019). Manually assessing an individual client's financial situation – including tax considerations, estate planning, and overall financial goals – is a time-consuming and inefficient task for retail banking. However, technological advancements and data analysis have enabled the development of more sophisticated methods. These include robot advisors – that leverage machine-learning algorithms – at scale (Kobets et al., 2020; Capponi et al., 2019).

Banks face a significant challenge in providing *personalized investment advice* due to strict data privacy laws and regulations, such as the GDPR (Mathews & Assefa, 2022) and the California Consumer Privacy Act. These laws limit the use of customer data, which is usually restricted to specific authorized purposes, such as managing their accounts or providing targeted marketing materials. Here, FL provides a potential solution to both problems. Models can be trained locally using a shared parameterized algorithm that utilizes information from other users without disclosing sensitive data (Chen et al., 2019a). Clients, such as asset managers, can use FL methods to jointly train a shared machine-learning model (Byrd & Polychroniadou, 2021) while keeping their data in their systems. Furthermore, FL offers significant benefits when applied to models trained on data from various sources – as it can account for a broader range of market patterns and investor behavior – leading to more accurate forecasts and better investment outcomes (Awan et al., 2019). In sum, FL approaches can aid in providing *personalized investment advice* by enabling adjustments and recommendations based on individual financial conditions and investment objectives (Dziarstek et al., 2004).

FL in the financial industry presents promising opportunities to provide customers with better investment options and services, including retail and wealth management. However, the utilization of adversarial FL models raises concerns regarding the ethical implications of driving other clients to copy their actions Luo et al. (2021). This approach introduces new security, transparency, and privacy challenges when dealing with sensitive customer financial information for investment advice (Padala et al., 2021). The need to access such sensitive data, including legal status, profession, and the number of children, further amplifies these concerns (Huang & Lin, 2005). Therefore, exploring and developing approaches that balance the benefits of FL and the ethical, privacy, security, and transparency concerns associated with training models using sensitive financial information are crucial.

11.3.5 Open Banking

The rise of *open banking* has given customers more control over their banking data (Long et al., 2020). This shift has created new opportunities for data marketplaces and financial products and services where a rights-based framework that gives customers control over their data is more appropriate (Leong, 2020). However, the financial industry still faces the general problem of data sharing: On the one hand, consumers are hesitant to share their data, and on the other hand, privacy regulations limit the utilization of shared data (Brodsky & Oakes, 2017). These obstruct the exploitability of open banking. Here, FL could assist and answer some of these issues by offering valuable solutions to address data-sharing challenges in the financial industry, particularly in the context of open banking.

Notably, the exploration by WeBank has demonstrated how FL can be applied to payment management, application programming interface (API) integration, and other practical challenges within the open banking environment (see WeBank et al., 2018). These advancements highlight the significant potential of FL in addressing practical issues and unlocking business opportunities in open banking. By enabling decentralized model training without collecting private data, FL aligns with the preferences of customers who prioritize training models on their own devices rather than selling their data (Pallant et al., 2022). Additionally, FL facilitates carefully considering variations and biases in each user's data, including social, economic, political, and behavioral factors (Abadi et al., 2016).

In open banking and other large-scale systems involving multiple firms, incentive management is a critical challenge that needs to be addressed to motivate data owners to engage in FL and assess each participant's contribution (Kang et al., 2019; Khan et al., 2020; Yang et al., 2019a; Zhan et al., 2020). Various incentives, such as user-defined utility, charging by access times, and monetary rewards, have been explored in the literature (Han et al., 2022; Li et al., 2023). However, addressing incentive management alone cannot make FL a practical and effective solution in such systems. Other significant challenges must be tackled for users, ultimately enhancing financial services and customer experiences in the open banking ecosystem.

11.4 Adoption Challenges

The challenges surrounding the implementation of FL include concerns about privacy, trust, intellectual property rights, ownership, security, and governance – which are especially important in collaborative environments within competitive markets (Berente et al., 2021). While FL benefits each party by allowing them to share information derived from datasets privately, the degree of each party's contribution depends on the types of problems and environments they bring together. Trustworthy environments are established through appropriate governance in business settings (Sambamurthy & Zmud, 1999); they set the terms of collaboration, participation, and contribution.

Subsequently, we discuss three fields of challenges pertaining to FL adoption: first, that of technology readiness. Second, we turn to IT governance. At last, we consider the natural competitive dynamics of data markets in the financial industry which, too, may pose challenges to adoption.

11.4.1 Technology Readiness

FL has a unique opportunity in the financial sector, yet most of the advancement is still limited to the academic setting. Significant challenges must be tackled for the financial sector to be able to see its benefits:

Data heterogeneity Users may come from different FIs with multiple bank accounts, credit cards, and investment portfolios, while others may only have a checking account, and even the same user may have different information in different institutions (Yang et al., 2019b).

Model heterogeneity is a challenge when different FIs choose and run a model with personalized architectures. For example, a wealth management firm may require a model that focuses on high-net-worth individuals, while a retail bank may require a model that focuses on more general consumer banking. This challenges how their central server can aggregate information across FIs with heterogeneous models (Long et al., 2020).

Statistical heterogeneity due to diverse user behavior is another challenge in FL, where each user's data may vary in its hidden distribution and spending patterns that change given regional conditions or investment preferences leading to different patterns in their financial data (Montani, 2008).

Furthermore, with the development of FL and its collaborative nature, it is crucial to look into concerns of bias and fairness (Zhang et al., 2020; Huang et al., 2022) in federated models to prevent malicious movements from the clients toward their particular interests. In conclusion, while there are solid academic grounds for FL in the financial industry, empirical industrial research is urgently needed to solve real-world issues.

11.4.2 Governance

Governance is understood as the "organizing logic through which the management of data" takes place, including its "collection, storage, processing, using, sharing, and destroying" (Janssen et al., 2020). Formerly, governance pertains to decision rights, accountability, and incentives (Weill & Ross, 2004). To guarantee that these tasks are completed in a safe, moral, and responsible manner, governance must set clear policies and guidelines. Decision rights play a crucial role in FL governance. They determine who has the authority to make decisions regarding the FL process, such as model selection, hyperparameter tuning, and data participation. The clear allocation of decision rights can help avoid conflicts and ensure that the FL system operates smoothly.

Decision Rights Khatri and Brown (2010) establish that decision rights largely determine "who can make [decisions] and therefore influence how data is accessed, controlled, used and benefited from." Decision rights generally define the locus of centralization (i.e., the "locus of authority"), that is, to what extent decision-making power is concentrated (centralized) or dispersed (decentralized) among participants or stakeholders (Sambamurthy & Zmud, 1999). The degree of centralization, then, is contingent on factors such as the governance mode, geographic dispersion, diversification mode, and breadth, as well as the absorptive capacity of IT.

In practice, decision-making structures must be conceptualized and designed according to the setting in which IT is implemented. For instance, in environments that use FL technology, the server coordinator, which may be a trusted third party like a central bank, a joint venture, or an industry consortium, plays a critical role. This party defines access rights and operating standards that increase overall trust in the technology and market functioning by ensuring that all participants adhere to the agreed-upon rules and regulations. All participants should trust the central server coordinator regarding its tasks before any collaboration and sharing of data assets occurs. This approach helps bridge the gap between individual interests and collective goals, creating a collaborative environment where all parties benefit from shared insights while maintaining the confidentiality and integrity of their data.

Accountability is critical in autonomous AI systems and refers to the ability to monitor decisions and hold agents accountable for their actions. This includes accountability for data handling, model performance, and compliance with regulations and privacy policies. The obscurity of AI models is a concern, making it challenging to scrutinize and explain algorithmic activity (Martin, 2019). This obscurity is especially problematic in FL, which can further darken the AI black box due to increased privacy-preserving features and the federated nature of the system. Keeping inputs confidential has a detrimental effect on audibility, making accountability difficult. Institutional enactment of accountability through legal frameworks and policies could offer profitable opportunities to address this challenge (Weitzner et al., 2008).

Incentives Two problems related to the alignment of incentives in FL can be highlighted. The first problem relates to free riding, where participants benefit from the shared model without making valuable contributions. Incentive schemes that reward participants for contributing to the learning protocol could prevent free riding and malicious actors (Richardson et al., 2020). Incentive schemes that use distributed ledger technology (DLT)-based tokens have also been proposed (Thiebes et al., 2021). The second problem pertains to the temporal mismatch between the training of models and the commercialization of the shared model, which creates an incentive problem for data owners' continued participation. An incentive scheme that progressively rewards and incentivizes clients within a federation could address this problem (Yu et al., 2020). The scheme aims to maximize collective utility while minimizing inequality among data owners regarding the payoff received and their waiting time for receiving payoffs.

11.4.3 Competition

In highly competitive electronic markets, the challenge is to strike a balance between collaboration and competition. Competitive pressure can drive the adoption of ITs (Zhu & Kraemer, 2005; Chan et al., 2012), but businesses are increasingly turning toward collaborative and cooperative strategies such as joint ventures and consortium partnerships to gain a competitive edge (Teo & Pian, 2003; Chen and Tsou, 2007; Chiu & Yang, 2019; Hemphill, 2003). Collaborative technologies like FL can contribute to this development, but the creation of trust among participants is crucial for adoption (Salam, 2017; Chong et al., 2009). For the successful adoption of FL, firms need to define and determine how competitive advantages will be formed and understand how trust between participants is fostered. However, there are two crucial challenges to adoption: pricing and the potential formation of cartels or oligopolies.

Pricing The success of collaborative markets is contingent on the definition of common "rules of the game." Productive collaboration in electronic markets is linked to the cost-benefit of participating in an FL environment. Compensation for participants' contributions in an equitable manner is necessary for the success of collaborative markets. The variability of data in FL is crucial, as models require statistically new data to increase their accuracy and widen their field of view. Therefore, pricing in FL can be conceptualized in terms of both the training time and the value of contributions, which raises issues like accommodating participant expectations, valuing contributions to the shared model, and balancing contribution rewards relative to performance.

Oligopolies The second challenge to adoption from the perspective of markets pertains to the nature of competitive markets. Related work has highlighted how these can induce selfish, rational, and, at times, unethical firm behavior (Ghoshal, 2005). On the one hand, FL can be used as an attack vector for businesses to maliciously undermine each other and disrupt the gains from collaboration. On the other hand, amid the dynamics of collaboration in competition (coined "coopetition" (Hoess et al., 2024)), there is considerable risk of collusion and the potential formation of cartels and oligopolies (Goyal & Joshi, 2003). While data is an integral part of business operations and drives organizations' individual behavior, the sharing of information as derivatives of data can reinforce antitrust and anticompetitive behavior (Parker et al., 2019; Rusche, 2019; Schneider, 2020). Take, for instance, a market of the leading social media companies who collaborate within a consortium to train FL models for targeted advertising. Minor contributions are close to worthless in this setting, which leads to the exclusion of smaller companies and large firms to gobble up more market share(Mitra & Baid, 2020). Admittedly, such an environment is primed for the formation of data cartels and oligopolies (Goyal & Joshi, 2003): Only large firms form strategic alliances with each other over equally large contributions.

11.5 Outlook

In this chapter, we presented the core opportunities that FL presents to the financial industry. These include the ability to leverage decentralized data sources to increase the quantity and diversity of data available for model training, the potential to improve model accuracy and reduce the risk of overfitting by training models on data from multiple sources, and the ability to maintain data privacy and security by keeping sensitive data within organizational boundaries. Then, we explored five different applications of FL in the financial industry – credit risk assessment, systemic risk and portfolio overlap, fraud detection, personalized investment advice, and open banking. Through these examples, we demonstrate how FIs can combine data from multiple sources to improve the accuracy of their models, inform decisions, and predict liabilities while maintaining data privacy. In sum, we argue that FL presents a powerful opportunity to leverage decentralized data sources while maintaining data privacy and security. The applications of FL in the financial industry are vast and promising. We conclude that FL has the potential to revolutionize the way FIs approach data-driven decision-making and that it will be an important area of research and development in the future.

References

Abadi, M., Chu, A., Goodfellow, I., McMahan, H. B., Mironov, I., Talwar, K., & Zhang, L. (2016). Deep learning with differential privacy. In *Proceedings of the ACM SIGSAC Conference on Computer and Communications Security* (pp. 308–318). https://doi.org/10.1145/2976749.2978318

Adadi, A. (2021). A survey on data-efficient algorithms in big data era. *Journal of Big Data, 8*. https://doi.org/10.1186/s40537-021-00419-9

Almanifi, O. R. A., Chow, C.-O., Tham, M.-L., Chuah, J. H., & Kanesan, J. (2023). Communication and computation efficiency in federated learning: A survey. *Internet of Things*, *22*, 100742. https://doi.org/10.1016/j.iot.2023.100742

Altman, E. I., & Saunders, A. (1997). Credit risk measurement: Developments over the last 20 years. *Journal of Banking & Finance*, *21*(11), 1721–1742. https://doi.org/10.1016/S0378-4266(97)00036-8

Aral, S., & Weill, P. (2007). IT assets, organizational capabilities, and firm performance: How resource allocations and organizational differences explain performance variation. *Organization Science*, *18*(5), 763–780. https://doi.org/10.1287/orsc.1070.0306

Awan, S., Li, F., Luo, B., & Liu, M. (2019). Poster: A reliable and accountable privacy-preserving federated learning framework using the blockchain. In *Proceedings of the 2019 ACM SIGSAC Conference on Computer and Communications Security* (pp. 2561–2563). ACM. https://doi.org/10.1145/3319535.3363256

Banabilah, S., Aloqaily, M., Alsayed, E., Malik, N., & Jararweh, Y. (2022). Federated learning review: Fundamentals, enabling technologies, and future applications. *Information Processing & Management*, *59*(6), 103061. https://doi.org/10.1016/j.ipm.2022.103061

Bansal, A., Kauffman, R. J., & Weitz, R. R. (1993). Comparing the modeling performance of regression and neural networks as data quality varies: A business value approach. *Journal of Management Information Systems*, *10*(1), 11–32. https://doi.org/10.2307/40398029

Basel Committee on Banking Supervision. (1999). Credit risk modelling: Current practices and applications. https://www.bis.org/publ/bcbs49.htm

Basel Committee on Banking Supervision. (2018). Pillar 3 disclosure requirement – updated framework. https://www.bis.org/bcbs/publ/d455.pdf

Berente, N., Gu, B., Recker, J., & Santhanam, R. (2021). Managing artifical intelligence. *MIS Quarterly*, *45*(3), 1433–1450. https://aisel.aisnet.org/misq/vol45/iss3/16/

Bessis, J. (2011). *Risk management in banking*. John Wiley & Sons.

Bonawitz, K., et al. (2017). Practical secure aggregation for privacy-preserving machine learning. In *Proceedings of the ACM SIGSAC Conference on Computer and Communications Security* (pp. 1175–1191). https://doi.org/10.1145/3133956.3133982

Brodsky, L., & Oakes, L. (2017). Data sharing and open banking. https://www.mckinsey.com/~/media/McKinsey/Industries/Financial%20Services/Our%20Insights/Data%20sharing%20and%20open%20banking/Data-sharing-and-open-banking.pdf

Byrd, D., & Polychroniadou, A. (2021). Differentially private secure multi-party computation for federated learning in financial applications. In *Proceedings of the 1st International Conference on AI in Finance*. ACM. https://doi.org/10.1145/3383455.3422562

Campbell, C., et al. (2003). Estimating dataset size requirements for classifying DNA microarray data. *Journal of Computational Biology*, *10*, 119–142. https://doi.org/10.1089/106652703321825928

Capponi, A., Ólafsson, S., & Zariphopoulou, T. (2019). Personalized robo-advising: Enhancing investment through client interactions. *Consumer Behavioral Finance eJournal*. https://doi.org/10.1287/mnsc.2021.4014

Chan, F. T., Yee-Loong Chong, A., & Zhou, L. (2012). An empirical investigation of factors affecting e-collaboration diffusion in SMEs. *International Journal of Production Economics*, *138*(2), 329–344. https://doi.org/10.1016/j.ijpe.2012.04.004

Chen, F., Luo, M., Dong, Z., Li, Z., & He, X. (2019a). Federated meta-learning for recommendation. https://arxiv.org/abs/1802.07876

Chen, J.-S., & Tsou, H.-T. (2007). Information technology adoption for service innovation practices and competitive advantage: The case of financial firms. *Information Research*, *12*(3). https://files.eric.ed.gov/fulltext/EJ1104803.pdf

Chen, M., Mao, S., & Liu, Y. (2014). Big data: A survey. *Mobile Networks and Applications*, *19*, 171–209. https://doi.org/10.1007/s11036-013-0489-0

Chen, N., Ribeiro, B., & Chen, A. (2016). Financial credit risk assessment: A recent review. *Artificial Intelligence Review*, *45*. https://doi.org/10.1007/s10462-015-9434-x

Chen, R., Stewart, W. F., Sun, J., Ng, K., & Yan, X. (2019b). Recurrent neural networks for early detection of heart failure from longitudinal electronic health record data: implications for temporal modeling with respect to time before diagnosis, data density, data quantity, and data type. *Circulation: Cardiovascular Quality and Outcomes*, *12*(10). https://doi.org/10.1161/circoutcomes.118.005114

Chiu, C.-N., & Yang, C.-L. (2019). Competitive advantage and simultaneous mutual influences between information technology adoption and service innovation: Moderating effects of environmental factors. *Structural Change and Economic Dynamics*, *49*, 192–205. https://doi.org/10.1016/j.strueco.2018.09.005

Chong, A. Y.-L., Lin, B., Ooi, K.-B., & Raman, M. (2009). Factors affecting the adoption level of C-commerce: An empirical study. *Journal of Computer Information Systems*, *50*(2), 13–22. https://doi.org/10.1080/08874417.2009.11645380

Dziarstek, C., et al. (2004). A user-aware financial advisory system. *Multikonferenz Wirtschaftsinformatik*. *2*, 217–229. https://www.fim-rc.de/Paperbibliothek/Veroeffentlicht/136/wi-136.pdf

European Central Bank. (2009). Financial stability review. https://www.ecb.europa.eu/pub/financial-stability/fsr/shared/pdf/ivbfinancialstabilityreview200912en.pdf?a3fef6891f874a3bd40cd00aef38c64f?a3fef6891f874a3bd40cd00aef38c64f

European Central Bank. (2010). Memorandum of understanding on the exchange of information among national central credit registers for the purpose of passing it on to reporting institutions. https://www.ecb.europa.eu/pub/pdf/other/moucreditregistersen.pdf

Galindo, J., & Tamayo, P. (2000). Credit risk assessment using statistical and machine learning: Basic methodology and risk modeling applications. *Computational Economics*, *15*, 107–43. https://doi.org/10.1023/A:1008699112516

Garnier, J., Papanicolaou, G., & Yang, T.-W. (2013). Diversification in financial networks may increase systemic risk. In *Handbook on Systemic Risk* (p. 432). Cambridge University Press. https://doi.org/10.1017/CBO9781139151184.022

Garrido, G. M., Sedlmeir, J., Uludağ, Ö., Alaoui, I. S., Luckow, A., & Matthes, F. (2022). Revealing the landscape of privacy-enhancing technologies in the context of data markets for the IoT: A systematic literature review. *Journal of Network and Computer Applications*, *207*, 103465. https://doi.org/10.1016/j.jnca.2022.103465

Ghoshal, S. (2005). Bad management theories are destroying good management practice. *Academy of Management Learning & Education*, *4*, 75–91. https://doi.org/10.5465/AMLE.2005.16132558

Gibbons, C., Richards, S., Valderas, J. M., & Campbell, J. (2017). Supervised machine learning algorithms can classify open-text feedback of doctor performance with human-level accuracy. *Journal of Medical Internet Research*, *19*(3). https://doi.org/10.2196/jmir.6533

Goyal, S., & Joshi, S. (2003). Networks of collaboration in oligopoly. *Games and Economic Behavior*, *43*(1), 57–85. https://doi.org/10.1016/S0899-8256(02)00562-6

Gregory, R. W., Henfridsson, O., Kaganer, E., & Kyriakou, H. (2021). The role of artificial intelligence and data network effects for creating user value. *Academy of Management Review*, *46*(3), 534–551. https://doi.org/10.5465/amr.2019.0178

Gualdi, S., Cimini, G., Primicerio, K., Di Clemente, R., & Challet, D. (2016). Statistically validated network of portfolio overlaps and systemic risk. *Scientific Reports*, *6*(1), 39467. https://doi.org/10.1038/srep39467

Han, J., et al. (2022). Heterogeneity-aware adaptive federated learning scheduling. In *International Conference on Big Data* (pp. 911–920). IEEE. https://doi.org/10.1109/BigData55660.2022.10020721

Heitfield, E. (2009). Parameter uncertainty and the credit risk of collateralized debt obligations. https://doi.org/10.2139/ssrn.1190362

Hemphill, T. (2003). Cooperative strategy, technology innovation and competition policy in the united states and the european union. *Technology Analysis & Strategic Management*, *15*(1), 93–101. https://doi.org/10.1080/0953732032000046079

Hoess, A., Lautenschlager, J., Sedlmeir, J., Fridgen, G., Schlatt, V., & Urbach, N. (2024). Toward seamless mobility-as-a-service. *Business & Information Systems Engineering*. https://doi.org/10.1007/s12599-024-00856-9

Huang, E. Y., & Lin, C.-Y. (2005). Customer-oriented financial service personalization. *Industrial Management & Data Systems*, *105*(1), 26–44. https://doi.org/10.1108/02635570510575171

Huang, W., Li, T., Wang, D., Du, S., Zhang, J., & Huang, T. (2022). Fairness and accuracy in horizontal federated learning. *Information Sciences*, *589*, 170–185. https://doi.org/10.1016/j.ins.2021.12.102

Inhoffen, J., Wierts, P., van Lelyveld, I., & Bootsma, N. (2019). Indirect interconnectedness – portfolio overlap in the euro area. In *Global Monitoring Report on Non-Bank Financial Intermediation 2018* (pp. 36–38). Financial Stability Board. https://hdl.handle.net/1871.1/e96eba0c-fc39-4907-9e0b-a81a9a5cd2c3

Israël, J.-M., Damia, V., Bonci, R., & Watfe, G. (2017). The analytical credit dataset – a magnifying glass for analysing credit in the euro area. https://doi.org/10.2139/ssrn.2985442

Janiesch, C., Zschech, P., & Heinrich, K. (2021). Machine learning and deep learning. *Electronic Markets*, *31*(3), 685–695. https://doi.org/10.1007/s12525-021-00475-2

Janssen, M., Brous, P., Estevez, E., Barbosa, L. S., & Janowski, T. (2020). Data governance: Organizing data for trustworthy artificial intelligence. *Government Information Quarterly*, *37*(3), 101493. https://doi.org/10.1016/j.giq.2020.101493

Jordan, M. I., & Mitchell, T. M. (2015). Machine learning: Trends, perspectives, and prospects. *Science*, *349*(6245), 255–260. https://doi.org/10.1126/science.aaa8415

Kairouz, P., et al. (2021). Advances and open problems in federated learning. *Foundations and Trends® in Machine Learning*, *14*(1–2). https://doi.org/10.1561/2200000083

Kang, J., Xiong, Z., Niyato, D., Xie, S., & Zhang, J. (2019). Incentive mechanism for reliable federated learning: A joint optimization approach to combining reputation and contract theory. *IEEE Internet of Things Journal*, *6*(6), 10700–10714. https://doi.org/10.1109/JIOT.2019.2940820

Khan, L. U., Pandey, S. R., Tran, N. H., Saad, W., Han, Z., Nguyen, M. N. H., & Hong, C. S. (2020). Federated learning for edge networks: Resource optimization and incentive mechanism. *IEEE Communications Magazine*, *58*(10), 88–93. https://doi.org/10.1109/MCOM.001.1900649

Khatri, V., & Brown, C. V. (2010). Designing data governance. *Communications of the ACM*, *53*(1), 148–152. https://doi.org/10.1145/1629175.1629210

Kobets, V., Yatsenko, V., Mazur, A., & Zubrii, M. (2020). Data analysis of personalized investment decision making using robo-advisers. *Nauka ta Innovacii*. https://doi.org/10.15407/scine16.02.080

Konečný, J., McMahan, B., Ramage, D., & Richtárik, P. (2016). Federated optimization: Distributed machine learning for on-device intelligence. https://arxiv.org/abs/1610.05492

Lamport, L., Shostak, R. E., & Pease, M. C. (1982). The Byzantine generals problem. *Transactions on Programming Languages and Systems*, *4*(3), 382–401. https://doi.org/10.1145/357172.357176

Lee, C. M., Delgado Fernandez, J., Potenciano Menci, S., Rieger, A., & Fridgen, G. (2023). Federated learning for credit risk assessment. In *Proceedings of the 56th Hawaii International Conference on System Sciences* (pp. 386–395). https://hdl.handle.net/10125/102676

Leite, R. A., Gschwandtner, T., Miksch, S., Gstrein, E., & Kuntner, J. (2015). Visual analytics for fraud detection and monitoring. In *IEEE Conference on Visual Analytics Science and Technology* (pp. 201–202). https://doi.org/10.1109/VAST.2015.7347678

Leong, E. (2020). Open banking: The changing nature of regulating banking data – a case study of Australia and Singapore. *Banking & Finance Law Review*, *35*(3). https://papers.ssrn.com/sol3/papers.cfm?abstract_id=3678458

Li, L., Fan, Y., Tse, M., & Lin, K.-Y. (2020a). A review of applications in federated learning. *Computers & Industrial Engineering*, *149*, 106854. https://doi.org/10.1016/j.cie.2020.106854

Li, T., Sahu, A. K., Talwalkar, A., & Smith, V. (2020b). Federated learning: Challenges, methods, and future directions. *IEEE Signal Processing Magazine*, *37*(3), 50–60. https://doi.org/10.1007/978-3-030-85559-8_13

Li, X., Zhao, S., Chen, C., & Zheng, Z. (2023). Heterogeneity-aware fair federated learning. *Information Sciences*, *619*, 968–986. https://doi.org/10.1016/j.ins.2022.11.031

Long, G., Tan, Y., Jiang, J., & Zhang, C. (2020). Federated learning for open banking. In *Federated Learning: Privacy and Incentive* (pp. 240–254). Springer. https://doi.org/10.1007/978-3-030-63076-8_17

Lopez-Rojas, E. A., & Axelsson, S. (2016). A review of computer simulation for fraud detection research in financial datasets. In *Future Technologies Conference* (pp. 932–935). https://doi.org/10.1109/FTC.2016.7821715

Luo, X., Wu, Y., Xiao, X., & Ooi, B. C. (2021). Feature inference attack on model predictions in vertical federated learning. In *Proceedings of the 37th International Conference on Data Engineering* (pp. 181–192). IEEE. https://doi.org/10.1109/ICDE51399.2021.00023

Martin, K. (2019). Designing ethical algorithms. *MIS Quarterly Executive*, *18*(2), 5. https://doi.org/10.17705/2msqe.00012

Mathews, S. M., & Assefa, S. A. (2022). Federated learning: Balancing the thin line between data intelligence and privacy. https://arxiv.org/abs/2204.13697

McKinsey & Company. (2022). Making financial services available to the masses through AI. https://www.mckinsey.com/industries/financial-services/our-insights/making-financial-services-available-to-the-masses-through-ai#/

McMahan, B., Moore, E., Ramage, D., Hampson, S., & y Arcas, B. A. (2017). Communication-efficient learning of deep networks from decentralized data. In *Proceedings of the 20th International Conference on Artificial Intelligence and Statistics*, volume 54 of *Proceedings of Machine Learning Research* (pp. 1273–1282). PMLR. https://proceedings.mlr.press/v54/mcmahan17a/mcmahan17a.pdf

McMahan, B., Ramage, D., Talwar, K., & Zhang, L. (2018). Learning differentially private recurrent language models. In *International Conference on Learning Representations*. https://openreview.net/pdf?id=BJ0hF1Z0b

Mitra, P., & Baid, K. (2020). Targeted advertising for online social networks. In *Proceedings of the First International Conference on Networked Digital Technologies* (pp. 366–372). IEEE. https://doi.org/10.1109/NDT.2009.5272165

Mohammed, R. A., Wong, K.-W., Shiratuddin, M. F., & Wang, X. (2018). Scalable machine learning techniques for highly imbalanced credit card fraud detection: A comparative study. In *Trends in Artificial Intelligence: 15th Pacific Rim International Conference on Artificial Intelligence* (pp. 237–246). Springer. https://doi.org/10.1007/978-3-319-97310-4_27

Montani, S. (2008). Exploring new roles for case-based reasoning in heterogeneous AI systems for medical decision support. *Applied Intelligence*, *28*(3), 275–285. https://doi.org/10.1007/s10489-007-0046-2

Myalil, D., Rajan, M. A., Apte, M., & Lodha, S. (2021). Robust collaborative fraudulent transaction detection using federated learning. In *20th International Conference on Machine Learning and Applications* (pp. 373–378). IEEE. https://doi.org/10.1109/ICMLA52953.2021.00064

Najafabadi, M., Villanustre, F., Khoshgoftaar, T., Seliya, N., Wald, R., & Muharemagic, E. (2015). Deep learning applications and challenges in big data analytics. *Journal of Big Data*, *2*. https://doi.org/10.1186/s40537-014-0007-7

Napirata, S., Sedlmeir, J., Rieger, A., Fridgen, G., & Zimmermann, S. (2023). The competition effect of decentralized platforms: An analytical model. In *Proceedings of the 44th International Conference on System Sciences*. AIS. https://aisel.aisnet.org/icis2023/sharing_econ/sharing_econ/16/

Nilsson, A., Smith, S., Ulm, G., Gustavsson, E., & Jirstrand, M. (2018). A performance evaluation of federated learning algorithms. In *Proceedings of the Second Workshop on Distributed Infrastructures for Deep Learning*. ACM. https://doi.org/10.1145/3286490.3286559

Padala, M., Damle, S., & Gujar, S. (2021). Federated learning meets fairness and differential privacy. In *Neural Information Processing: 28th International Conference* (pp. 692–699). Springer. https://doi.org/10.1007/978-3-030-92310-5_80

Pallant, J. I., Pallant, J. L., Sands, S. J., Ferraro, C. R., & Afifi, E. (2022). When and how consumers are willing to exchange data with retailers: An exploratory segmentation. *Journal of Retailing and Consumer Services*, *64*, 102774. https://doi.org/10.1016/j.jretconser.2021.102774

Parker, G., Petropoulos, G., & Alstyne, M. v. (2019). Digital platforms and antitrust. In *The Oxford Handbook of Institutions of International Economic Governance and Market Regulation*. Oxford Academic. https://doi.org/10.1093/oxfordhb/9780190900571.013.34

Paruchuri, H. (2017). Credit card fraud detection using machine learning: A systematic literature review. *ABC Journal of Advanced Research*. https://i-proclaim.my/journals/index.php/abcjar/article/view/547/505

Philip Chen, C., & Zhang, C.-Y. (2014). Data-intensive applications, challenges, techniques and technologies: A survey on big data. *Information Sciences*, *275*, 314–347. https://doi.org/10.1016/j.ins.2014.01.015

Riccetti, L. et al. (2022). Agent-based multi-layer network simulations for financial systemic risk measurement: A proposal for future developments. *International Journal of Microsimulation*, *15*(2), 44–61. https://doi.org/10.34196/IJM.00262

Richardson, A., Filos-Ratsikas, A., & Faltings, B. (2020). Budget-bounded incentives for federated learning. In *Federated Learning* (pp. 176–188). Springer. https://doi.org/10.1007/978-3-030-63076-8_13

Roose, K. (2022). We need to talk about how good A.I. is getting. https://www.nytimes.com/2022/08/24/technology/ai-technology-progress.html

Rückel, T., Sedlmeir, J., & Hofmann, P. (2022). Fairness, integrity, and privacy in a scalable blockchain-based federated learning system. *Computer Networks*, *202*, 108621. https://doi.org/10.1016/j.comnet.2021.108621

Rusche, C. (2019). Data economy and antitrust regulation. *Intereconomics: Review of European Economic Policy*, *54*(2), 114–119. https://doi.org/10.1007/s10272-019-0804-5

Salam, M. (2017). The mediating role of supply chain collaboration on the relationship between technology, trust and operational performance an empirical investigation. *Benchmarking: An International Journal*, *24*(2), 298–317. https://doi.org/10.1108/bij-07-2015-0075

Sambamurthy, V., & Zmud, R. W. (1999). Arrangements for information technology governance: A theory of multiple contingencies. *MIS Quarterly* (pp. 261–290). https://doi.org/10.2307/249464

Schmähl, W. (1999). Fundamental decisions for the reform of pension systems. *International Social Security Review*, *52*(3), 45–55. https://doi.org/10.1111/1468-246x.00045

Schneider, G. (2020). Designing pro-competitive research data pools: Which EU competition remedies for research data silos in digital markets? *Yearbook of Antitrust and Regulatory Studies*, *12*, 161–186. https://doi.org/10.7172/1689-9024.YARS.2020.13.21.6

Shin, J., Li, Y., Liu, Y., & Lee, S.-J. (2022). FedBalancer: Data and pace control for efficient federated learning on heterogeneous clients. In *Proceedings of the 20th Annual International Conference on Mobile Systems, Applications and Services*, MobiSys '22 (pp. 436–449). ACM. https://doi.org/0.1145/3498361.3538917

Tarashev, N. (2010). Measuring portfolio credit risk correctly: Why parameter uncertainty matters. *Journal of Banking & Finance*, *34*(9), 2065–2076. https://doi.org/10.1016/j.jbankfin.2010.01.017

Teo, T., & Pian, Y. (2003). A contingency perspective on Internet adoption and competitive advantage. *European Journal of Information Systems*, *12*, 78–92. https://doi.org/10.1057/palgrave.ejis.3000448

Thiebes, S., Lins, S., & Sunyaev, A. (2021). Trustworthy artificial intelligence. *Electronic Markets*, *31*(2), 447–464. https://doi.org/10.1007/s12525-020-00441-4

Vanderford, R. (2022). U.S., U.K. collaborate to spur innovation in tech used to combat money-laundering. https://www.wsj.com/articles/u-s-u-k-collaborate-to-spur-innovation-in-tech-used-to-combat-money-laundering-11655161935

Walczak, S. (2001). An empirical analysis of data requirements for financial forecasting with neural networks. *Journal of Management Information Systems*, *17*(4), 203–222. https://doi.org/10.1080/07421222.2001.11045659

Wang, T., Rausch, J., Zhang, C., Jia, R., & Song, D. (2020). A principled approach to data valuation for federated learning. In *Federated Learning: Privacy and Incentive* (pp. 153–167). Springer. https://doi.org/10.1007/978-3-030-63076-8_11

WeBank et al. (2018). Federated learning white paper v1.0.

Weill, P., & Ross, J. W. (2004). *IT governance: how top performers manage IT decision rights for superior results*. Harvard Business Press.

Weitzner, D. J., Abelson, H., Berners-Lee, T., Feigenbaum, J., Hendler, J., & Sussman, G. J. (2008). Information accountability. *Communications of the ACM, 51*(6), 82–87. https://doi.org/10.1145/1349026.1349043

Xiong, Z., et al. (2021). Facing small and biased data dilemma in drug discovery with enhanced federated learning approaches. *Science China Life Sciences, 65*, 529–539. https://doi.org/10.1007/s11427-021-1946-0

Yang, Q., Liu, Y., Chen, T., & Tong, Y. (2019a). Federated machine learning: Concept and applications. *ACM Transactions on Intelligent Systems and Technology, 10*(2), 1–19. https://doi.org/10.1145/3298981

Yang, Q., Liu, Y., Cheng, Y., Kang, Y., Chen, T., & Yu, H. (2019b). Federated transfer learning. In *Federated Learning* (pp. 83–93). Springer. https://doi.org/10.1007/978-3-031-01585-4_6

Yang, W., Zhang, Y., Ye, K., Li, L., & Xu, C. (2019c). FFD: A federated learning based method for credit card fraud detection. In *BigData congress*. https://doi.org/10.1007/978-3-030-23551-2_2

Yu, H., et al. (2020). A sustainable incentive scheme for federated learning. *IEEE Intelligent Systems, 35*(4), 58–69. https://doi.org/10.1109/MIS.2020.2987774

Zhan, Y., Li, P., Qu, Z., Zeng, D., & Guo, S. (2020). A learning-based incentive mechanism for federated learning. *IEEE Internet of Things Journal, 7*(7), 6360–6368. https://doi.org/10.1109/JIOT.2020.2967772

Zhang, C., Xie, Y., Bai, H., Yu, B., Li, W., & Gao, Y. (2021). A survey on federated learning. *Knowledge-Based Systems, 216*, 106775. https://doi.org/10.1016/j.knosys.2021.106775

Zhang, D. Y., Kou, Z., & Wang, D. (2020). FairFL: A fair federated learning approach to reducing demographic bias in privacy-sensitive classification models. In *International Conference on Big Data* (pp. 1051–1060). IEEE. https://doi.org/10.1109/BigData50022.2020.9378043

Zhu, K., & Kraemer, K. L. (2005). Post-adoption variations in usage and value of e-business by organizations: Cross-country evidence from the retail industry. *Information Systems Research, 16*(1), 61–84. https://doi.org/10.1287/isre.1050.0045

Chapter 12
Decentralization Beyond Disintermediation: The Case of Central Bank Digital Currencies

Nadia Pocher and Johannes Sedlmeir

Abstract Over the past 10 years, private and public actors have been experimenting with the application of blockchain and distributed ledger technologies (DLTs) in the financial sector. In particular, central banks have explored different approaches toward the issuance of digital versions of cash – i.e., *retail* central bank digital currencies (CBDCs) – and toward improving interinstitutional transfers and settlements – i.e., *wholesale* CBDC systems. These projects put forward challenging techno-regulatory questions related to the associated system architecture to meet end user and institutional demands. This includes compliance with data protection rules and financial integrity safeguards, such as anti-money laundering (AML) and counter terrorist financing (CFT). Often, these goals seem conflicting, so CBDC models require a careful design of the corresponding technology stack. We argue how supplementary cryptographic components, such as decentralized digital identities and zero-knowledge proofs (ZKPs), can support both centralized and decentralized deployments of CBDCs. Accordingly, this chapter explores the techno-regulatory building blocks of CBDC designs and outlines different design choices that have been discussed, therefore challenging the narrative that necessarily associates decentralization with disintermediation.

12.1 Introduction

The advent of cryptocurrencies, stablecoins, and—more recently—decentralized finance (DeFi) (see also Chap. 8) has inspired a new way of conceiving money and payments. While the Bitcoin whitepaper (Nakamoto, 2008) presented a novel means to keep consistent and tamper-proof information records without trusting a centralized party in an open (permissionless) setting, the hype that followed the ubiquitous application of blockchains and DLTs promised a new decentralized, allegedly more

N. Pocher (✉) · J. Sedlmeir
Interdisciplinary Centre for Security, Reliability and Trust (SnT), University of Luxembourg, Luxembourg, Luxembourg
e-mail: nadia.pocher@uni.lu; johannes.sedlmeir@uni.lu

G. Fridgen et al. (eds.), *Decentralization Technologies*, Financial Innovation and Technology, https://doi.org/10.1007/978-3-031-66047-4_12

democratic way of managing data (Tapscott & Tapscott, 2017; Beck et al., 2017). In a financial context, these expectations rely on the opportunity of exchanging value digitally peer-to-peer (P2P)—although from a technical perspective the distributed ledger takes the role of a collectively operated third party, while P2P messaging only involves the bilateral exchange of information. In this context, creating digital representations of assets and managing ownership rights with cryptographic keys—typically by means of blockchains and smart contracts instead of dedicated financial intermediaries—are often termed tokenization (Sunyaev et al., 2021). Tokenization, in turn, has incubated a rich ecosystem, called DeFi, that replicates many financial services without financial institutions (Gramlich et al., 2023). When compared to the degree of intermediation in the incumbent financial system, and to existing mechanisms to comply with regulation, this new paradigm represents a conceptual disruption (Cong & He, 2019).

We are now more than 14 years after the first Bitcoin transaction, and ideas for applications of blockchain technology have spilled over from the sphere of cryptocurrencies and DeFi into the institutional domain (see also Chap. 8). Central banks started investigating how to leverage this emerging cryptographic decentralization technology to improve interinstitutional transfers and to provide digital fiat money to be used by the general public (Agur et al., 2022). This development also addresses the decrease in the use of cash as a means of payment in many advanced economies, a trend accelerated by the COVID-19 pandemic (Zamora-Pérez, 2022). Additional competition from the private sector through BigTech payment services and so-called global stablecoin projects urged monetary authorities to provide an alternative to safeguard their monetary policy and independence. A survey by the Bank for International Settlements (BIS) reveals that 90 % of central banks are considering developing a CBDC (Kosse & Mattei, 2022). The Bahamas, China, Nigeria, and Jamaica have already launched their CBDCs, but most jurisdictions are still discussing the alleged opportunities provided by CBDCs and evaluating corresponding design options.

A vast body of literature details the drivers behind CBDC explorations and discusses the characteristics of the various models (e.g., Adrian & Mancini-Griffoli, 2019; Allen et al., 2020b; Chen & Siklos, 2022). Building on previous work, in particular Gross et al. (2021), Pocher and Veneris (2022a), and Michalopoulos et al. (2024), this chapter focuses on the way decentralized designs and decentralization technologies can be deployed in these institutional settings to obtain novel functionalities that make a CBDC different from prevalent forms of electronic money. Accordingly, it addresses the techno-regulatory impacts of embedding a given property in a CBDC design. A typical but disputed narrative identifies DLT-based decentralized designs as a means to strengthen resilience and availability, to improve the degree of interoperability and flexibility, to facilitate financial inclusion, and to counter surveillance threats (e.g., Auer et al., 2020). We aim to unpack each of these features and assess their advantages and shortcomings from the perspective of the specific institutional use case. It should be noted that in the context of each of the stated promises, decentralization can have very different forms. We will try to disentangle dimensions that can be discussed separately and that are sometimes mixed or misinterpreted. For instance, while a CBDC system's fault-tolerance (i.e., availability and immutability) guarantees can be improved through the replication inherent to DLT, a blockchain-based system also rules out fine-granular access control mechanisms (Sedlmeir et al., 2022). Privacy-oriented CBDCs that protect sensitive information also should store sensitive data in a decentralized way to avoid honeypots, but here decentralization means local processing and storage on the involved transaction partners' end devices, not replication in a blockchain network. Only certain evidence that the rules of the monetary system are abided by in transactions should be disclosed to relevant stakeholders and, therefore, replicated (Gross et al., 2021). As such, a blockchain-based CBDC design that protects sensitive information can naturally be deployed also in a centralized setting. In addition, the discussion needs to be situated in the topical realm of safeguarding compliance with diverse regulatory regimes, such as data protection, AML, and CFT measures (Pocher, 2023; Allen et al., 2020a).

Against this backdrop, this chapter is structured as follows: Sect. 12.2 provides fundamentals on CBDCs. We explore their interplay with regulatory requirements in the area of data protection and AML/CFT in Sect. 12.3, heeding also cross-border issues. Section 12.4 pinpoints the interconnections between compliance and CBDC designs, considering overall scope, offline functionalities, and privacy guarantees. Section 12.5 concludes the chapter.

12.2 Central Bank Digital Money: Fundamentals

Over the past two decades, methods of payment transmission have been digitized in various ways to support the digital transformation of society and the economic globalization. Other chapters of this book (e.g., Chap. 8) focus on private sector initiatives in digital finance, a field that is witnessing novel solutions by traditional players as well as the emergence of new stakeholders in the form of payment service providers (PSPs), BigTech, and FinTech companies (Carstens, 2021). Innovations in this domain typically affect what is called "commercial bank money" or "electronic money (e-money)," the combination of which represents the majority of money in circulation in advanced economies today. In a complementary fashion, this chapter explores the institutional activity performed by central banks and monetary authorities. In particular, it focuses on the increasing interest displayed in the tokenization of "central bank money."

12.2.1 Traditional Central Bank Money

The monetary base—M0 or base money in economic jargon—consists of two sets of central bank money. As the name suggests, central bank money is issued by the central bank, as opposed to private money, which covers both commercial bank money and e-money. On the one hand, *general purpose money*, also known as *fiat money* or (physical) cash, is the official "sovereign" (i.e., set as such by a sovereign law) currency available to the public with legal tender status (ITU-T Focus Group on Digital Currency, 2019). On the other hand, central banks hold deposits of commercial banks and payment institutions in specific accounts. These deposits are referred to as *bank reserves* and are used for interbank settlements. The typical process for such settlements is known as real-time gross settlement (RTGS), where transfer instructions occur one-to-one and are executed on a real-time basis by writing to a corresponding centralized ledger controlled by a central bank (European Cental Bank, 2022). The experiments to digitize central bank money have so far explored both these directions, where in the case of the RTGS, typically more organizations get access to the already digital system.

Both fiat money transactions and interinstitutional settlements have a domestic and an international dimension. Accordingly, cross-border transactions may involve not only wholesale transfers for settlement purposes but also retail transfers (Themistocleous et al., 2023). While the latter make up for the vast majority of payment transactions, wholesale transactions comprise almost their entire value (Financial Stability Board, 2021; Fanti & Pocher, 2022). It follows that the methods of creation and/or circulation of money can be looked at from different standpoints, depending on the specific cases. We outline the impact in terms of fundamental typologies of CBDC projects and pilots below.

12.2.2 Types of CBDC Projects and Objectives

The overarching distinction in CBDC literature embodies the difference between the two categories of central bank money and the domestic or cross-border dimension. Hence, institutional projects in the CBDC realm can be grouped as follows:

Retail CBDC schemes introduce digital fiat money, available to the public for everyday use. Their transformative character lies in the democratization of the (sovereign) currency transmission channel in the sense that it gives citizens direct access to fiat money without a bank acting as an intermediary. Retail CBDC systems can be characterized as "one-tier" (end-users directly interact with the central bank, also known as "direct" or "one-layered" structure) or "two-tier" (intermediaries, such as commercial banks and other PSPs provide an interface for engaging in CBDC transactions and for its distribution, also known as "two-layered") (Allen et al., 2020a; Pocher & Veneris, 2022a). As such, in one-tier retail CBDCs, citizens can directly submit authorized payment requests to the central bank, which updates its ledger representing citizens' ownership relations with regard to units of the currency accordingly. However, the vast majority of ongoing retail CBDC projects adopt a two-tier model, where the central bank issues the CBDC and PSPs distribute it to end-users and provide account-related services (European Central Bank, 2019). Meanwhile, the issuance and distribution the issuance and distribution of retail CBDCs raise key issues of monetary stability, efficiency, regulatory compliance, and security (Pocher & Veneris, 2022a). Related work on retail CBDCs is situated in the wave of fascination for devising an electronic version of cash that originated after the launch of Bitcoin and the decrease in the use of cash in some jurisdictions (Zamora-Pérez, 2022). Meanwhile, the development of cryptocurrencies and smart contract platforms, which further expand the opportunities of applications in DeFi (Gramlich et al., 2023), e.g., in the form of stablecoins (Ante et al., 2021), further stimulated corresponding institutional projects.

Wholesale CBDC models, on the other hand, focus on the systems of interinstitutional—e.g., interbanking—settlements, and their objective is to update and/or complement existing solutions for central bank deposits. It was the first type of CBDC projects being explored around 2014 (Wilkins, 2014; Poenisch, 2014), and a substantial set of projects have ever since involved major central banks all over the world. From 2021 onward, many of these projects have been conducted within the framework of the activities of the BIS Innovation Hub (Fanti & Pocher, 2022).

Cross-border CBDC projects are driven by the growing importance of international payments from both a wholesale and a retail perspective. Currently, cross-border payments often rely on multilayered networks of correspondent banking, which involves various intermediaries that own correspondent accounts with one another (Rice et al., 2020). While this reciprocal system eases the flow of funds, and the SWIFT network provides a standardized messaging solution to communicate the relevant instructions (Robinson et al., 2023), the involved banks need to clear and settle fund transfers individually. Thus, cross-border payments are typically less efficient and more expensive than domestic ones (OMFIF and CCB, 2023). Cross-border CBDC projects focus on developing cross-border models and/or interconnections between different domestic CBDC schemes—e.g., by exploring "multi-CBDCs" as interoperable digital platforms to automate and integrate validity checks while reducing the need for intermediaries and, therefore, transaction friction, latency, and fees (Fanti & Pocher, 2022). As blockchains can provide a non-proprietary and, therefore, neutral platform for digital interactions (Sedlmeir et al., 2022), it is not surprising that DLT plays a major role in these efforts (Themistocleous et al., 2023).

12.3 Financial Privacy and Transparency

The digitization of money and payments at the hand of private and/or public stakeholders happens in a highly regulated environment. Within the latter, various interests and values are protected by different legal frameworks and upheld by the activity of various institutions (see also Chap. 2). To start with, the framework of "monetary law" is the one that provides the legal foundation for the use of monetary value in society and the relevant qualification as legal tender. From this perspective, it is interesting to note how the issuance of digital fiat money ostensibly requires amendments to the domestic laws of most jurisdictions that have so far experimented with the idea (Bossu et al., 2020). Accordingly, the European Commission (EC) has made a proposal for a Regulation that covers essential aspects of the digital euro to allow the European Central Bank (ECB) to issue it as a novel form of central bank money (European Commission, 2023).

However, while this type of reform may seem relatively straightforward when there is a clear policy decision to issue a CBDC, other regulatory issues appear more convoluted. In particular, the world of money and payments features a long-established tension between financial transparency and financial privacy (Allen et al., 2020a), which is enshrined by regulatory frameworks to avoid the exploitation of the financial system for illegal purposes and ensure the confidentiality of financial data, respectively (Pocher, 2023). Although the presence of this ambivalent objective precedes digital technologies and the advent of cryptocurrencies, specific questions arise in this domain when considering CBDCs. This is due to the fact that the design of a CBDC displays a two-way relationship with regulatory requirements. On the one hand, technical choices impact the possibility of complying with a set of diverse legal regimes, such as those to safeguard data protection and the effectiveness of AML/CFT safeguards. Because the popularity of cryptocurrencies based on transparent blockchain networks has led to rapid progress in the design of privacy-focused payment systems (e.g., Barbereau et al., 2023; Ben-Sasson et al., 2014; Wüst et al., 2022; Nadler & Schär, 2023), the presence and feasibility of these anonymous payment methods exert pressure on the designs being discussed also in the regulated environment (Bank for International Settlements, 2023; European Central Bank, 2019). Many considerations pertaining to these and adjacent legal fields are heavily debated and considered during the design phase of the respective CBDC models (Bossu et al., 2020; Oliver Wyman Forum, 2022; Pocher & Veneris, 2022b).

12.3.1 Data Protection and Financial Privacy

CBDCs and digital payments at large arguably display a considerable vulnerability to aiding mass monitoring, profiling, surveillance, endangering the mechanisms to protect against the misuse of personal information, and threatening data protection, security, and safety (Chaum, 1985; Garratt & van Oordt, 2021; Goodell et al., 2021). When tackling the exposure of sensitive information, it is important to distinguish between privacy—i.e., a citizen's control of how much data enters the system and how it is managed—and data protection—i.e., defining who has access to specific data and preventing unauthorized access to it after it has been collected (Goodell et al., 2021; Fanti & Kostiainen, 2022). From an information system (IS) perspective, privacy in general is a highly multifaceted concept (see also Chap. 6). From a legal perspective, privacy and data protection are tied but refer to two separate rights. The former is recognized as a universal human right by the Universal Declaration of Human Rights (UN General Assembly, 1948) and is also enshrined by the European Convention of Human Rights (Council of Europe, 1950). Both the right to privacy and to data protection are recognized as fundamental human rights in the European Union (EU) by the Charter of Fundamental Rights of the European Union (European Parliament, Council and Commission, 2012).

In the EU, the protection of personal data is addressed extensively, primarily by the General Data Protection Regulation (GDPR), which has extensive cross-border impacts, and by the Data Protection Law Enforcement Directive (LED) (see Chap. 2). Indeed, EU and non-EU-based entities handling, accessing, or processing personal data of EU residents must comply, and the transfer of personal data to third countries is subject to strict conditions (Fanti & Pocher, 2022). But also other jurisdictions have privacy and data protection laws, such as the United States (US) Privacy Act and the Gramm-Leach-Bliley Act (Hanus & Relyea, 1975; Congress of the United States, 1999). Nevertheless, as recently displayed by the debate on the new EU-US Data Privacy Framework (European Data Protection Board, 2023), other jurisdictions can feature a very different and fragmented approach, often resulting in fewer safeguards (Fanti & Pocher, 2022).

In CBDC schemes, the main concerns related to the potential for data abuse arise from the presence of a compound of data on transaction partners and amounts, metadata (e.g., geolocation and time), and its connection to additional data sources, such as social media in a context that possibly features a combination of actors including government and public bodies as well as commercial players. While such data aggregation is not uncommon in the private sector, the risk of possible surveillance by public institutions and a potential aggravation in the course of "replacement" of physical cash that does not leave any digital traces have caused substantial concerns among citizens and civil rights organizations (Tronnier et al., 2022). Consequently, it is pivotal to understand the concept of CBDC-related privacy in a broad fashion (Rennie & Steele, 2021): Although CBDC privacy is often treated as a single comprehensive concept, from a practical perspective, it concerns different actors involved in the system, including central banks, PSPs, regulators, law enforcement, and retailers (Pocher, 2023). Design choices that affect privacy-related properties include but are not limited to system access and use policies, the establishment of public-private roles in guarding identity and transaction data, the definition of conditions under which public entities can retrieve and process such data and corresponding metadata, as well as if, how, and when to share data with private stakeholders (Carstens, 2021; Oliver Wyman Forum, 2022).

As such, the implemented technologies require adequate and specific controls to protect personal data (Michalopoulos et al., 2024; Tronnier et al., 2022; Gross et al., 2021). This is particularly true for blockchains, in which information is replicated and, therefore, exposed to all participants in the network (Butijn et al., 2020) (see also Chap. 3). In the absence of advanced cryptographic safeguards, a CBDC based on a public permissionless blockchain could become the "most privacy-invading citizen surveillance tool we have ever seen" (Jagati, 2020). Even a private permissioned blockchain (see also Chap. 3) will often expose too much sensitive data to third parties and poses unnecessary attack vectors, as it suffices to attack the weakest node to obtain a copy of the relevant sensitive information (Schlatt et al., 2022b). Following up on the mentioned difference among jurisdictions, local data privacy preferences and the discrepancies between regulatory frameworks across the world also inevitably lead to CBDC initiatives that embody specific inclinations (Carstens, 2021; Fanti & Pocher, 2022).

12.3.2 AML/CFT Compliance, Financial Transparency, and Data Sharing

In addition to privacy and data protection aspects, financial institutions and PSPs fall within the categories of "regulated entities" that must comply with AML/CFT regulations. This means they are required to provide active cooperation to law enforcement agencies and make efforts to prevent, unveil, and/or report suspicious activities (Financial Action Task Force, 2012; European Commission, 2015). The same regime would likely be applicable to central banks in one-tier retail CBDC models and to the financial intermediaries involved in two-tiered schemes. The AML/CFT regime consists of a multilayered set of laws, regulations, and procedures that lay out preventive and repressive measures to hamper criminals from enjoying illicit profits, financing terrorism and proliferation, and sanctioning the breach of relevant compliance obligations (Financial Action Task Force, 2012) (see Chap. 2). National efforts are overseen and coordinated by the Financial Action Task Force (FATF), the global standard-setter in this domain. The FATF is an intergovernmental policy-making, monitoring, and enforcement body that provides guidance mainly by means of its Recommendations (Financial Action Task Force, 2017).

The AML/CFT framework is grounded on the risk-based approach (RBA), which means compliance measures must be tuned to the principle of proportionality and resources must be commensurate to the nature of the different risks. It follows that the decision on the extent of data to collect to meet their obligations is largely thrust on regulated entities. Corresponding obligations on regulated entities include customer due diligence (CDD) duties such as know-your-customer (KYC) (see also Chap. 7), thus entailing identification and verification of customers' identities, checks of personal and business information, ongoing monitoring and transaction scrutiny, data retention, and suspicious transaction reporting (Schlatt et al., 2022a). Hence, regulated entities have a significant responsibility in balancing transparency and privacy in their everyday activities (Fanti & Pocher, 2022). Based on the current international standards, and in line with existing CDD processes performed by banks, a selection of categories of data would need to be processed—i.e., collected and retained for 5 years starting from the end of the business relationship or occasional transaction—within a CBDC system for the sake of AML/CFT compliance (Fanti & Pocher, 2022): (1) *Information on customers and beneficial owners*, including identification and contact data (for individuals, usually name, surname, ID/passport number, nationality, date of birth; for legal entities, typically country of incorporation, nature of the entity's business, entity's directors, beneficial owners); (2) *Account data*, including details such as the intended purpose of the account and the expected location of transactions, valuable for monitoring; and (3) *Transaction information*, e.g., records and patterns, including sender, receiver, amount, and modality, associated metadata such as timestamps and IP addresses. Subsets of this information may then be shared with various stakeholders involved in the system (Financial Action Task Force, 2017). Examples of patterns are (Fanti & Pocher, 2022):

- Pre-suspicion sharing with service providers like analytics and RegTech companies for compliance checks and monitoring (Grassi & Lanfranchi, 2022; Papantoniou, 2022) or other financial firms;
- Post-suspicion sharing, in which a regulated entity sends suspicious transaction reports (STRs) to the national financial intelligence units (FIUs), and the FIU sends intelligence to other competent authorities;
- Aggregate sharing, where the central bank would submit aggregated data to the authorities for supervision and/or statistical purposes. Typically, such aggregated data usually does not involve personal data, while it can be financial (e.g., balance sheet) or operational (e.g., number of a type of transactions);
- Supervisory access to data, which includes routine checks and information sharing between supervisors, national FIUs, and law enforcement agencies (LEAs);
- Other frameworks for the use of data collected and retained for other reasons, such as for tax purposes, to different extents. Usually, these other authorities access data previously shared by regulated entities with AML/CFT bodies.

12.3.3 Trade-Offs by Design

The tension between confidentiality and transparency is well exemplified by the struggle to safeguard privacy and data protection while ensuring AML/CFT compliance. Related work identifies an inherent tension between the priorities of these regimes, since the detection and investigation of money laundering involve the exchange of substantial amounts of data about transaction parties and individual behavior, and CDD processes require customers' sensitive personal information. This has caused a situation where consumers enjoy little privacy vis-à-vis institutions and regulators—e.g., even if it is forbidden to use data collected for AML/CFT for business purposes, financial institutions may not always be strictly required to abide by data minimization (Mahari et al., 2022). In principle, the type of information that falls under privacy and data protection regimes is broader than what falls under AML/CFT. However, the data types collected for AML/CFT purposes, chiefly related to identifying individuals and monitoring operations and transactions, pose evident privacy and data protection risks in a CBDC scheme (Fanti & Pocher, 2022). At the same time, from the perspective of regulators, it is also of utmost importance to avoid that such an instrument, prospectively ubiquitous, can make criminals more efficient in abusing the financial system for illicit purposes (Mahari et al., 2022).

The full realization of such twofold vulnerability also presents a significant and unprecedented opportunity when designing CBDC models. Leveraging the large-scale interest and multi-stakeholder involvement in these explorations, in fact, central banks and policy-makers can operationalize their specific and multidimensional objectives during the design phase of the CBDC. Indeed, it is evident that CBDC designs entail different trade-offs, one of them being the one between privacy and transparency in financial transactions (Auer et al., 2023; Bank for International Settlements, 2023). These balances can be appropriately set by engaging in dialogues with regulators, supervisors, and industry members and by performing public consultations. In some cases, it may even be possible to improve the degree of privacy without substantial losses on the transparency or accountability side by employing PETs (see also Chap. 6) (Gross et al., 2021; Michalopoulos et al., 2024). Yet, identifying such potentials again requires interactions with all stakeholders.

From an operational perspective, whenever we refer to the interplay between technical and regulatory compliance, we are grounding our argument on the assumption that the latter can be embedded into the technology itself. The notion of compliance-by-design is increasingly spreading in the field of law and technology and is at the root of those design-based regulatory and compliance techniques that aim to foster socially and legally desirable outcomes (Pocher, 2023; Hoess et al., 2024; Pocher & Veneris, 2022b). The concept of heeding compliance aspects starting from the early stages of the design of a system is enticing (Zetzsche et al., 2020; Casanovas et al., 2022) and means that regulation can be approached proactively rather than reactively by addressing the design itself, which also includes the software artifact. Besides their close link to the legitimacy of the CBDC projects that chose to deploy such methods, we argue that regulatory and compliance dynamics should be explicitly positioned within the design process. Moreover, the ex ante definition of conditions under which a certain transaction is compliant can be considered a prerequisite for the use of some PETs, such as ZKPs: If it is not possible to prove compliance, it seems that auditability in the sense of the opportunity to access transaction details ex post in the case of a closer examination is required. In this case, for an anonymous transaction, some third party requires access to the transaction details, and hence privacy guarantees for the user would not be unconditional and fully controllable (Gross et al., 2021).

12.4 Design Options and Regulatory Compliance

This section provides selected examples of key techno-regulatory design considerations. With respect to traditional forms of digital money, CBDC models provide a rich variety of design choices. This extends to deciding who can access the currency, how to distribute it, how payments are handled, and the role and management of users' (digital) identities. As such, technical, organizational, and governance-related design choices can and must be made (Fanti & Pocher, 2022). For the most part, these choices are not binary but placed on a spectrum (Michalopoulos et al., 2024). Moreover, technical design options can be used to operationalize policy and regulatory objectives. Hence, the latter can and should drive the CBDC design (Mahari et al., 2022). Ongoing CBDC projects provide insights into the rich selection of available technical options to cover the design space. In the following, we will discuss design choices for the following layers: (Sect. 12.4.1) ledger architecture, (Sect. 12.4.2) transport layer, (Sect. 12.4.3) wallets, (Sect. 12.4.4) means of transaction representation, and (Sect. 12.4.5) identity management. In parallel, we discuss the stakeholders involved in terms of data sharing and resulting privacy-transparency trade-offs.

12.4.1 Ledger Architecture

CBDC research has largely, albeit not exclusively, focused on leveraging the implementation of some type of DLT to overcome what is often framed as shortcomings of incumbent technologies used for payments (Auer & Böhme, 2020). In particular, DLT is often argued to facilitate frictionless settlement, global interoperability, high levels of security, and low latency, automated transfers while diminishing the role of intermediaries as well as the need for trust between the parties involved (Sethaput & Innet, 2023). For a critical infrastructure such as payments, the fault tolerance introduced by blockchain networks indeed seems appealing. Since many CBDC projects have been developed in partnership with private sector companies in the FinTech sphere, CBDC models often feature enterprise-grade permissioned blockchains. These systems are often considered a good fit for these institutional use cases as they allow for control of the identity of participating entities and can elevate accountability guarantees (OMFIF and CCB, 2023). However, permissioned blockchains still exhibit considerable shortcomings as compared to a centralized ledger (that could be managed by the central bank) when it comes to performance, deployment complexity, and access control (Sedlmeir, 2023).

In principle, a CBDC system could be based on a permissionless blockchain network, building on a decentralized infrastructure where only the monetary supply is governed by the central bank in the form of the token smart contract defining the CBDC's properties (Gogol et al., 2023). However, this approach arguably introduces a series of complexities and limitations that would discourage the permissionless approach in a system with at least one trusted party—i.e., the central bank—unless significant evolutions of the technology were to improve the suitability of the permissionless option for a CBDC system, e.g., from a scalability, transaction costs, or privacy perspective. As of today, most of the available projects have assumed the existence of a central authority and a permissioned system—i.e., one managed by a single trusted entity or group thereof (The White House, 2022).

12.4.2 Transport Layer and Architecture of the Model

Design choices related to the transport layer consider the possible roles taken on by intermediaries. They specify the conditions under which end users have the option of transferring money P2P and define who has access to the payment system technology at which level. Potential intermediaries that may be involved in transaction processing beyond the central bank comprise, among others, commercial banks and other third-party entities. These stakeholders may engage in "issuing currency, distributing currency, custody and wallets for currency, validating transactions, settling transactions, provisioning access (e.g., user accounts, KYC), providing user interfaces, providing customer service, conducting fraud detection, conducting AML/CFT compliance, and resolving disputes" (The White House, 2022).

In this context, some CBDC core architecture considerations are subject to variations, depending on whether the focus is on retail or wholesale projects. In addition, some specific considerations emerge in cross-border scenarios. From a first standpoint, retail CBDC models can be classified depending on the stakeholders involved—i.e., public and/or private. Furthermore, the distinction between one-tier and two-tier architectures corresponds to the transport layer (see also Sect. 12.2) (Auer & Böhme, 2021; Carstens, 2021). The implementation of a *direct* model requires central banks to maintain a relationship with the general public. Typically, however, activities such as customer onboarding fall outside the scope of their competencies and would require them to start offering a range of services that are ordinarily – and perhaps more efficiently—performed by PSPs (Gross et al., 2021). Evidently, this could generate a duplication of resources that is far from efficient. Hence, many retail CBDC proof-of-concepts and pilots focus on a *two-tier* scenario where users interact with intermediaries for certain processes—e.g., for opening and managing their accounts (Pocher & Zichichi, 2022; Pocher & Veneris, 2022a).

The role of stakeholders beyond the central bank can vary as well. For instance, in *hybrid* and *intermediated* models, the transactions are managed by the private sector—i.e., users interact with intermediaries—but the CBDC represents a direct claim on the central bank and the latter keeps the relevant ledger. On the contrary, in *synthetic* schemes, the CBDC represents a claim on financial institutions, similar to what happens with commercial bank money and e-money. As such, the system seems similar to that of a stablecoin offered by a private actor and backed by its reserve account with the central bank (Pocher & Veneris, 2022a). Another key question relates to the responsibility for compliance duties, KYC, account management, identity, and transaction checks. While in a one-tier CBDC structure the central bank would need new resources and expertise (Bossu et al., 2020), two-tier models allow compliance to be outsourced to PSPs and commercial banks, who may in turn be obliged to manage these processes directly or be allowed to further delegate these duties. Hence, two-tier structures may be favored by central banks, as they do not traditionally interact directly with public end users but rather with private financial institutions. This intermediated access model is favored to leverage existing customer-facing services and to avoid redundant compliance-related efforts. From this perspective, public-private cooperation was argued to help reduce risks and costs, as central banks do not ordinarily manage onboarding, customer service, dispute resolution, technology maintenance, transaction monitoring, and compliance processes (Sidorenko et al., 2021; Auer & Böhme, 2020). Accordingly, a practical and efficient architecture may take a hybrid form, with central banks issuing CBDCs and the private sector handling onboarding and payment-related services (Auer & Böhme, 2020).

From a second perspective, cross-border CBDC projects can be designed to feature either a single ledger or multiple interconnected ledgers. On the one hand, single-ledger systems are beneficial from an interoperability and ease of implementation standpoint. On the other hand, in architectures that interconnect existing ledgers, cross-border transactions must be recorded on both parties' ledgers—e.g., through cross-chain atomic swaps (Gogol et al., 2023). Most projects with available documentation seem to focus on interconnecting separate ledgers. The literature displays how multi-CBDC projects are particularly challenging when it comes to balancing privacy and transparency. This is not only for technical reasons, where heterogeneity makes secure computation approaches particularly challenging to implement, but also related to the interplay between various regulatory and geopolitical influences. Also in this setting, the relevant stakeholders may opt for various technical choices, obviously exerting various impacts depending on the properties of the system (Fanti & Pocher, 2022).

12.4.3 Wallet Types

All CBDC architectures can deploy different types of wallets, through which end users' devices interact with the ecosystem. As with other digital wallets, CBDC wallets represent the interface to perform financial transactions and serve the function of authenticating the user and, therefore, ensuring that transactions are only performed if they were authorized by the corresponding sender (Allen et al., 2020b). To this end, users store private keys used to sign transactions digitally, or a password to gain access to their CBDC account managed by the central bank or a third party (e.g., a PSP). From a concrete perspective, CBDC projects can opt for different solutions when it comes to wallet options (Pocher & Zichichi, 2022; Pocher & Veneris, 2022b). One common characterization distinguishes account-based wallets, for which access is tied to an identity system and authentication is performed via identity verification—e.g., a security code sent to a previously registered user—and token-based wallets, which tie tokens directly to their controlling cryptographic key pairs (Auer & Böhme, 2020; Carstens, 2021). Yet, this classification falls short in covering all potential CBDC designs (Garratt et al., 2020) and is also ambiguous: For instance, account updates can be represented as spending a token and receiving a new one (Gross et al., 2021).

Another distinction can be made regarding the level of security provided by a wallet. Hardware wallets rely on specific tamper-proof cryptographic chips (e.g., secure elements) that can protect cryptographic keys and also ensure the correct processing of bilateral payments (e.g., in an offline interaction) (Michalopoulos et al., 2024), while a software-based wallet makes use of cryptography and security protocols without dedicated hardware protection, which may be more suitable for large-scale deployment (Working Group E-CNY People's Bank of China, 2021). Furthermore, wallets are characterized as custodial when a third party operates the wallet and holds the private keys on the user's behalf, while in noncustodial wallets, end users hold the private keys directly (Barbereau & Bodó, 2023). Noncustodial wallets can offer cash-like privacy features in digital transactions (Michalopoulos et al., 2024). While token-based CBDCs can be held by custodians on behalf of end users, account-based CBDCs are intrinsically based on the relationship with a custodian (Goodell et al., 2021). Moreover, sometimes distinctions between parent wallets and sub-wallets are made. This difference relates to authorization—i.e., the holder could have a main wallet as a parent wallet and open sub-wallets to set payment limits or conditions that, in turn, ensure a certain degree of privacy, or to use other features (Working Group E-CNY People's Bank of China, 2021). A parent wallet, therefore, reminds of a bank account for the use of fiat currency, while sub-wallets resemble prepaid cards linked to the account and equipped with a limited amount of fiat.

Lastly, a necessary requirement for CBDCs is to be usable even when their end users are temporarily unable to access the Internet (Michalopoulos et al., 2024). Usually, the strategy is to develop solutions that allow storing small amounts of CBDCs units that can meet the needs of daily and common transactions (e.g., grocery shopping, petrol) even when connectivity to the network is not available. Alternatively, it is possible to issue CBDC-cards for offline payments, which can be loaded with a small number of CBDC tokens when the user's wallet is online (Allen et al., 2020b). At first glance, offline payments may be considered less problematic than remote payments, as the physical presence required for engaging in offline payments puts a potential illicit user at risk. However, because reliable proofs of proximity are hard to achieve (Ranganathan & Capkun, 2017), we should consider the possibility of masking remote payments as proximity payments, suggesting that offline payments may require similar risk mitigation measures as remote payments with cash-like privacy (Michalopoulos et al., 2024).

If one of the drivers of CBDC initiatives is the intention to mirror the user experience of cash, it is not surprising that token-based CBDCs were argued to be more conducive to goals of financial inclusion and access to central bank money than account-based ones. Yet, hybrid constructions can internally use an account-based structure and make use of a token-based envelope to anonymize transactions in a similar way as Zcash, building on unspent *accout* instead of the unspent transaction output (UTXO) model (Gross et al., 2021). Moreover, token-based systems without identity binding seem to provide a lower degree of flexibility in the tension field between privacy and transparency, as they may suffer from the easy transferability of corresponding cryptographic keys. Nonetheless, it was argued that CBDC implementation offers the perfect opportunity to mitigate some of the new risks by embedding sophisticated AML/CFT detection and anti-fraud solutions (Oliver Wyman Forum, 2022). It is also clear that if a CBDC initiative underestimates compliance during the design phase, this does not mean users and regulated entities will be allowed to operate beyond such principles. Instead, one can expect compliance burdens to be shifted to private entities offering CBDC-related services to the end users. These observations lead to preferring either a two-tiered structure or one where the CBDC itself offers strong anonymity, but regulators would still likely impose compliance on service providers converting CBDCs to other currencies. Evidently, a central bank may also undertake the costly compliance effort itself.

12.4.4 Transaction Representation

Some types of DLTs, such as Bitcoin or Cardano, make use of a type of data representation based on UTXOs—i.e., an address-based or token-based model. Another common approach to representing and changing ownership relations of digital assets uses an account-based record-keeping system, which provides more opportunities, specifically in combination with smart contracts. In UTXO-based models, there are no accounts at the protocol level. In Bitcoin, the balance of a wallet equals the outputs not yet spent. At first glance, the UTXO-based model seems more compatible with privacy mechanisms and efficient (parallel) transaction processing, while the account-based one appears more compatible with flexible smart contract functionality, transparency, and accountability. However, it turns out that the privacy guarantees provided by the UTXO model are very weak (Biryukov & Tikhomirov, 2019). On the other hand, there are many tools for providing privacy in account-based models, so simplicity may remain the only good reason for a UTXO-based approach. There are also hybrid models, and it is possible to create interoperable ledgers that run different transaction models (Fanti & Pocher, 2022). Consequently, in general, the classification into UTXO or token-based CBDC systems and account-based systems seems neither particularly clear nor particularly helpful.

From a related perspective, a CBDC model has to decide not only which of the participating nodes receive, store, and process transactions but also the way data is represented and made available to them. These options govern the way to encode transactions with respect to the data flow to various stakeholders. In particular, in most CBDC designs, transactions are directly processed by nodes. In private transactions, in many designs, either nodes store and process obfuscated (e.g., hashed) transactions, or they do neither of the two. This has significant security implications, since it requires making stronger trust assumptions on the validation process (Fanti & Pocher, 2022).

12.4.5 Identity Management

Identity management plays a crucial role in CBDCs. The identity of an organization decides its role and data access rights, while users can be held accountable through their identity bound to specific tokens or turnover limits. In public permissionless blockchains with no centralized authority, the nodes that maintain the network "operate without association to a particular given identity" (Wang & De Filippi, 2020). On the contrary, in permissioned systems, there is a centralized entity/consortium that identifies the nodes, and the relevant key pairs are typically associated with real-world identities. As mentioned before, CBDC models often feature enterprise (permissioned) blockchains. In this environment, CBDC research provides guidelines for identity management—i.e., which data to collect on end users and with which parties to share it. In particular, a report by the Oliver Wyman Forum (2022) creates a taxonomy for the various relationships between the CBDC system and the individual identities of the users. From this perspective, the relationship can be:

- *anonymous*: when the individual is not known to the central bank, distributors, or other counterparties, and it is extremely difficult to determine real-world identities on the basis of the accessible data;
- *pseudonymous*: when, although real-world identities are not recorded, a unique identifier is linked to each transaction and authorized parties can determine real-world identities for purposes such as law enforcement and investigation;
- *knowable*: when real-world identities are known to the central bank and/or to distributors and are linked to all accounts and transactions.

Accordingly, user privacy trade-offs have been found to range between complete anonymity—i.e., when a distributor assigns a system identifier that is not tied to the user's real-world identity and obscured from transactions—to fully identity-based services. The way identity is managed influences the level of individual privacy substantially. For instance, the existence of an independent—i.e., outside the central bank's perimeter—national ID system arguably allows for a centralized system that does not change a jurisdiction's privacy approach (Oliver Wyman Forum, 2022).

In this context, the privacy of the users can be assessed with reference to the central bank, if the system is centralized, or also in relation to the distributor(s). This is far from trivial: In public surveys, privacy protection usually ranks as a top priority in payments (Tronnier et al., 2022), and it is known that individuals do not only care about what data is collected but also with whom it is shared and for what purpose. The participants in the CBDC system—e.g., central bank, distributors, and PSPs—can be granted different levels of visibility into user data (Oliver Wyman Forum, 2022). In addition, multiple solutions can be adopted within the same CBDC scheme, and a regime of anonymity and pseudonymity can be provided for low-value transactions and low-balance wallets, possibly coupled with the limit to hold only one CBDC wallet, and in conjunction with an identity-compliant wallet (Gross et al., 2021), while "step-up authentication" mechanisms can allow additional risk-based checks (Pocher & Veneris, 2022b; Pocher & Zichichi, 2022; Oliver Wyman Forum, 2022). In this context, decentralized digital identities (see Chap. 4) can be very useful, as their cryptography-based design allows for the seamless use in privacy-oriented protocols (e.g., ZKPs), and their integration in regulated environments with support for high levels of assurance may be very useful to achieve the required degree of "all-or-nothing non-transferability" (Gross et al., 2021; Feulner et al., 2022).

12.5 Conclusion

CBDCs offer a rich design space that can combine different centralized and decentralized components. In this chapter, we shed light on the different design choices—including stakeholders, architectures, and technologies—a central bank may make, and argue that these design choices require close calibration with the intended regulation. We also discuss in detail the implications of these design choices on the tension between privacy and transparency. In light of the foregoing, one can identify two main points of discussion. Firstly, the role the feature of decentralization and relevant technologies can play in CBDC systems and the meaning of the concept of decentralization within institutional projects. Secondly, the way in which the twofold relationship of decentralized designs and regulatory provisions requires a careful cross-disciplinary approach to their development to ease an interplay that is often burned by miscommunication. As the new concept of CBDCs lies at the crossroads between different disciplines—most notably economics, policy, technology, law, finance, and sociology—new definitions, research methods, and designs are necessary but also difficult to come up with (Pocher & Veneris, 2022a).

How to best design a CBDC remains an open question that raises manifold technical, organizational, and governance-related questions. In addition, the chosen design affects the privacy and transparency properties of the model. The literature has identified how CBDC models display trade-offs between anonymity and transparency in CBDCs and that various designs can embed different balances between confidentiality and auditability (Pocher & Veneris, 2022b). If digital fiat money is advertised as a cash substitute, any desire for privacy should not threaten the integrity of the financial system. Undeniably, policy-makers are caught between offering CBDC users the highest degree of anonymity, making identity data hardly accessible to the public and the private sector, and establishing identity-based services. In different jurisdictions, this clash is also influenced by aspects that are not CBDC-related—e.g., the attitude toward data protection and digital identity management (Oliver Wyman Forum, 2022). Although a privacy-transparency tension is inherent to CBDCs, the relationship emerges as a trade-off (Pocher & Veneris, 2022b). To establish the desired balance, it is possible to rely on technology (e.g., cryptographic techniques) and/or on regulation that sets data governance policies (e.g., usage or access limitations). While the first option seems more resilient and tamper-proof (e.g., because of a certain degree of independence from political changes), policy measures are more flexible and can adapt to societal needs (Oliver Wyman Forum, 2022).

References

Adrian, T., & Mancini-Griffoli, T. (2019). The rise of digital money. *Annual Review of Financial Economics*, *13*, 57–77. https://doi.org/10.1146/annurev-financial-101620-063859

Agur, I., Ari, A., & Dell'Ariccia, G. (2022). Designing central bank digital currencies. *Journal of Monetary Economics*, *125*, 62–79. https://doi.org/10.1016/j.jmoneco.2021.05.002

Allen, J. G., Rauchs, M., Blandin, A., & Bear, K. (2020a). Legal and regulatory considerations for digital assets. https://www.jbs.cam.ac.uk/faculty-research/centres/alternative-finance/publications/legal-and-regulatory-considerations-for-digital-assets

Allen, S., et al. (2020b). Design choices for central bank digital currency: Policy and technical considerations. NBER Working Paper 27634. https://doi.org/10.3386/w27634

Ante, L., Fiedler, I., & Strehle, E. (2021). The influence of stablecoin issuances on cryptocurrency markets. *Finance Research Letters*, *41*, 101867. https://doi.org/10.1016/j.frl.2020.101867

Auer, R., & Böhme, R. (2020). The technology of retail central bank digital currency. *BIS Quarterly Review* (pp. 85–100). https://www.bis.org/publ/qtrpdf/r_qt2003j.pdf

Auer, R., Böhme, R., Clark, J., & Demirag, D. (2023). Mapping the privacy landscape for central bank digital currencies. *Communications of the ACM*, *66*(3), 46–53. https://doi.org/10.1145/3579316

Auer, R., & Böhme, R. (2021). Central bank digital currency: the quest for minimally invasive technology. BIS Working Papers No 948. https://www.bis.org/publ/work948.pdf

Auer, R., Cornelli, G., & Frost, J. (2020). Rise of the central bank digital currencies: Drivers, approaches and technologies. BIS Working Papers No 880. https://www.bis.org/publ/work880.htm

Bank for International Settlements. (2023). Project Tourbillon: Exploring privacy, security and scalability for CBDC. https://www.bis.org/publ/othp80.pdf

Barbereau, T., & Bodó, B. (2023). Beyond financial regulation of crypto-asset wallet software: In search of secondary liability. *Computer Law & Security Review*, *49*, 105829. https://doi.org/10.1016/j.clsr.2023.105829

Barbereau, T., Ermolaev, E., Brennecke, M., Hartwich, E., & Sedlmeir, J. (2023). Beyond a fistful of tumblers: Toward a multi-layered taxonomy of Ethereum-based crypto-asset mixers. In *Proceedings of the 44th International Conference on Information Systems*. https://aisel.aisnet.org/icis2023/cyber_security/cyber_security/13/

Beck, R., Avital, M., Rossi, M., & Thatcher, J. B. (2017). Blockchain technology in business and information systems research. *Business & Information Systems Engineering*, *59*, 381–384. https://doi.org/10.1007/s12599-017-0505-1

Ben-Sasson, E., Chiesa, A., Garman, C., Green, M., Miers, I., Tromer, E., & Virza, M. (2014). Zerocash: Decentralized anonymous payments from Bitcoin. In *Symposium on Security and Privacy* (pp. 459–474). IEEE.

Biryukov, A., & Tikhomirov, S. (2019). Deanonymization and linkability of cryptocurrency transactions based on network analysis. In *IEEE European Symposium on Security and Privacy (EuroS&P)* (pp. 172–184).

Bossu, W., Itatani, M., Margulis, C., Rossi, A., Weenink, H., & Yoshinaga, A. (2020). Legal aspects of central bank digital currency: Central bank and monetary law. International Monetary Fund. https://www.imf.org/-/media/Files/Publications/WP/2020/English/wpiea2020254-print-pdf.ashx

Butijn, B.-J., Tamburri, D. A., & van den Heuvel, W.-J. (2020). Blockchains: A systematic multivocal literature review. *ACM Computing Surveys, 53*. https://doi.org/10.1145/3369052
Carstens, A. (2021). Digital currencies and the future monetary system. In *Hoover Institution Policy Seminar* (Vol. 89). https://www.bis.org/speeches/sp210127.pdf
Casanovas, P., de Koker, L., & Hashmi, M. (2022). Law, socio-legal governance, the Internet of Things, and Industry 4.0: A middle-out/inside-out approach. *MDPI, 5*(1), 64–91. https://doi.org/10.3390/j5010005
Chaum, D. (1985). Security without identification: Transaction systems to make Big Brother obsolete. *Communications of the ACM, 28*, 1030–1044. https://doi.org/10.1145/4372.4373
Chen, H., & Siklos, P. L. (2022). Central bank digital currency: A review and some macro-financial implications. *Journal of Financial Stability, 60*, 100985. https://doi.org/10.1016/j.jfs.2022.100985
Cong, L. W., & He, Z. (2019). Blockchain disruption and smart contracts. *The Review of Financial Studies, 32*(5), 1754–1797. https://doi.org/10.1093/rfs/hhz007
Congress of the United States. (1999). Gramm-Leach-Bliley Act. https://www.govinfo.gov/app/details/PLAW-106publ102
Council of Europe. (1950). European Convention of Human Rights. https://www.echr.coe.int/documents/convention_eng.pdf
European Central Bank. (2019). Exploring anonymity in central bank digital currencies. https://www.ecb.europa.eu/paym/intro/publications/pdf/ecb.mipinfocus191217.en.pdf
European Cental Bank. (2022). Real-time gross settlement. https://www.ecb.europa.eu/paym/target/consolidation/profuse/shared/pdf/RTGS_UDFS_v3.0_clean_221014.bg.pdf
European Central Bank (2023) Stocktake on the Digital Euro. Summary report on the investigation phase and outlook on the next phase. https://www.ecb.europa.eu/euro/digital_euro/timeline/profuse/shared/pdf/ecb.dedocs231018.en.pdf
European Commission. (2015). Directive EU 2015/849 of the European Parliament and of the Council of 20 May 2015 on the prevention of the use of the financial system for the purposes of money laundering or terrorist financing, amending Regulation EU No 648/2012 of the European Parliament and of the Council, and repealing Directive 2005/60/EC of the European Parliament and of the Council and Commission Directive 2006/70/EC Text with EEA relevance. https://eur-lex.europa.eu/legal-content/EN/TXT/?uri=celex%3A32015L0849
European Commission. (2023). Digital euro package. https://finance.ec.europa.eu/publications/digital-euro-package_en
European Data Protection Board. (2023). EDPB welcomes improvements under the EU-U.S. Data Privacy Framework, but concerns remain. https://edpb.europa.eu/news/news/2023/edpb-welcomes-improvements-under-eu-us-data-privacy-framework-concerns-remain_en
European Parliament, Council and Commission. (2012). Charter of Fundamental Rights of the European Union. http://data.europa.eu/eli/treaty/char_2012/oj
Fanti, G., & Kostiainen, K. (2022). Missing key: The challenge of cybersecurity and central bank digital currency. Atlantic Council. https://www.atlanticcouncil.org/wp-content/uploads/2022/06/Missing_key.pdf
Fanti, G., & Pocher, N. (2022). Privacy in cross-border digital currency: A transatlantic perspective. In *Frankfurt Forum on European–US GeoEconomics*. https://www.atlanticcouncil.org/wp-content/uploads/2022/09/Privacy_in_cross-border_digital_currency-_A_transatlantic_approach__-.pdf
Feulner, S., Sedlmeir, J., Schlatt, V., & Urbach, N. (2022). Exploring the use of self-sovereign identity for event ticketing systems. *Electronic Markets, 32*, 1759–1777. https://doi.org/10.1007/s12525-022-00573-9
Financial Action Task Force. (2012). The FATF recommendations. Last amended November 2023. https://www.fatf-gafi.org/en/publications/Fatfrecommendations/Fatf-recommendations.html
Financial Action Task Force. (2017). Private sector information sharing. https://www.fatf-gafi.org/en/publications/Fatfgeneral/Guidance-information-sharing.html
Financial Stability Board. (2021). Targets for addressing the four challenges of cross-border payments. https://www.fsb.org/wp-content/uploads/P131021-2.pdf

Garratt, R. J., Lee, M. J., Malone, B., & Martin, A. (2020). Token-or account-based? A digital currency can be both. https://ideas.repec.org/p/fip/fednls/88550.html

Garratt, R. J. & van Oordt, M. R. C. (2021). Privacy as a public good: A case for electronic cash. *Journal of Political Economy*, *129*(7), 2157–2180. https://doi.org/10.1086/714133

Gogol, K., Messias, J., Schlosser, M., Kraner, B., & Tessone, C. (2023). Cross-border exchange of CBDCs using layer-2 blockchain. https://arxiv.org/abs/2312.16193

Goodell, G., Al-Nakib, H. D., & Tasca, P. (2021). A digital currency architecture for privacy and owner-custodianship. *Future Internet*, *13*. https://doi.org/10.3390/fi13050130

Gramlich, V., Guggenberger, T., Principato, M., Schellinger, B., & Urbach, N. (2023). A multivocal literature review of decentralized finance: Current knowledge and future research avenues. *Electronic Markets*, *33*. https://doi.org/10.1007/s12525-023-00637-4

Grassi, L., & Lanfranchi, D. (2022). Regtech in public and private sectors: the nexus between data, technology and regulation. *Journal of Industrial and Business Economics* (pp. 449–471). https://doi.org/10.1007/s40812-022-00226-0

Gross, J., Sedlmeir, J., Babel, M., Babel, M., Bechtel, A., Schellinger, B., & Schellinger, B. (2021). Designing a central bank digital currency with support for cash-like privacy. https://papers.ssrn.com/sol3/papers.cfm?abstract_id=3891121

Hanus, J. J., & Relyea, H. C. (1975). A policy assessment of the Privacy Act of 1974. *American University Law Review*, *25*, 555. https://heinonline.org/HOL/LandingPage?handle=hein.journals/aulr25&div=32&id=&page=

Hoess, A., Pocher, N., Tamara, R.H., & Fridgen, G. (2024). Towards a design science research process for legal compliance by design. PACIS 2024 Proceedings. https://aisel.aisnet.org/pacis2024/track04_dessci/track04_dessci/3

ITU-T Focus Group on Digital Currency. (2019). Terms of reference of Focus Group Digital Currency including digital fiat currency. https://www.itu.int/en/ITU-T/focusgroups/dfc/Documents/TOR-FG-DFC.pdf

Jagati, S. (2020). CBDCs with a twist: The public-private solutions needed for adoption. Cointelegraph. https://cointelegraph.com/news/cbdcs-with-a-twist-the-public-private-solutions-needed-for-adoption

Kosse, A., & Mattei, I. (2022). Gaining momentum – results of the 2021 BIS survey on central bank digital currencies. http://www.bis.org/publ/bppdf/bispap125.htm

Mahari, R., Hardjono, T., & Pentland, A. (2022). Aml by design: Designing a central bank digital currency to stifle money laundering. *MIT Science Policy Review*. https://doi.org/10.38105/spr.j0hildxtyi

Michalopoulos, P., Olowookere, O., Pocher, N., Sedlmeir, J., Veneris, A., & Puri, P. (2024). Compliance design options for offline CBDCs: Balancing privacy and AML/CFT. In *Proceedings on the 6th International Conference on Blockchain and Cryptocurrency*. http://www.doi.org/10.1109/ICBC59979.2024.10634398.

Nadler, M., & Schär, F. (2023). Tornado Cash and blockchain privacy: A primer for economists and policymakers. *Federal Reserve Bank of St. Louis Review*, *105*(2), 122–136. https://doi.org/10.20955/r.105.122-36

Nakamoto, S. (2008). Bitcoin: A peer-to-peer electronic cash system. https://bitcoin.org/bitcoin.pdf

Oliver Wyman Forum. (2022). Retail central bank digital currency: From vision to design. https://www.oliverwymanforum.com/content/dam/oliver-wyman/ow-forum/future-of-money/Retail-Central-Bank-Digital-Currency-From-Vision-to-Design.pdf

OMFIF & CCB. (2023). The role of blockchain in banking. Future prospects for cross-border payments. https://www.omfif.org/blockchainbanking/

Papantoniou, A. (2022). Regtech: steering the regulatory spaceship in the right direction? *Journal of Banking and Financial Technology*, *6*(16). https://doi.org/10.1007/s42786-022-00038-9

Pocher, N. (2023). *Distributed Ledger Technologies between Anonymity and Transparency: AML/CFT Regulation of Cryptocurrency Ecosystems in the EU*. PhD thesis, Alma Mater Studiorum Università di Bologna, Universitat Autònoma de Barcelona, KU Leuven. https://lirias.kuleuven.be/retrieve/706912

Pocher, N., & Veneris, A. (2022a). Central bank digital currencies. In *Handbook on Blockchain* (pp. 463–501). Springer. https://doi.org/10.1007/978-3-031-07535-3_15
Pocher, N., & Veneris, A. (2022b). Privacy and transparency in CBDCs: A regulation-by-design AML/CFT scheme. *IEEE Transactions on Network and Service Management, 19*(2), 1776–1788. https://doi.org/10.1109/TNSM.2021.3136984
Pocher, N., & Zichichi, M. (2022). Towards CBDC-based machine-to-machine payments in consumer IoT. In *Proceedings of the 37th ACM/SIGAPP Symposium on Applied Computing* (pp. 308–315). https://doi.org/10.1145/3477314.3507078
Poenisch, H. (2014). Introducing digital currencies to the global interbank settlement system. *International Monetary Review 1917*. http://www.imi.ruc.edu.cn/EN/uploads/2019/12/IMI-Working-Paper-No.-1917-EN.pdf
Ranganathan, A., & Capkun, S. (2017). Are we really close? Verifying proximity in wireless systems. *IEEE Security & Privacy, 15*(3), 52–58. https://doi.org/10.1109/MSP.2017.56
Rennie, E., & Steele, S. (2021). Privacy and emergency payments in a pandemic: How to think about privacy and a central bank digital currency. *Law, Technology and Humans, 3*, 6–17. https://doi.org/10.5204/lthj.1745
Rice, T., von Peter, G., & Boar, C. (2020). On the global retreat of correspondent banks. *BIS Quarterly Review*. https://papers.ssrn.com/sol3/papers.cfm?abstract_id=3561184
Robinson, G., Dörry, S., & Derudder, B. (2023). Global networks of money and information at the crossroads: Correspondent banking and SWIFT. *Global Networks, 23*(2), 478–493. https://doi.org/10.1111/glob.12408
Schlatt, V., Sedlmeir, J., Feulner, S., & Urbach, N. (2022a). Designing a framework for digital KYC processes built on blockchain-based self-sovereign identity. *Information & Management, 59*. https://doi.org/10.1016/j.im.2021.103553
Schlatt, V., Sedlmeir, J., Traue, J., & Völter, F. (2022b). Harmonizing sensitive data exchange and double-spending prevention through blockchain and digital wallets: The case of e-prescription management. *Distributed Ledger Technologies: Research and Practice, 2*. https://doi.org/10.1145/3571509
Sedlmeir, J. (2023). *Blockchain Adoption in Organizations: Technical Barriers and Potential Solutions*. PhD thesis, University of Bayreuth. https://doi.org/10.15495/EPub_UBT_00007183
Sedlmeir, J., Lautenschlager, J., Fridgen, G., & Urbach, N. (2022). The transparency challenge of blockchain in organizations. *Electronic Markets, 32*, 1779–1794. https://doi.org/10.1007/s12525-022-00536-0
Sethaput, V., & Innet, S. (2023). Blockchain application for central bank digital currencies (CBDC). *Cluster Computing, 26*(4), 2183–2197. https://doi.org/10.1007/s10586-022-03962-z
Sidorenko, E. L., Sheveleva, S. V., & Lykov, A. A. (2021). Legal and economic implications of central bank digital currencies (CBDC). In *Innovative Economic Symposium* (pp. 496–502). Springer. https://doi.org/10.1007/978-3-030-60929-0_63
Sunyaev, A., et al. (2021). Token economy. *Business & Information Systems Engineering, 63*, 457–478. https://doi.org/10.1007/s12599-021-00684-1
Tapscott, A., & Tapscott, D. (2017). How blockchain is changing finance. *Harvard Business Review, 1*(9), 2–5. https://doi.org/https://capital.report/Resources/Whitepapers/40fc8a6a-cdbd-47e6-83f6-74e2a9d36ccc_finance_topic2_source2.pdf
The White House. (2022). Technical design choices for a U.S. central bank digital currency system. https://www.whitehouse.gov/wp-content/uploads/2022/09/09-2022-Technical-Design-Choices-US-CBDC-System.pdf
Themistocleous, M., Rupino da Cunha, P., Tabakis, E., & Papadaki, M. (2023). Towards cross-border CBDC interoperability: Insights from a multivocal literature review. *Journal of Enterprise Information Management, 36*(5), 1296–1318. https://doi.org/10.1108/JEIM-11-2022-0411
Tronnier, F., Harborth, D., & Hamm, P. (2022). Investigating privacy concerns and trust in the digital Euro in Germany. *Electronic Commerce Research and Applications, 53*, 101158. https://doi.org/10.1016/j.elerap.2022.101158

UN General Assembly. (1948). Universal Declaration of Human Rights. https://www.refworld.org/legal/resolution/unga/1948/en/11563

Wang, F., & De Filippi, P. (2020). Self-sovereign identity in a globalized world: Credentials-based identity systems as a driver for economic inclusion. *Frontiers in Blockchain, 2*. https://doi.org/10.3389/fbloc.2019.00028

Wilkins, C. (2014). Speech: Money in a digital world. https://www.bankofcanada.ca/2014/11/money-digital-world/

Working Group E-CNY People's Bank of China. (2021). Progress of research & development of e-CNY in China. http://www.pbc.gov.cn/en/3688110/3688172/4157443/4293696/2021071614584691871.pdf

Wüst, K., Kostiainen, K., Delius, N., & Capkun, S. (2022). Platypus: A central bank digital currency with unlinkable transactions and privacy-preserving regulation. In *Proceedings of the 29th ACM SIGSAC Conference on Computer and Communications Security* (pp. 2947–2960).

Zamora-Pérez, A. (2022). Guaranteeing freedom of payment choice: Access to cash in the Euro area. https://www.ecb.europa.eu/pub/economic-bulletin/articles/2022/html/ecb.ebart202205_02~74b1fc0841.en.html#toc

Zetzsche, D. A., Arner, D. W., & Buckley, R. P. (2020). Decentralized finance. *Journal of Financial Regulation, 6*, 172–203. https://doi.org/10.1093/jfr/fjaa010

Part IV
Discussion and Outlook

Chapter 13
Reflections on Decentralization in Decentralized Financial Applications

Martin Brennecke, Eduard Hartwich, Emanuela Podda, and Alexander Rieger

Abstract Interest in decentralized financial applications continues to grow. But as adoption accelerates, so do concerns about (re-)centralization driven by regulatory and economic considerations. In this chapter, we take a closer look at these concerns. In particular, we analyze how regulatory requirements can lead to more centralized responsibilities and how economic considerations on different levels of the decentralized finance (DeFi) technology stack can limit the degree of technical decentralization.

13.1 Introduction

Interest in decentralized finance (DeFi) applications has grown in recent years, and they increasingly make their way into the financial services industry (Hartwich et al., 2024). Financial technology providers and traditional finance (TradFi) institutions now offer DeFi applications that range from capital and asset management, over banking and insurance, to international trade (Gramlich et al., 2023). Due to regulatory pressures, these "institutional" applications are often more centralized than their decentralized counterparts, such as Bitcoin and other cryptocurrencies.

M. Brennecke (✉) · E. Hartwich
Interdisciplinary Centre for Security, Reliability and Trust (SnT), University of Luxembourg, Luxembourg, Luxembourg
e-mail: martin.brennecke@uni.lu; eduard.hartwich@uni.lu

E. Podda
Department of Computer Science, SPDP Lab, Università degli Studi di Milano, Milan, Italy

Interdisciplinary Centre for Security, Reliability and Trust (SnT), University of Luxembourg, Luxembourg, Luxembourg
e-mail: emanuela.podda@unimi.it

A. Rieger
Sam M. Walton College of Business, University of Arkansas, Fayetteville, AR, USA
e-mail: arieger@uark.edu

G. Fridgen et al. (eds.), *Decentralization Technologies*, Financial Innovation and Technology, https://doi.org/10.1007/978-3-031-66047-4_13

Decentralization is also under attack by economic centralization pressures on different levels of the DeFi technology stack.

In this chapter, we explore the underlying dynamics of these centralization pressures. We begin with a brief review of the history of DeFi applications and then explore how different legal requirements arising from anti-money laundering (AML) and combating the financing of terrorism (CFT) regulation as well as the General Data Protection Regulation (GDPR) can lead to more centralized offers by financial technology providers and TradFi institutions in the European Union (EU) and beyond. In the second part of this chapter, we then explore how economic considerations on different levels of the technology stack (incl. hardware and software) lead to more technical centralization of DeFi applications.

13.2 A Short History of DeFi Applications

The idea for DeFi applications was born with the introduction of Bitcoin, which kickstarted innovations that resulted, among others, in the development of the Ethereum blockchain (Arnold et al., 2019; Hartwich et al., 2023). Ethereum revolutionized the field with the introduction of Turing-complete smart contracts. These contracts paved the way for the creation of advanced digital, cryptographically secured financial assets that could be used in various financial services, such as payment and insurance (see also Chaps. 3 and 8).

However, these digital assets were mainly accessible to tech-savvy users. To open the market, i.e., the "DeFi World," to a broader audience, centralized exchanges (CEXs) emerged. CEXs converged control over DeFi on- and off-ramps to a concentrated number of stakeholders (Jeng, 2024). To counteract these centralization tendencies and reignite the original spirit of decentralization, various individuals and start-ups developed DeFi services and decentralized autonomous organization (DAO)-based applications that extend beyond CEXs (Gramlich et al., 2023; Brennecke et al., 2022).

Inspired by the initial success of CEXs and DeFi services, financial technology providers and TradFi institutions started to also move into the crypto space (Rapoza, 2023). For example, PayPal supports the transfer of cryptocurrencies between PayPal accounts and other wallets or CEXs (PayPal, 2024a). It also enables its customers in the United States to use cryptocurrencies to pay for online purchases (PayPal, 2024b). Other financial service providers, in turn, enable their customers to trade cryptocurrencies on their trading platforms either via their cryptocurrency exchange (Baden-Württembergische Wertpapierbörse, 2024), via exchange-traded products (BlackRock, 2024), or derivatives (Börse Stuttgart, 2024). Furthermore, credit institutions such as MasterCard and VISA have started offering DeFi services such as payments via multi-token networks, credential issuance, and stablecoin settlement (Mastercard, 2024; Visa, 2024). These "institutional" DeFi applications often promise better accessibility, security, and user support. However, their "convenience" gains usually come with consolidated control and a clear allocation of roles and responsibilities.

13.3 Regulatory Tendencies Toward Centralization

From a regulatory perspective, DeFi services span across traditional geographical boundaries of national jurisdictions (Zetzsche et al., 2020). This cross-jurisdictional nature can make it difficult to reconcile DeFi with various legal requirements (Salami, 2021). In this section, we take a closer look at some of these requirements as well as how they can push DeFi applications toward more centralization. We focus our analysis on the EU's AML/CFT rules affecting financial technology providers and TradFi institutions (especially Directive EU 2018/843, 2018 and Directive EU 2019/1153 (2019)), as well as the GDPR (Regulation EU 2016/679, 2016) rules.

These two bodies of legislation pursue different objectives. With a margin of national appreciation, the EU's AML/CFT rules are designed to improve client identification, access to financial and bank account information, and better information exchange with investigators and law enforcement authorities. In fact, Directive EU 2018/843 and Directive EU 2019/1153 (2019) tend toward the identifiability of transacting customers. The GDPR, in turn, is designed to protect the data privacy rights of clients, tending toward de-identification and de-identifiability.

More specifically, the AML/CFT rules aim to minimize the risks of money laundering, terrorism financing, and other illicit activities (Barbereau et al., 2023). Under these rules, customers are required to submit identification documents to open bank accounts prior to engaging in investment activities. Moreover, the EU's AML/CFT rules – together with Directive EU 2019/1153 (2019) – demand that TradFi institutions monitor client activities to identify money laundering and terrorism financing risks. They may also be obliged to grant national financial intelligence units (FIUs) access to client data in cases of suspected money laundering or financing of terrorism risks (Brewczyńska, 2021). These rules naturally imply that "institutional" DeFi applications may not offer full privacy and "end-to-end (E2E) encryption" of transactions. In particular, these rules are difficult to observe with DeFi applications that only require users to have a non-custodial crypto wallet without proper user verification and exact correlation with real-world identities, even if new machine-learning approaches are increasingly able to address these limitations (Pocher et al., 2023).

At first glance, the objectives of the GDPR may be easier to reconcile with DeFi applications than those of the EU's AML/CFT rules. The GDPR establishes a comprehensive and general set of obligations for data controllers and data processors that are aimed at reducing reidentification risks. But at a second glance, many of these obligations can be very difficult to observe for DeFi applications as the GDPR had been conceived for the centralized collection, processing, and storage of personal data (Finck, 2019). Examples include but are not limited to lawfulness of data processing, purpose limitation and data minimization, transparency of processing, data confidentiality, and accountability (Regulation EU 2016/679, 2016).

These challenges become particularly apparent when it comes to DeFi applications provided by DAOs. These organizations typically distribute responsibilities between a large set of pseudonymous data controllers. In theory, DAOs could be conceived as data controllers (viz., joint controllers), who determine the purpose and means of processing personal data as well as being the addressees of the data subjects' claims. DAOs could also establish the responsibilities of the network participants, relying on legal agreements and other legal instruments. In practice, however, it is uncertain how such constructs would be perceived by regulators and law enforcement.

The result is that participating in DAOs or using their DeFi applications comes with substantial legal risks. If decisive roles and responsibilities cannot be identified, the result is everyone's joint responsibility. Also, the higher the degree of decentralization, the more challenging it is to hold others accountable for errors and failures from the operation of the protocol, for any intent or gross negligence in ensuring *prosumers'* protection, and from a cybersecurity perspective (Kirimhan, 2023).

In effect, DeFi applications will often be difficult to reconcile with the applicable regulatory frameworks. While these challenges can be addressed, the cheapest option will often result in a higher degree of centralization, as users are often driven by economic considerations.

13.4 Economic Tendencies Toward Centralization

Such economic considerations can be found on various levels of the DeFi technology stack. To unpack these mechanisms, we take a closer look at the software and hardware used in providing and accessing DeFi applications. While software-related centralization often results from user preferences, hardware-related technical centralization is often driven by infrastructure providers. Both types of centralization limit the degree of technical decentralization and make it easier for attackers to exploit vulnerabilities. While some vulnerabilities may only affect individual users, large shares of vulnerable hardware or software may create risks for the entire network.

Software-related centralization tendencies include but are not limited to the clients and wallets used to access blockchain networks (Sai et al., 2021). In the DeFi context, clients refer to "implementation[s] of a decentralized ledger technology that verifies data against the protocol rules and keeps the network secure" (Ethereum.org, 2024d, p. 1). Using Ethereum as an example, one may distinguish between execution and consensus clients. An execution clients "listens to new transactions broadcasted to the network, executes them [the Ethereum Virtual Machine], and holds the latest state and database of all current Ethereum data" (Ethereum.org, 2024d, p. 1). A consensus client, in turn, "implements the proof-of-stake consensus algorithm" (Ethereum.org, 2024d, p. 1).

As of March 2024, the Ethereum network can be accessed with a variety of execution clients, including Geth, Nethermind, and Besu (Ethereum.org, 2024d). However, Geth holds a supermajority share of 70% over potential alternatives, while Nethermind and Besu hold 18% and 9% shares, respectively (Clientdiversity.org, 2024). While client diversity is considered to be a value proposition for many actors participating in DeFi ecosystems, higher levels of execution client diversity are difficult to achieve, as they would create additional costs for users and developers.

Given the Ethereum community's awareness that client centralization could turn into a systemic risk, it placed particular importance on client diversity when it transitioned to the proof of stake (PoS) consensus mechanism (Ethereum.org, 2024a, 2024b) (see also Chaps. 14). As a result, users can now use various different options, including but not limited to Prysm, Lighthouse, Teku, and Nimbus (Ethereum.org, 2024d). As of March 2024, Prysm and Lighthouse hold shares of around 29–41% and 33–44%, respectively, while Teku and Nimbus hold a share of around 16–19% and 5–9%, respectively (Clientdiversity.org, 2024).

Another element prone to centralization is digital wallets (Ethereum.org, 2024c). Recently, non-custodial wallets that can only be accessed by their owner – rather than a regulated entity that would have to comply with applicable regulatory requirements – gained popularity, with MetaMask taking a significant share of the overall market (ConsenSys Software, 2023). As with execution client centralization, it can be difficult to roll back this wallet centralization and encourage developers and users to diversify. Overall, there are few incentives for participating stakeholders to redevelop specific solutions already implemented in available clients and wallets.

Similar centralization tendencies exist on the hardware level (Sai et al., 2021), ranging from application-specific integrated circuits (ASICs) for proof of work (PoW) mining to cloud service providers (CSPs) and staking pools in PoS staking. ASICs are specialized chips that significantly outperform other PoW mining hardware. They thus came to dominate the mining operations in PoW blockchains, leading to centralization on the producer and user side. ASICs production is highly centralized, as their manufacturing requires specialized knowledge and machinery. Given the resulting supply restrictions and their limited use outside of cryptocurrency mining, ASICs are often owned by a professional minority of miners with the necessary financial resources (Barbereau et al., 2022; Yazıcı et al., 2023). Recent models of Bitcoin mining thus indicate that it is likely that an equilibrium characterized by a "highly concentrated ownership of mining equipment" (Arnosti & Weinberg, 2022, p. 1) will emerge.

In the context of PoS-based blockchains, most clients and wallets are hosted by CSPs, and large shares of staking activities are conducted by or as part of staking pools. Data provided by Grafana (2024), for instance, indicates that as of March 2024, around 3000 out of 11,700 active Ethereum nodes are associated with internet protocol routing prefixes issued by just 4 network operators. Centralized hosting is often a direct result of CSPs promising lower hosting costs, potentially higher availability, and better security measures. Centralization tendencies in staking, in turn, result from the economic decisions of users aiming to share the risks involved in earning rewards from the verification and validation of transactions in the network. By relying on staking pools, all participating parties share the rewards if one party is rewarded for their staking activities. Shortly before the Merge in 2022, Lido, Coinbase, and Kraken held a cumulative 50% share of staked Ether (Jha, 2022). This tendency continued to persist, even after the Ethereum Merge, when Coinbase and Lido added up to 40% of blocks in Ethereum (Luo, 2022).

Such relative centralization may, directly and indirectly, impact the system's vulnerability to specific attacks (Schlatt et al., 2023). Regarding the direct impact, high degrees of centralization are risky, as they enable a relatively small number of network participants with weighty vote or node operation shares to potentially exert undue influence on the operation or governance of the overall system. Beyond the direct impact, loci of centralization may also be a target for attacks themselves, thereby creating risks to the overall system. Abellán Álvarez et al. (2024) provide a summary of thresholds for specific attacks on both PoW- and PoS-based blockchains.

In summary, there are strong economic tendencies toward centralization on various levels of the DeFi technology stack. Many of these tendencies are driven by users and organizations that naturally tend to choose clients and wallets that are easy to use and offer reasonable security guarantees. However, while their ease of use reduces the cost or effort associated with familiarizing oneself with a client or wallet, improved security could reduce subsequent costs due to data leakage or malicious attacks. The same holds for hardware-related centralization, where users and organizations choose the data storage and mining hardware offering the best return on investment.

13.5 Conclusion

As DeFi applications grow in popularity, maintaining their decentralization becomes more difficult. Financial technology providers and TradFi institutions need to comply with various regulations that often introduce centralization pressures. Moreover, economic considerations increasingly lead to centralization in the DeFi technology stack.

In this chapter, we provide a closer look at these centralization pressures for both regulatory and economic reasons. Our analysis is particularly useful for management and organization researchers and those analyzing the regulatory environment and economic pressures surrounding DeFi applications. For decision-makers in the public sector, we highlight the effects of recent measures taken by regulators in the EU. For decision-makers in the private sector, we offer valuable insights into the history of DeFi applications, as well as current opportunities and limitations related to decentralization in financial applications.

References

Abellán Álvarez, I., Gramlich, V., & Sedlmeir, J. (2024). Unsealing the secrets of blockchain consensus: A systematic comparison of the formal security of proof-of-work and proof-of-stake. In *Proceedings of the 39th Symposium on Applied Computing*. ACM. https://doi.org/10.1145/3605098.3635970

Arnold, L., et al. (2019). Blockchain and initial coin offerings: Blockchain's implications for crowdfunding. In *Business Transformation through Blockchain* (pp. 233–272). Springer. https://doi.org/10.1007/978-3-319-98911-2_8

Arnosti, N., & Weinberg, S. M. (2022). Bitcoin: A natural oligopoly. *Management Science*, *68*(7), 4755–4771. https://doi.org/10.1287/mnsc.2021.4095

Baden-Württembergische Wertpapierbörse. (2024). Trade on the official crypto exchange of Börse. Stuttgart. https://www.bsdex.de/en/

Barbereau, T., Ermolaev, E., Brennecke, M., Hartwich, E., & Sedlmeir, J. (2023). A fistful of Ethereum-based mixers: Towards a multi-layered taxonomy. In *Proceedings of the 44th International Conference on Information Systems*. AIS. https://aisel.aisnet.org/icis2023/cyber_security/cyber_security/13/

Barbereau, T., Smethurst, R., Papageorgiou, O., Rieger, A., & Fridgen, G. (2022). DeFi, not so decentralized: The measured distribution of voting rights. In *Proceedings of the 55th Hawaii International Conference on System Sciences* (pp. 6043–6052). http://hdl.handle.net/10125/80074

BlackRock. (2024). iShares Bitcoin Trust (IBIT). https://www.blackrock.com/us/financial-professionals/investment-strategies/bitcoin-investing#About-IBIT

Brennecke, M., Guggenberger, T., Schellinger, B., & Urbach, N. (2022). The de-central bank in decentralized finance: A case study of MakerDAO. In *Proceedings of the 55th Hawaii International Conference on System Sciences* (pp. 6073–6082). AIS. http://hdl.handle.net/10125/80077

Brewczyńska, M. (2021). Financial intelligence units: Reflections on the applicable data protection legal framework. *Computer Law & Security Review*, *43*(105612). https://doi.org/10.1016/j.clsr.2021.105612

Börse Stuttgart. (2024). Wie Sie Bitcoin und andere Kryptowährungen bei uns handeln können. https://www.boerse-stuttgart.de/de-de/handel/kryptowaehrungen-handeln/

Clientdiversity.org. (2024). Ethereum client distribution. https://clientdiversity.org

ConsenSys Software. (2023). MetaMask surpasses 10 million MAUs. https://consensys.net/blog/press-release/metamask-surpasses-10-million-maus-making-it-the-worlds-leading-non-custodial-crypto-wallet/

Directive EU 2018/843. (2018). Directive EU 2018/843 of the European Parliament and of the Council of 30 May 2018 amending Directive EU 2015/849 on the prevention of the use of the financial system for the purposes of money laundering or terrorist financing, and amending Directives 2009/138/EC and 2013/36/EU. https://eur-lex.europa.eu/eli/dir/2018/843/oj

Directive EU 2019/1153. (2019). Directive (EU) 2019/1153 of the European Parliament and of the Council of 20 June 2019 laying down rules facilitating the use of financial and other information for the prevention, detection, investigation or prosecution of certain criminal offences, and repealing Council Decision 2000/642/JHA. http://data.europa.eu/eli/dir/2019/1153/oj

Ethereum.org. (2024a). The Beacon chain. https://ethereum.org/en/roadmap/beacon-chain/

Ethereum.org. (2024b). Client diversity. https://ethereum.org/en/developers/docs/nodes-and-clients/client-diversity/

Ethereum.org. (2024c). Ethereum wallets. https://ethereum.org/en/wallets/

Ethereum.org. (2024d). Nodes and clients. https://ethereum.org/en/developers/docs/nodes-and-clients/

Finck, M. (2019). Blockchain and the general data protection regulation: Can distributed ledgers be squared with European data protection law? Publications Office of the European Union. https://doi.org/10.2861/535

Grafana. (2024). Ulisse – Ethereum network topology explorer. https://chainbound.grafana.net/public-dashboards/b39ed764b36548a2a74024eab3de2fe3

Gramlich, V., Guggenberger, T., Principato, M., Schellinger, B., & Urbach, N. (2023). A multivocal literature review of decentralized finance: Current knowledge and future research avenues. *Electronic Markets, 33*(1). https://doi.org/10.1007/s12525-023-00637-4

Hartwich, E., Ollig, P., Fridgen, G., & Rieger, A. (2023). Probably something: A multi-layer taxonomy of non-fungible tokens. *Internet Research, 34*(1), 216–238. https://doi.org/10.1108/INTR-08-2022-0666

Hartwich, E., Roth, T. H., Rieger, A., Zavolokina, L., & Fridgen, G. (2024). Negotiation and translation between discursive fields: A study on the diffusion of decentralized finance. In *Proceedings of the European Conference of Information Systems*. AIS. https://aisel.aisnet.org/ecis2024/track20_adoption/track20_adoption/4

Jeng, L. (2024). The 're-centralization' trap: Global regulation in 2024. https://www.forbes.com/sites/lindajeng/2024/01/10/blockchain-regulation-in-2024-the-re-centralization-trap/

Jha, P. (2022). Ethereum at the center of centralization debate as SEC lays claim. https://cointelegraph.com/news/ethereum-at-the-center-of-centralization-debate-as-sec-lays-claim

Kirimhan, D. (2023). Importance of anti-money laundering regulations among prosumers for a cybersecure decentralized finance. *Journal of Business Research, 157*, 113558. https://doi.org/10.1016/j.jbusres.2022.113558

Luo, X. (2022). Ethereum already showing signs of increased centralization. https://finance.yahoo.com/news/eth-may-already-showcasing-increased-203531239.html

Mastercard. (2024). Scaling and securing the crypto ecosystem together. https://www.mastercard.com/global/en/business/issuers/crypto.html

PayPal. (2024a). How do I transfer my crypto? https://www.paypal.com/us/cshelp/article/how-do-i-transfer-my-crypto-help822

PayPal. (2024b). How to use crypto at checkout? https://www.paypal.com/us/cshelp/article/how-to-use-crypto-at-checkout-help571

Pocher, N., Zichichi, M., Merizzi, F., Shafiq, M. Z., & Ferretti, S. (2023). Detecting anomalous cryptocurrency transactions: An AML/CFT application of machine learning-based forensics. *Electronic Markets, 33*. https://doi.org/10.1007/s12525-023-00654-3

Rapoza, K. (2023). Traditional banking is poised to take bigger stake in crypto space. Forbes. https://www.forbes.com/sites/digital-assets/2023/10/26/traditional-banking-is-poised-to-take-bigger-stake-in-crypto-space/

Regulation EU 2016/679. (2016). Regulation EU 2016/679 of the European Parliament and of the Council of 27 April 2016 on the protection of natural persons with regard to the processing of personal data and on the free movement of such data, and repealing Directive 95/46/EC. http://data.europa.eu/eli/reg/2016/679/oj

Sai, A. R., Buckley, J., Fitzgerald, B., & Gear, A. L. (2021). Taxonomy of centralization in public blockchain systems: A systematic literature review. *Information Processing & Management, 58*(4). https://doi.org/10.1016/j.ipm.2021.102584

Salami, I. (2021). Challenges and approaches to regulating decentralized finance. *American Journal of International Law Unbound, 115*, 425–429. https://doi.org/10.1017/aju.2021.66

Schlatt, V., Guggenberger, T., Schmid, J., & Urbach, N. (2023). Attacking the trust machine: Developing an information systems research agenda for blockchain cybersecurity. *International Journal of Information Management, 68*(102470). https://doi.org/10.1016/j.ijinfomgt.2022.102470

Visa. (2024). Unlocking crypto opportunities. https://usa.visa.com/solutions/crypto.html

Yazıcı, A. F., Olcay, A. B., & Arkalı Olcay, G. (2023). A framework for maintaining sustainable energy use in Bitcoin mining through switching efficient mining hardware. *Technological Forecasting and Social Change, 190*(122406). https://doi.org/10.1016/j.techfore.2023.122406

Zetzsche, D. A., Arner, D. W., & Buckley, R. P. (2020). Decentralized finance. *Journal of Financial Regulation, 6*(2), 172–203. https://doi.org/10.1093/jfr/fjaa010

Chapter 14
On the Energy Consumption of a Decentralized Financial Sector

Matthias Babel, Vincent Gramlich, Felix Paetzold, and Till Zwede

Abstract The financial sector has seen a trend toward more decentralization, especially led by the introduction and prevalence of blockchain. However, decentralization technologies may increase energy consumption through the use of potentially less optimized hardware, replication, and consensus-related operations, as well as further cryptographic overhead when involving privacy enhancing technologies (PETs). Blockchain technology is usually at the center of criticism related to electricity consumption, manifesting in sensationalized headlines such as "Bitcoin [or blockchain] uses more electricity than country X." In this chapter, we focus on important distinctions that need to be made when analyzing the electricity consumption of a blockchain. We show that while for proof of work (PoW) blockchains, electricity consumption is an inherent feature and may justify such headlines; the energy intensity of blockchains with other consensus mechanisms is multiple orders of magnitude lower. We also argue that for these blockchains non-PoW blockchains and decentralized systems in general, a trade-off between the security achieved through decentralization and energy consumption exists, as the additional electricity consumption compared to centralized systems can mainly be attributed to redundant computations introduced by decentralization. Lastly, we discuss different approaches to managing the tension between decentralization and electricity consumption.

M. Babel · F. Paetzold · T. Zwede
University of Bayreuth, Bayreuth, Germany

Fraunhofer FIT – Branch Business Information Systems Engineering, Bayreuth, Germany
e-mail: matthias.babel@fit.fraunhofer.de; felix.paetzold@fim-rc.de; till.zwede@fim-rc.de

V. Gramlich (✉)
Frankfurt University of Applied Sciences, Frankfurt am Main, Germany

Fraunhofer FIT – Branch Business Information Systems Engineering, Bayreuth, Germany
e-mail: vincent.gramlich@fim-rc.de

G. Fridgen et al. (eds.), *Decentralization Technologies*, Financial Innovation and Technology, https://doi.org/10.1007/978-3-031-66047-4_14

14.1 Introduction

The digitalization of our world entails a growing use of information systems like cloud computing, artificial intelligence, and the Internet of Things. Besides the numerous advantages, such as the high availability, automatability, verifiability, and new possibilities that are opened up by these digital and technological advances, there are also growing concerns about the implications and costs of their extensive and rapidly increasing usage. The large energy consumption of information technology, where data centers alone consume over 1% of global final energy, has raised concerns, especially as the energy sector plays a key role in the climate crisis (Masanet et al., 2020). A digital technology that is particularly often at the center of the discussion around electricity consumption is Bitcoin or blockchain technology in general. Controversial scientific publications even claim that Bitcoin alone may be responsible for breaking the 1.5° target set by the Paris Agreement in 2015 (Mora et al., 2018). While this may arguably be a grave overstatement, the notion that this type of blockchain technology can be accountable for significant shares of global energy consumption is valid.

Meanwhile, the financial sector has been undergoing a major transformation induced by digitalization, shifting to fully digital payment and settlement infrastructures. As part of this trend, the financial industry is now looking toward decentralized financial systems. This trend was initially triggered by the emergence of blockchain technology and further amplified by the advent of decentralized finance (DeFi), a decentralized financial system based on public blockchains and smart contracts (Gramlich et al., 2022, 2023). Recently, this development has seen another push through the convergence of traditional centralized finance (CeFi) and emerging DeFi, which is leading the global financial sector to adopt decentralized technologies and mechanisms, e.g., in the continual evolution of their infrastructure and services (see also Chap. 1). However, decentralization in the financial sector has raised concerns about the consequences on its electricity consumption and sustainability, especially through the use of blockchain technology. In recent years, it has been widely proclaimed that blockchain solutions consume a lot of electricity and, therefore, cause a major negative impact on the environment (International Energy Agency, 2024; Gallersdörfer et al., 2020). While this is undoubtedly true for some blockchain solutions, many approaches have shown to be less electricity-intensive. Overall, the decentralization technologies featured in this book mainly comprise blockchain technology, decentralized digital identities, federated learning (FL), and PETs. There are a few distinct underlying mechanisms when considering the additional electricity consumption that these technologies introduce over their centralized alternative. The first mechanism is the additional computational overhead that these technologies introduce. This is particularly relevant for PETs. For example, encryption and decryption require additional computational steps and the generation of zero-knowledge proofs (ZKPs) (see Chap. 6) can induce computational overhead that is multiple orders of magnitude higher than the original computation or assertion that is to be proven. The second cause for additional electricity consumption is the offloading of computations from highly efficient servers to less efficient end devices. This is, for example, the case for decentralized identity solutions where, in many cases, encryption, decryption, or even proof generation needs to be handled by mobile phones instead of hyperscale computing centers that handle the computations and communications in centralized identity solutions and which can be orders of magnitude more electricity efficient in computing due to highly specialized and optimized hardware as well as better management of idle time (Shehabi et al., 2016). The last reason for additional electricity consumption is redundant execution which is especially relevant in the context of blockchains and other distributed ledger technologies. In these systems, the same set of transactions is processed and stored by multiple network participants, so-called nodes, which multiplies the computational effort of the system and, thus, its electricity consumption. Blockchains that use the PoW consensus mechanism have an additional cause for electricity consumption that strongly differentiates from the others. This cause is the economic incentives that are created in PoW blockchains for consensus participants to use computational power, i.e., electricity consumption, to obtain a share in the voting rights and thus, a share of the rewards that are paid out to participants. This tie is also the most significant driver for electricity consumption of decentralized technologies in general, and blockchain technology in particular.

Among decentralization technologies, blockchains are arguably the largest electricity consumers, using around 0.4% of the global final energy (International Energy Agency, 2024). Furthermore, their electricity consumption aspects are arguably the most complex due to the interplay of economic and technical factors. This is why this chapter specifically focuses on the electricity consumption of blockchains. We explain how design decisions influence the electricity consumption of blockchain solutions and provide insights into what this means for the future of a decentralized financial system. By doing so, we hope to contribute to a more nuanced understanding of the relationship between decentralization and environmental sustainability in the financial sector. In improving the understanding of this topic, we hope to foster the development of a blockchain-based, decentralized financial system that can support economic growth (Gramlich et al., 2023) while preserving our planet's resources.

This chapter contains two main sections. Section 14.2 will give an overview of the electricity consumption of blockchains and how it can be influenced by different design choices. Afterward, Sect. 14.3 outlines the most significant trade-offs between decentralization and the electricity consumption of blockchains in particular but also for decentralized systems in general. Subsequently, we discuss how these findings can be leveraged to manage and optimize the environmental sustainability of decentralization in the financial system (Sect. 14.4). We conclude in Sect. 14.5 with a summary of the most important takeaways and a call for future investigation and development by practitioners and researchers.

14.2 Determining the Electricity Consumption of Blockchain Networks

Due to the decentralized nature of a blockchain network, there is no single distinct source of electricity consumption that can be directly measured. Instead, the network's total electricity consumption consists of the sum of the individual electricity consumption of all components (Sedlmeir et al., 2020a; Stoll et al., 2019). Furthermore, these participants and their electricity consumption are not homogeneous but can vary strongly. They depend on factors such as their role in the network, their hardware, and location-based specificities (e.g., electricity prices, infrastructure, climate) that affect the cooling of data centers) (Sai & Vranken, 2024; de Vries, 2022). However, as we will point out, among all parameters the consensus mechanism has the most significant influence on electricity consumption in blockchain networks. Therefore, in Sect. 14.2.1, we first examine the electricity consumption of PoW networks as their cause for electricity consumption differs from other consensus mechanisms, which we group under non-PoW and discuss in Sect. 14.2.2.

14.2.1 Proof of Work

PoW is the consensus mechanism used in the Bitcoin network and often used by other early public permissionless networks. However, it is also the most electricity-intensive mechanism. This high power consumption is mainly due to the way consensus is reached in these PoW blockchains. In order to gain voting rights in the consensus mechanism and thus a greater chance of proposing a new block and earning rewards, complex hash puzzles and other computationally intensive tasks must be solved. Higher financial rewards thus incentivize higher investments in computational power. As such, the high energy consumption of PoW is by design, determined by economic dependencies rather than technical inefficiencies (Sedlmeir et al., 2020a).

The decentralized nature of a permissionless blockchain makes it impossible to directly determine the electricity consumption of a PoW network. Independent entities can enter the network and participate in its subsystems, leading to an unknown number of miners who make individual decisions about their mining operations, such as the hardware and the underlying infrastructure used. These decisions significantly influence the amount of electricity consumed (Sedlmeir et al., 2020b). However, the design choices made when instantiating the PoW algorithm can impose certain constraints that affect the mining-related activities and, hence, the main driver of the network's electricity consumption (de Vries, 2020). Based on these insights and observable actions in the network, one can measure the electricity consumption of a PoW-network. The existing methods for measuring a network's electricity consumption can be classified into two categories: *bottom-*

up (commonly defining a lower bound for electricity consumption) and *top-down* (commonly defining an upper bound for electricity consumption). The following sections will present these two approaches.

Bottom-up Approach To estimate a blockchain network's electricity consumption, one common approach is to analyze the publicly observable hash rate of the network and the amount of electricity that miners consume to generate this hash rate. Using this approach, the network's electricity consumption can be approximated by multiplying the network's hash rate with the electricity consumed per hash by the miners:

$$\text{electricity consumption } = \text{hash rate} \times \text{average electric energy required per hash}$$

In other words, the network's total *electricity consumption* is the *network's hash rate* (hashes/second) multiplied with the *average electric energy* used by the mining process (J/hash). Because this model depends on two variables that can be observed relatively well – the network's total hash rate and the distribution of energy efficiency among the used mining hardware, it provides relatively robust estimations compared to other methods (Sedlmeir et al., 2020a; Stoll et al., 2019).

The first variable, the *network's hash rate*, can be accurately calculated from observed data through the current mining difficulty combined with the average time block. But the second variable, the *electricity consumption per hash* by the miners, i.e., the efficiency of the mining hardware, cannot be measured directly at the network level (Sedlmeir et al., 2020b). Consequently, the literature proposes various approaches for determining this value.

One method calculates a lower bound on electricity consumption by assuming that miners exclusively use the most efficient hardware available (Krause & Tolaymat, 2018; Sedlmeir et al., 2020b). While this approach provides a robust and simple method, it has been criticized for its tendency to significantly underestimate actual electricity consumption (de Vries, 2020; Koomey, 2019). Another approach involves approximating the average efficiency of active mining devices to obtain a more accurate estimation of the actual electricity consumption. For this purpose, sales figures provided by manufacturers of suitable mining hardware can be used as a basis for deriving the distribution of used devices in the network (de Vries, 2020). A further approach determines the expected lifespan of mining hardware (de Vries, 2019). This assumption implies that miners continue to use their equipment until it reaches a point where it is no longer economically viable compared to more electricity-efficient alternatives (de Vries, 2019, 2020). However, the empirical reliability of the result obtained from both approaches is questioned due to their lack of accuracy in predicting the hardware's lifespan (Sai & Vranken, 2024).

A calculation based solely on network hash rate and hardware efficiency only considers the direct electricity consumption of the mining hardware and neglects the electricity consumption of the infrastructure required for performing mining operations, such as cooling or network infrastructure. Stoll et al. (2019) and de Vries (2018) account for this additional electricity requirement by multiplying the total energy consumption calculated from a network's hash rate with a power usage effectiveness (PUE) factor.

Top-down Approach The top-down approach assumes that all mining participants behave in an economically rational way: Miners don't spend more than their expected revenue (Lei et al., 2021). Thus, this method allows an estimation of the upper limit for the electricity consumption of a blockchain network. It is essentially based on the relationship between income and expenses:

$$\text{total mining revenue} \geq \text{total mining costs.}$$

Based on this assumption, it is possible to estimate the electricity consumption by considering the maximum expenditure miners are willing to allocate toward electricity, given their total mining revenue and their expenses. When a miner solves a hash puzzle correctly, they receive the associated *block rewards* (an incentive for creating a new block) and *transaction fees* as a prize, with the amount – in network native currency – determined by the consensus mechanism. This currency can be sold for fiat money on exchanges and thus be converted into the currency in which miners pay for their expenses (typically fiat currency such as the Euro or USD):

$$\text{total mining revenue} = \text{block reward} + \text{transaction fees.}$$

Like the metric of the hash rate utilized in the bottom-up approach, the *total mining revenue* can be determined from public data. *Transaction fees* and *block rewards* are paid in the network's native currency, whose value is determined by the current exchange rate. The mining revenue, influenced by *transaction fees*, *block rewards*, and exchange rates, sets an upper limit on their budget for electricity and other expenses (Stoll et al., 2019). In addition to *block reward* and *transaction fees*, miners can earn additional revenue streams, such as *maximal extractable value (MEV)* – also denoted as miner extractable value – by using their ability to decide which transactions are included in a new proposed block (Daian et al., 2020).

Similarly to the *average electric energy required per hash* variable in the bottom-up approach, the total mining cost in the network is not directly observable and depends on the expenses of individual mining operations. Therefore, it is necessary to make assumptions regarding the miners' costs. The *electricity cost* acts as the main factor determining how much hash power miners are willing to contribute. Miners weigh their expected revenue against current electricity prices; based on this calculus, they may opt to adjust the hash rate offered or the electricity consumed by their mining devices (Sedlmeir et al., 2020a).

$$\text{Total mining costs} = (\text{electricity consumption} \times \text{electricity prices}) + \text{other expenses.}$$

An important variable in this formula is the *electricity prices* miners pay. As such data is currently lacking (Sai & Vranken, 2024), estimations often assume prices between 0.05 and 0.10 USD/kWh. However, by assuming a global electricity price, regional differences (e.g., due to a high share of hydropower) or seasonal differences (e.g., cheaper electricity during the rainy season) are not considered (Sedlmeir et al., 2020a; Sun et al., 2022). To address regional price differences, one may consider the average electricity prices paid by households from different countries (Küfeoğlu & Özkuran, 2019; Shi et al., 2023). However, country-level allocation alone may not be sufficient to factor in regional differences adequately. Additionally, it should be noted that miners usually pay a lower electricity price than private consumers as the majority of the hash rate originates from industrial-scale miners. As a result, employing household electricity prices results in an underestimate of the network's electricity usage (de Vries, 2022).

Other expenses, such as investments in new hardware or infrastructure and personnel expenses, limit the amount a miner can spend on electricity. It is essential to consider these additional costs associated with mining that reduce the proportion of revenue miners can allocate to electricity consumption. For example, de Vries (2018) estimates, based on the required investment costs, that miners spend about 60% of their revenues on electricity.

By inserting the first two formulas into the last and rearranging it, we finally obtain the formula for the upper limit of electricity consumption of PoW-based blockchains in a certain time frame (Sedlmeir et al., 2020a):

$$\text{electricity consumption} \leq \frac{(\text{total mining revenue} - \text{other expenses})}{\text{electricity price}}.$$

Therefore, we can conclude that from an economic perspective, an upper bound for the electricity consumption of a PoW blockchain can be determined by total mining revenue, other expenses of miners, and the electricity prices they pay.

14.2.2 Non-Proof of Work

As discussed in the previous sections, the PoW consensus mechanism forms the basis of Bitcoin – the first blockchain implementation – and has been adopted by many other distributed ledgers since. However, with the continuous advancement of decentralized technologies, a variety of other consensus mechanisms have been developed with different operating principles and, thus, different characteristics. Networks employing *non-PoW* consensus mechanisms consume considerably less electricity than PoW-based networks (Crypto Carbon Ratings Institute, 2022c; de Vries, 2022). In PoW-based systems, computational work and therefore electricity consumption are the scarce resource that has to be invested by network nodes to solve hash puzzles to obtain voting rights in the consensus mechanism. By using other scarce resources, like currency ownership (proof of stake (PoS)) or restricted access (as in a proof of authority (PoA)-based network), to participate in the consensus, non-PoW systems eliminate the requirement for high-electricity consumption inherent in a PoW-based network. As a consequence, these blockchains have significantly lower electricity demands per transaction when compared to PoW-based blockchains, as exemplified by Ethereum's transition from PoW to PoS in September 2022. This so-called Merge reduced electricity consumption by about 99.998% (Crypto Carbon Ratings Institute, 2022c). However, noticeable differences exist between the total electricity consumption of various non-PoW networks, mainly due to the expenses required for maintaining nodes (Platt et al., 2021). Thus, the total electricity consumption of a non-PoW-based network can be approximated by a multiplication of the number of the active nodes and a node's average electricity consumption:

$$\text{total electricity consumption} = \text{number of nodes} \cdot \text{node avg. electricity consumption.}$$

In contrast to PoW mining, the computational complexity and frequency of proposing and verifying new blocks in non-PoW systems are generally low and have a minimal impact on a node's overall electricity consumption. Similarly, the number of transactions per block does not significantly affect the computational complexity of block proposition or verification (Platt et al., 2021). Therefore, the average electricity consumption of a non-PoW node mainly depends on its idle load consumption, which primarily relies on the hardware used, with the lower bound of the hardware configuration determined by the minimum requirements needed to operate a node. These minimum hardware requirements hinge on the network's design decisions, such as transaction complexity and optional functions like stake delegation (Gallersdörfer et al., 2022). For instance, Solana nodes run multiple separate smart contracts in parallel, enhancing the network's performance but also demanding significant computational resources from the nodes.

The second variable of system-wide electricity consumption, the *overall number of nodes participating*, can also hardly be determined directly in public blockchain networks, although permissioned blockchains at least allow control over the number of nodes participating in the consensus. However, reasonable estimations can be carried out for most networks. One exemplary approach that works for many PoS networks is to use the number of publicly known "validator" nodes and approximate the number of corresponding full nodes, though other network types have to be approached with different heuristics. The factor of corresponding full nodes greatly depends on a network's hardware requirements. Consequently, demanding higher hardware requirements will generally reduce the number of active nodes, as higher investment costs discourage potential node operators from participating (Gallersdörfer et al., 2022). Therefore, while increasing the electricity consumption per node, higher hardware requirements generally decrease the number of operating nodes. Thus, higher hardware requirements can reduce or increase the network's total electricity consumption, depending on the increase of electricity consumption per node and the decrease in the number of nodes caused by higher requirements. Additionally, some networks may require nodes consisting of multiple dedicated systems. For instance, in the Cardano network, a participating node requires multiple separate devices. Therefore, the network's actual number of active devices should be three times the number of validator nodes (Platt et al., 2021).

Recent studies used the aforementioned approach to analyze some of the most relevant PoS-based networks (Crypto Carbon Ratings Institute, 2022c,a,b; Gallersdörfer et al., 2022). While accurate or at least good approximations of the number of active nodes are readily available for these networks, there is no information available on the average electricity consumption of the nodes. To approximate that variable, these studies measured the electricity consumption of various hardware configurations, from constrained to high-performance devices, in a controlled test bed environment. The studies then estimated a distribution of hardware configurations capable of running the node software of a given network in order to estimate a node's average electricity consumption.

In addition to the number and average electricity consumption of its nodes, the total electricity consumption of a system depends on several additional factors that can increase or decrease its overall efficiency. For one, the electricity consumption of the entire blockchain system also depends on the underlying network infrastructure, which is generally not taken into account in related work, leading to a potential underestimation of its total electricity consumption (Lei et al., 2021). However, this issue can be addressed by a power efficiency factor similar to the estimates used for PoW-based networks (Shi et al., 2023). Furthermore, efficiency measures in the overall hardware used and its organization can significantly impact the overall electricity consumption of the system. One example is computation as a service, e.g., through hyperscale cloud infrastructures, which reduces the idle electricity consumption of a system compared to dedicated hardware by distributing it across multiple systems. This results in less accountable idle consumption for individual nodes and leads to an overall decrease in electricity consumption of the node (Castro et al., 2019; Rieger et al., 2022). On the other hand, a node operator may opt for a redundant server architecture, with multiple identical nodes running in parallel to ensure high availability guarantees, adding additional electricity consumption to the network.

14.3 Trade-Off: Decentralization and Electricity Consumption

An analysis of the electricity consumption of blockchains, whether PoW- or non-PoW-based, provides a compelling example of the additional environmental costs of decentralizing a system. In general, nodes of a blockchain store the whole blockchain and verify, i.e., rerun, all transactions that are included in new incoming blocks. Thus, the same job that could be done by one party in a fully centralized system is done by all participants, and this redundancy in data storage and processing results in an increase in total computational load and electricity consumption by a factor that is equal to the number of nodes. This redundancy ensures the integrity and availability of the system.

In a fully centralized system without redundancy, only one party bears the computational load and associated electricity costs. However, it is essential to acknowledge that the financial sector often employs a mix of centralized and decentralized elements. For example, credit card companies like Visa centralize transaction approvals but interact with various decentralized elements such as banks, payment processors, and end users (Stearns, 2011). Switching to a fully decentralized system in such a context would still represent an increase in electricity costs, and these costs would scale in proportion to the level of redundancy introduced. Therefore, the electricity costs of adopting a decentralized system could be multiple times those of the current, semi-centralized models in the financial sector. However, there are several trade-offs between maximizing the integrity as well as the availability of a system and the degree of redundancy and its electricity consumption. These trade-offs are well illustrated by non-PoW blockchains (Platt et al., 2021), but the higher-level concept can be applied to decentralized systems more broadly.

14.3.1 Reducing Redundancies (Number of Nodes)

A higher number of nodes leads to a higher degree of redundancy, which in turn increases the electricity consumption linearly. Reducing the number of nodes is the most straightforward measure to reduce the electricity consumption of the system (Gallersdörfer et al., 2022). This is a direct trade-off with the integrity and availability of a system, since reducing redundancy directly affects both.

In a blockchain, the integrity of the system depends on the majority of the consensus participants behaving honestly. Some consensus mechanisms tolerate up to 33% adversarial participants, meaning that 67% of the voting power in the consensus mechanism must act honestly to maintain system integrity and its functionality for honest participants. The data availability of the system only requires one honest and running node. However, to maximize data availability, every possible participant in the system should be able to contact an honest node at any time, which means that more than one is desirable for availability purposes.

In most cases, ensuring the integrity of the consensus mechanism is more challenging than ensuring the availability of the system. This adds a layer of complexity to the trade-off between decentralization and electricity consumption. That is, ensuring a system's integrity may require greater redundancy – and hence greater electricity expenditure – than simply ensuring its availability. Increasing the number of participants can enhance the likelihood of an honest majority. However, the system can also achieve reliability by restricting participation to known, trustworthy actors. In permissioned blockchains, for instance, the consensus mechanism is operated by selected parties that could be publicly known entities or institutions. These chosen participants may have a good reputation at stake, or better-aligned incentives with the services – for example, if they are system users who would incur significant losses from its failure. Such nuanced decisions can reduce the number of nodes required and hence lead to a reduction in the electricity consumption of the system without compromising the integrity or availability of the system (dena, 2023). Thus, the reliability and availability of the system do not only depend on the number of nodes but also on entities operating the nodes which can be directly chosen in a permissioned blockchain.

14.3.2 Reducing the Degree of Redundancy on Every Node

Besides the reduction of the number of nodes that were discussed above, the redundancy in the overall system can also be reduced by decreasing the degree of redundancy of the nodes. Instead of all nodes storing the whole blockchain and processing all transactions, nodes could also just store a certain amount or process a specific share of transactions. This is denoted as *sharding*, a concept already known from more classical database management systems. In the context of blockchain, sharding is a process that metaphorically breaks one homogenous blockchain into multiple shards, which are then operated by different subgroups of nodes. One version of this concept, called *Danksharding*, is currently being implemented for Ethereum, which shards a certain type of blockchain data storage (Ethereum Foundation, 2023). Danksharding introduces a new data type that is not stored by all nodes but instead split across the nodes, utilizing erasure coding (Hall-Andersen et al., 2024). This allows for the reconstruction of the data if a certain share of nodes provides their codes, making the availability of the data dependent on a small set of honest nodes instead of just one. Sharding blockchain data allows for reduction in computational load and especially required storage without sacrificing the availability of the data and is thus a great strategy for reducing energy consumption, especially if combined with approaches that require additional data storage, e.g., roll-ups (dena, 2023). This concept can also be applied to the transaction processing (i.e., execution layer) of a blockchain. This is denoted as execution sharding where individual transactions are not processed and verified by all consensus participants but only those responsible for the respective shard. However, in contrast to data sharding, this compromises the integrity guarantees of the blockchain as the security of an individual shard is lower than the security of the unsharded blockchain as a whole. Additionally, this concept is not easily applicable to all consensus mechanisms, i.e., for PoW it is unclear how miners can be bound to an individual shard (Sedlmeir et al., 2020a). Therefore, execution sharding remains a rather theoretical concept.

14.3.3 Creating More Centralized Subsystems (Side Chains and Roll-Ups)

The third option to reduce electricity consumption is also based on reducing redundancy by creating subsystems. In the context of blockchains, this can be realized in two different ways that differ in terms of the governance of the less decentralized subsystem and its connection to the more decentralized main system. *Side chains* are blockchains that have their own consensus mechanism but often have strong connectivity to the main blockchain, i.e., funds or information can easily be transferred from the main blockchain to the side chain and vice versa. Additionally, many side chains also store a summary of their state on the main blockchain to benefit from its higher integrity. However, bridging between the two systems with separate consensus mechanisms can introduce technical or counterparty risks.

Roll-ups typically do not have their own consensus mechanism but instead are typically run by a single operator or a small consortium. Among the various roll-up techniques, two prominent approaches have gained substantial attention: optimistic roll-ups and ZK-roll-ups, also named validity roll-ups (Sguanci et al., 2021). Optimistic roll-ups operate on the principle of assuming that most transactions are valid without immediate verification, thereby reducing energy costs by offloading the computational burden from the blockchain. In this approach, transactions are initially processed off-chain in a "roll-up," and multiple transactions are aggregated into a single batch. These batches are then periodically submitted to the blockchain. If no disputes are raised within a specified challenge period, the transactions are considered valid and included in the blockchain's state. However, in the event of a dispute, the challenger must provide a proof of a faulty transaction, based on the batched transaction data. While optimistic roll-ups offer significant scalability improvements, they rely on the assumption that honest behavior predominates, making them vulnerable to potential malicious actors. ZK roll-ups, on the other hand, prioritize privacy and security by employing advanced cryptographic techniques known as ZKPs. In this approach, transactions are aggregated and processed off-chain, similarly to optimistic roll-ups. However, instead of relying on the assumption of honest behavior, ZK-roll-ups use ZKPs to cryptographically verify the correctness of the entire batch of transactions without revealing their content. This cryptographic assurance guarantees the validity of transactions without the need for on-chain verification, significantly improving scalability while maintaining security and privacy.

Side chains and roll-ups create smaller subsystems in big blockchain ecosystems which result in less redundancy, i.e., less additional electricity costs (Sedlmeir et al., 2020a). Since side chains have in most cases their own, more centralized, consensus mechanisms that govern the transactions of that subsystem, they entail less redundancy while sacrificing some of the availability and integrity guarantees of the underlying blockchain. Both optimistic and ZK roll-ups can bring electricity savings. While ZK roll-ups minimize the required data and transactions on the main blockchain, they incur more computational overload for the roll-up operator due to the effort required for proof generation (dena, 2023). Overall, these more centralized subsystems can be used to process transactions whose requirements on system availability and integrity are lower than the security guarantees provided by the main blockchain. Therefore, they can be processed in a subsystem with slightly weaker security guarantees, which enables the system as a whole to process more transactions while maintaining or even decreasing the computational load, i.e., electricity consumption, of the majority of the nodes.

14.4 Discussion

The introduction of decentralized systems in the financial sector has seen substantial progress in recent years. Corresponding decentralization technologies have the purpose of creating trustworthy systems with inherent safety and availability. However, their integration into the financial sector has given rise to questions about their environmental sustainability based on a perception of high electricity intensity.

First, it has to be said that the electricity consumption of blockchains is very heterogeneous and depends greatly on many design decisions. The design decision with the biggest impact on electricity consumption is that of the consensus mechanism. As we have illustrated in Sect. 14.2.1, the electricity consumption of PoW-based blockchains is mainly determined by the energy required to solve computational-intensive puzzles, making the PoW consensus mechanism inherently electricity-intensive. Meanwhile, the main additional electricity consumption of non-PoW blockchains compared to centralized solutions comes from redundant processing and storage of transactions. Using a consensus mechanism other than PoW generally uses less than 1% of the energy required for PoW and thus is a more sustainable alternative, as previously evidenced by the Ethereum network's Merge to PoS. However, even within non-PoW systems, there can be strong differences in terms of their electricity consumption, which are attributable to different design choices as outlined in Sect. 14.3.

However, decentralization generally does not necessarily imply redundancy, as is the case in blockchain technology. Other decentralization technologies can introduce different forms of additional electricity consumption. For instance, in decentralized digital identities, identity information is saved and computed on edge devices such as mobile phones. Here, the location and underlying platform for storage, networking, and computations changes, while the amount generally stays the same. The same observation applies to edge computing, a paradigm that brings computation and data storage closer to the sources of data. The emerging FL applications, for example, translate this into the training of a joint machine learning (ML) model on several individual devices, each using its own data set for training. Additionally, most of these decentralized approaches need PETs to comply with regulatory and individual data protection requirements. For the described blockchain approaches, this means guaranteeing verifiability and immutability of information while managing transparency, for example, through ZKPs. Similarly, with decentralized digital identities, PETs are useful to enable better control and nuance in information sharing, i.e., a more precise selection of the information that is exchanged. For instance, in FL, these technologies allow for the trustworthiness of the trained model while keeping the underlying, sensitive training data secret (Rückel et al., 2022).

Generally, these PETs come at the cost of additional computing requirements on the edge. However, any approach that uses edge computing may suffer from efficiency losses due to a lower power usage efficiency, e.g., the efficiency with which electricity is translated into computing power. This efficiency is generally higher in bigger computing clusters such as hyper-scale cloud infrastructure, which can sequence operations far more efficiently to avoid and manage idle time and operate in a far more efficient power window, including the efficiency of cooling Shehabi et al. (2016). Depending on their implementation, these additional computational efforts may or may not be offset by alleviating the necessity of redundant computations on other devices. This is, for example, the case in zero-knowledge roll-ups, which verify transactions and computations through a single succinct non-interactive argument of knowledge (SNARK) which is then only verified by other network nodes, eliminating the need to redundantly compute these transactions on each node. However, for cases in which decentralization means computing on the edge, such as FL or decentralized digital identities, these PETs usually add additional computation without alleviating additional processing elsewhere but with the added benefit of information sovereignty and privacy (see Chap. 6).

These emerging decentralized concepts, however, are still in their infancy and rapidly evolving, and thus, research and practice have gathered little actionable knowledge to date. Therefore, further research is needed on the environmental impact of systems using these technologies and evaluating the resulting trade-offs between environmental impact and the security of such systems. Overall, while the implementation of decentralization measures may increase electricity consumption, the broader efficiency savings within the financial sector may be able to offset this effect (see, e.g., Rieger et al., 2022). While decentralized networks such as Ethereum offer a broader range of functionality today, they consume significantly less electricity than systems like American Express and still handle a significant volume of transactions, though at a lower transaction rate (Cambridge Centre for Alternative Finance, 2022). In other contexts, such as the labeling of electricity, approaches using ZK roll-ups and shielded transactions have been shown to increase transaction throughput and reduce bandwidth and storage requirements greatly (Babel et al., 2022). Exploring the viability of such concepts in financial transactions poses an opportunity for future research.

14.5 Conclusion

This chapter has explored the impact of decentralized technologies on electricity consumption in the financial sector and shed light on the role of the most important design options of decentralized systems. In conclusion, using the example of blockchains, we highlighted that the decentralization of the financial system comes with additional electricity consumption. However, the magnitude of and the reasons for these costs can strongly vary, within a single technology, such as blockchain, and between the different decentralization technologies. This, as pointed out throughout this chapter, showcases that the use of decentralized technologies is a complex and multifaceted topic with both opportunities and challenges.

The impact of the use of decentralized systems on the financial sector's environmental sustainability could prove noteworthy. Therefore, it is important to make adequate design decisions in their implementation to minimize the negative effects while aptly leveraging the opportunities of decentralized technologies. Besides the most important design choice on the consensus mechanism, the deliberate design of the degree of decentralization, degree of redundancy per node, and more centralized subsystems creates additional degrees of freedom to optimize such systems toward the minimal negative impact on environmental sustainability while fulfilling security requirements regarding system integrity and availability. In sum, decentralization, no matter on which layer of the system or to which degree, rather aims at providing different forms and levels of integrity and availability. A deliberate decision on how system requirements on these aspects can be fulfilled in the most efficient way is necessary to leverage the potentials of decentralization technologies while minimizing the drawbacks, especially regarding additional electricity consumption.

This chapter comes with some challenges and limitations. For once, reliable quantitative data on the current direct environmental impact of the financial sector's digital systems to which we could compare future, decentralized systems, is mostly absent. However, it is certain that large financial systems, even if centralized, already have redundancies to ensure their availability. Thus, the redundancy introduced by blockchain would need to be compared with the already existing, less coordinated redundancy. Additionally, regulatory challenges and the lack of standardization in decentralized systems may pose obstacles to the widespread adoption of these technologies. Furthermore, a holistic comparison of decentralized and centralized systems cannot be limited to the system itself but needs to account for their impact on the application they are used in. For example, the use of decentralized systems offers the possibility for entirely new business processes within and across organizations and new services for all types of customers, which could, in turn, have a net positive effect on sustainability. Lastly, while the electricity consumption of blockchain networks, especially those using the PoW consensus mechanism, has received significant attention from researchers, there is currently no definite quantified consensus on the electricity consumption of other decentralization technologies.

In conclusion, as the decentralization of the financial system continues to move forward, the impact of decentralized systems on sustainability grows as well. Therefore, conscious design decisions that minimize the direct influence on environmental aspects such as electricity consumption are becoming increasingly relevant. Continued research and development in this area will be critical in realizing the full potential of decentralization technologies to enable a more sustainable financial sector in the future. Furthermore, deliberate decision-making in the design of decentralized systems, considering the associated trade-off between decentralization on different levels and layers and the additional electricity costs, is necessary to ensure the integrity and availability of such systems while confining their environmental impact.

References

Babel, M., Gramlich, V., Körner, M.-F., Sedlmeir, J., Strüker, J., & Zwede, T. (2022). Enabling end-to-end digital carbon emission tracing with shielded NFTs. *Energy Informatics*, *5*(1). https://doi.org/10.1186/s42162-022-00199-3

Cambridge Centre for Alternative Finance. (2022). Cambridge Bitcoin Electricity Consumption Index. https://ccaf.io/cbnsi/cbeci

Castro, P., Ishakian, V., Muthusamy, V., & Slominski, A. (2019). The rise of serverless computing. *Communications of the ACM*, *62*(12), 44–54. https://doi.org/10.1145/3368454

Crypto Carbon Ratings Institute. (2022a). Energy efficiency and carbon footprint of the Polygon blockchain. https://carbon-ratings.com/dl/polygon-report-2022

Crypto Carbon Ratings Institute. (2022b). Energy efficiency and carbon footprint of the TRON blockchain. https://carbon-ratings.com/dl/tron-report-2022

Crypto Carbon Ratings Institute. (2022c). The Merge: Implications on the electricity consumption and carbon footprint of the Ethereum network. https://carbon-ratings.com/dl/eth-report-2022

Daian, P., et al. (2020). Flash Boys 2.0: Frontrunning in decentralized exchanges, miner extractable value, and consensus instability. In *Symposium on Security and Privacy* (pp. 910–927). https://doi.org/10.1109/SP40000.2020.00040

de Vries, A. (2018). Bitcoin's growing energy problem. *Joule*, *2*(5), 801–805. https://doi.org/10.1016/j.joule.2018.04.016

de Vries, A. (2019). Renewable energy will not solve Bitcoin's sustainability problem. *Joule*, *3*(4), 893–898. https://doi.org/10.1016/j.joule.2019.02.007

de Vries, A. (2020). Bitcoin's energy consumption is underestimated: A market dynamics approach. *Energy Research & Social Science*, *70*, 101721. https://doi.org/10.1016/j.erss.2020.101721

de Vries, A. (2022). Cryptocurrencies on the road to sustainability: Ethereum paving the way for Bitcoin. *Patterns* (pp. 100633). https://doi.org/10.1016/j.patter.2022.100633

dena. (2023). Rethinking blockchain's electricity consumption: A guide to electricity-efficient design of decentralized data infrastructure. https://future-energy-lab.de/app/uploads/2023/10/GUIDE_Rethinking_Blockchains_Energy_Consumption.pdf

Ethereum Foundation. (2023). Danksharding. https://ethereum.org/en/roadmap/danksharding/

Gallersdörfer, U., Klaaßen, L., & Stoll, C. (2020). Energy consumption of cryptocurrencies beyond Bitcoin. *Joule*, *4*(9), 1843–1846. https://doi.org/10.1016/j.joule.2020.07.013

Gallersdörfer, U., Klaaßen, L., & Stoll, C. (2022). Energy efficiency and carbon footprint of proof of stake blockchain protocols. https://carbon-ratings.com/dl/pos-report-2022

Gramlich, V., Guggenberger, T., Principato, M., Schellinger, B., & Urbach, N. (2023). A multivocal literature review of decentralized finance: Current knowledge and future research avenues. *Electronic Markets*, *33*(11). https://doi.org/10.1007/s12525-023-00637-4

Gramlich, V., et al. (2022). Decentralized Finance (DeFi): Foundations, applications, potentials, and challenges. https://www.fim-rc.de/wp-content/uploads/2022/07/Whitepaper__DeFi__English_Version_2022_07_15.pdf

Hall-Andersen, M., Simkin, M., & Wagner, B. (2024). FRIDA: Data availability sampling from FRI. https://eprint.iacr.org/2024/248

International Energy Agency. (2024). Data centres and data transmission networks. https://www.iea.org/energy-system/buildings/data-centres-and-data-transmission-networks

Koomey, J. (2019). Estimating Bitcoin electricity use: A beginner's guide. https://www.coincenter.org/app/uploads/2020/05/estimating-bitcoin-electricity-use.pdf

Krause, M. J., & Tolaymat, T. (2018). Quantification of energy and carbon costs for mining cryptocurrencies. *Nature Sustainability*, *1*(11), 711–718. https://doi.org/10.1038/s41893-018-0152-7

Küfeoğlu, S., & Özkuran, M. (2019). Bitcoin mining: A global review of energy and power demand. *Energy Research & Social Science*, *58*, 101273. https://doi.org/10.1016/j.erss.2019.101273

Lei, N., Masanet, E., & Koomey, J. (2021). Best practices for analyzing the direct energy use of blockchain technology systems: Review and policy recommendations. *Energy Policy*, *156*, 112422. https://doi.org/10.1016/j.enpol.2021.112422
Masanet, E., Shehabi, A., Lei, N., Smith, S., & Koomey, J. (2020). Recalibrating global data center energy-use estimates. *Science*, *367*(6481), 984–986. https://doi.org/10.1126/science.aba3758
Mora, C., Rollins, R. L., Taladay, K., Kantar, M. B., Chock, M. K., Shimada, M., & Franklin, E. C. (2018). Bitcoin emissions alone could push global warming above 2°C. *Nature Climate Change*, *8*(11), 931–933. https://doi.org/10.1038/s41558-018-0321-8
Platt, M., Sedlmeir, J., Platt, D., Xu, J., Tasca, P., Vadgama, N., & Ibanez, J. I. (2021). The energy footprint of blockchain consensus mechanisms beyond Proof-of-Work. In *Proceedings of the 21st International Conference on Software Quality, Reliability and Security Companion* (pp. 1135–1144). https://doi.org/10.1109/QRS-C55045.2021.00168
Rieger, A., Roth, T., Sedlmeir, J., & Fridgen, G. (2022). We need a broader debate on the sustainability of blockchain. *Joule*, *6*(6), 1137–1141. https://doi.org/10.1016/j.joule.2022.04.013
Rückel, T., Sedlmeir, J., & Hofmann, P. (2022). Fairness, integrity, and privacy in a scalable blockchain-based federated learning system. *Computer Networks*, *202*, 108621. https://doi.org/10.1016/j.comnet.2021.108621
Sai, A. R., & Vranken, H. (2024). Promoting rigor in blockchain energy and environmental footprint research: A systematic literature review. *Blockchain: Research and Applications*, *5*, 100169. https://doi.org/10.1016/j.bcra.2023.100169
Sedlmeir, J., Buhl, H. U., Fridgen, G., & Keller, R. (2020a). The energy consumption of blockchain technology: Beyond myth. *Business & Information Systems Engineering*, *62*(6), 599–608. https://doi.org/10.1007/s12599-020-00656-x
Sedlmeir, J., Buhl, H. U., Fridgen, G., & Keller, R. (2020b). Recent developments in blockchain technology and their impact on energy consumption. *Informatik Spektrum*, *43*(6), 391–404. https://doi.org/10.1007/s00287-020-01321-z
Sguanci, C., Spatafora, R., & Vergani, A. M. (2021). Layer 2 blockchain scaling: A survey. https://arxiv.org/abs/2107.10881
Shehabi, A., et al. (2016). United States data center energy usage report. https://eta-publications.lbl.gov/sites/default/files/lbnl-1005775_v2.pdf
Shi, X., Xiao, H., Liu, W., Lackner, K. S., Buterin, V., & Stocker, T. F. (2023). Confronting the carbon-footprint challenge of blockchain. *Environmental Science & Technology*, *57*(3), 1403–1410. https://doi.org/10.1021/acs.est.2c05165
Stearns, D. L. (2011). *Electronic value exchange: Origins of the VISA electronic payment system*. Springer.
Stoll, C., Klaaßen, L., & Gallersdörfer, U. (2019). The carbon footprint of Bitcoin. *Joule*, *3*(7), 1647–1661. https://doi.org/10.1016/j.joule.2019.05.012
Sun, W., Jin, H., Jin, F., Kong, L., Peng, Y., & Dai, Z. (2022). Spatial analysis of global Bitcoin mining. *Scientific Reports*, *12*(1), 10694. https://doi.org/10.1038/s41598-022-14987-0

SPRINGER NATURE

GPSR Compliance

The European Union's (EU) General Product Safety Regulation (GPSR) is a set of rules that requires consumer products to be safe and our obligations to ensure this.

If you have any concerns about our products, you can contact us on ProductSafety@springernature.com

In case Publisher is established outside the EU, the EU authorized representative is:

Springer Nature Customer Service Center GmbH
Europaplatz 3
69115 Heidelberg, Germany

The manufacturer's authorised representative in the EU is Springer
Nature Customer Service Centre GmbH, Europaplatz 3, 69115 Heidelberg,
Germany. If you have any concerns regarding our products, please
contact ProductSafety@springernature.com

Printed and bound by CPI Group (UK) Ltd, Croydon, CR0 4YY
30/09/2026
02225567-0014